Optimise

Teacher's Book Premium Pack

B2

macmillan education

Welcome

ABOUT *OPTIMISE*

- *Optimise* is a fantastic new secondary-level exam-preparation course for 21st century learners. The course is designed to prepare teenagers for international exams (First (FCE) for Schools, etc.) or local state exams.
- *Optimise*'s highly respected team, including authors Malcolm Mann and Steve Taylore-Knowles, and Course Consultant, Karen Ludlow share their exam expertise and many years of experience of official exams to ensure that your students achieve exam success.
- *Optimise* offers attractive images, stimulating, age-appropriate topics and carefully guided skills development, which prepare students for everyday life as well as exams.
- *Optimise*'s print and digital package gives you the flexibility to choose the approach that works best for your teaching situation: from print to blended to a fully interactive digital approach.

For students

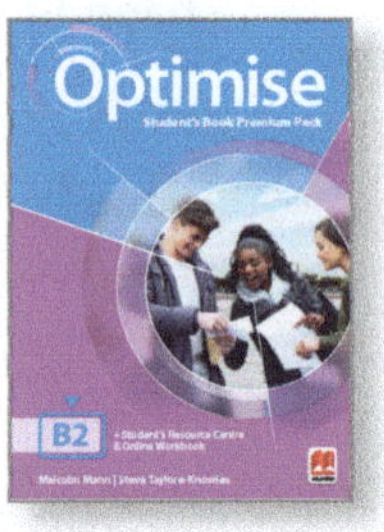

Student's Book or Digital Student's Book

See pages 4–13 for details of the Student's Book content.

See page 14 for more on the Digital Student's Book.

Workbook with/without answer key or Online Workbook

See pages 17–20 for details of the Workbook content.

See page 21 for more on the Online Workbook.

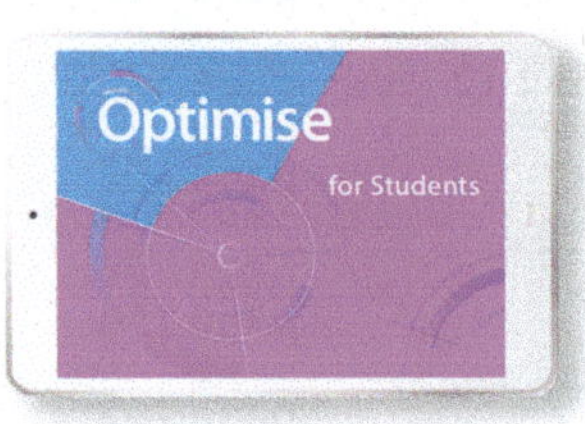

Student's Resource Centre

See page 22 for a full list of resources available on the Student's Resource Centre.

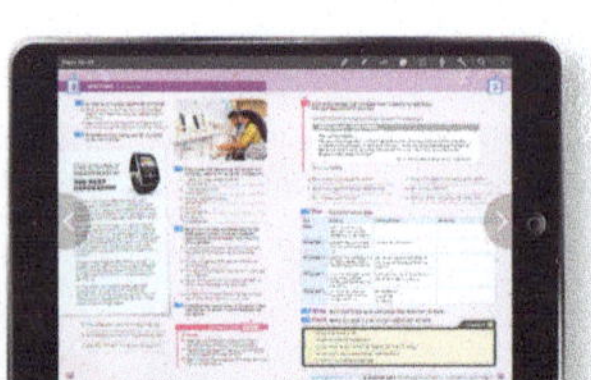

Student's eBook

An eBook version of the Student's Book is included.

For teachers

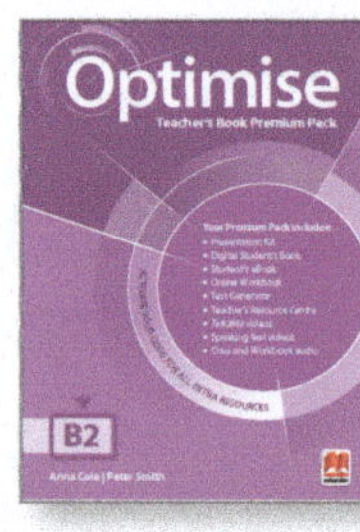

Teacher's Book

Your Teacher's Book Premium Pack includes:

- Presentation Kit
- Digital Student's Book
- Student's eBook
- Online Workbook
- Test Generator
- Teacher's Resource Centre
- *Talk2Me* videos
- Speaking test videos
- Class and Workbook audio

See pages 22–23 for details of the worksheets and tests available.

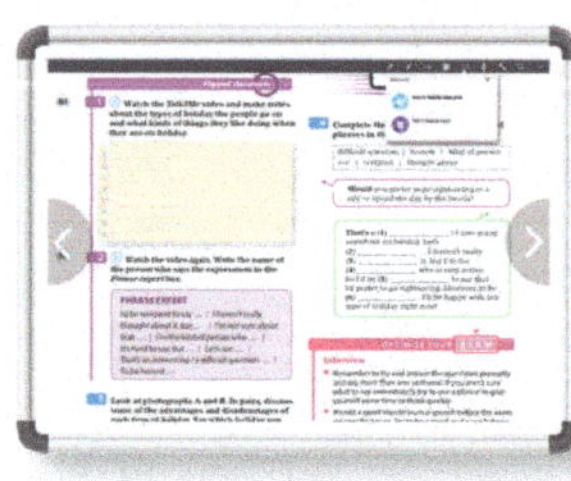

Presentation Kit

See page 15 for more information about the Presentation Kit.

Teacher's Resource Centre
Digital Student's Book
Online Workbook
Test Generator
Student's eBook

See page 22 for a full list of resources available on the Teacher's Resource Centre.

Class Audio CDs

Class audio on CDs. Also available on the Resource Centres.

ABOUT THE *OPTIMISE* AUTHORS

Malcolm Mann and Steve Taylore-Knowles have written a number of exam courses for teenagers, including the highly successful *Laser* series. They are also the series editors of Macmillan's *Improve your Skills for First (FCE)* and *Improve your Skills for Advanced (CAE)* series.

Malcolm

Malcolm lives and works in Athens, Greece. He's responsible for the production of the LAAS exam suite, and is a former Chairperson of TESOL Greece.

Steve

Steve lives and works in the UK. He is a former Cambridge oral examiner and also provides government-endorsed teacher training in many countries throughout Europe, Asia and South America.

A MESSAGE FROM THE *OPTIMISE* AUTHORS

Thank you for choosing to use *Optimise*.

Optimise is an exam course with a difference.

In *Optimise*, we effectively combine exam training, language development and 21st century skills to prepare students not only for language exams, but also for life beyond the classroom.

Below we have listed our principles and the key features which we believe make *Optimise* an outstanding exam-preparation course.

We very much hope you and your students enjoy using *Optimise B2* and benefit from its motivating content, syllabus and structure.

All the very best for the school year!

Malcolm and Steve

Principles

The following principles are at the heart of the *Optimise* series:

- **Motivation:** The more that 21st century teens can be motivated by engaging and interesting content (texts, topics, tasks, etc.), the more likely they are to improve their skills, and develop their linguistic competence.
- **Practice:** Exam practice is essential. In order for students to feel confident and perform at their optimum, they need to be familiar with exam tasks. Language and exam skills tested in the exam have to be practised and developed.
- **Guidance:** The most effective way to help students develop their language and exam skills is to deal with them in a systematic and guided way, through a carefully-planned course syllabus.
- **Coverage:** Vocabulary does not only consist of individual words; it also includes collocations, phrasal verbs, idioms, word formation and word patterns, as well as topic vocabulary, which all need to be covered comprehensively.
- **Support:** Students require expert guidance and support in order to produce exam-level pieces of writing. The process of writing involves different drafts, proofreading and feedback, and is essential in helping students develop their skills.
- **Consolidation:** Regular consolidation makes a vital contribution towards ensuring students understand and retain the information they need in order to prepare for exams.
- **Personalisation:** Personalisation is key in enabling students to relate the material in their Student's Book to their own lives, opinions and culture.

Key features

- An extensive range of print and digital materials, providing you with a variety of flexible options for your students.
- Strong focus on exam-skills development, with each lesson focusing on a specific skill and offering detailed advice on how to complete the task effectively.
- Resource Centres for both students and teachers, with a wide variety of worksheets including CLIL and Culture, Grammar and Vocabulary.
- Unit tests, Progress tests, End-of-year test, all set at two levels – Standard and Higher – are available as PDFs and also adaptable to suit your own requirements on the Test Generator.
- A Placement test to check your students' level and a Diagnostic test to highlight students' strengths and weaknesses.
- First (FCE) for Schools Practice tests: one at the back of the Workbook and another complete Practice test available on the Teacher's Resource Centre as a printable PDF.
- Systematic language and exam-preparation development throughout every lesson.
- Personalisation tasks to foster 21st century skills, such as critical analysis, collaboration and learning strategies, presented through the Think, Research, Culture, Learn and Me features.
- *Talk2Me* videos in every Speaking lesson present functional language through interesting vox pops videos. The Flipped classroom approach is suggested as an alternative approach for this video to encourage learner autonomy and create more time to focus on activating the target language.
- A Speaking test video with an examiner shows a pair of students completing all four parts of a speaking test. This video is exploited in the *Optimise your speaking* section of the Student's Book *Optimise your exams* pages, along with an additional worksheet on the Resource Centre.
- Systematic Writing lessons which include a writing model, a paragraph planner and a writing exam task, along with a post-writing Checklist for students to refer to.
- A Progress check, after every two units, reviews the grammar and vocabulary of the preceding two units and includes a self-assessment tool for students to chart their learning.

Course components

STUDENT'S BOOK | Reading lesson

Every unit starts with a 2-page Reading lesson.

8 The world around us

READING | Multiple matching | A nature article

1 **In pairs or as a group, answer the questions.**

1 Which areas of your country are known for their natural beauty?
2 What can people visiting those areas expect to experience?

2 **Read the article quickly. Match each person with an overall opinion of the park. There is one extra sentence you do not need.**

A Aiden King: ____
B Chloe Morton: ____
C Nakaaya Kikwete: ____
D Manuel Garcia: ____

1) It faces challenges from different threats and its amazing natural wealth needs to be protected.
2) It doesn't deserve the reputation it has for outstanding beauty and amazing wildlife.
3) It impressed me with its natural beauty, but it also made me think about what is important.
4) It was interesting, but it didn't mean as much to me as it could have done with more information.
5) It helped me to connect with other people and what their lives were like in the past.

3 **Find phrases in the article for expressing attitude and opinion that mean the same as phrases 1–5.**

1 I thought it was …
____
2 As you might expect, …
____
3 In my opinion, …
________________, ________________
4 … my personal opinion is …
____
5 … I am certain that …
____

OPTIMISE YOUR EXAM

Multiple matching

- In this task, the writer's attitudes and opinions are often important. Look for key phrases that show this, e.g. *To my mind …, My own view is …*
- Also look for adjectives and descriptive phrases that show attitude and opinion, e.g. *it was (…) that really stuck with me, breathtaking, stunning.*

80

Unit topics and themes chosen to be interesting and engaging for teenage students.

The opening spread of each unit has a colourful and impactful image connected to the unit topic, which can be used at the start of the lesson to stimulate on-topic discussion.

Clear labelling of the exam task and text type in the lesson will help you and your learners.

All Reading lessons include an *Optimise your exam* feature, which gives students tips and strategies to help them prepare for the lesson exam task.

READING 8

NATIONAL PARKS

Four young people tell us about visiting a national park in their country.

A Mammoth Cave National Park, Kentucky, USA

Aiden King

The Mammoth Cave National Park is an extensive underground system of caves of which about 400 miles have been explored. I found it really impressive, and some of the rock formations are incredible. If I'd known more about the history before going, I'd have got more out of it. Not surprisingly, rocks get a little tedious after a while without a context, and unlike other national parks, there isn't a great deal of wildlife. It all seemed rather laid on for visitors, so it was a relief to go on a 'wild' tour, which takes you to some of the less-developed parts of the cave system. Crawling in small spaces in mud you can get a real sense of what it must have been like for the early explorers. Local legends say that wanted criminals used to hide in the caves!

B Great Barrier Reef Marine Park, Australia

Chloe Morton

The Great Barrier Reef has become one of the global symbols of just how fragile nature can be. There's no doubt that the reef is something we have to preserve very carefully for future generations. The diversity of life in the area is breathtaking! I had an exciting opportunity to help out with a team of marine scientists to see what effect human activity is having on the reef. The area is divided up into zones and there are limits on different activities within each zone. This minimises the impact of some activities, such as diving, while still allowing people to enjoy the stunning natural beauty of the reef. If we had done something like that years ago, the reef would be in a much better state now! Unfortunately, past mistakes and a changing climate mean that parts of the reef are struggling to recover. Let's hope we can improve its cultivation for the future.

Nakaaya Kikwete

C Serengeti National Park, Tanzania

The Serengeti National Park is world famous for the fact that one and a half million wildebeest migrate 600 miles every year in search of fresh grass and water. For me, it was an epic sight, and the struggle of the wildebeest to survive in dangerous conditions (the rivers are full of crocodiles!) reminded me of the daily struggle to survive that many people in my country face. To my mind, national parks are there not only for the conservation of wildlife, but to inspire us to lead better lives. If you visited my country, you would see fantastic scenery and great natural beauty alongside difficult living conditions. It's vital that we explore ways in which our society can develop at the same time as preserving the spectacular natural resources we have. We can't encourage one at the expense of the other.

Manuel Garcia

Tikal is an amazing place with over 3,000 buildings from the Mayan civilisation! From about 900 BC to 900 AD, a major city of 100,000 people developed and you can still visit the ruins. The park is also home to jaguars and other animals. I visited with my class, and it was awesome to think we were walking in the footsteps of people from so long ago! The temples were very striking, but it was the courts for ball games that really stuck with me. It gave us some insight into what their lives were like. It's fascinating to think that they played sport just like us! We often look at constructions and monuments and think they represent what a culture was like, but my own view is that it's the ordinary aspects of everyday life that tell us a lot more.

D Tikal National Park, Guatemala

4 2.13 **For each question, choose from the people A–D. The people may be chosen more than once.**

Which person

thinks that parks have a function beyond the preservation of animals and monuments?	1
visited a place that is seen as a good example of problems faced by nature?	2
found a connection with the past through everyday experiences?	3
thinks they should have found out more before visiting?	4
was impressed by the range of different creatures in the park?	5
visited a place that preserves both wild creatures and a way of life?	6
preferred to see a side of the place that most tourists don't see?	7
thinks that important buildings don't tell the complete story of people's lives?	8
thinks we should have done things differently in the past?	9
draws a parallel between the natural world and human society?	10

5 **Find these words and phrases in the article. Work out what they mean from the context.**

fragile (adj) | insight (n) | inspire (v)
laid on (phr v) | minimise (v) | preserve (v)
striking (adj) | tedious (adj)

THINK | RESEARCH | CULTURE | LEARN | ME

Think about a national park in your country. How does it compare to those in the text? Tell the class about it.

► **Workbook Unit 8:** Reading, pages 60–61, exercises 1, 2, 3 81

Reading texts focus on stimulating, out-of-the-ordinary topics, which will be of interest to teenage students.

Every Reading lesson has an exam task. These tasks are level-appropriate and reflect the tasks students are likely to encounter in most official exams.

All lessons include references to the Workbook, and other relevant reference material.

Every unit has two separate Grammar lessons.

8 GRAMMAR 1 | Conditionals (2): second, third and mixed conditionals

Grammar in context

Look at these sentences from the article on page 81. Are they talking about hypothetical events or events that have happened?

If you visited my country, you would see great natural beauty alongside difficult living conditions.

If I'd known more about the history before going, I'd have got more out of it.

If we had done something like that years ago, the reef would be in a much better state now!

REMEMBER

- The second conditional refers to the hypothetical present result of an unlikely or impossible present condition, e.g. *If I were you, I would visit the incredible caves.*
- The third conditional refers to the hypothetical past result of a past condition, e.g. *If I hadn't spoken to Annie, I wouldn't have known about her trip.*
- One type of mixed conditional refers to the hypothetical present result of a past condition, e.g. *If I had taken any photos, I would show them to you.* Another type refers to the hypothetical past result of a present condition, e.g. *If I were in better shape, I would have gone on the trek.*
- Instead of *if*, we can use an inversion. This is more formal, e.g. ***Had I not*** *gone on the trip, I wouldn't have seen the amazing natural park.*

▶ See Grammar reference, Unit 8, page 156

1 Choose the correct word or phrase to complete each sentence.

1 If you went on safari, do you think you ____ it?
a) enjoyed b) would enjoy
2 If I had visited the caves, I ____ it very interesting.
a) would have found b) would find
3 What ____ if we built a new recycling plant?
a) happened b) would happen
4 If you were in charge, ____ dropping litter illegal?
a) did you make b) would you make
5 If humans hadn't destroyed their natural habitats, Bengal tigers ____ endangered.
a) would have been b) wouldn't be
6 My sister ____ a zookeeper if our parents hadn't encouraged her.
a) wouldn't become b) wouldn't have become

2 Complete the questions using the prompts. Add any words you need and make any necessary changes.

1 If you knew your favourite animal was in danger of extinction, ____________?
(you / do)
2 Had you not come here today, ____________?
(you / do / instead)
3 If you had been born in another country, ____________?
(your life / be different)
4 If you could travel back in time, ____________?
(you / like / see)
5 Had you known about the effects of climate change, ____________?
(you / start recycling / years ago)
6 If you could be any animal, ____________?
(you / be)

3 Write the correct form of the verb or verb phrase from the box in each gap.

be (× 2) | be aware | bring | have | learn | not save | see | survive | want

EXTINCTION CAUSED BY HUMANS

If you (1) ____________ to see a dodo today, you would search in vain of course. The dodo was discovered by Europeans on the island of Mauritius in 1598 and was extinct by 1680. If it hadn't been flightless, perhaps it (2) ____________. However, it was unable to escape sailors, who hunted and ate the bird. Apparently it wasn't particularly tasty, so the dodo population might have recovered from hunting, if the sailors (3) ____________ rats, cats and dogs to the island. Perhaps the dodo (4) ____________ here today if those animals hadn't eaten the birds and their eggs.

Sadly, the dodo's story is not uncommon. But perhaps if humans (5) ____________ of the effects of climate change, hunting and even tourism on many species, there (6) ____________ so many critically endangered species. However, there are some stories that bring hope to animals close to extinction. If you (7) ____________ the news 15 years ago, you (8) ____________ that the Iberian lynx was in danger of becoming extinct. Today, thanks to the efforts made through conservation initiatives, the population has slowly increased to a healthier level. (9) ____________ conservationists not made such an effort, the species (10) ____________.

82 ▶ **Workbook Unit 8:** Grammar 1, page 62, exercises 1, 2, 3

Every Grammar lesson presents a different grammar point.

The *Grammar in context* box introduces the grammar lesson by asking students to identify the target structures in a context they have already seen.

Exercises are staged so as to be progressively more challenging as students work through the lesson.

GRAMMAR 2 | Unreal past and past wishes 8

Grammar in context

Look at these sentences from the audio in the listening lesson. For each one, decide whether the clause in bold refers to the present or the past.

1 *It's time* ***we did something about it.***
present / past
2 *I wish* ***more people knew about geothermal energy.***
present / past
3 *I wish* ***I had got involved sooner.***
present / past

REMEMBER

- After some phrases and in some types of sentence, we use past tenses to refer to the present, a general situation or the future. This includes:
  - *It's (high) time …*, e.g. *It's high time we* ***lived*** *a greener life.*
  - *Suppose …*, *Imagine …* and *What if …?*, e.g. *Imagine there* ***were*** *no elephants.*
  - *would rather + you/he/she/it/we/they*, e.g. *I'd rather we* ***didn't*** *waste so much food.*
  - second conditional sentences, e.g. *We'd help the planet if we* ***recycled*** *more.*
  - *wish* and *if only*, e.g. *I wish people* ***cared*** *more about the environment.*
  - we can use *would* with *wish* to express criticism, e.g. *I wish you* ***wouldn't*** *do that!*
  - we can use *could* with *wish* to express hypothetical ability, e.g. *I wish I* ***could*** *go camping this weekend, but I can't.*
  - for wishes about the past (regrets), we use past perfect, e.g. *I wish people* ***had thought*** *about climate change years ago.*

▶ See Grammar reference, Unit 8, page 157

1 Complete the sentences using the verbs in brackets in the correct form.

1 It's time we ____________ **(stop)** polluting our streams and rivers.
2 Don't you wish you ____________ **(have)** a lower carbon footprint?
3 We'd produce less toxic waste if we ____________ **(burn)** less fossil fuel.
4 Don't you wish you ____________ **(know)** the benefits of living a green life years ago?
5 If only there ____________ **(be)** some way of reducing the effects of global warming.
6 Suppose you ____________ **(try)** to live a low-carbon life. Would you enjoy it?

2 Rewrite the sentences in different ways using the words given.

1 Please don't throw your litter on the ground. **RATHER**
____
2 I shouldn't have bought such a large motorbike. **WISH**
____
3 We should manufacture more electric cars in order to help the environment. **HIGH**
____
4 I want to wave a magic wand and solve climate change, but I can't. **COULD**
____
5 People should realise that we have to use more renewable energy. **TIME**
____
6 Do you want people to take the threat to the environment more seriously? **WOULD**
____

3 Write a verb from the box in the correct form in each gap. Add any other words you need.

can | face | get | go | have | provide | start | think

Extreme green!

What if your family (1) ____________ rid of the car, the air-conditioning unit, the tumble dryer, the fridge and almost everything else that uses energy in the home? Suppose you never (2) ____________ on holiday or you (3) ____________ to wear extra clothes in bed to keep warm because you had no heating. Those are just a few of the things that people who live an extreme green life have done to try to keep their carbon footprint as low as possible, and many of them wish they (4) ____________ earlier.

Of course, we all wish we (5) ____________ use less energy, and for many of us it's high time we (6) ____________ of ways to cut down on our energy use. However, few of us are prepared to deliberately keep our house cold in the winter and grow all our own food. We'd much rather supermarkets (7) ____________ us with everything we need, but the food in shops has often travelled a long way to get there. These 'food miles' increase your carbon footprint. Perhaps it's about time we (8) ____________ up to reality and thought more carefully about the effect our everyday actions have on the environment.

THINK | RESEARCH | CULTURE | LEARN | ME

Could you live an extreme green life? What would you find most difficult?

In what ways could you make your life greener than it is now?

▶ **Workbook Unit 8:** Grammar 2, page 63, exercises 1, 2 85

Remember boxes on the grammar pages present additional information in a clear way for students to remember, and end with a signpost to the *Grammar reference* at the back of the Student's Book, where further explanations and examples are provided.

Whenever possible, short texts are included on the grammar pages, to give your students the opportunity to see and practise grammar in realistic contexts.

Grammar personalisation activities suggest ways to use the grammar in a personal context.

The Vocabulary lesson in each unit has three separate word sets, one of which is always topic vocabulary.

Each lesson has three clearly-labelled vocabulary areas.

Topic vocabulary sections increase students' lexical knowledge in topics that commonly appear in exams.

Phrasal verbs are taught in every unit to extend students' vocabulary as well as serving to prepare them for language that commonly appears in exams.

Word patterns help students increase their vocabulary competence and prepare for a number of different exam tasks.

VOCABULARY | Topic vocabulary | Phrasal verbs | Word patterns 8

Words connected with *environmental issues*

1 2.14 **Write a word from the box in each gap to make phrases. Listen and check.**

change | development | effect | energy | footprint | layer | toxic | warming

1 global ______
2 climate ______
3 greenhouse ______
4 ______ waste
5 carbon ______
6 renewable ______
7 sustainable ______
8 ozone ______

2 Write a phrase from Exercise 1 in each gap. There may be more than one correct answer.

1 To measure ______, you need to look at weather patterns over many years.
2 A person's ______ is a measure of the amount of carbon dioxide that is produced by their actions and its effect on the environment.
3 We need ______ so that our economy can grow without damaging the environment.
4 One of the harmful products produced by industrial processes is ______.
5 Some countries may face serious problems if ______ is more than 2°C.
6 Wind power and wave power are excellent sources of ______.
7 The ______ in the atmosphere protects us from dangerous ultraviolet light.
8 The ______ is when the warmth from the sun is trapped in the atmosphere.

Phrasal verbs

3 2.15 **Write a phrasal verb from the box in the correct form to replace the words in brackets in each sentence. Listen and check.**

call for | chop down | clean up | die out | do away with | run out | throw away | wipe out

1 Some animal species ______ (became extinct) due to human activities.
2 People ______ (are demanding) urgent action on climate change.
3 Will we just keep using oil until it all ______ (finishes)?
4 We all have a responsibility to help ______ (tidy) our beaches.
5 If we're not careful, our actions are going to ______ (completely destroy) the wild elephant.
6 I think we should ______ (abolish) cars that produce lots of pollution in city centres to protect the environment.
7 When we ______ (destroy) trees, we remove the natural habitat of a number of species.
8 Don't just ______ (put in the rubbish) your old bottles. Recycle them!

Words + prepositions

4 2.16 **Choose the correct preposition to complete each sentence. Use the words in italics to help you. Listen and check.**

1 Water pollution can be *harmful* **at / to** fish and animals that live along the river.
2 The Sumatran rhino is *threatened* **from / by** hunters.
3 Without the ozone layer, we would be *exposed* **by / to** UV rays that can cause cancer.
4 Do you think we do enough to *protect* animals **by / from** illegal activity?
5 Which countries will be most *affected* **by / with** climate change?
6 Using drinking water to water the garden is a *waste* **from / of** natural resources!

THINK | RESEARCH | CULTURE | LEARN | ME

Choose one of the phrases in Exercise 1 and find out more about it. Tell the class what you discover.

▶ Vocabulary reference, page 166 ▶ Workbook Unit 8: Vocabulary, page 63, exercises 1, 2, 3 83

Lessons include details of the *Vocabulary reference* at the back of the Student's Book. This provides reference materials to support students during vocabulary tasks and also acts as a revision tool.

TOPIC VOCABULARY | Words connected with *environmental issues*

Word	Example sentence
carbon footprint (n)	We're trying to reduce our carbon footprint by using our bikes more and the car less.
climate change (n)	We need to take climate change more seriously, or our world is going to become a very different place.
global warming (n)	If we don't do something about global warming, some islands are going to disappear under the sea.
greenhouse effect (n)	The greenhouse effect means our planet is becoming warmer than it should be.
ozone layer (n)	Although we can't see it, the ozone layer protects us from dangerous UV radiation.
renewable energy (n)	We need to rely more on renewable energy like solar panels to generate electricity.
sustainable development (n)	Governments are now more concerned about sustainable development, but they still don't do enough to control economic growth.
toxic waste (n)	There is a lot of industry there and the river and sea are polluted with toxic waste.

The Listening lesson in each unit focuses on a specific exam skill and always includes an exam task.

All class audio material is available on CDs as well as being provided on the Resource Centres.

Listening lessons always feature a specific exam skill and provide support and guidance to help students develop the skill further.

The initial task helps students to start thinking about the topic of the lesson in more depth.

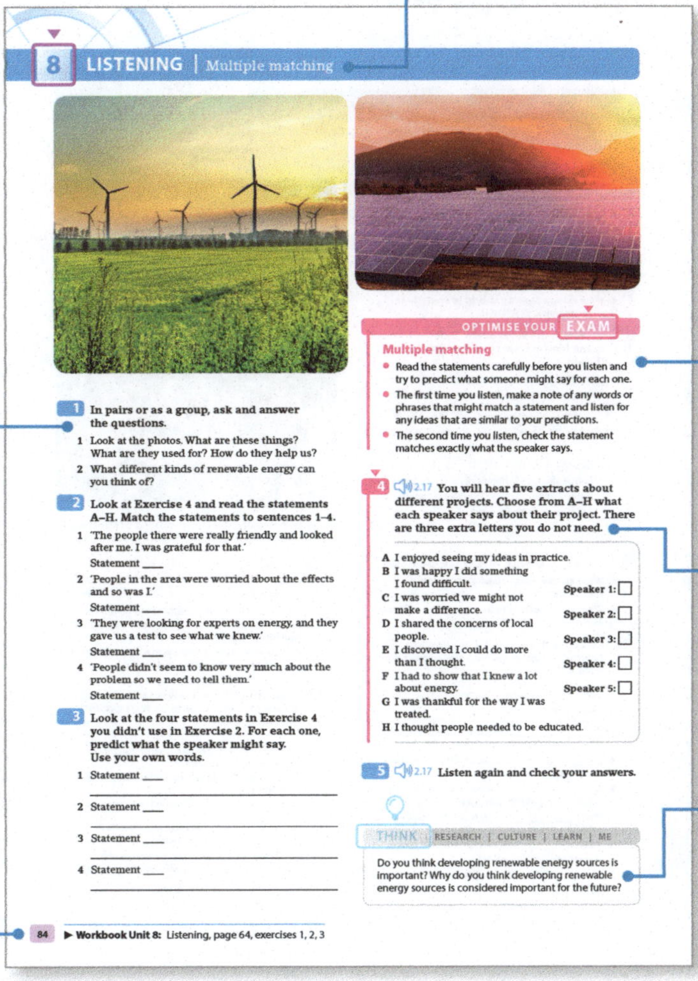

8 LISTENING | Multiple matching

1 In pairs or as a group, ask and answer the questions.

1 Look at the photos. What are these things? What are they used for? How do they help us?
2 What different kinds of renewable energy can you think of?

2 Look at Exercise 4 and read the statements A–H. Match the statements to sentences 1–4.

1 'The people there were really friendly and looked after me. I was grateful for that.'
Statement ___
2 'People in the area were worried about the effects and so was I.'
Statement ___
3 'They were looking for experts on energy, and they gave us a test to see what we knew.'
Statement ___
4 'People didn't seem to know very much about the problem so we need to tell them.'
Statement ___

3 Look at the four statements in Exercise 4 you didn't use in Exercise 2. For each one, predict what the speaker might say. Use your own words.

1 Statement ___
2 Statement ___
3 Statement ___
4 Statement ___

OPTIMISE YOUR EXAM

Multiple matching

- Read the statements carefully before you listen and try to predict what someone might say for each one.
- The first time you listen, make a note of any words or phrases that might match a statement and listen for any ideas that are similar to your predictions.
- The second time you listen, check the statement matches exactly what the speaker says.

4 2.17 You will hear five extracts about different projects. Choose from A–H what each speaker says about their project. There are three extra letters you do not need.

A I enjoyed seeing my ideas in practice.
B I was happy I did something I found difficult.
C I was worried we might not make a difference.
D I shared the concerns of local people.
E I discovered I could do more than I thought.
F I had to show that I knew a lot about energy.
G I was thankful for the way I was treated.
H I thought people needed to be educated.

Speaker 1: ☐
Speaker 2: ☐
Speaker 3: ☐
Speaker 4: ☐
Speaker 5: ☐

5 2.17 Listen again and check your answers.

THINK | RESEARCH | CULTURE | LEARN | ME

Do you think developing renewable energy sources is important? Why do you think developing renewable energy sources is considered important for the future?

84 ▶ **Workbook Unit 8:** Listening, page 64, exercises 1, 2, 3

The *Optimise your exam* box in the Listening lessons always gives students advice on how to approach this kind of task.

Every Listening lesson includes an exam task which allows students an opportunity to apply the advice given in the preceding *Optimise your exam* box.

Personalisation tasks at the end of the Listening lessons relate to the unit topic, giving students a chance to develop the topic further.

There is a reference to the relevant Workbook pages at the end of each Listening lesson.

Talk2Me video in every Speaking lesson

Speaking lessons include a video which features target functional language.

Speaking lessons focus on one of four task types which students will need to develop in preparation for a speaking test.

All Speaking lessons suggest using an optional Flipped classroom approach, in which students watch the video and complete some exercises at home in order to prepare for the lesson.

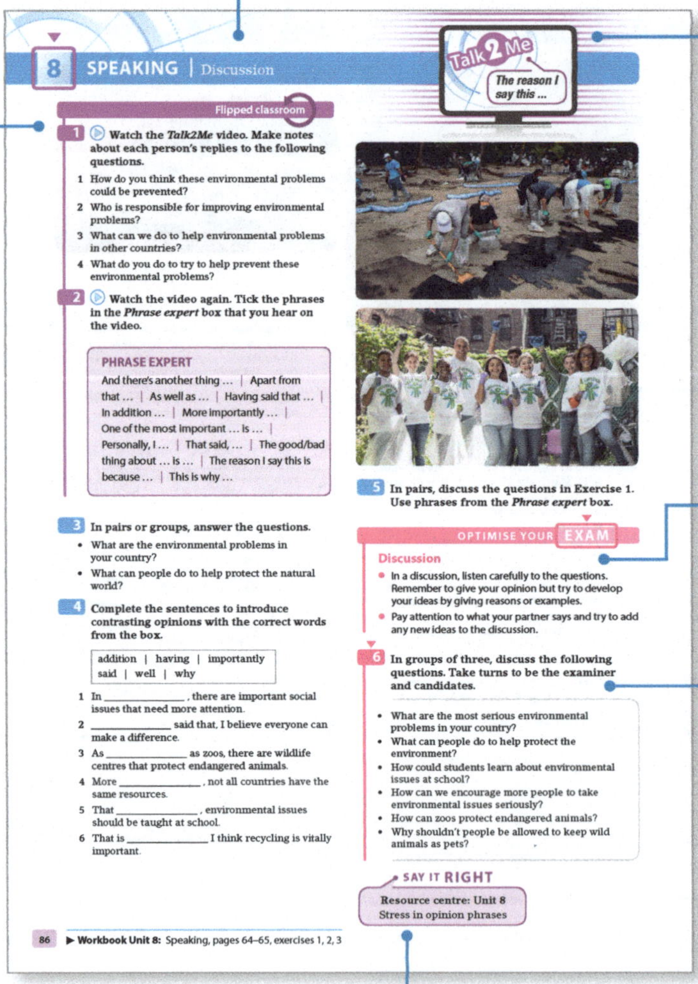

8 SPEAKING | Discussion

Talk2Me — The reason I say this …

Flipped classroom

1 Watch the *Talk2Me* video. Make notes about each person's replies to the following questions.

1 How do you think these environmental problems could be prevented?
2 Who is responsible for improving environmental problems?
3 What can we do to help environmental problems in other countries?
4 What do you do to try to help prevent these environmental problems?

2 Watch the video again. Tick the phrases in the *Phrase expert* box that you hear on the video.

PHRASE EXPERT

And there's another thing … | Apart from that … | As well as … | Having said that … | In addition … | More importantly … | One of the most important … is … | Personally, I … | That said, … | The good/bad thing about … is … | The reason I say this is because … | This is why …

3 In pairs or groups, answer the questions.

- What are the environmental problems in your country?
- What can people do to help protect the natural world?

4 Complete the sentences to introduce contrasting opinions with the correct words from the box.

addition | having | importantly | said | well | why

1 In __________, there are important social issues that need more attention.
2 __________ said that, I believe everyone can make a difference.
3 As __________ as zoos, there are wildlife centres that protect endangered animals.
4 More __________, not all countries have the same resources.
5 That __________, environmental issues should be taught at school.
6 That is __________ I think recycling is vitally important.

5 In pairs, discuss the questions in Exercise 1. Use phrases from the *Phrase expert* box.

OPTIMISE YOUR EXAM

Discussion

- In a discussion, listen carefully to the questions. Remember to give your opinion but try to develop your ideas by giving reasons or examples.
- Pay attention to what your partner says and try to add any new ideas to the discussion.

6 In groups of three, discuss the following questions. Take turns to be the examiner and candidates.

- What are the most serious environmental problems in your country?
- What can people do to help protect the environment?
- How could students learn about environmental issues at school?
- How can we encourage more people to take environmental issues seriously?
- How can zoos protect endangered animals?
- Why shouldn't people be allowed to keep wild animals as pets?

SAY IT RIGHT

Resource centre: Unit 8
Stress in opinion phrases

86 ▶ Workbook Unit 8: Speaking, pages 64–65, exercises 1, 2, 3

All Speaking lessons include a *Talk2Me* video, featuring native speakers. They discuss topics related to the unit, modelling target functional language, which students then practise and use in their final task.

The *Optimise your exam* box develops the lesson skill in order to prepare students for the exam task that follows.

The lesson ends in a speaking-test task consolidating the skill developed on this page.

Every unit contains a *Say it right* feature, which develops a specific aspect of pronunciation that appears in one of the lessons. The worksheet for this is available on the Resource Centre.

STUDENT'S BOOK | Use of English lesson

All Use of English lessons provide comprehensive coverage of all aspects of grammar and vocabulary that students need in order to prepare for exams.

Every Use of English lesson is based on a specific task type that students will be tested on in Use of English exams.

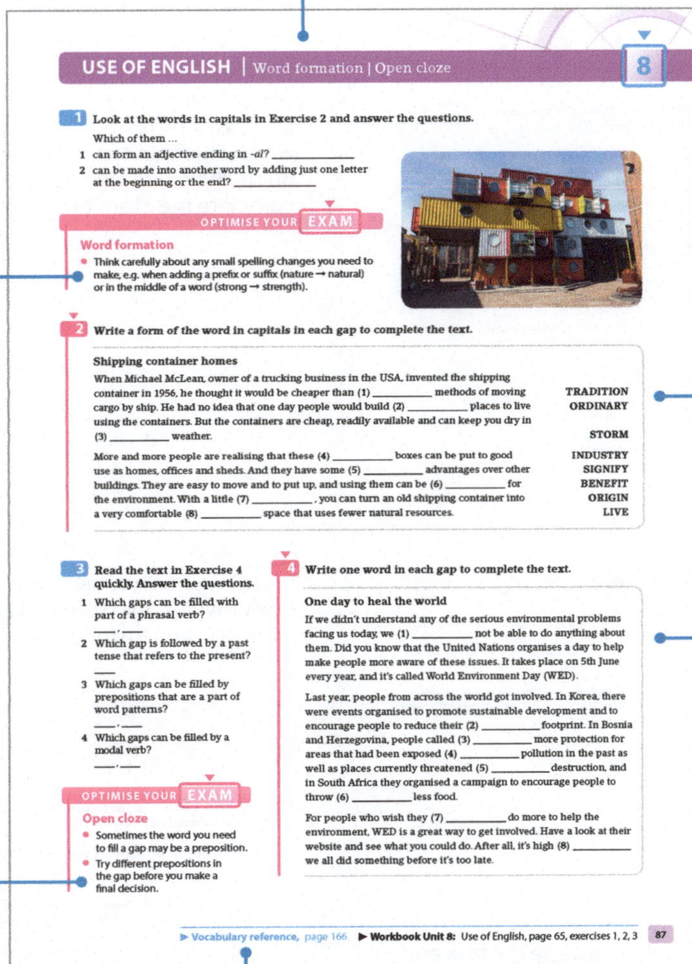

USE OF ENGLISH | Word formation | Open cloze

8

1 **Look at the words in capitals in Exercise 2 and answer the questions.**

Which of them ...

1 can form an adjective ending in *-al*? __________
2 can be made into another word by adding just one letter at the beginning or the end? __________

OPTIMISE YOUR EXAM

Word formation

- Think carefully about any small spelling changes you need to make, e.g. when adding a prefix or suffix (nature → natural) or in the middle of a word (strong → strength).

2 **Write a form of the word in capitals in each gap to complete the text.**

Shipping container homes

When Michael McLean, owner of a trucking business in the USA, invented the shipping container in 1956, he thought it would be cheaper than (1) __________ methods of moving cargo by ship. He had no idea that one day people would build (2) __________ places to live using the containers. But the containers are cheap, readily available and can keep you dry in (3) __________ weather.

More and more people are realising that these (4) __________ boxes can be put to good use as homes, offices and sheds. And they have some (5) __________ advantages over other buildings. They are easy to move and to put up, and using them can be (6) __________ for the environment. With a little (7) __________, you can turn an old shipping container into a very comfortable (8) __________ space that uses fewer natural resources.

TRADITION
ORDINARY
STORM
INDUSTRY
SIGNIFY
BENEFIT
ORIGIN
LIVE

3 **Read the text in Exercise 4 quickly. Answer the questions.**

1 Which gaps can be filled with part of a phrasal verb? ___, ___
2 Which gap is followed by a past tense that refers to the present? ___
3 Which gaps can be filled by prepositions that are a part of word patterns? ___, ___
4 Which gaps can be filled by a modal verb? ___, ___

OPTIMISE YOUR EXAM

Open cloze

- Sometimes the word you need to fill a gap may be a preposition.
- Try different prepositions in the gap before you make a final decision.

4 **Write one word in each gap to complete the text.**

One day to heal the world

If we didn't understand any of the serious environmental problems facing us today, we (1) __________ not be able to do anything about them. Did you know that the United Nations organises a day to help make people more aware of these issues. It takes place on 5th June every year, and it's called World Environment Day (WED).

Last year, people from across the world got involved. In Korea, there were events organised to promote sustainable development and to encourage people to reduce their (2) __________ footprint. In Bosnia and Herzegovina, people called (3) __________ more protection for areas that had been exposed (4) __________ pollution in the past as well as places currently threatened (5) __________ destruction, and in South Africa they organised a campaign to encourage people to throw (6) __________ less food.

For people who wish they (7) __________ do more to help the environment, WED is a great way to get involved. Have a look at their website and see what you could do. After all, it's high (8) __________ we all did something before it's too late.

▶ Vocabulary reference, page 166 ▶ **Workbook Unit 8:** Use of English, page 65, exercises 1, 2, 3 87

The *Optimise your exam* box develops the lesson skill in order to prepare students for the exam task that follows.

Every unit features a Word formation exam task and another exam task.

All the common Use of English exam tasks are covered: multiple-choice cloze, open cloze, word formation and sentence transformation.

Any extra material in the *Vocabulary reference* which is relevant to the Use of English lesson is signposted at the bottom of the page.

Every unit ends with a two-page Writing lesson.

Writing lessons focus on the different types of writing that students may be expected to produce in an exam situation.

8 **WRITING** | An article

1 In pairs or as a group, answer the questions.

1 What is happening in the photo?
2 What things could young children do to help protect the environment?

2 Read this article and answer the questions in your own words.

Teaching the next generation

If you're anything like me, you love nature. Perhaps you also worry about problems like climate change and the greenhouse effect. One important question is how can we teach students about those problems from an early age?

The first thing we should consider is making sure that schools all go green. For example, we're encouraged to recycle paper at our school. This is important due to the fact that schools generally use a lot of paper. Young students would be able to see the difference their behaviour makes in a practical way.

Another great way to teach very young children is to get them involved in a local environmental project. This includes cleaning up a local river, or picking up litter that people have thrown away. This can be very educational as the students are shown how their local environment is affected by different issues.

So, I would encourage everyone to make sure that future generations understand more about the way nature is threatened by some of our actions. We need them to grow up caring for the environment.

Every Writing lesson includes a model, which students can use to inform and guide their own writing when they complete the exam task later in the lesson.

1 How does the writer try to make a personal connection with the reader?
2 How many points does the writer mention? How is each point introduced?
3 How does the writer summarise and conclude the article?

3 Find two ways in which the writer introduces examples. What other phrases for introducing examples do you know?

1 ______
2 ______
Other phrases: ______

4 Find two ways in which the writer introduces reasons. What other phrases for introducing reasons do you know?

1 ______
2 ______
Other phrases: ______

OPTIMISE YOUR EXAM

An article

- When you write an article, you should try to make a connection with the reader.
- You can refer to your own experience using phrases such as *If you are like me, …, Have you ever noticed that …?* or *In my experience, …*
- Remember to give specific reasons and examples in your article to make it more interesting for the reader.

In Writing lessons, the *Optimise your exam* box provides guidance and advice to help students prepare for the lesson exam task.

88

8

5 Look at this writing task and make notes to answer the questions. Use your imagination if necessary.

You see this advert in an English-language magazine for young people.

ARTICLES WANTED

Many ordinary people don't care for the environment as much as they could. We want to change that! Send us your articles explaining the two most important things ordinary people can do to help the environment. The best articles will appear in a special issue and win a prize!

Write your article.

Students analyse the task and make notes to prepare for the writing in each unit.

1. What is one thing ordinary people can do to help the environment? (e.g. produce less waste)

Is there a good example you can use? (e.g. Buy products with less packaging.)

Give a reason why this helps. (e.g. It means less waste to burn or bury.)

2. What is another thing they can do?

Is there a good example you can use?

Give a reason why this helps.

6 Plan Make a paragraph plan.

Part	Purpose	Useful phrases	My notes
Title	show clearly what you are writing about		
Paragraph 1	make a connection with the reader	*If you're anything like me …* *In my experience …* *Have you ever noticed that …*	
Paragraph 2	make your first point – give specific reasons and examples	*The first thing we should consider …*	
Paragraph 3	make a second point – support your point with examples	*Another great way to …*	
Paragraph 4	summarise your article to encourage action from your reader	*So, I would encourage everyone to …* *To summarise …*	

After writing, students are encouraged to check their work carefully.

7 Write Write your article in an appropriate style. Write 140–190 words.

8 Check Before you hand in your article, complete this checklist.

There is a Checklist at the end of every Writing lesson so that students take responsibility for reviewing and assessing their work.

Checklist

- ◯ I've given my article a title.
- ◯ I've written at least four paragraphs.
- ◯ I've given examples and reasons for each main point I've made.
- ◯ I've checked my spelling and grammar.
- ◯ I've made a connection with the reader.
- ◯ I've encouraged action from my reader.

▶ Writing reference, page 169 ▶ **Workbook Unit 8:** Writing, page 66, exercises 1, 2, 3, 4 and Progress check 8, page 67 89

In the *Writing reference*, there are model writing texts for each task type. The Workbook offers further writing practice.

There is a two-page Progress check after every two units.

PROGRESS CHECK UNITS 7–8

GRAMMAR AND VOCABULARY

The *Progress checks* cover grammar and vocabulary from the preceding two units.

The first task is always an exam-type task.

1 Write a form of the word in capitals in each gap.

PHOTO SAFARIS

The safari was (1) __________ a hunting expedition, and even today some people still travel to Africa to hunt. However, most people now join photo safaris. On these trips, you get to see the (2) __________ range of wildlife that Africa has to offer, while at the same time improving your photography. Before you go, the instructors will advise you on the best (3) __________ to take, and while on the safari, the guides will show you the best locations to 'shoot' animals. But it's important to remember that not all of the areas are (4) __________ to tourists, and you also might need a lot of time and (5) __________ to see some of the rarer animals.

But whatever you see, going on a trip like this can (6) __________ improve your photography. And it's not just animals. A photo safari can also be a great opportunity to get to know some of the local people and experience (7) __________ activities such as dancing or cooking. And if your photos are good enough, you may even be able to show them in an (8) __________ when you get home!

ORIGIN
ORDINARY
EQUIP
ACCESS
PATIENT
SIGNIFY
TRADITION
EXHIBIT

__/8

2 Put the verbs into the correct form to complete the sentences.

1 I wish you __________ me that you were going to be late last night! (tell)
2 What would you do if you __________ an injured animal by the side of the road? (find)
3 I'd rather you __________ the dog for a walk before you play games. (take)
4 What would happen if we __________ something to take carbon dioxide from the air? (invent)
5 What do you think would __________ if you hadn't stopped the car in time? (happen)
6 If you hadn't trained as an artist, what job would you __________ now? (do)
7 If only you __________ to me when I advised you not to do it! (listen)
8 I think Esme would __________ the exam if she'd worked a bit harder. (pass)
9 It's time people __________ killing rhinos for their horns. (stop)
10 I'd never go hunting, even if you __________ me a million pounds! (pay)

__/10

3 Choose the correct word or phrase.

1 The scientist started to sketch her ideas **off / out / up** on a paper napkin.
2 Do you think our supply of clean water will ever run **away / out / over**?
3 Sophie tore the letter **down / through / up** and threw it onto the floor.
4 Isn't it time we did **away / back / off** with power stations that run on coal?
5 There won't be any trees left if we continue to chop them **away / down / off** like this!
6 You probably won't like this show at first, but it'll grow **from / in / on** you.
7 I'm going to volunteer to help clean **away / over / up** the local beaches.
8 Some animals will be wiped **back / off / out** if we don't act now!
9 The audience called **for / in / on** the actors to return to the stage.
10 The government have drawn **away / off / up** a proposal to protect endangered species.

__/10

90

4 If a sentence is correct, tick it. If a sentence is incorrect, underline the mistake and correct it.

1 Even it was tough, I finally managed to climb to the top of the mountain. __________
2 I can't wait until I'm enough old to ride a motorbike. __________
3 There really isn't somewhere I'd rather be than right here, right now. __________
4 It wouldn't have been such a bad picnic if it hadn't rained for hours. __________
5 Don't you sometimes wish that you don't have to do all this homework? __________
6 The producer was very pleased with herself because the film was a success. __________
7 Van Gogh didn't sell many paintings during his life, although he was very talented. __________
8 The interviewer asked me where I saw me in five years' time. __________
9 Are you really such upset you can't accept Damien's apology? __________
10 Jen and Will really enjoyed himself at the art exhibition. __________

__/10

The *Progress checks* end with an exam-type task.

5 Complete the second sentence so it has a similar meaning to the first. Do not change the word given. Use two to five words, including the word given.

1 Was the extinction of the dinosaurs a result of climate change? OUT
Did the dinosaurs __________ climate change?
2 Mum regrets letting Dad learn to play the trombone! LET
Mum wishes __________ Dad learn to play the trombone!
3 We all wanted to go to the beach because it was so hot. SUCH
It was __________ we all decided to go to the beach.
4 Can humans be harmed by air pollution? TO
Is air pollution __________ humans?
5 We missed the auction because you arrived so late! IF
We wouldn't have missed the auction __________ so late!
6 Finally, it became clear that the man sitting next to me was the choreographer. OUT
The man sitting next to me __________ the choreographer.

__/12

Total score __/50

There is a total of 50 marks for every *Progress check*.

Every *Progress check* ends with an *Exam skills can-do* checklist. This gives students the opportunity to assess what they can now do, having completed two more units of their Student's Book, and also provides references of where to look if there are any areas students feel they need to review.

EXAM SKILLS

Tick the statements that are true for you. Review the skills in the unit if you need more help.

I can ...	Unit/page
☐ understand implication in a news article	Unit 7 p70
☐ understand the speaker's purpose in conversations	Unit 7 p74
☐ express my preferences and give reasons in a photo task	Unit 7 p76
☐ create adverb forms and use different grammatical structures accurately	Unit 7 p77
☐ create an engaging narrative in a story	Unit 7 p78
☐ understand the writer's attitude and opinion in a nature article	Unit 8 p80
☐ predict and anticipate a speaker's opinion in short extracts	Unit 8 p84
☐ qualify my opinion in a discussion	Unit 8 p86
☐ identify spelling changes when working with prefixes and suffixes and use prepositions accurately	Unit 8 p87
☐ give reasons and examples in an article	Unit 8 p88

91

The 12-page *Optimise your exams* section at the back of the Student's Book brings together exam strategies for each of the key skills, plus advice on how to perform well under exam conditions.

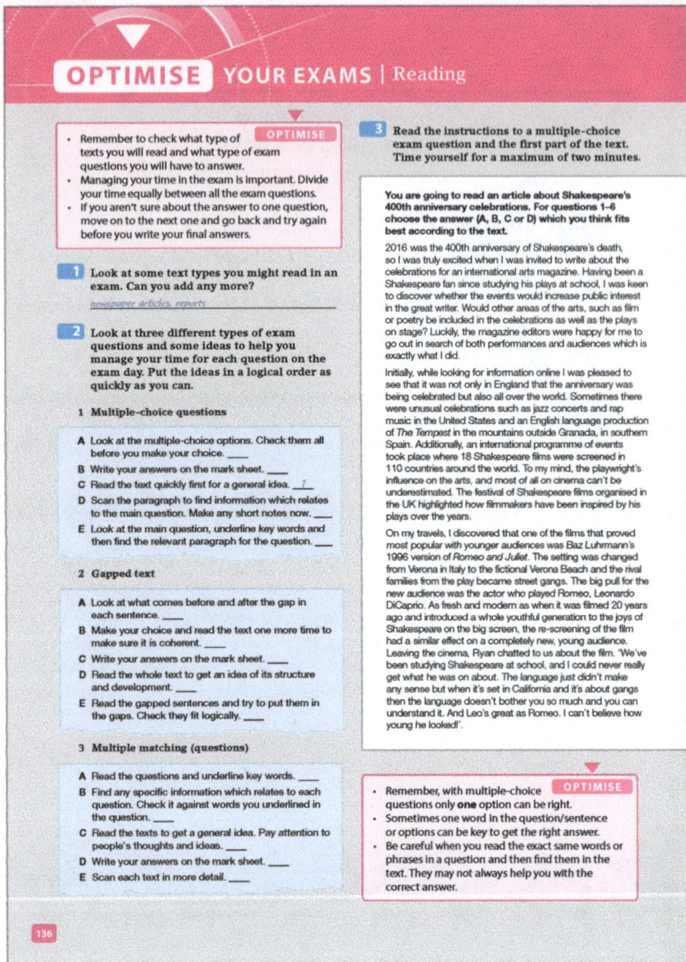

OPTIMISE YOUR EXAMS | Reading

OPTIMISE
- Remember to check what type of texts you will read and what type of exam questions you will have to answer.
- Managing your time in the exam is important. Divide your time equally between all the exam questions.
- If you aren't sure about the answer to one question, move on to the next one and go back and try again before you write your final answers.

1 Look at some text types you might read in an exam. Can you add any more?

newspaper articles, reports

2 Look at three different types of exam questions and some ideas to help you manage your time for each question on the exam day. Put the ideas in a logical order as quickly as you can.

1 Multiple-choice questions

A Look at the multiple-choice options. Check them all before you make your choice. ___
B Write your answers on the mark sheet. ___
C Read the text quickly first for a general idea. *1*
D Scan the paragraph to find information which relates to the main question. Make any short notes now. ___
E Look at the main question, underline key words and then find the relevant paragraph for the question. ___

2 Gapped text

A Look at what comes before and after the gap in each sentence. ___
B Make your choice and read the text one more time to make sure it is coherent. ___
C Write your answers on the mark sheet. ___
D Read the whole text to get an idea of its structure and development. ___
E Read the gapped sentences and try to put them in the gaps. Check they fit logically. ___

3 Multiple matching (questions)

A Read the questions and underline key words. ___
B Find any specific information which relates to each question. Check it against words you underlined in the question. ___
C Read the texts to get a general idea. Pay attention to people's thoughts and ideas. ___
D Write your answers on the mark sheet. ___
E Scan each text in more detail. ___

3 Read the instructions to a multiple-choice exam question and the first part of the text. Time yourself for a maximum of two minutes.

You are going to read an article about Shakespeare's 400th anniversary celebrations. For questions 1–6 choose the answer (A, B, C or D) which you think fits best according to the text.

2016 was the 400th anniversary of Shakespeare's death, so I was truly excited when I was invited to write about the celebrations for an international arts magazine. Having been a Shakespeare fan since studying his plays at school, I was keen to discover whether the events would increase public interest in the great writer. Would other areas of the arts, such as film or poetry be included in the celebrations as well as the plays on stage? Luckily, the magazine editors were happy for me to go out in search of both performances and audiences which is exactly what I did.

Initially, while looking for information online I was pleased to see that it was not only in England that the anniversary was being celebrated but also all over the world. Sometimes there were unusual celebrations such as jazz concerts and rap music in the United States and an English language production of *The Tempest* in the mountains outside Granada, in southern Spain. Additionally, an international programme of events took place where 18 Shakespeare films were screened in 110 countries around the world. To my mind, the playwright's influence on the arts, and most of all on cinema can't be underestimated. The festival of Shakespeare films organised in the UK highlighted how filmmakers have been inspired by his plays over the years.

On my travels, I discovered that one of the films that proved most popular with younger audiences was Baz Luhrmann's 1996 version of *Romeo and Juliet*. The setting was changed from Verona in Italy to the fictional Verona Beach and the rival families from the play became street gangs. The big pull for the new audience was the actor who played Romeo, Leonardo DiCaprio. As fresh and modern as when it was filmed 20 years ago and introduced a whole youthful generation to the joys of Shakespeare on the big screen, the re-screening of the film had a similar effect on a completely new, young audience. Leaving the cinema, Ryan chatted to us about the film. 'We've been studying Shakespeare at school, and I could never really get what he was on about. The language just didn't make any sense but when it's set in California and it's about gangs then the language doesn't bother you so much and you can understand it. And Leo's great as Romeo. I can't believe how young he looked!'.

OPTIMISE
- Remember, with multiple-choice questions only **one** option can be right.
- Sometimes one word in the question/sentence or options can be key to get the right answer.
- Be careful when you read the exact same words or phrases in a question and then find them in the text. They may not always help you with the correct answer.

136

4 Watch two students each talking about a different set of photographs. Answer the questions while you watch.

1 How many photographs are there in each set of exam questions? ___
2 How long does each student have to talk about the photographs and answer the question about them? ___
3 Can both students see their partner's set of photographs? Why / Why not? ___
4 How long does the other student have to answer an additional question about their partner's photos? ___
5 Can the students talk together about the photographs or questions? ___

OPTIMISE
- Timing is important in a speaking exam. The examiner will guide you but make sure you know exactly how much time you have to answer each part of a question, usually around one minute.
- You often talk about photos in a speaking exam. Remember to listen carefully. In this task, it's important to **compare** the photos, not describe them in detail.
- Try to find two or three similarities or differences between the photos. This will help you extend the first part of your answer.
- Then answer the question about the photographs. Give your opinion or a reason for your answer: *I think / don't think … because …* Use any examples in the photographs to help you focus.

5 Work in pairs. Student A look at set 1 photographs. Student B look at set 2 photographs. Make a note of any words or expressions related to your set. Then find some similarities or differences between them. You have three minutes to write down your ideas. Compare your lists and add any more ideas together.

What are the advantages of studying in these different ways? 1

How might the people be feeling? 2

Example: classroom

Set 1

formal style class room, inside, informal/relaxed way to study, outside, students collaborating, sharing, project work

In the first photo we can see a more formal style classroom with a teacher talking and the students are inside whereas/but/while in the second photo the students are outside, talking together, and sharing ideas, it might be a project …

6 Work in pairs. Take turns to talk about the set of photographs you made notes about and answer the question. Time your partner for one minute. How well do they manage the time? How could they improve?

OPTIMISE
- In a speaking exam you usually get a mark for grammar and vocabulary.
- Try to use a variety of different structures, words and expressions. Try not to repeat yourself too much.
- Use a variety of linking words or phrases to help you structure what you say.

141

Optimise your exams features:

- Sections dedicated to each of the exam papers.
- Exercises to improve students' understanding of common exam tasks.
- Clear targeted advice on how to approach specific exam tasks.
- Exercises to encourage analysis of sample answers.
- Details of common FAQs regarding specific exam papers.
- A *Speaking test* video in which real candidates complete an authentic Speaking test, to watch and analyse.
- Sample writing plans to compare and critique.
- Information about how the test is marked.
- Advice on how much time to spend on different parts of the exams.

STUDENT'S BOOK | Reference material

There is a bank of reference material at the back of the Student's Book, designed to support students as they work through the lessons, and also intended to act as a revision tool when required.

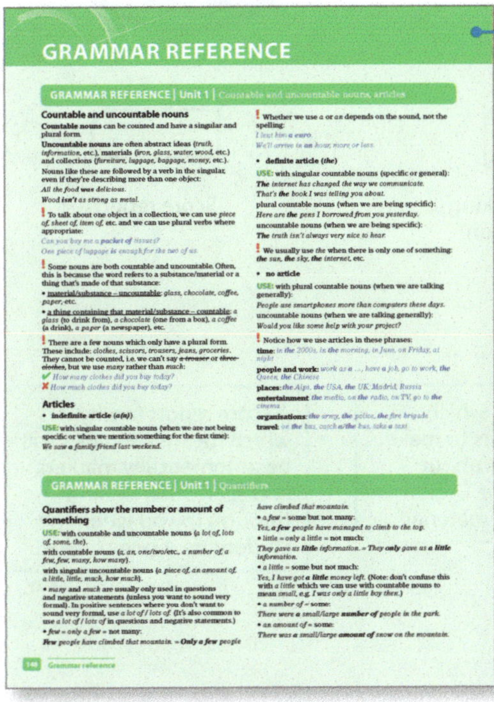

The *Grammar reference* pages provide more detailed explanations of the grammar points covered in every unit, along with example sentences showing how the structures can be used.

All three vocabulary sections from each unit are expanded upon in the *Vocabulary reference*. The sections on Topic vocabulary, Phrasal verbs, Collocations, Word patterns and Idioms all include example sentences. The Word formation sections from the Use of English lessons include a list of derivatives.

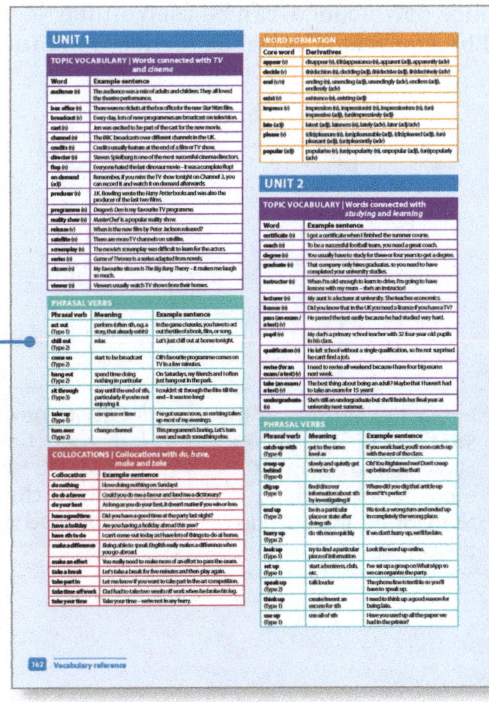

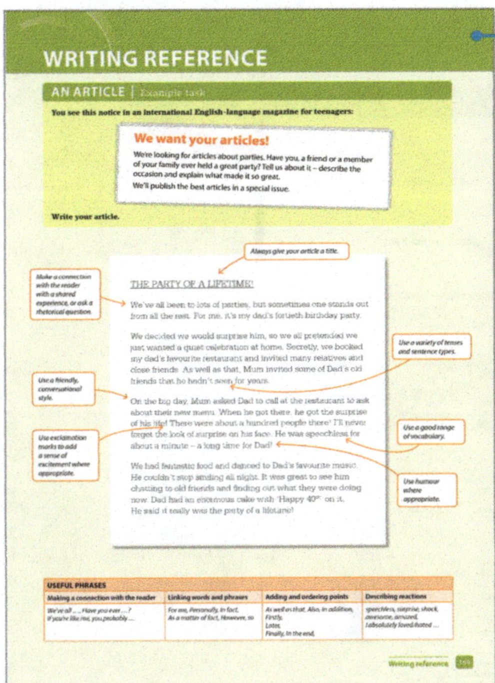

There is a model text for each writing genre, with annotations to highlight key points that students need to remember. Every *Writing reference* page also includes a bank of 'Useful phrases'.

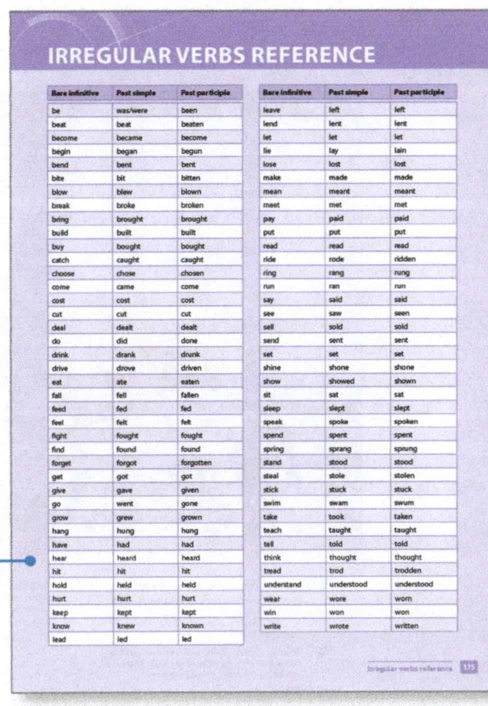

A list of irregular verbs used throughout the Student's Book is provided at the end of the reference material.

DIGITAL STUDENT'S BOOK SB

Includes an access code for the Student's Resource Centre

The *Optimise* Digital Student's Book offers students the possibility of an interactive learning experience, which engages the class as a whole and enables lessons to be dynamic and motivating. The material is easily downloadable and, once downloaded, can be used offline.

The *Optimise* Digital Student's Book includes:

Interactive Student's Book Activities
Interactive versions of the Student's Book activities, allowing the option of more flexible learning both inside and outside the classroom situation.

Complete class audio / **Integrated video**
Easy-to-navigate digital reproduction of the Student's Book pages which includes embedded audio and video material.

Note-taking function
A notes facility, which enables students to make their own notes about all aspects of the Digital Student's Book material.

Score report
A score report facility, which means exercises will be automatically marked and scores will be sent through to you when the student next goes online.

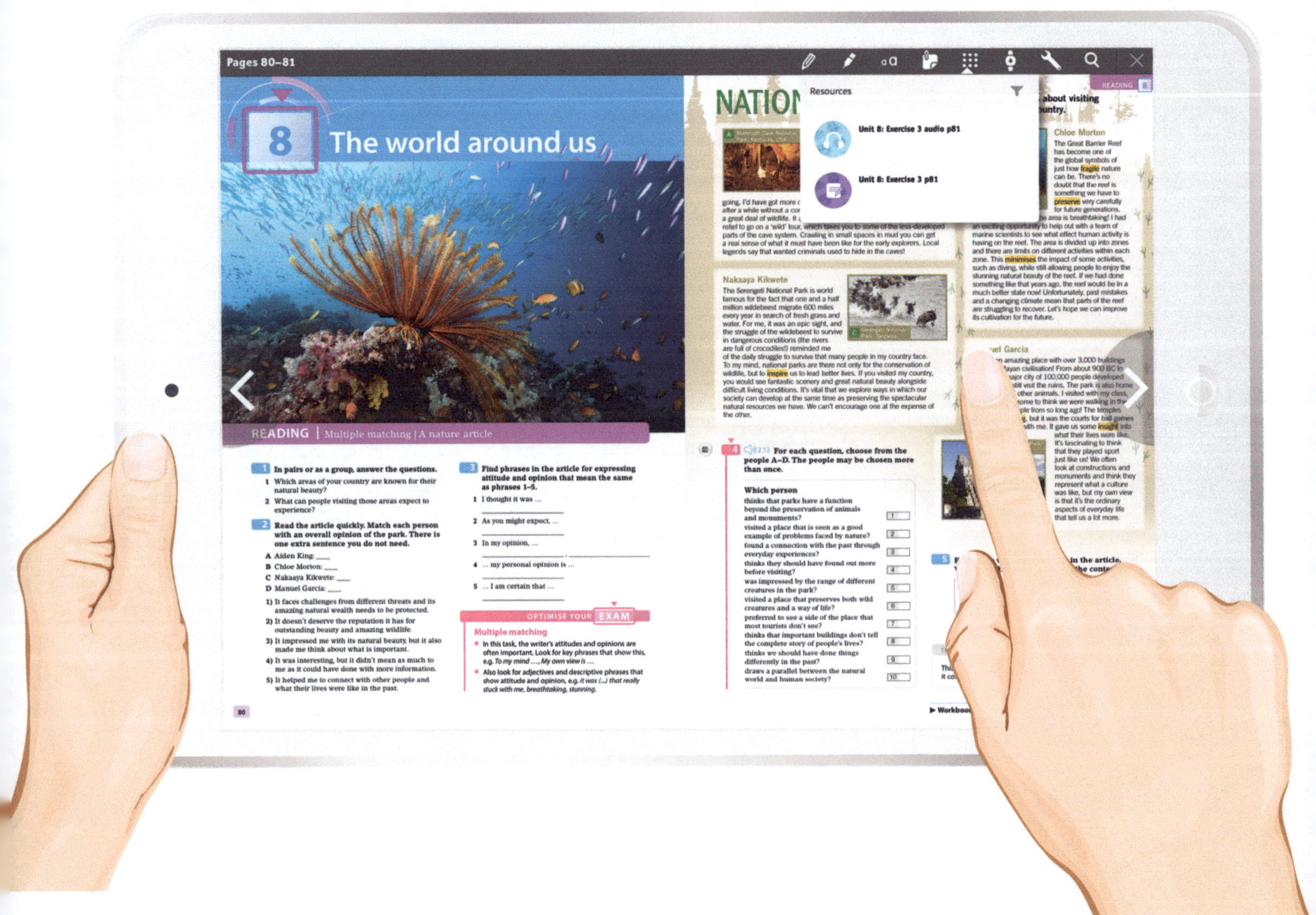

PRESENTATION KIT

Includes digital versions of the Student's Book and Workbook

You can use the *Optimise* Presentation Kit in the classroom to promote interactive, heads-up lessons, allowing for the option of collaborative learning. The Presentation Kit provides you with a versatile, digital presentation and teaching tool. Built-in functionality enables you to annotate and customise your presentation in advance, making the lesson more suited to the needs of your class. The Presentation Kit can be easily downloaded and, once downloaded, can be used offline.

The *Optimise* Presentation Kit includes:

Interactive Student's Book activities

Interactive versions of the Student's Book activities, giving you the opportunity to complete activities and check answers as a whole class.

Complete Class and Workbook audio / **Integrated video**

All class audio and video material, which can be played instantly by clicking on the hotspots throughout the Presentation Kit material.

Student's Book and Workbook Answer key feature

Answer keys for the Student's Book and Workbook are embedded within each activity, meaning you can show the next answer at the touch of a button. Additional answer key pop-ups are also provided, with suggested answers for open activities.

Note pad feature

A notes facility, enabling you to add your own comments on the material. This helps you deliver more effective and engaging lessons.

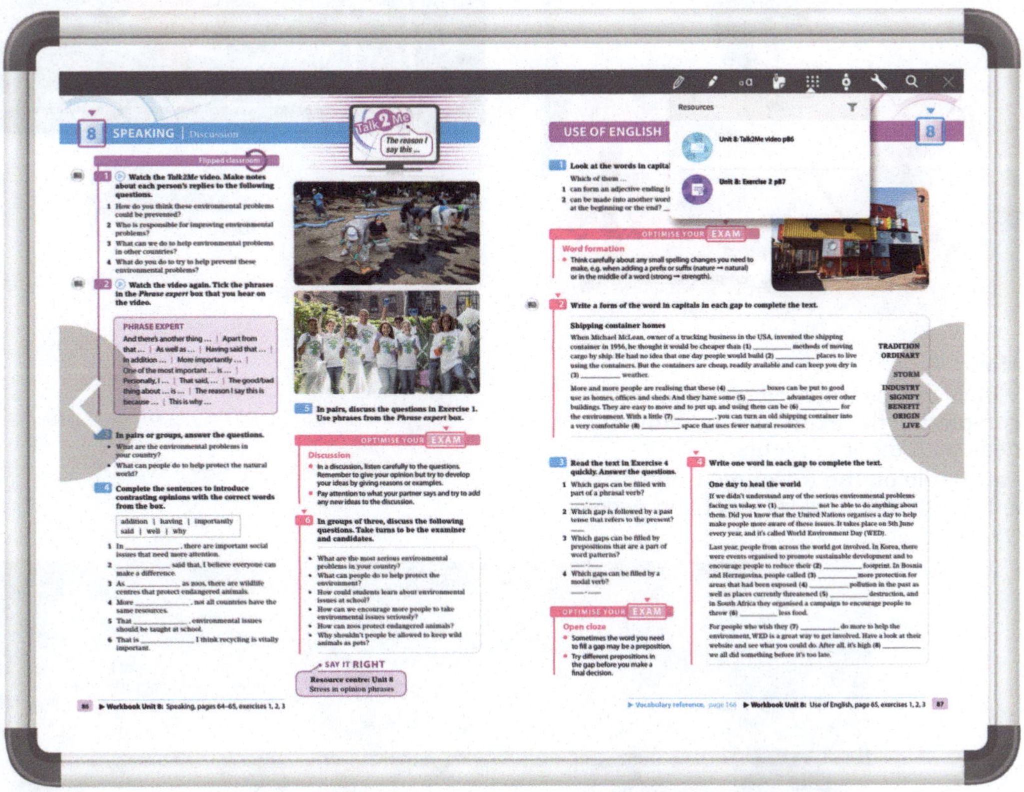

VIDEOS

Use in class or for self-study

Optimise videos provide comprehensive support for students to develop their speaking skills. The course features two different video strands, both of which are flexible and versatile resources that can be used in a number of different ways to support and extend listening and speaking skills.

Talk2Me

1 *Talk2Me* videos

Every Speaking lesson includes a *Talk2Me* video. These exciting vox pops videos feature a presenter talking to teenagers and young people about a variety of engaging subjects.

The videos present key functional language in a natural and original context.

Flipped classroom

Flipped classroom option

You can choose to use the Flipped classroom approach for these videos and set them for homework. Students watch the videos and complete the exercises in the Student's Book at home to prepare for the Speaking lesson. This allows more class time to activate the functional language and develop fluency for the exam task.

Classroom option

Of course, the videos can be watched together as a class with students completing the exercises individually or sharing their ideas with other students.

The videos are available on the Resource Centre and are accompanied by additional worksheets, transcripts and answer keys.

2 Speaking test videos

Optimise includes Speaking test videos as part of the *Optimise your exams* section. The videos provide students with a chance to observe the performance of candidates doing complete Speaking tests under exam conditions.

Watching and discussing the video also enables students to have a greater understanding of the format and processes involved in speaking tests, giving them more confidence and helping them to feel better prepared for the exam.

WORKBOOK | Reading lesson

Complete *Optimise Practice test* at the back of the Workbook

Each Workbook unit has eight pages, with a section for each separate lesson in the Student's Book, and one page for an end of unit Progress check.

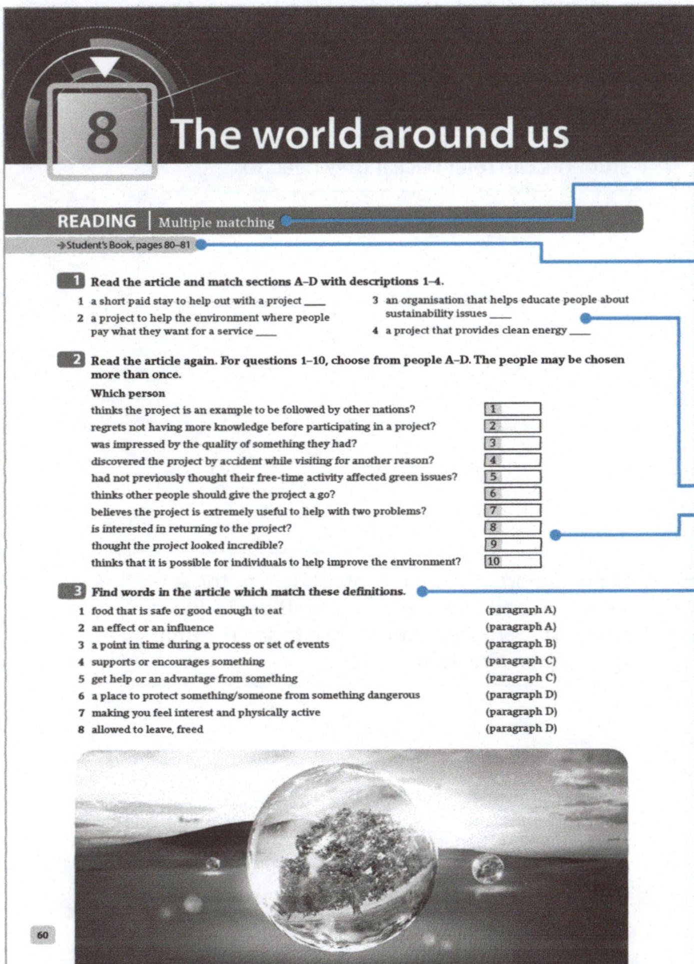

8 The world around us

READING | Multiple matching

→Student's Book, pages 80–81

1 Read the article and match sections A–D with descriptions 1–4.

1 a short paid stay to help out with a project ___
2 a project to help the environment where people pay what they want for a service ___
3 an organisation that helps educate people about sustainability issues ___
4 a project that provides clean energy ___

2 Read the article again. For questions 1–10, choose from people A–D. The people may be chosen more than once.

Which person

thinks the project is an example to be followed by other nations? 1
regrets not having more knowledge before participating in a project? 2
was impressed by the quality of something they had? 3
discovered the project by accident while visiting for another reason? 4
had not previously thought their free-time activity affected green issues? 5
thinks other people should give the project a go? 6
believes the project is extremely useful to help with two problems? 7
is interested in returning to the project? 8
thought the project looked incredible? 9
thinks that it is possible for individuals to help improve the environment? 10

3 Find words in the article which match these definitions.

1 food that is safe or good enough to eat (paragraph A)
2 an effect or an influence (paragraph A)
3 a point in time during a process or set of events (paragraph B)
4 supports or encourages something (paragraph C)
5 get help or an advantage from something (paragraph C)
6 a place to protect something/someone from something dangerous (paragraph D)
7 making you feel interest and physically active (paragraph D)
8 allowed to leave, freed (paragraph D)

60

All exam skills match the corresponding Student's Book lesson.

Every unit includes a reference to the corresponding Student's Book lesson.

Exercises check students' comprehension of the reading text and are designed to develop students' reading skills.

New vocabulary from the Workbook reading text is highlighted.

The world around us 8

www.helpi....

HELPING THE WORLD

Read about these exciting projects to help nature and the environment

A Amelie Barton

You might think that malnourishment – not having enough to eat to lead a healthy and active life – only affects people in the developing world, but the shocking truth is that in the UK over three million people suffer from it every year. Yet, every year 40% of our food – food that could be eaten – ends up in landfills, where it produces harmful greenhouse gases. Not only that, it's a huge waste of all the resources like water and energy that went into producing it. That's why I was so excited to eat at 'Skipchen' in Bristol – the meal was stunning! Everything they cook is donated or found in supermarket skips – supermarkets throw out tons of food every day because it is past its sell-by date although it is still edible. The volunteer staff collect it and make delicious meals with whatever they've found, so the menu varies daily. Customers pay what they want or eat for free if they can't afford to pay. More restaurants like this are opening all over the country. In my view, it's a brilliant way of reducing our impact on the environment and feeding people.

B Miguel Blanco

I went to Ouarzazate in Morocco because I'm a huge fan of *Game of Thrones* and wanted to visit the film location there. When I came across what will be the largest solar power plant in the world there, I was amazed. The first stage of this exciting development is now working and it's awesome to look at – in fact, it's so big, you can see it from space! It's made of 500,000 curved mirrors that reflect and concentrate the sunlight onto a pipe filled with liquid, heating it to over 370 °C. This hot liquid is combined with water to turn wheels in huge machines called turbines to generate energy. When it's completed, the plant aims to produce 38% of the country's energy and provide 1.1 million people with clean electricity, and it will save Morocco hundreds of thousands of tons of carbon emissions every year. That's an impressive achievement – let's hope more countries do the same.

C Luke Davis

I love sailing, but I'd never considered how it could affect the environment. For me, taking part in some activities for my Duke of Edinburgh Award* organised by The Green Blue really opened my eyes. The Green Blue, an environmental programme, promotes the sustainable use of coastal waters, lakes and rivers by boating and water sports participants. They also help boating businesses to be 'green'. On my project we learnt lots of practical ways to be more environmentally friendly, such as improving water quality and preventing non-native species of marine life accidentally being carried to Britain by boats – they can seriously damage the environment and local species. To my mind, everyone who goes out on the water would benefit from looking at The Green Blue's online resources or participating in one of their educational projects.

D Erin Roberts

Too many people believe that protecting the environment isn't something one person can do, but my own view is that anyone can make a difference. That's why I volunteered at the Matang Wildlife Centre in Borneo on a fascinating conservation and protection project. The centre is a refuge for orangutans that have been injured, rescued or lost their parents due to deforestation, mining and forest fires. I learnt a lot about providing the animals with stimulating environments to encourage natural behaviour so the animals can be released back into the wild. I wish I'd known more before going, as I'd have been able to help more. I enjoyed looking after the animals and helping to create an organic farm so the centre can grow enough food to feed the animals. It cost £1,280 to go for two weeks, but it was an incredible experience. I'll try and go again when I can!

*The Duke of Edinburgh Award is the world's leading youth achievement award, giving millions of 14- to 24-year-olds the opportunity to be the very best they can be.

61

The Reading lessons feature a full-length reading text.

Engaging images attract students' attention and interest in the text.

8 **GRAMMAR 1** | Conditionals (2): second, third and mixed conditionals

→Student's Book, page 82 →Grammar reference, Student's Book, page 156

Grammar lessons throughout the Workbook reflect the material covered in the Student's Book and provide students with more opportunities to consolidate and practise the structures.

The page number of the Student's Book *Grammar reference* is included in the Workbook so that students can refer back if they need to.

1 Choose the correct words.

1 What **happened / would happen** if one day we suddenly had no fresh water on Earth?
2 There would be more elephants now if they **hadn't been / weren't** hunted for their tusks.
3 If I **go / went** to an area of natural beauty, I wouldn't leave any rubbish behind.
4 **Had / Has** the government considered the future, it would have introduced more laws to combat global warming.
5 They wouldn't be looking for the tiger, if the zookeeper **locked / had locked** the cage!
6 If we **didn't burn / hadn't burnt** fossil fuels, the world would be a very different place.
7 If Max hadn't become a vet, he would **be / have been** a marine scientist instead.
8 We could **film / have filmed** the lions if we had had a video camera with us.

2 Read situations 1–6 and complete the conditional sentences.

1 We didn't protect the animals and they died out.
Had ______ the animals, they ______ .
2 You're not in Africa so you don't know what's happening.
If ______ in Africa, you ______ happening.
3 They destroyed the forest and now the animals have nowhere to live.
If they ______ the forest, the animals ______ somewhere to live now.
4 We didn't realise solar power was cheaper so we didn't get solar panels.
If we ______ solar power was cheaper, we ______ solar panels.
5 I went on the safari and I saw giraffes in the wild.
Had I ______ on the safari, I ______ giraffes in the wild.
6 I'm not at the environment lecture because no-one told me about it.
I ______ at the environment lecture now if someone ______ me about it.

3 Rewrite the underlined sentences as conditionals.

THE EXXON VALDEZ OIL SPILL

On March 24, 1989, the oil tanker Exxon Valdez had just left the Valdez Marine Terminal in Alaska full of crude oil. At midnight, (1) the ship hit a reef, which tore a hole in it. Investigators later discovered that (2) the accident happened because the crew were tired. The result was that over 40 million litres of oil entered the water, which is roughly the same amount as 17 Olympic-sized swimming pools. A bad situation was then made worse when (3) a storm hit the area and spread the oil widely. Eventually, (4) the oil covered the coastline and thousands of animals died.

Exxon ended up paying around two billion dollars to clean up the oil spill. (5) Not all of the oil has gone and many Alaskan beaches are still polluted with oil just inches below the surface. Unfortunately, (6) we can't remove it so that the beaches are clean again.

1 If ______
2 Had ______
3 If ______
4 Had ______
5 If ______
6 If ______

62

Every grammar section contains two or three exercises, and where possible texts are included, giving students another chance to see the unit grammar in a realistic context.

The world around us 8

8 **VOCABULARY** | Topic vocabulary | Phrasal verbs | Word patterns

→Student's Book, page 83 →Vocabulary reference, Student's Book, page 166

The corresponding page of the *Vocabulary reference* is included throughout the Workbook wherever relevant.

Each of the three vocabulary sections is covered separately in the Workbook, giving your students another chance to reinforce their lexical knowledge.

1 The words in bold are in the wrong place. Complete the phrases by writing the words on the correct line.

1 global **development** ______
2 greenhouse **change** ______
3 renewable **warming** ______
4 toxic **energy** ______
5 carbon **layer** ______
6 climate **effect** ______
7 ozone **footprint** ______
8 sustainable **waste** ______

2 Match to make sentences. Use the words in italics to help you.

1 Many plant and animal species are in danger of *dying* ___
2 Naturally, oil-producing countries don't want us to *do* ___
3 I don't think our leaders understand that time is *running* ___
4 People are far too lazy to recycle so they just *throw* ___
5 It's a tragedy for the planet when companies *chop* ___
6 Because they are huge, there's no way we can *clean* ___
7 If sea levels rise too much, they will eventually *wipe* ___
8 Our seas are being polluted and the situation *calls* ___

a) *away with* fossil fuels.
b) *for* immediate action.
c) *out* for us to save the planet.
d) *down* forests to make way for roads.
e) *away* very useful materials.
f) *up* the oceans.
g) *out* entire cities.
h) *out* and need our protection.

3 Complete the dialogue with the words in the box.

by (× 2) | from | of | to (× 2)

Jade: For our presentation on environmental problems, I was thinking we could talk about water and how using it irresponsibly is a waste (1) ______ natural resources, but the rest of the class might find it boring.
Ben: Yes, probably. What if we focus on an animal instead? So many are threatened (2) ______ climate change. We could talk about the polar bear.
Jade: OK, but first we'll need to explain what causes climate change and why it's harmful (3) ______ animals.
Ben: Right. We'll explain how global temperatures are affected (4) ______ human activities, and then we'll discuss the connection between rising temperatures and the melting polar ice caps.
Jade: Yes, and how that is an example of habitat loss. To finish, we could discuss ways of protecting animals (5) ______ habitat loss.
Ben: Do you mean other animals, in addition to the polar bear? If we did that, we would have to talk about the specific dangers they're exposed (6) ______ , and then the presentation would be too long.
Jade: You're right. Let's just stick to the polar bears.

A second grammar section in the Workbook corresponds to the second grammar lesson in the Student's Book.

8 **GRAMMAR 2** | Unreal past and past wishes

→Student's Book, page 85 →Grammar reference, Student's Book, page 157

1 Choose the correct words.

1 It's high time the government **invested / had invested** more money in green technology.
2 Suppose there were no more fossil fuels. What would we **do / have done** without them?
3 If we can afford it, I'd rather we **had bought / bought** an electric car.
4 If only everyone **shares / shared** our concerns for the environment.
5 I wish people **wouldn't leave / have left** their rubbish on the beach.
6 I wish we **can / could** go on an African safari and see elephants and lions.

2 Complete the sentences with the correct form of the verbs in brackets.

1 I wish you ______ so much water. **(not waste)**
2 If only the ship ______ a reef. **(not strike)**
3 I'd rather you ______ all the lights on. **(not leave)**
4 You know, it's high time you ______ an interest in the environment. **(take)**
5 Do you wish we ______ recycling cans a lot sooner? **(start)**
6 I wish I ______ to the beach clean-up, but I'm studying. **(go)**

63

Exercises in the Workbook are staged so as to be progressively more challenging.

WORKBOOK | Listening lesson | Speaking lesson | Use of English lesson

8 LISTENING | Multiple matching

→ Student's Book, page 84

The listening exam skill in the Student's Book is practised again in the Workbook.

1 Match the underlined phrases in the sentences to their meanings.

1 I can't believe they knocked down the old library to make way for a new car park. ___
2 It just goes to show how little the council understands about conservation. ___
3 If you think the environment isn't in danger, you have your head in the sand. ___
4 After the heavy storm, I went to the beach and there was not a soul around. ___
5 Washing empty cartons before putting them in the recycling bin is a pain in the neck. ___

a) refuse to think about unpleasant facts
b) no-one present
c) provide a space for
d) very annoying
e) proves that something is true

2 Look at Exercise 3 and read the sentences. Match them to sentences 1–8.

1 It affects the whole world. ___
2 Every living thing has its value. ___
3 You wouldn't believe how bad it was. ___
4 Households throw away too much rubbish. ___
5 It's no use pretending it's not happening. ___
6 Everyone needs to get involved. ___
7 They're always complaining about the rain. ___
8 Joining an online campaign doesn't really do much. ___

The Workbook listening exercises have their own dedicated audio material, available on the Resource Centres and on the Online Workbook.

3 11 You will hear five people on a radio programme talking about their concerns for the environment. Choose from the list (A–H) what each speaker says about it. There are three extra letters you do not need.

A It's difficult to comprehend the scale of a disaster.
B A combined effort is needed to save the planet.
C Online petitions tend to have little success.
D Environmental pollution has a truly global impact.
E People worry about the weather more than they should.
F It's clear that certain problems cannot be denied anymore.
G It's important that we maintain the variety of life on earth.
H We are producing more and more waste in our homes.

Speaker 1 ☐
Speaker 2 ☐
Speaker 3 ☐
Speaker 4 ☐
Speaker 5 ☐

Workbook exercises give students more practice in exam-type tasks.

8 SPEAKING | Discussion

→ Student's Book, page 86

1 Match the words and phrases to do with the environment that are connected.

1 carbon dioxide ___
2 endangered species ___
3 forests ___
4 global warming ___
5 harmful products ___
6 land and water ___
7 ozone layer ___
8 solar power ___

a climate change
b UV rays
c die out
d toxic waste
e renewable energy
f carbon footprint
g natural resources
h natural environment

2 Complete the sentences with the phrases in the box.

and there's another thing | apart from that | as well as | having said that | in addition | more importantly | the good thing about | this is why

1 We should protect forests for a number of reasons. Firstly, they're beautiful places, but much ___________, these natural environments produce oxygen and are home to many animals.
2 The destruction of the ozone layer in the atmosphere is very dangerous for our health because exposure to UV light can lead to skin cancer. ___________ too – UV light is harmful for our eyes.

As the Workbook is designed for independent use, the speaking lessons consist of written exercises specifically designed to provide essential preparation that will further improve students' speaking skills.

3 ___________ solar power is that it is a renewable form of energy, so it will never run out. Another advantage is it's clean and doesn't pollute the atmosphere.
4 People are very aware of environmental problems such as carbon dioxide in the atmosphere. ___________, however, most people haven't done anything to reduce their own carbon footprint.
5 There are too many endangered species. I recently found out that tigers ___________ elephants could die out completely in our lifetime unless we do something to save them.
6 Climate change is a huge threat to our planet. ___________ governments around the world must work together to fight climate change and its terrible consequences.
7 Toxic waste is polluting the oceans and killing sea life. ___________, this harmful product is poisoning the land that we need to grow food on.
8 Water is a valuable natural resource, so I try not to waste it when, for example, I'm doing the dishes. ___________ though, I don't know how else to be environmentally friendly at home.

8 USE OF ENGLISH | Word formation | Open cloze

→ Student's Book, page 87

Workbook exercises give students the chance to examine and practise language in more detail.

1 Look at the gaps in the sentences and decide if they need a verb (V), an adjective (ADJ), an adverb (ADV) or a noun (N).

1 I returned to the island after the earthquake. Nothing looked the same. In fact, the place was ___________. ___
2 While gold could be found, the area was ___________ active. But then the mines closed down and people left the town. ___
3 Luckily for the elephant, an ___________ gamekeeper spotted the poachers and contacted the police who caught them. ___
4 The architect came up with a wonderful ___________ design for the new animal enclosure at the zoo. ___
5 Surely something as important as the ___________ of the wetlands should be supported by all the political parties. ___
6 As the wild animal struggled to free itself, the hunter's net ___________ even more around it. ___
7 The catastrophic oil spill near the coast of Florida received extensive ___________ on TV and in the newspapers. ___
8 We would like to install solar panels on our roof, but the problem is ___________ – they're just too expensive. ___

2 Complete the sentences in Exercise 1 with the words in the box in the correct form.

afford | conserve | cover | future | industry | observe | recognise | tight

3 Write a form of the word in capitals in each gap to complete the text.

The Use of English lessons in the Workbook include an exam-type task, so students get a further opportunity to apply the language skills they developed in the Student's Book lesson.

The variety of life on Earth is known as biodiversity. All species of plants, animals and micro-organisms, their (1) ___________ make-up and different ecosystems, such as deserts, rainforests and coral reefs, are all part of our (2) ___________-diverse Earth. (GENE, BIOLOGY)

Biodiversity is vital for many reasons. A larger number of plant species means a bigger variety of crops so that hunger does not (3) ___________ us. (THREAT)

In addition, greater diversity creates natural (4) ___________ for all forms of life. (SUSTAIN)

Diverse ecosystems can make a quicker recovery from (5) ___________ events such as floods or fires. (PREDICT)

They are also responsible for protecting our water resources and the (6) ___________ of nutrients in the soil. (STORE)

So, although we are the (7) ___________ species on the planet, we still need to be concerned about the (8) ___________ of diversity. (DOMINATE, PRESERVE)

8 **WRITING** | An article

→Student's Book, pages 88–89 →Writing reference, Student's Book, page 169

Details of the *Writing reference* in the Student's Book are included, so students can easily refer back to it.

1 Read the exam advice and choose the correct words.

1 When you write an article, you **should / shouldn't** try to make a connection with the reader.
2 Give **possible / specific** reasons and examples to make your article more interesting for the reader.
3 It **is / isn't** a good idea to refer to your own experience to draw the reader in.

Writing lessons begin by re-focusing students on the exam advice given in their Student's Book.

Learning from school gardens

If you're anything like me, you believe that growing your own food is an important way to reduce your carbon footprint. Perhaps you also think that it is something everyone should learn at school. In my experience, school gardens have many benefits.

The first thing we should consider is that a school garden supports the development of life skills as students have to work together to make and maintain it. These include problem-solving, taking responsibility, working well in groups, good communication and respecting other people's needs.

Another great way to use school gardens is to help students learn about the world they live in. For example, students can learn about sustainable living and how they can help look after the environment. In addition, growing and eating their own food is a good opportunity to make students aware of the importance of food choices, personal health and well-being.

So, I would encourage all secondary schools to start or continue using school gardens. To summarise, students learn a tremendous amount from working in them and they are good for the environment.

The Workbook includes a model answer in addition to the one found in the Student's Book.

2 Read the article. Are the statements T (True) or F (False)?

1 The writer does not try to make a personal connection with the reader. T / F
2 The first main point is that school gardens can help teach life skills. T / F
3 The second main point is that school gardens are good for the environment. T / F

3 Rewrite the sentences using the words given. Make any necessary changes.

1 Many students don't get enough exercise. Driving to school is not a good idea. **SO**
____
____
2 Students could use other forms of transport to get exercise. Cycling, walking or using a scooter are other forms of transport. **SUCH AS**
____
____
3 Car shares are a good idea. They reduce the number of cars on the road. **DUE TO THE FACT THAT**
____
4 Car shares also reduce pollution. They are good for the environment. **BECAUSE**
____

Exercises in the Workbook will help students to consolidate and develop their writing skills in general.

4 Read the information in the box and make notes. Use the ideas in Exercise 3 or your own ideas and include useful phrases. Then write your article.

You see this advert in an English-speaking magazine for young people.

Articles wanted
Too many students travel to school by car – and too many cars on the road isn't good for the environment. We want to change that! Send us your articles explaining two ways students could travel to school instead and what the benefits are. We will publish the best articles!

Part	Purpose	My ideas (including useful phrases)
Paragraph 1	make a connection with the reader	
Paragraph 2	make your first point – give reasons and examples	
Paragraph 3	make your second point – give reasons and examples	
Paragraph 4	summarise your article to encourage action from your reader	

Students are not always required to do a complete writing task in the Workbook. Instead they will sometimes be asked to write or complete sentences, write a paragraph or complete a paragraph plan.

66

The world around us 8

PROGRESS CHECK

Every Workbook lesson ends with a one-page *Progress check*.

1 Complete the texts with the words and phrases in the boxes. For each text there are some extra words and phrases you do not need.

1 call for | climate change | die out | do away with | exposed to | global warming | greenhouse effect | ozone layer | protected from | threatened by | wipe out

Aerosol sprays have created a hole in the (1) ____________ above our atmosphere. When it is intact, we are (2) ____________ dangerous solar rays. But when we are (3) ____________ them, they can cause skin cancer. Governments passed laws to (4) ____________ the dangerous chemicals in the sprays. Many people thought that would be the end of the problem, but it wasn't. Industrial processes are largely responsible for the (5) ____________ phenomenon that has caused temperatures to rise. (6) ____________ is a very serious problem because ecosystems often can't respond to extreme weather patterns quickly enough. When they don't, species can (7) ____________. Once that happens, they can never be replaced.

2 affected by | carbon footprint | chopped down | cleaned up | harmful to | renewable energy | run out | sustainable development | throw away | toxic waste | waste of

Everyone has a responsibility to reduce their individual (8) ____________. You can choose to have (9) ____________ for your needs at home, for example, solar panels that convert the sun's rays into electricity. This is clean energy so it isn't (10) ____________ the atmosphere. Secondly, it will never (11) ____________ because the sun provides an endless supply of light. You can also be careful with water. Don't take long showers as they're a(n) (12) ____________ this natural resource. Don't (13) ____________ paper products – they can be recycled. This is good because it means fewer trees are (14) ____________ to produce paper. These are just a few ideas and you can find out more online.

2 Complete the sentences with the correct form of the verbs in brackets.

1 If you ____________ the newspapers, we could have sent them for recycling. (**not throw away**)
2 I wish you ____________ the car when the shops are only a five-minute walk away. (**not take**)
3 Don't you think it's time you ____________ recycling glass, paper and aluminium? (**start**)
4 What ____________ if electric cars were affordable enough for every family to own one? (**happen**)
5 If he ____________ more carefully before lighting the fire, he wouldn't be in trouble now. (**think**)
6 I'd rather we ____________ more trees instead of building a swimming pool. (**plant**)
7 You would learn a lot about sustainability if you ____________ that video I sent you. (**watch**)
8 If only people ____________ more willing to change their lifestyle to help the environment. (**be**)
9 I wish I ____________ at that beach, but the sea there is too dirty and it's not safe. (**swim**)
10 If only we ____________ alternative energy sources decades ago. (**develop**)

The *Progress Check* always has one exercise based on the vocabulary from the unit, and one exercise based on the unit grammar.

Cumulative progress 1 2 3 4 5 6 7 8 9 10 11 12

3 Write one word in each gap to complete the text.

EARTH WITHOUT HUMANS

If (1) ________ was a sudden, worldwide catastrophe and humans were wiped (2) ________, what would happen to our planet? According to the TV series *Life After People*, some very terrifying things. In just a few hours there wouldn't be any lights on because power plants would (3) ________ out of fuel. A few days later underground train systems would flood because the pumps keeping water out of the tunnels would stop (4) ________. About a month later, things would get much (5) ________. That's when (6) ________ waste from nuclear power stations would be released into the atmosphere and the soil. It would be (7) ________ poisonous that any remaining animals would die. Eventually, plants would cover the world and it would be like humans and animals had never (8) ________ at all.

67

The final part of the *Progress check* is a *Cumulative progress* exercise, which includes vocabulary and grammar items from any of the preceding units.

ONLINE WORKBOOK OWB

For students PLUS Gradebook for teachers

The *Optimise* Online Workbook includes all the print Workbook content in a fully-interactive digital format, which students can use for independent self-study.

The *Optimise* Online Workbook includes:

- Interactive Workbook activities
- Complete Workbook audio
- Automated marking for instant feedback
- Gradebook

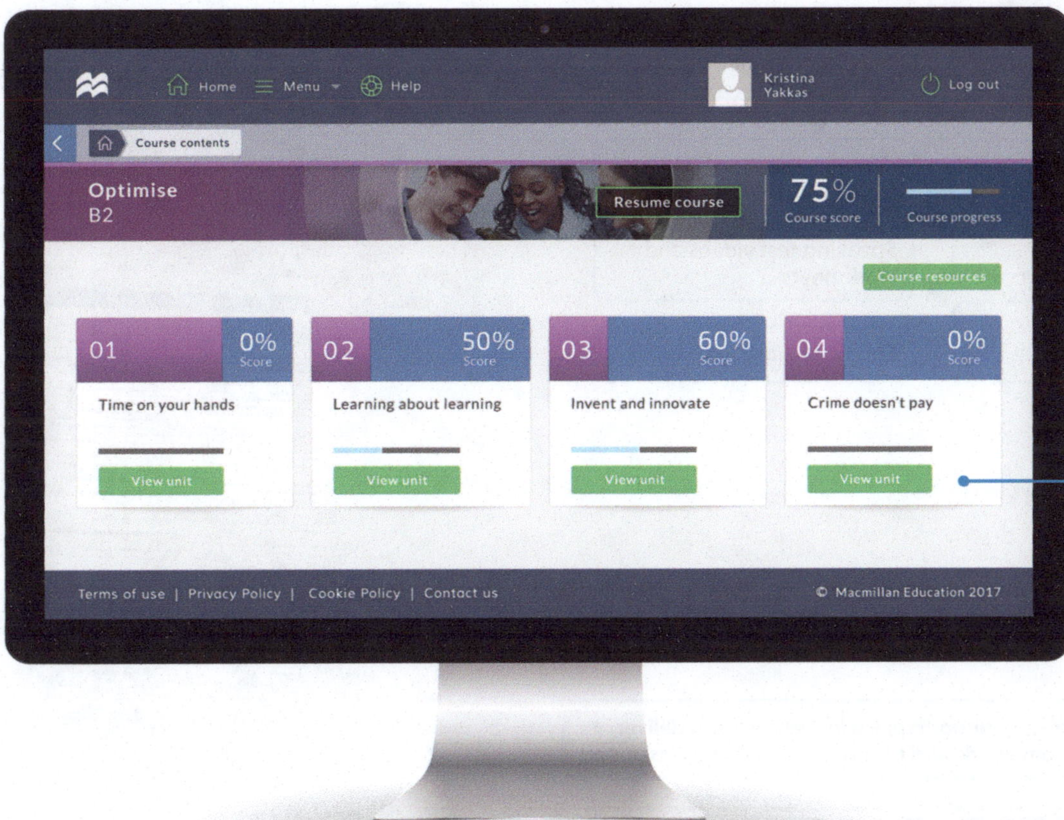

The automatic Gradebook facility will save you valuable marking time.

The Online Workbook enables you to manage multiple classes in a single location, and the content-locking facility gives you control over how you manage the tasks for your class.

Students have the chance to make multiple attempts at answering questions, enabling them to effectively consolidate their learning.

Scores are automatically collated and clearly displayed in the Gradebook, so it is easy to compare students and classes. Students' progress can be monitored at a glance, highlighting areas where they may require additional support.

The messaging and notification features allow you to correspond with your students, send homework reminders, and notify your classes when scores are available.

Detailed feedback on scores and progress creates a highly personalised self-study environment.

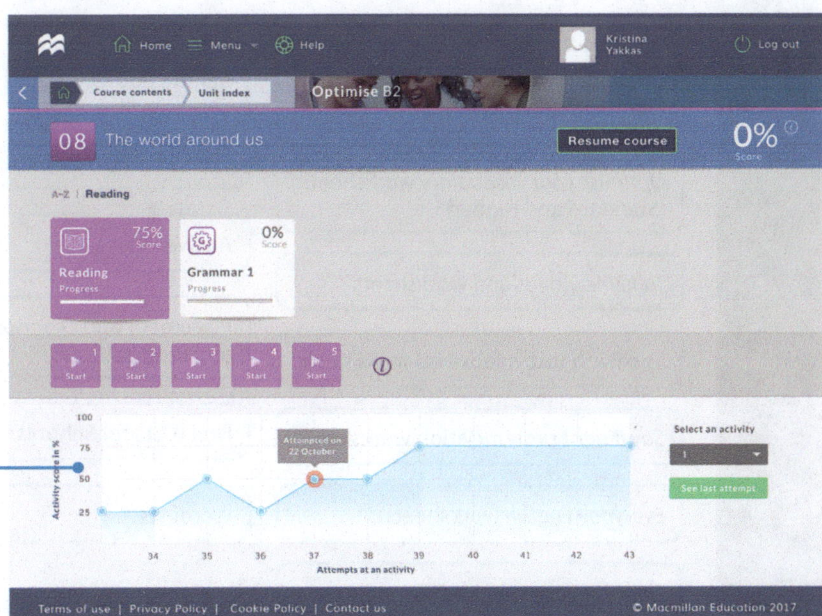

TEACHER'S AND STUDENT'S RESOURCE CENTRES

For teachers and students

The *Optimise* Resource Centres offer a huge bank of additional downloadable material and tests that have been designed to comprehensively support and enhance the core Student's Book and Workbook material.

For students, the Student's Resource Centre provides complementary materials to consolidate learning and encourage independent study.

STUDENT'S RESOURCE CENTRE

- *Optimise your grammar* worksheets (Standard and Higher)
- *Optimise your vocabulary* worksheets (Standard and Higher)
- *Talk2Me* videos and worksheets
- *Say it right* pronunciation worksheets
- Culture and CLIL worksheets
- Speaking test videos and worksheets
- Class and Workbook audio

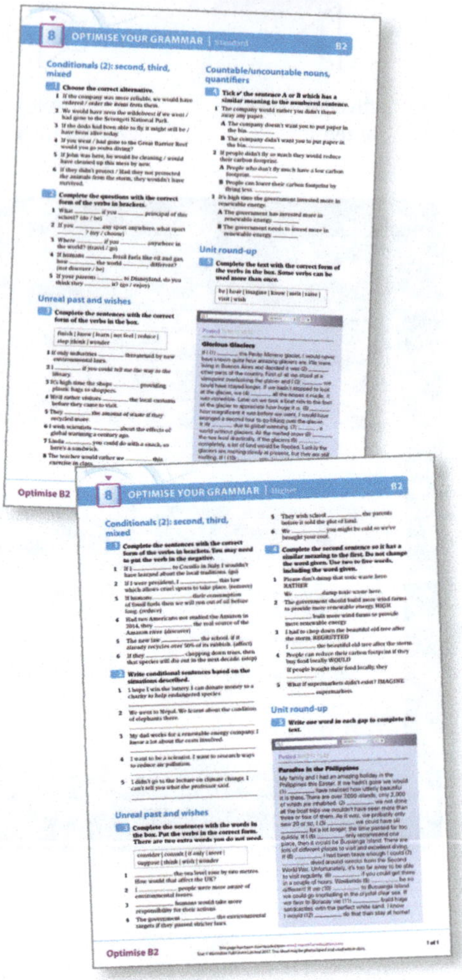

The Teacher's Resource Centre is your go-to place for resources to deliver dynamic lessons, assign for homework, and to support you in the classroom.

TEACHER'S RESOURCE CENTRE

- *Optimise your grammar* worksheets (Standard and Higher)
- *Optimise your vocabulary* worksheets (Standard and Higher)
- *Talk2Me* videos and worksheets
- Speaking test videos and worksheets
- *Say it right* pronunciation worksheets
- *Everyday English* worksheets
- Grammar communication worksheets
- Culture and CLIL worksheets
- Class and Workbook audio
- Answer keys
- Placement and Diagnostic tests, Unit and Progress tests
- First (FCE) for Schools Practice test
- Wordlists

TESTING MATERIALS

Complete testing package

Optimise provides an extensive range of testing materials, which can be used throughout the school year to assess your students' progress and to prepare them for exams.

Printable tests

Optimise offers a comprehensive range of printable tests, available on the Teacher's Resource Centre in PDF format.

All the *Optimise* tests correspond to the course level.

Tests are aligned closely to the CEFR and to competency levels for international and state exams.

Tests include:

- *Diagnostic* and *Placement tests*
- *Unit tests*, *Progress tests* and *End-of-year tests* (Standard and Higher)
- *First (FCE) for Schools* practice tests:
  - an *Optimise Practice test* at the back of the Workbook
  - *First (FCE) for Schools Practice test* on the Teacher's Resource Centre, which can be taken under test conditions

Complete answer keys, audio and audioscripts are provided for all tests.

Test Generator

The *Optimise* Test Generator allows you to create customised tests from the pre-prepared Unit and Progress tests.

- Tests are aligned to CEFR levels.
- The content reflects Reading, Writing, Speaking, Use of English and Listening tasks from international and state exams.
- The Test Generator comes with the option to save tests in progress and to preview them before printing.
- With Standard and Higher levels available, it also allows for maximum flexibility in choosing the test content.

Teacher support

PREPARING STUDENTS FOR EXAMS

Knowing your exam

- It's important that students become as familiar as possible with the different parts of the exam they are preparing for and understand what is required of them in each exam task.
- Carry out timed practice tests regularly with your students. As well as being excellent training, it's also an important way of highlighting specific areas for improvement.
- *Optimise* includes two Practice tests: one at the back of the Workbook and another on the Teacher's Resource Centre.
- After each test, draw up a class checklist of basic reminders or issues related to the exam.
- The *Optimise your exams* section at the back of the Student's Book provides a list of questions about different exam sections; this can be used for discussion and to create the class checklist.
- Many students associate exams with stress and panic, but if they are well prepared, students will generally feel more confident and that will show through in their performance.

Reading and Use of English preparation

- It's important that students develop key strategies for dealing with a variety of question types. These include skimming, scanning, understanding a writer's purpose, identifying reference words and understanding text logic.
- Encourage students to refer to dictionaries or the *Grammar* and *Vocabulary references* at the back of the Student's Book. However, students also need to learn strategies for working independently, as reference material cannot be used in exams.
- Students should create an efficient system for recording all new vocabulary they learn. Encourage them to think about how they can record words and phrases in as much detail as possible.
- Remind students that spelling is important, especially in tasks such as Word formation.
- Encourage students to read a variety of texts outside the classroom, e.g. online articles, graded readers, short stories and novels. This should help to increase their knowledge of vocabulary, grammatical structures and writing styles.
- Ask students to share ideas for recording and learning vocabulary, and to give short presentations about what they have read or learnt outside the classroom.

PREPARING STUDENTS FOR EXAMS

Writing preparation

- Writing in another language can be challenging for most young students, so make sure they choose tasks which are close to their interests or experiences whenever possible.
- Make sure students always read the question carefully and underline the key points. If they don't answer the question, or include all relevant information, they may lose marks.
- Remind students to think carefully about who they are writing for, and if the style required will be formal or informal.
- Encourage students to work in pairs or groups to discuss and brainstorm ideas in class and to make a clear plan before writing. This is especially useful for essays, where students may have to include some of their own ideas and opinions related to a topic.
- Timing is important in a real exam and practice under timed conditions in class is the best way to prepare students for writing tasks. If an essay task is to be completed in 40 minutes, students should spend approximately 5–10 minutes planning, and leave 5 minutes at the end for re-reading and checking spelling and punctuation. They should avoid counting every word in the exam.
- Students need to write within the correct word limit. Under-writing may mean they haven't answered the whole question and overwriting can mean they have repeated ideas, included irrelevant information or not organised the piece of writing very well.
- Tell students to read each other's pieces of writing to give them ideas and develop their own writing further.

Listening preparation

- It's important that students develop key strategies for dealing with a variety of listening question types. These include predicting information, identifying attitudes and opinions, and note-taking. Students should also practise identifying distractors in questions, to help them avoid choosing the wrong answer.
- Classroom discussions can help prior to doing a listening task. For example, ask students what they think the speakers will talk about, and if they will hear any specific information, such as times, names, dates and places.
- It can also be useful to vary the focus of a task in class before students attempt a set of exam questions. For example, students could listen once to give an overall summary of what was said on the audio, then listen again for specific information.
- When listening to short extracts, students need to look carefully at multiple-choice options in questions and underline key words. This will help them to focus on the important points in a question and identify key words and phrases.
- When listening to longer extracts, encourage students to listen for the overall idea(s) first before they focus on the actual words and phrases. Make sure students listen to stressed or key words that have an important message, rather than focusing on every individual word.
- Encourage students to listen to audio material outside class, for example on English-language digital radio or TV stations. They also need to hear a variety of accents, styles and age groups.

Speaking preparation

- Some students may feel especially nervous about taking a speaking exam, so one way to reassure them is to make them familiar with the structure of the exam they are going to take.
- In some speaking exams, students are tested in pairs or groups of three and there are two examiners: one interlocutor, who speaks to the candidates and directs the test as well as giving marks, and one assessor, who marks the students on specific criteria.
- It is important for students to understand the different types of interaction that will take place. For example, students need to know when they will speak alone and when they will speak with their partner or with the interlocutor.
- All classroom activities that encourage students to discuss issues in pairs or groups will give them practice in skills they will need in an exam, such as starting and ending a discussion, asking for and giving opinions, agreeing and disagreeing, developing arguments, and giving examples and reasons for opinions.
- Remind students that they don't have to agree with each other when doing a speaking task, but that they should use appropriate language for disagreeing politely.
- When practising any activities for speaking, encourage students to speak clearly and to ask for clarification if they don't understand or aren't sure about something.
- Ask students to work in pairs or groups to create their own set of questions about topics, such as school and free time interests, family and friends, sports, travel, etc. They can compare questions and interview each other.
- Encourage students to expand on their ideas and give examples or reasons when speaking.
- Give students as much practice as possible in talking for the required amount of time for each part of the test. They can time each other in class in order to improve on this.
- Make sure students know there isn't a correct answer to a question and they don't need to be experts on a topic.
- When they are speaking with a partner, encourage them to help each other and be supportive. It's a good idea for students to practise different tasks with different classmates and also to spend time speaking to other students they feel comfortable with.

TEACHING MIXED-ABILITY CLASSES

Introduction

All classes have students of different abilities and with a range of different learning needs. The teacher's challenge is to engage the more advanced students at the same time as helping those who are finding lessons more difficult. Here are some practical tips to create a more inclusive classroom.

Group dynamics

Begin the whole class together with a lead-in activity to provide a sense of community and a foundation for the levelled tasks that will follow. Lead-in activities preview, present and practise language in a way that lends itself perfectly to whole-class, multi-level instruction. At the end of a lesson, always bring the class back together and assign a whole-class activity.

Group, pair and individual work

Vary the way students work in the class to address different levels and needs. Organise students to work in pairs, small groups and teams. It is less stressful for weaker students to work with other classmates because they have more time to think about tasks, and students can help and learn from each other.

In some schools, it may be possible to divide classes into two groups according to ability. The two groups can be given the same work to complete, or they can work on differentiated material.

Games and activities, such as brainstorming vocabulary, help to increase collaboration in the mixed-ability classroom. For example, ask students to work together to produce spidergrams as a way to help them remember topic vocabulary.

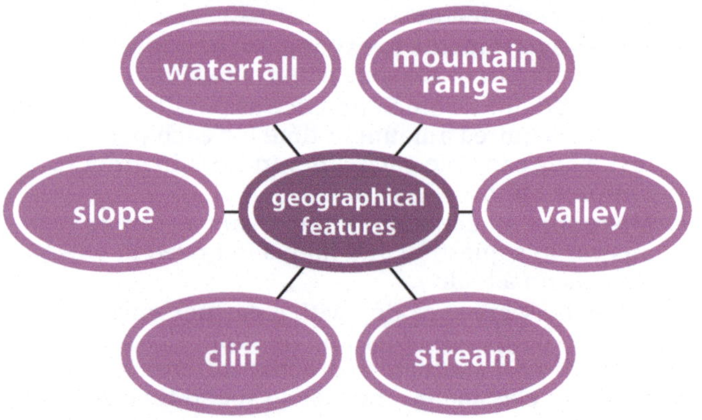

No matter what the level of the student, they all get better results through collaboration than they would have got by working on their own.

Pair work is usually successful in the mixed-ability classroom because it is easy to control and there is greater student participation. Depending on the task, decide how you organise your students into pairs: students with a similar level can work together at their own pace, or a stronger student can pair with a weaker student and help to support them. There are plenty of opportunities for pair work throughout *Optimise*.

Individual work allows for variations in speed and level. By giving a time limit rather than a quantity-of-work limit (e.g. *'Do as much as you can in three minutes.'* instead of, *'Do exercise 3.'*), students are able to work at their own pace.

Specific strategies for dealing with above-level students

- **Reading**

Set students more challenging work to keep the more advanced students motivated. For example, they could write their own comprehension questions to ask the class, select six new words from the reading text to write definitions for and learn, or create their own sentences or short texts using new vocabulary from the reading text.

Ask more advanced students to write or say a short summary of the text with their books closed.

- **Grammar and Vocabulary**

Ask stronger students to deduce the meaning of new words from the context and to elicit grammar rules by looking at the language in context.

Demand a higher level of fluency and accuracy from the students.

Encourage students to support weaker classmates by explaining the grammar point to them or by clarifying the meaning of a new vocabulary item.

- **Listening**

Ask students to summarise what they heard after listening to it the first time (as a whole class or in pairs).

Encourage students to write their own comprehension questions to ask the class.

- **Speaking**

Demand a higher level of fluency and accuracy and ask students to justify and defend their opinions.

Practise paraphrasing and brainstorm other phrases to use in the functional language.

Encourage students to write their own dialogues to act out in pairs.

- **Writing**

Indicate where something could be said in a more interesting or more complex way, and give creative tasks that students can do at their level.

Encourage peer correction by asking them to look at each other's work and suggest improvements. However, where more advanced students are reviewing work from below-level students, always make sure they are sensitive and constructive in their advice.

TEACHING MIXED-ABILITY CLASSES

Specific strategies for dealing with below-level students

- **General classroom organisation**

Make sure weaker students don't sit at the back, where it's more difficult for you to make eye contact with them.

Give clear instructions and check students have understood the task before they begin. For more complex tasks, ask stronger students to do an example of the task to check understanding.

- **Reading**

Ask weaker students easier questions, alternating with harder questions for stronger students.

Simplify multiple-choice tasks by reducing the number of options. Then gradually increase to exam level.

- **Grammar and Vocabulary**

Simplify gap-fill tasks by introducing optional answers, so students can identify the correct answer rather than having to produce it.

Be selective in your error correction and praise students for what they have managed to do, regardless of what others have produced.

Use homework to address weaknesses and consolidate classwork by using the mixed-ability Grammar and Vocabulary worksheets on the Teacher's Resource Centre.

- **Listening**

Pause the audio regularly to check understanding and explain if anything remains unclear. For more difficult texts, provide audioscripts after the first two listenings.

- **Speaking**

Provide useful phrases and model answers for less-able students to use as a basis for their answers.

- **Writing**

Additional model answers can assist students with their writing tasks. For students who need more support, provide a gapped or jumbled model answer for them to complete or put in order instead of asking them to write a text from scratch.

Mixed-ability features in *Optimise*

The **Mixed-ability** features in the *Optimise* Teacher's Book help to engage different groups of students using the same class material as the starting point, but with multi-level instruction. This way, you avoid increased preparation time, and the student group can still work together for most of the class.

As well as the **Mixed-ability** features in the *Optimise* Teacher's Book, the **Optional extension** and **Fast finishers** boxes also offer teachers a range of suggestions for ways to differentiate activities for stronger students.

Mixed ability

Pair up weaker students and give them the option of only reading two sections and working together to answer the questions. Challenge more advanced students who finish early by asking them to write three questions about the text. These can then be given to another early finisher to answer and then passed back to the original student for marking.

Optional extension

Before students give each other advice on how to improve their email, you could go over some key points on how to give effective feedback.

Only positive feedback: students only make suggestions about what their partner might add to or develop in his/her email. Feedback should give students a clear idea of how to improve.

Give a reader response: encouraging students to say what they expect to read in the email.

Limit feedback: A few main ideas is enough; three or four specific, clear ideas at the most.

Fast finishers

Write these definitions on the board and ask students to find the words or phrases in the text in Exercise 3.

one of two children born at the same time to the same mother

be friends with someone

to have the same interests or opinions

Answers

twins

get on with someone

have a lot in common

The *Optimise* Teacher's Resource Centre provides additional Grammar and Vocabulary worksheets in addition to the Unit and Progress tests, all available at two levels (Standard and Higher).

The *Optimise* Test Generator also allows teachers to custom-build their own tests according to their students' needs.

Encourage students to use the Online Workbook. Students get immediate feedback on their work and they can do the tasks as many times as necessary in order to get them correct. It's perfect for students of all abilities.

TEACHING TIPS

Here are some useful teaching tips for you to refer to throughout the school year.

Encouraging language development

Optimise B2, positioned at CEFR level B2, provides your students with an excellent opportunity to consolidate and build on the language they have learnt up to this point. The material is rich with new vocabulary and presents comprehensive coverage of a full range of grammar structures. Lessons include a wide range of strategies that you can use to help your students develop their language. Exploiting all this material in as many ways as possible will help to consolidate the language and make students comfortable and confident about using it in other contexts.

Useful expressions

One important aspect of language development which you can help your students focus on at this level is learning expressions. Expressions are high-frequency, multi-word phrases that function as a unit. Very often, expressions are pronounced as if they were one word. Fixed expressions, such as expressions of opinion, perform specific functions and they can't always be defined by looking them up in a dictionary as individual words. Such expressions are important in helping students improve their fluency. If they can learn these fixed expressions, students can develop language competency by transferring them to a variety of different contexts.

It is often the case that students learn these expressions, use them in the class and then go back to using just one expression they were already familiar with. Point out to students they can gain more points in an oral exam if they use a variety of expressions.

Developing accuracy and fluency in speaking

Accuracy is the ability to produce correct sentences with correct grammar and vocabulary. Fluency is the ability to read, speak or write easily, smoothly and with the correct intonation. The accuracy/fluency question depends on the purpose of the activity students are doing in the class. Controlled and semi-controlled speaking practice such as drills and information exchanges are working on accuracy. More open discussion should focus on fluency.

In general, try not to correct speaking too often in class as it interrupts the student's train of thought and can undermine their confidence. It's important to encourage students to talk and to keep talking. It's useful to note down errors while students are speaking then to take a few minutes at the end of class for a quick feedback session.

Memory and learning

Students are far more likely to remember words that they have analysed or focused on in some way than words they have learnt in isolation. If they have learnt the word in context and have fully understood it, rather than just learning it based upon a definition, it is much easier for students to remember the word in the long-term. Ask your students how they learn words best – do they need to hear them, see them written down or write them down themselves? Some students memorise vocabulary by associating new words with ideas or anecdotes. Good learners create mnemonic devices such as short phrases, tunes or poems to support their learning. In order to internalise vocabulary, students should also review vocabulary regularly. For strong lexical ability, students need to study vocabulary in context and that is best done by reading in English. Try to encourage your students to do this as much as possible. You could invite them to bring English books and magazines to class for group discussion or presentations. When your students come across a new word, encourage them to look at its place in the sentence, and to look at the words that appear either side of it. Remind them to think about the context and who the text is written for, and to look out for word patterns. They should always try to deduce meaning, but where they can't, point out that it's fine to use a dictionary as a tool for vocabulary building.

Teacher-talking time

As a teacher, you're always aware of how much time you spend speaking during the lesson. This is especially important in speaking lessons, where the key purpose is to encourage students to speak. That's not to say your speech isn't invaluable in providing models for pronunciation, functional language and appropriate discourse. But sometimes a large amount of teacher-talking time can slow the pace of a lesson and students can lose concentration and become bored or disinterested.

Some useful strategies to avoid this are:

- Wait for an answer when you ask a question. Students need 'thinking' time.
- Ask open-ended questions (e.g. *Wh-* questions) to encourage students to give longer answers, e.g. *What did you do last weekend?* instead of *Did you have a good weekend?*
- Vary the way students get feedback: they can check activities in pairs, for example.
- Encourage students to give explanations instead of giving them yourself.
- Present students with clear examples and guided questions so that they do not need to be 'told'. Guided discovery is a better and more rewarding way for students to learn.
- A useful guideline is to limit your talking to 30% of class time and no more than ten minutes at a time.

TEACHING TIPS

Pairwork

Pairwork is another opportunity for students to practise their speaking skills. Pairwork activities enable all students to have much more speaking time than if each student had an individual turn at speaking. When students are working in pairs, it also provides teachers with a chance to walk round and listen, and to give advice to students in a more discreet and personal way, rather than in front of the whole class.

If you ask students to work in pairs, they are likely to pair up with their friends or the person they sit nearest. It's a good idea to put students into 'new' pairs from time to time, so they can work with classmates of different abilities and with different approaches.

Certain speaking skills are necessary when working with another person, so it's useful to teach phrases that help students interrupt politely (*Yes, I agree, but … / May I … So you think …*, etc.).

Another idea to put students at their ease when they're speaking is to play some quiet music in the background. This helps students feel less self-conscious.

Personalisation

Students are more likely to want to speak when they are speaking about something they personally know about, are interested in or have experienced. Personalisation is important in learning a second language as it makes language more meaningful and therefore memorable to learners. There are plenty of personalisation opportunities throughout *Optimise*. Where possible, extend and adapt other activities to give students even more speaking opportunities.

Developing writing skills

Students are required to produce different genres of writing whilst preparing for exams. Nevertheless, the basic steps for all writing tasks are the same. This is reinforced by the approach used throughout *Optimise* – ***Plan, Write, Check***.

There are some extra points to keep in mind when helping students with writing tasks:

Before beginning to write, students need to consider the purpose of the text and who the text is for, as both things will affect the tone (*formal or informal*).

During the ***Plan*** phase, students should brainstorm ideas (they can make lists, mind maps, or use question words as prompts: *Why? What? Where? When? How? Who?*). Students then need to choose and order their final ideas. It is important to encourage students to spend time on this stage as it makes the writing task easier.

Next is the ***Write*** phrase. Students write a first draft as quickly as they can, including all the main points from the brainstorming phase. They should make sure they include all required information and that they fully answer the question.

The final stage is the ***Check*** phase, where students need to look closely at spelling, grammar, punctuation and word choice. They can use the *Optimise* **Checklist** for this.

Classroom management

It can be particularly challenging with larger class groups to keep all students engaged in the lesson.

Here are some ideas to consider:

- Move around and teach the class from different points in the classroom to give the students the feeling of being in the middle of the 'action' rather than an observer. Moving around the class makes the room feel smaller and encourages student involvement. It also means students who are furthest away from the front of the classroom can feel more involved.
- Check understanding regularly, and give students feedback to clarify points they haven't understood.
- Set up some class routines (weekly homework assignments of 30 minutes, class discussions every Friday, etc.). Where possible, involve students in deciding what these routines should be.
- Find ways to link what students have learnt to the exam, so they can clearly see their progress and the fact that they are achieving a common goal.
- Give regular short tests and dictations.
- Change the pace of the lesson from time to time and change delivery methods (speaking, using IWB, playing video, etc.)
- Start lessons by writing a lesson outline on the board so students know what to expect.
- Give fast finishers something to do (see the unit teaching notes for suggestions) or direct them to the Workbook.

Games

As a useful change of pace, and sometimes to refocus students, games can be an excellent teaching tool. Students generally enjoy games and tend to remember more as a result. Vocabulary games are helpful for practising and reviewing language. Always make the 'rules' clear, and check understanding before playing the game. For example, after explaining what to do, ask the students to explain the game back to you. Or demonstrate the game by playing it yourself with a few students while the others watch.

When planning games you need to consider what your aims and objectives are. Games are particularly useful for reviewing work from the previous lesson, checking what students know before teaching a new language item, practising a new language item you have just presented, warming up at the beginning of the lesson or filling in at the end of a lesson. There are a variety of games suggested throughout the *Optimise* teaching notes.

LISTENING	SPEAKING	USE OF ENGLISH	WRITING
Predicting missing information Sentence completion	Talking about habits and routines Interview Talk2Me	Word formation Open cloze	Creating an appropriate style An article
Listening for agreement and disagreement Multiple choice (extracts)	Agreeing and disagreeing Collaborative task Talk2Me	Word formation Sentence transformation	Expressing and justifying opinion An essay
Listening for opinion and attitude (1) Multiple matching	Comparing and contrasting Photo task Talk2Me	Word formation Multiple-choice cloze	Making recommendations A review
Listening for synonyms (1) True/false	Expressing and justifying opinions Discussion Talk2Me	Word formation Sentence transformation	Giving reasons and examples (1) A letter / An email
Listening for relevant information Multiple choice (single extract)	Speculating about a situation Photo task Talk2Me	Word formation Open cloze	Formality (1) A letter / An email
Avoiding unnecessary detail Sentence completion	Making suggestions Collaborative task Talk2Me	Word formation Multiple-choice cloze	Making suggestions A letter / An email
Listening for purpose Multiple choice	Expressing preference and giving reasons Photo task Talk2Me	Word formation Sentence transformation	Creating a good narrative A story
Predicting and anticipating Multiple matching	Qualifying your opinion Discussion Talk2Me	Word formation Open cloze	Giving reasons and examples (2) An article
Recognising difference in meaning True/false/not stated	Talking about experiences Interview Talk2Me	Word formation Multiple-choice cloze	Using descriptive language A story
Understanding responses to questions Multiple choice	Reaching a decision Collaborative task Talk2Me	Word formation Open cloze	Introducing and concluding An essay
Listening for synonyms (2) Sentence completion	Answering questions promptly Interview Talk2Me	Word formation Sentence transformation	Formality (2) A letter / An email
Listening for opinion and attitude (2) Multiple choice (extracts)	Managing a discussion Discussion Talk2Me	Word formation Multiple-choice cloze	Using your imagination A review

▸ USE OF ENGLISH p 144–145 ▸ WRITING p 146–147

Student's Resource Centre

- *Talk2Me* videos
- Speaking test videos
- *Optimise your grammar* worksheets
- *Optimise your vocabulary* worksheets
- *Say it right* pronunciation worksheets
- Culture and CLIL worksheets
- Class and Workbook audio

1 Time on your hands

UNIT AIMS

Exam preparation in Unit 1:

- understand the overall structure and meaning of a text
- predict missing information
- talk about free time
- add prefixes and suffixes and use them in a word-formation exercise
- understand phrasal verbs and apply them in an open-cloze exercise
- engage the reader in an article

TEACHER'S PRESENTATION KIT

- *Talk2Me* videos
- Speaking test videos
- Class and Workbook audio
- Workbook pages and answer key

UNIT OVERVIEW

Student's Book / Digital Student's Book SB		Workbook / Online Workbook OWB
LESSON / EXAM TASK	**EXAM SKILLS / LANGUAGE FOCUS**	**CONSOLIDATION**
Reading **Gapped text**	Understanding references (1) A magazine article	Workbook, pp 4–5, Exercises 1, 2, 3, 4 Unit 1, Reading, Exercises 1, 2, 3, 4
Grammar 1	Countable and uncountable nouns, articles	Workbook, p 6, Exercises 1, 2 Unit 1, Grammar 1, Exercises 1, 2
Vocabulary	Words connected with *TV* and *cinema* Phrasal verbs Collocations with *do*, *have*, *make* and *take*	Workbook, pp 6–7, Exercises 1, 2, 3 Unit 1, Vocabulary, Exercises 1, 2, 3
Listening **Sentence completion**	Predicting missing information	Workbook, p 8, Exercises 1, 2, 3 Unit 1, Listening, Exercises 1, 2, 3
Grammar 2	Quantifiers	Workbook, p 7, Exercises 1, 2, 3 Unit 1, Grammar 2, Exercises 1, 2, 3
Speaking **Interview**	Talking about habits and routines	Workbook, pp 8–9, Exercises 1, 2, 3 Unit 1, Speaking, Exercises 1, 2, 3
Use of English **Word formation** **Open cloze**	Prefixes and suffixes Phrasal verbs	Workbook, p 9, Exercises 1, 2 Unit 1, Use of English, Exercises 1, 2
Writing **An article**	Creating an appropriate style	Workbook, p 10, Exercises 1, 2, 3, 4 Unit 1, Writing, Exercises 1, 2, 3, 4
		Workbook, p 11, Progress check and Cumulative progress Progress check and Cumulative progress

Additional material

PRESENTATION KIT	TEACHER'S / STUDENT'S RESOURCE CENTRE RC	TEST GENERATOR
Talk2Me video *In an average week, I …*	**Unit 1 worksheets:** *Optimise your grammar* (Standard and Higher), *Optimise your vocabulary* (Standard and Higher), *Talk2Me* video, *Say it right* **Units 1–2 worksheets:** CLIL, Culture, Everyday English (TRC only), Grammar communication (TRC only)	Unit Test 1 (Standard and Higher)

READING
Gapped text | A magazine article

→ Student's Book, pages 4–5 SB

Lesson aims

- Focus on gapped text
- Practise a gapped-text exam task

Lead-in

Elicit the meaning of the unit title ***Time on your hands*** (*to have more time available than you need, e.g. Now her children have gone to university, she has a lot more time on her hands.*). Draw students' attention to the photo and ask them what they think the lesson is going to be about (*leisure and entertainment*).

1 In pairs or groups, students ask and answer the questions. Elicit answers in open class and try to develop a class discussion.

Suggested answers

1 Students' own answers

2 Actor, actress, director, producer, make-up artist, camera operator, etc.

2 Ask students to complete the exercise. Remind them to always start by reading the introduction to the task and the title of the text, and then read the text first to get an overall impression and understanding of it.

Time this activity (three minutes) and give updates, e.g. *One minute to go … Only thirty seconds left*. Check answers in open class.

Answers

Paragraph 1 **c** Paragraph 2 **g** Paragraph 3 **a** Paragraph 4 **f**
Paragraph 5 **d** Paragraph 6 **e** Paragraph 7 **b**

3 Ask students to complete the exercise. Draw students' attention to the example.

Answers

A They
B This, it, they
C It's, they
D its
E They, them
F he
G You'll, you, you

Language note

Point out to students that the pronoun must agree in gender and number with the noun (or another pronoun) to which it refers.

Students are often tested on the knowledge of how texts are structured in reading exams and good use of pronoun reference in their writing will earn them marks. Typically tested pronouns at this level include:

Subject pronouns: *he, she,* etc. Object pronouns: *her, him,* etc. Possessive pronouns: *hers, his,* etc. Possessive adjectives: *her, his,* etc. Relative pronouns: *which, that, whose,* etc. Demonstrative pronouns: *this, that,* etc.

OPTIMISE YOUR EXAM

Gapped text

Ask students to read the tips.

- In this type of exam task, students should always read the title and the gapped text first in order to gain an overall idea of the structure and the meaning of the text. They should pay attention to the information and ideas before and after each gap as well as throughout the whole of the gapped text. Remind students to read the text again as a whole before making their final decision.
- In gapped-text exam tasks, students are tested on text structure, cohesion and coherence. Rather than concentrating on individual sentences, students need to be able to follow the development of ideas through the text as a whole, using their understanding of text coherence and cohesion devices, e.g. time expressions, exemplification, repetition, concordance of tenses, pronouns, etc.
- Point out that in a reading exam, students should always check that the extra sentence doesn't fit in any of the gaps. In class, always ask your students to tell you why a particular part of the text matches a question. This helps them check their choices carefully. Remind them that they should try not to leave any questions unanswered.

▼ Exam task

4 1.01 **Note: The reading text is also available on the audio CD. You may want to have students listen and read the text before doing the exam task.**

Ask students to complete the exercise. Check answers in open class. Elicit what evidence helped students decide on their answers.

Answers

1 F (*Nobody can do it for you … You're the only one with your particular vision.*)

2 D (*They're the ones who can make action movies and large-scale epics.*)

3 A (*… and it's easy to find advice and information on courses online.*)

4 G (*And you have to learn to work with what you've got … 'No matter where you are located on this earth, you can film.'*)

5 B (*test screen your film … That doesn't mean that you have to change your vision to keep people happy.*)

6 E (*Film festivals and competitions are a great way to do this … get feedback on what is successful*)

Cultural note

Luke Jaden is an actor and director, known for *Wolf Who Cried Boy* (2015), *King Ripple* (2015) and *The Listing* (2015), and the critically acclaimed documentary, *Madman or Martyr* (2014). Jaden first wanted to be an actor. At 13 years old, he worked as an extra and acted in some films and TV commercials. He first made an impression as a director locally with *Madman or Martyr*, which began as a project at his school in Beverly Hills.

5 Ask students to complete the exercise. Check their answers.

Suggested answers

blockbuster (n): a very successful film

budget (n): the amount of money a person or organisation has to spend on something

cast (n): all the performers in a film

determined (adj): not willing to let anything prevent you from doing what you have decided to do

enrol (v): officially register as a student on a course

epic (n): a style of large-scale film-making on a big budget, often focused on a heroic character

messing around (phr v): behaving in a relaxed way

overcome (v): succeed in dealing with a problem or difficulty

special effects (n): an illusion created for films by props, camerawork, computer graphics, etc.

trailer (n): an extract from a film used for advance publicity

willing (adj): ready to do something

Mixed ability

Divide the class into small groups of mixed-level students. Ask them to divide up the task of looking up words in the dictionary and pool their knowledge. Elicit the definitions in open class for other students to say the answers and check pronunciation.

Optional extension 1.01

Play the recorded text and ask students to underline all the reference words in the text, and what they refer to. Ask students to compare in pairs before you check in open class.

Answers

Paragraph 1: whose (young people)

Paragraph 2: it (make your movie)

Paragraph 3: that (making the movie), They (Hollywood), it (your movie)

Paragraph 4: that (get the best results), this (making a silent movie)

Paragraph 5: who (people)

Paragraph 6: it (your movie)

Paragraph 7: this (get your movie in front of a wider audience), They (film festivals and competitions)

THINK | RESEARCH | CULTURE | LEARN | **ME**

Students could write comments in class or for homework. In pairs or groups, students could read out their posts for others to comment on and ask follow-up questions.

Homework

OWB

Assign students Reading exercises 1, 2, 3 and 4 on pages 4–5 of their Workbook.

Optional extension

Ask students to make a list of top ten tips for becoming famous as a screenwriter or director. Students then share their ideas in open class.

GRAMMAR 1

Countable and uncountable nouns, articles

→ Student's Book, page 6 SB

Lesson aims

- Understand the correct usage of countable and uncountable nouns and articles
- Practise using countable and uncountable nouns and articles

Lead-in

Play ***Board race***. Divide the board into two halves and the class into two teams. Students stand up in two lines in front of their halves of the board. One team writes uncountable nouns on their side of the board and the other team writes countable nouns. The person at the front of each line writes something in their category, passes the pen to the person behind them and goes to the back of the line. This continues until you say 'Stop'. The team with the most correct words in their category wins.

Grammar in context

Ask students to complete the task. Refer them to the *Remember* box if they need help. Check answers in open class and ask students to associate the nouns with the descriptions in the *Remember* box.

Remind students that they can find more information in the Grammar reference, Unit 1, page 148. This should be the first source students refer to when they have any questions or doubts.

Answers

1 Many young film-makers enrol on a course to learn basic skills.

2 It's easy to find advice and information on courses online.

3 They provide a fantastic opportunity to see your work on the big screen and get feedback on what is successful.

1 Ask students to complete the exercise. Check their answers and ask them to explain any difference in meaning if a noun can be both countable and uncountable.

Answers

countable: leisure activity, book, house, table

uncountable: baggage, clothes, entertainment, equipment, knowledge, money, music, news, trousers

both: coffee (C: a cup of coffee, UC: the substance / coffee); film (C: a movie, UC: the substance; the artistic field / film); glass (C: a container made of glass, UC: the substance / glass); interest (C: a hobby, UC: the abstract idea / interest); metal (C: an example, such as gold, etc., UC: the substance / metal); time (C: an occasion, one occurrence of something, UC: the abstract idea / time); truth (C: a fact that is believed by most people to be true, UC: the abstract idea / truth)

Language note

Remind students that certain nouns have a plural form (ending in *-s*) but a singular meaning, e.g. *No news is good news*. Highlight that some uncountable nouns are plural. They have no singular form with the same meaning and cannot be used with numbers, e.g. *clothes* (other examples are: *police, customs, thanks, trousers, jeans, pyjamas, pants, scissors, spectacles, glasses, etc.*).

Extra support

Ask students to think of example sentences for the words that can be both countable and uncountable.

Suggested answers

Coffee: *I'd like a coffee, please.* (C); *Would you like some coffee?* (UC)

Film: *I love horror films.* (C); *He did his best work in film.* (UC)

Glass: *Have a glass of water.* (C); *Glass is breakable.* (UC)

Interest: *Her main interests are music and dance.* (C); *The money was repaid with interest.* (UC)

Metal: *Silver and gold are expensive precious metals.* (C); *His belt is made of metal.* (UC)

Time: *Did you have a good time?* (C); *How much time does it take?* (UC)

Truth: *Many truths came out in our discussion.* (C); *There is a lot of truth in what you say.* (UC)

2 Ask students to complete the exercise. Check their answers in open class.

Answers

1 I went to a great show at the theatre last week with a group of friends.

2 Music is a big part of my life and I like listening to the latest tracks on the radio.

3 Lisa saw a great interview on the internet with a local TV presenter.

4 Would you prefer to be an actor or a musician, or does working in entertainment not interest you?

5 The way we get our entertainment is changing quickly and lots of people watch films online now.

6 I'd rather go to the cinema and see a movie than stay at home and watch a programme on TV.

3 Ask students to complete the exercise. Ask them to compare in pairs before you check their answers in open class.

Answers

1 a **2** a **3** a **4** the **5** –/the **6** a **7** the **8** the **9** – **10** a **11** – **12** – **13** an

Optional extension

Play ***Noughts and crosses***. Draw a large 3 by 3 grid on the board. Number the boxes 1 to 9 and write some of the countable and uncountable nouns from the previous lesson in the boxes.

Divide the class into two teams, X and O. Flip a coin to see which team goes first.

In order for the team to receive the X or the O for the box they have chosen, they must make a correct sentence using *How much* or *How many*.

Alternate between the teams until one team has a line of three Xs or Os, or it is a draw.

THINK | RESEARCH | CULTURE | LEARN | ME

In pairs, students discuss the questions. Elicit answers in open class.

Homework

OWB

Assign students Grammar 1 exercises 1 and 2 on page 6 of their Workbook.

VOCABULARY

Topic vocabulary | Phrasal verbs | Collocations

→ Student's Book, page 7 SB

Lesson aims

- Understand the correct usage of:
  - words connected with TV and cinema
  - phrasal verbs
  - verb collocations

Lead-in

Write these prompts on the board: *What's your favourite TV series? What is it about? Why do you like it?*

In pairs, students take turns to discuss the questions. Elicit answers from different students in open class and write them on the board for students to refer to later in the lesson. Point out to students that these are typical questions in the first section of some speaking exams.

Words connected with *TV* and *cinema*

1 1.02 Ask students to complete the exercise. Play the audio for students to listen and check their answers. Elicit explanations for each word and check their pronunciation.

Answers/Audioscript

TV: broadcast, channel, on demand, programme, reality show, satellite, series, sitcom, viewer

cinema: box office, flop, release, screenplay

both: audience, cast, credits, director

Meanings

flop: a complete failure

on demand: programmes available via the internet, usually after they have been transmitted, to watch at your leisure

sitcom: a television or radio series about a particular group of characters who deal with situations in a humorous way

screenplay: a story someone writes for a film

2 Ask students to complete the exercise. Elicit answers from different students around the class. Highlight the passive infinitive form in the first sentence of the exercise (***to be* + past participle**).

Answers

1 released **2** sitcom / reality show **3** flop **4** credits **5** viewers **6** box office **7** on demand **8** director

Fast finishers

In pairs, students take it in turns to define words in Exercise 1 in a random order, making a 'beep' sound instead of the words connected to TV and cinema for their partner to guess.

Refer students to the Vocabulary reference, page 162, for more information on topic vocabulary.

Phrasal verbs

3 1.03 Ask students to complete the exercise. Play the audio for students to listen and check their answers.

Point out that there are phrasal verbs with one stress on the main verb (e.g. *sit through*) and phrasal verbs with two stresses (a main and a secondary stress) (e.g. *chill out*). Students will practise the pronunciation of phrasal verbs in the *Say it right* section on this page.

Answers/Audioscript

1 What time does the new reality show come *on*? I don't want to miss it.

2 Jen's just going to chill out this weekend and watch a few episodes of her favourite TV series. ✓

3 In last week's drama class we started acting out a new play. ✓

4 This programme is boring. Why don't you turn *over* and see what else is on?

5 My schoolwork takes up so much time that I don't really watch much TV. ✓

6 Tim likes to hang *out* with his friends at the weekend and play video games.

7 I sat through the film all the way to the end, even though I really wasn't enjoying it. ✓

Extra support

In pairs, or as a group, ask students to discuss the meaning of each of the phrasal verbs in Exercise 3.

Refer students to the Vocabulary reference, page 162, for more information on phrasal verbs.

Collocations with *do, have, make* and *take*

4 1.04 Remind students what collocations are before they do the activity (*a group of two or more words that usually go together and just sound 'right' to native English speakers*). In this exercise, students develop their intuition for how words work together.

Ask students to complete the exercise. Check their answers in open class.

Answers/Audioscript

1 have/take a break **2** have a good time **3** make a difference **4** have/take a holiday **5** have/take time off work **6** do nothing all day **7** make an effort **8** take part in **9** do someone a favour **10** do your best **11** have work to do **12** take your time

Language note

Do* and *make

The two verbs *do* and *make* are often confused. The meanings are similar, but there are some key differences.

do: Used with daily activities or jobs that do not result in a physical object, e.g. *do homework, do housework, do the ironing, do the washing.*

make: Used with creative activities that result in a physical object, e.g. *make a cake*. Point out that there are also many standard expressions such as *make the bed*.

5 Ask students to complete the exercise. Walk round the classroom to assist students and check for accuracy. Check their answers in open class.

Refer students to the Vocabulary reference, page 162, for more information on collocations.

Optional extension

In pairs or small groups, students write a classroom survey with the phrases from Exercise 4. Encourage your students to use a variety of question words when they write their survey. You can also review types of questions that are often used on surveys, e.g. *How do you feel about …?* and *Do you agree or disagree with the following statement?* and *How would you rate the following?*. Walk round and monitor, helping students with accuracy. Students find new partners and carry out the survey taking it in turns to ask and answer questions. Elicit interesting and unusual answers in open class to close the activity.

SAY IT RIGHT

Stress in phrasal verbs (1) TRC

For the *Say it right* pronunciation activity and instructions, go to the Teacher's Resource Centre.

THINK | RESEARCH | **CULTURE** | LEARN | ME

In pairs or small groups, students discuss the questions. Elicit answers in open class.

Homework

OWB

Assign students Vocabulary exercises 1, 2 and 3 on pages 6–7 of their Workbook.

LISTENING
Sentence completion

→ Student's Book, page 8 SB

Lesson aims

- Focus on sentence completion
- Practise a sentence-completion exam task

Lead-in

Write the lesson theme *circus* on the board. Write some facts in circles:

Roman times *clowns, acrobats, musicians, tightrope walkers*
Philip Astley *1768, England*
Cirque du Soleil *A ring or a circle in Latin*

Ask students to brainstorm the questions that could give the facts as answers. Elicit if students have been to a circus and what they think about them.

Possible questions

When did the circus originate? What type of performers are there in a circus? Who opened the first modern circus? When and where was the first modern circus? Do you know the name of a famous circus? Where does the word circus come from?

1 In pairs, students ask and answer the questions. Elicit ideas from different students around the class.

Answers

1 left-hand photo: someone juggling, right-hand photo: someone unicycling **2** Students' own answers

2 Ask students to complete the exercise. You could do the first item together, if appropriate. Elicit answers around the class and accept all sensible suggestions.

Suggested answers

1 his family, his parents, his mum, his dad, his school, his teacher **2** money, sleep, time **3** good-looking, clever, friendly

3 Ask students to complete the exercise. Check their answers and highlight that they should always check that what they write fits grammatically in a gap, e.g. singular or plural, and that it makes sense in the complete sentence.

Answers

1 5 **2** 1 **3** 10, 1 **4** 8 **5** 7 **6** 2, 7 **7** 9, 2 **8** 4 **9** 3 **10** 6

OPTIMISE YOUR EXAM

Sentence completion

Ask students to read the tips.

- An awareness of how this type of listening test works is key for scoring high marks. Students should know that the sentences follow the order of the listening. They should write the exact words they hear, but point out that the words surrounding the gaps in questions 1–10 are not worded in exactly the same way. Remind them not to change the words they hear and not to repeat words that they read.
- Point out that predicting missing information (as they did in exercises 2 and 3) can help students identify relevant points in a listening exam and guess unknown words and phrases more easily.

▼ Exam task

4 1.05 Play the track for students to listen and complete the exercise. Don't check answers at this stage, as students will listen again to check in Exercise 5.

5 1.05 Play the track again for students to check their answers. Remind them to always write something in the gap. In open class, discuss the specific clues that helped them choose their answers.

Answers

1 one of his relatives / a relative (*I went to see [a circus] with one of my relatives when I was 11.*)

2 curious (*None of my family knew anything about the circus, so they were a bit curious …*)

3 (physical) strength (*You need physical strength for some of the skills, and I didn't have much at the beginning!*)

4 running (*I found that running helped. It was something that my circus skills teacher advised me to take up.*)

5 slowly (*When you're learning a new routine, I find it helps to do it slowly at first. … Then you can do it faster …*)

6 the streets (*People love to see someone doing a few tricks while they're out shopping.*)

7 encouraging (*I was really nervous for my first ever performance and I'm sure lots of things went wrong. But people were really encouraging …*)

8 juggle (*I'm getting ready to learn a new skill*)

9 funny (*That's one of the hardest parts for a lot of performers*)

10 a clown (*That would let me use everything I know. And there's no feeling like making people laugh.*)

Extra support

Point out to students that none of the words or phrases in Exercise 3 were the correct answers. However, they helped show students what type of word or phrase to listen for. Ask students if this helped them do Exercise 4. Ask students to explain how they found the correct answers.

THINK | RESEARCH | CULTURE | **LEARN** | ME

Ask students to answer the question and, in open class, discuss the specific clues that helped them choose their answers (answers included in Answer key for Exercise 5).

Homework OWB

Assign students Listening exercises 1, 2 and 3 on page 8 of their Workbook.

GRAMMAR 2
Quantifiers

→ Student's Book, page 9 SB

Lesson aims

- Understand the correct usage of quantifiers
- Practise using quantifiers

Lead-in

Play ***First to five*** to revise vocabulary from the unit. Say different word categories (e.g. words connected with TV and cinema, phrasal verbs, collocations with *do, have, make* and *take,* words connected with the circus). Small groups compete to think of five words for each one. When they have five, they shout 'First to five'. Check their words, giving one point for each correct answer. The group with the most points wins.

Grammar in context

Ask students to complete the task. Check answers in open class and ask them to read more about quantifiers in the *Remember* box.

Remind students that they can find more information in the Grammar reference, Unit 1, page 148.

Answers

1 b **2** c

Language note

Quantifiers

We use these quantifiers with both countable and uncountable nouns: *all, any, enough, a lot of, lots of, more, most, no, none of, some.*

We use these quantifiers only with countable nouns: *both, each, either, (a) few, fewer, neither, several.*

We use *every* or *each* with a singular noun to mean *all*, e.g. *Each student was given a prize. / We go to our grandparents' house every year.* We often use *every* to talk about times like days, weeks, months and years.

When we talk about two people or things we use the quantifiers *both, either* and *neither*, e.g. *Both/All (of) the cinemas were closed. / All (of) the cinemas were closed. / Neither of the cinemas was open. / I don't think either of the cinemas was open.* Highlight that nouns with *either* and *neither* have a singular verb.

We use these quantifiers only with uncountable nouns: *a little, (not) much, a bit of.*

We often use *a great deal of / a good deal of* with abstract nouns such as *time, money*, etc.

1 Ask students to complete the exercise. Students compare in pairs before you check in open class.

Answers

1 some **2** a few **3** lots of **4** neither of **5** None of **6** Each **7** Both / Both of **8** all

2 Ask students to complete the exercise. Have students check in pairs before you check answers in open class.

Answers

1 have much **2** 's/is only a little time **3** does not / doesn't have many **4** Neither of us likes **5** gave me a bit of **6** a few friends / a few of my friends

3 Ask students to complete the exercise. Check answers in open class.

Answers

I've got <u>a</u> [some] really exciting news! I've finally got my drone! For those of you who don't know, drone flying is becoming really popular. In the past, <u>little</u> [few] people had drones, but now more and more of my friends are getting them – including me! My friend and I are going out this weekend to try it out and <u>neither</u> [neither of] us can wait!

Of course, you have to remember <u>few</u> [a few] things if you're going to fly a drone. Safety is very important, so make sure you can see your drone at <u>all of</u> [all] times. Also, remember that privacy is important to <u>a lots</u> [a lot / lots] of people, so don't fly over people's gardens or crowded public places taking photos.

I'll post pics here when I get it up in the air!

Mixed ability

Give less confident students the answers in a jumbled order to help them complete the exercise (*a few, all, few, a lot, some, neither of*).

Ask stronger students to write two comprehension questions. They can read them out to test other students' understanding of the text once everyone has finished the exercise.

Optional extension

Ask students to write two true sentences and one false sentence related to their life, using quantifiers from this lesson. In pairs, students take it in turns to guess which ones are true and which is false.

THINK | **RESEARCH** | CULTURE | LEARN | ME

If you have access to the internet, students can research information in class. Alternatively, they could prepare this for homework and present their information at the start of the next lesson.

Homework

Assign students Grammar 2 exercises 1, 2 and 3 on page 7 of their Workbook.

SPEAKING
Interview

→ Student's Book, page 10

Lesson aims

- Talk about free time
- Answer personal questions

The *Talk2Me* video in this unit focuses on free time. People talk about how much free time they have and what activities they usually do. Students answer some comprehension questions and then listen out for time expressions. The video can be used in one of two ways:

Flipped classroom

Flipped classroom option

Using this approach, students watch the video and complete the exercises for homework. This prepares students for the speaking lesson by introducing them to the topic and the key phrases to use in the exam task. Teachers who use this method will find they have more class time to spend on activating the target language and developing fluency for the final task.

Talk2Me worksheet

Ask students to also complete the *Talk2Me* worksheet on the Resource Centre for more detailed comprehension exercises and more practice of the key phrases.

Classroom option

1 Ask students to spend a minute or two reading the questions. Play the *Talk2Me* video for students to complete the exercise. Play the video again, if necessary, before checking their answers.

2 Play the *Talk2Me* video again, so students underline the phrases in the *Phrase expert* box. Pause the video from time to time if necessary. Check answers in open class.

Talk2Me worksheet

Ask students to also complete the *Talk2Me* worksheet on the Resource Centre for more detailed comprehension exercises and more practice of the key phrases.

Answers

The transcript and answer key for the *Talk2Me* video exercises and Worksheet can be found on the Teacher's Resource Centre.

Lead-in

Play ***Hot seat***. Divide the class into two teams. Ask a volunteer from team A to sit with his/her back to the board, facing their team. Choose words from the previous lesson and write the words on the board one by one. Team A defines the word for the volunteer student to guess in 1 minute. After 1 minute, it is the other team's turn to define the word, etc. The team that describes the most words in 1 minute wins the round.

Suggested words:

baggage, circus, blockbuster, trailer, special effects, news, entertainment, sitcom, acting, flop, series, channel, juggling, acrobat

3 In pairs or groups, students ask and answer the questions. Elicit answers from different students around the class.

Answers

Students' own answers

Extra support

Ask students to put the expressions in the *Phrase expert* box in order from most frequent to least frequent and add other adverbs and expressions they know. Check their answers.

Answer

always, frequently, usual/normal routine, on average, sometimes / quite often / at least once or twice a month, occasionally, hardly ever / I don't often / not very often, never / I don't ever

4 Ask students to complete the exercise. Check answers in open class.

Answers

1 normal **2** On **3** least **4** average **5** usual/normal, involves

Language note

Remind students that adverbs of frequency usually go before the main verb, or between the auxiliary and the main verb, but they come after the verb *to be*. The question phrase for adverbs of frequency is *How often …?*.

5 Ask students to complete the table. Elicit what other activities students do and how often they do them in open class.

Answers

Students' own answers

Optional extension

Find someone who: Students stand up and walk round to find out which students do the same activities as they do and how often they do them. Write these prompts on the board for less confident students: *Do you …? How often do you …?* and appropriate responses *So do I. / Nor do I.* You could put some music on in the background while students are doing this activity.

OPTIMISE YOUR EXAM

Interview

Ask students to read the tip.

- Remind students that official oral exams often start with a short conversation where students are asked to give personal information, including talking about their habits. Correct use of a variety of adverbs of frequency can make an early good impression.
- Highlight that in most official oral exams, there are no separate marks for the different stages in oral exams, so it can help nervous students to consider this section as a warm-up for the rest of the exam.

Exam task

6 In pairs, students complete the task. Elicit interesting or surprising answers from different students around the class.

Mixed ability

Set a competition and ask students to write as many different answers as they can in a three-minute time limit using adverbs and phrases of frequency (refer them to the *Phrase expert* box). Write the most interesting answers on the board. Less confident students can refer to the answers on the board to help them structure their answers.

Ask students to do Exercise 6. Walk round and monitor students, noting down errors and good use of language. Give feedback and write some key words on the board. Put students into new pairs and ask them to repeat the activity and improve their performance.

Homework

Assign students Speaking exercises 1, 2 and 3 on pages 8–9 of their Workbook. OWB

USE OF ENGLISH

Word formation | Open cloze

→ Student's Book, page 11 SB

Lesson aims

- Focus on word formation and practise a word-formation exam task
- Focus on open cloze and practise an open-cloze exam task

Lead-in

Play a memory game in which students use *a few* and *a little* with countable and uncountable shopping items.

Start the game with the sentence *I went to the supermarket and bought a few oranges and a little cheese.* Choose a student to repeat your sentence and add an item of their own using *a few* or *a little*. Continue round the class, with students remembering everything that's been said and adding items of their own.

1 Ask students to complete the exercise. Elicit answers from different students around the class.

Answers

1 (un)pleasant, (un)pleasurable, apparent, (un)impressive, existing
2 popular: (un)popularity, late: lateness
3 appear (appearance) and exist (existence)

OPTIMISE YOUR EXAM

Word formation

Ask students to read the tip.

- Remind students that sometimes they can only gain a sense of whether words are positive or negative by understanding the meaning of the whole text, not just the line including the gap.
- Point out that in word-formation tasks, students should be prepared to make up to two changes to a word, e.g. they may need to add a prefix and a suffix (e.g. *uninterrupted* from the prompt INTERRUPT).

Exam task

2 Ask students to complete the exercise. Ask them to compare in pairs before you elicit answers in open class.

Answers

1 pleasure **2** appearance **3** impressive **4** existence
5 popularity **6** decisions **7** endless **8** latest

Refer students to the Vocabulary reference, page 162, for more information on word formation.

3 Ask students to complete the exercise. Check answers in open class.

Answers

1 2, 5 **2** 4 **3** 8 **4** 1, 3, 6, 7

OPTIMISE YOUR EXAM

Open cloze

Ask students to read the tips.

- Phrasal verbs are frequently tested in open-cloze exam tasks, but it is hard to predict which ones. Students need to look out for missing verbs, prepositions or particles.
- Remind them not to leave the answer sheet blank for any question. If they don't know the correct answer, they should always make a guess.

Exam task

4 Ask students to complete the exercise. Check answers in open class.

Answers

1 in **2** takes **3** make **4** an **5** out **6** take **7** do **8** few

Fast finishers

Ask fast finishers to write one or two comprehension questions on the text in Exercise 4 to ask the class when everyone has finished.

Optional extension

Ask students to write personalised sentences with the phrasal verbs in Exercise 4.

Homework

OWB

Assign students Use of English exercises 1 and 2 on page 9 of their Workbook.

WRITING

An article

→ Student's Book, pages 12–13 SB

Lesson aims

- Focus on language in an article
- Plan and write an article

Lead-in

Play ***Hangman*** with some of the words from the unit. Invite students to come to the front to lead the game, if appropriate.

1 In pairs or as a group, students answer the questions. Elicit answers in open class.

Answers

1 The person is slacklining. **2** Students' own answers

2 Students complete the exercise. Check their answers.

Suggested answers

1 Doing tricks on a rope between two trees.

2 Using some special equipment and practising tricks such as walking on the rope.

3 It's fun with friends / you get to talk to people about it.

3 Ask students to complete the exercise. Check answers in open class.

Answers

1 b **2** a **3** b and c

4 Individually or in pairs, students complete the exercise. Walk round, monitoring students and helping them if necessary.

Suggested answer

Have you ever wondered how slacklining began? Well, it all started with tightrope walking, which was often a part of circus shows. In the 1970s, climbers came up with slacklining as a fun way of improving their balance. The hobby caught on and soon people started doing impressive tricks.

OPTIMISE YOUR EXAM

An article

Ask students to read the tips.

- Highlight how the writer instantly grabs the reader's attention by asking a rhetorical question (a question where you don't really expect an answer) in the first line, *Have you ever seen someone balancing on a rope between two trees?*, and again in the third paragraph *Why is it unusual?*, where you have to read on to find out what the writer is talking about.
- Remind students that examiners will really appreciate a well-structured article. Elicit why this student probably got very high marks for this article:
  – they address the reader directly (*Why not give it a go?*)
  – they use friendly informal language and have an interesting idea to write about
  – the vocabulary is rich and varied, e.g. *bouncing, amazed, bruises*
  – there is a clear and logical progression of ideas using linkers such as *first of all, secondly,* etc.
  – there is good use of pronoun referencing, e.g. *It's hard at first, but practice makes perfect!*

For more information on writing articles, refer students to the Writing reference, page 169.

▼ Exam task

5 Ask students to complete the exercise.

6 Plan Ask students to complete the paragraph plan using their notes from Exercise 5. You may want to look at students' plans, if possible, to check them and give advice and suggestions for improvement before students take the next step.

7 Write Ask students to write their article in an appropriate style in 140–190 words. Depending on time, it may be a good idea to set this and the subsequent checklist exercise for homework.

8 Check Ask students to complete the checklist before they hand in their article.

Homework

OWB

Assign students Writing exercises 1, 2, 3 and 4 on page 10 of their Workbook and Progress check 1 on page 11.

2 Learning about learning

UNIT AIMS

Exam preparation in Unit 2:

- deduce meaning from context in an online article
- identify attitude from speaker's tone of voice in conversations
- agree and disagree with someone else's opinions in a discussion
- add suffixes and negative prefixes and apply them in a word-formation exercise
- use contracted forms and apply them in a sentence-transformation exercise
- use phrases for agreeing and disagreeing in an essay

TEACHER'S PRESENTATION KIT

- *Talk2Me* videos
- Speaking test videos
- Class and Workbook audio
- Workbook pages and answer key

UNIT OVERVIEW

Student's Book / Digital Student's Book SB		Workbook / Online Workbook OWB
LESSON / EXAM TASK	**EXAM SKILLS / LANGUAGE FOCUS**	**CONSOLIDATION**
Reading **Multiple choice**	Deducing meaning from context An online article	Workbook, pp 12–13, Exercises 1, 2, 3 Unit 2, Reading, Exercises 1, 2, 3
Grammar 1	Tenses (1): present/past simple, *used to*, *would*, *be/get used to*	Workbook, p 14, Exercises 1, 2 Unit 2, Grammar 1, Exercises 1, 2
Vocabulary	Words connected with *studying* and *learning* Phrasal verbs Words + prepositions	Workbook, pp 14–15, Exercises 1, 2, 3 Unit 2, Vocabulary, Exercises 1, 2, 3
Listening **Multiple choice (extracts)**	Listening for agreement and disagreement	Workbook, p 16, Exercises 1, 2, 3, 4 Unit 2, Listening, Exercises 1, 2, 3, 4
Grammar 2	Tenses (2): present perfect simple, past perfect simple	Workbook, p 15, Exercises 1, 2 Unit 2, Grammar 2, Exercises 1, 2
Speaking **Collaborative task**	Agreeing and disagreeing	Workbook, p 17, Exercises 1, 2 Unit 2, Speaking, Exercises 1, 2
Use of English **Word formation** **Sentence transformation**	Suffixes and negative prefixes Contracted forms	Workbook, p 17, Exercises 1, 2, 3 Unit 2, Use of English, Exercises 1, 2, 3
Writing **An essay**	Expressing and justifying opinion	Workbook, p 18, Exercises 1, 2, 3, 4 Unit 2, Writing, Exercises 1, 2, 3, 4
Progress check	Check language progress for Units 1 and 2	Workbook, p 19, Progress check and Cumulative progress Progress check and Cumulative progress

Additional material

PRESENTATION KIT	TEACHER'S / STUDENT'S RESOURCE CENTRE RC	TEST GENERATOR
Talk2Me video *Neither do I …*	**Unit 2 worksheets:** *Optimise your grammar* (Standard and Higher), *Optimise your vocabulary* (Standard and Higher), *Talk2Me* video, *Say it right* **Units 1–2 worksheets:** CLIL, Culture, Everyday English (TRC only), Grammar communication (TRC only)	Unit Test 2 (Standard and Higher)

READING
Multiple choice | An online article

→ Student's Book, pages 14–15 SB

Lesson aims

- Focus on multiple choice
- Practise a multiple-choice exam task

Lead-in

Elicit the meaning of the unit title ***Learning about learning*** (*learning about different techniques to become a better learner*). Ask students what they think the lesson is going to be about (*education and learning*).

1 In pairs or groups, students ask and answer the questions. Elicit answers in open class and try to develop a class discussion on how much sleep students get and if they think they get enough.

Answers
Students' own answers

2 Ask students to complete the exercise. Check answers in open class.

Remind students that they need to be flexible and use different types of reading techniques in exams to help them quickly locate the answers and find specific information in the text. Highlight key techniques, such as keeping the concept clearly in mind as you scan, and using captions and different font sizes and colours to help locate specific information.

Answers
Students should tick: 1, 2, 4, 6

3 Ask students to complete the exercise. Ask them to compare their answers in pairs before you check in open class. Accept all sensible reasons.

Suggested answers

1 not allowing – If something is forbidden, it's not allowed. From the context, we can see that it's talking about '9 or 10 pm' when they 'should be feeling sleepy' but aren't.

2 awake – We're told it's 'hard for parents to stay awake' and this is contrasted with teens by using the phrase 'just when', meaning the teens are wide awake.

3 not getting enough sleep – It says the teens who used electronic devices also experienced sleep deprivation. The word 'also' shows us the previous teens experienced sleep deprivation too, and they 'were much more likely to need more than an hour to fall asleep, and were also more likely to sleep several hours less each night'.

4 start – If melatonin is a hormone that causes sleep and darkness affects melatonin production, it's most likely that darkness causes or leads to the production of melatonin rather than stopping it being produced.

OPTIMISE YOUR EXAM

Multiple choice

Ask students to read the tips.

- When students are tested on their ability to deduce the meaning of words from context in exams, there will always be clues in the text to help them do this. The next exercise will allow them to practise this exam technique. Point out that students should always check to see if the text actually defines the word or restates it. Sometimes the text gives examples that help explain the word in question.
- Highlight that the questions always follow the order of the text. A good exam technique is to stop after the first question and look at the options, and to continue like this until they have answered all the questions.
- Remind students that they should try not to leave any questions unanswered.

▼ Exam task

4 1.06 **Note: The reading text is also available on the audio CD. You may want to have students listen and read the text before doing the exam task.**

Ask students to complete the exercise. Check in open class and elicit evidence for their answers.

Answers

1 B (*... just as they should be feeling sleepy*)

2 C (*... also experienced some sleep deprivation ... Greg Dickson, 16, is a prime example.*)

3 B (*... either didn't improve or actually fell behind*) (Point out to students that option A is true, but it's not what the experiment is designed to show.)

4 D (*... the brain consolidates and practises what has been learnt while you're asleep*)

5 C (*... often called 'the sleep hormone'*)

6 D (*... you shouldn't sleep until noon on a Saturday. That simply confuses the body.*)

Fast finishers

Ask students to find words in the text to match these definitions.

the period of your life when you are no longer young but are not yet old

make something happen

to end or finish something gradually

Answers
middle age trigger wind down

Optional extension 1.06

Play the recorded text and ask students to underline all the words and expressions related to being asleep and awake. Ask them to compare in pairs before you check in open class. In pairs or small groups, students could make a list of top tips to have a good sleep. In open class, they then read out their tips for others to comment on and vote, by raising their hands, on the best tip.

Answers

bedtime, sleep, wake up, feel refreshed, sleep patterns, good night's sleep, fresh and energised, body clock, 'forbidden zone', prop you up, feel sleepy, stay awake, most alert, go to bed, fall asleep, sleep deprivation, before bed, go to sleep, get up, lack of sleep, have a good sleep, be asleep, get a good night's rest, binge-sleep (pronounced /bɪndʒ/), get up

Homework OWB

Assign students Reading exercises 1, 2 and 3 on pages 12–13 of their Workbook.

GRAMMAR 1

Tenses (1): present/past simple, *used to, would, be/get used to*

→ Student's Book, page 16 SB

Lesson aims

- Understand the correct usage of the present and past simple, *used to, would* and *be/get used to*
- Practise using the present and past simple, *used to, would* and *be/get used to*

Lead-in

Write these jumbled sentences on the board and ask students to reorder them:

the / you / binge-sleep / weekend / Did / at / ?

How / did / night / sleep / last / many / you / hours / ?

morning / you / in / feel / Do / sleepy / always / the / ?

In pairs, students ask and answer the questions. Walk round, monitoring students for good use of the present and past simple tenses.

Answers

Did you binge-sleep at the weekend? How many hours did you sleep last night? Do you always feel sleepy in the morning?

Grammar in context

Ask students to complete the task. Refer them to the *Remember* box if they need help. Check answers in open class.

Remind students that they can find more information in the Grammar reference, Unit 2, page 149.

Answers

1 present simple questions: What do you do in the hour …? / How many hours' sleep do you get …? / Do you wake up …? / But how does this lack of sleep affect learning? **present simple negatives:** I don't feel like going to sleep after that. / And I really don't feel like getting up the next morning

2 past simple negative: didn't improve **past simple irregular forms:** students were taught a series of skills (passive) / and then slept for various lengths of time / more accurate they became / who then had a good sleep / who got less than / or actually fell behind

1 Ask students to complete the exercise. Check their answers.

Answers

1 is, learn **2** went, enjoyed **3** don't usually stand **4** didn't you come, Were you **5** says **6** starts, don't like, we're / we are

Language note

Highlight that neither *used to* nor *would* can be used to refer to single actions in the past. For example, it would not be possible to use either form in this sentence: *I moved to Barcelona in 2001.* When students describe habitual actions and temporary or repeated events in the past, it's a good idea to try to vary their choice between *used to, would* and the past simple to make their descriptions more interesting.

An important difference between *used to* and *would* is that *would* is not used with stative verbs such as *love, be, understand* and *feel*. The use of *would* is more restricted than that of *used to*. Advise students that if they aren't sure which one to use, it's best to choose *used to*.

Remind students that the contracted form of *would* is *'d* and that *would* is also used in the second conditional.

Point out that *be/get used to, used to* and *would* are often tested in Use of English exams.

Remind students that they can find more information in the Grammar reference, Unit 2, page 149.

2 Ask students to complete the exercise. Check their answers in open class. Elicit if it is possible to use *would* in question 1 (yes, *wear* is not a stative verb).

Answers

1 used to wear **2** ✓ **3** Did you use **4** never used to like **5** I'm really used to doing **6** I'm still getting used to doing

Optional extension

Write these prompts on the board:

1 something you used to like doing but don't like so much now

2 something you used to do often but don't do so frequently now

3 something you are used to doing, even if it's not a lot of fun

4 something you still haven't got completely used to doing yet

Ask students to write sentences about each one. In pairs, students compare their sentences. Elicit some examples in open class.

3 Ask students to complete the exercise. Ask them to compare in pairs before you check their answers in open class. Elicit if it is possible to use *would* instead of *used to* (gap 2) (no, *believe* is a stative verb).

Answers

1 are **2** to **3** not **4** were **5** were **6** did **7** was

Mixed ability

Give less confident students the prepositions in a jumbled order (*not, were* × 2, *was, to, are, did*). Challenge more advanced students who finish early by asking them to select three new items of vocabulary, look them up in their dictionaries and write them up on the board, with definitions.

Fast finishers

Ask fast finishers to write one or two comprehension questions on the text in Exercise 3 to ask the class when everyone has finished.

Homework

OWB

Assign students Grammar 1 exercises 1 and 2 on page 14 of their Workbook.

VOCABULARY

Topic vocabulary | Phrasal verbs | Word patterns

→ Student's Book, page 17 SB

Lesson aims

- Understand the correct usages of:
  - words connected with studying and learning
  - phrasal verbs
  - words + prepositions

Lead-in

Divide the students into two teams. Call out letters randomly (don't use the letter *X*) and ask teams to think of a word they've learnt so far which begins with that letter. Students put up their hand if they know a word. Choose the first student who puts their hand up and ask him/her to say the word. If it is correct, their team gets a point. Play for a set time. At the end, the team with the most points wins.

Words connected with *studying* and *learning*

1 1.07 Ask students to complete the exercise. Play the audio for students to listen and check their answers. Elicit explanations for each word and check their pronunciation.

Answers/Audioscript

1 This allows you to do something, such as drive a car. *licence*
2 This is a piece of paper showing you've achieved something. *certificate*
3 This is a course of study that you take at university. *degree*
4 We've got a test tomorrow so I'm going to *revise* tonight.
5 Jason's going to *take* his first guitar exam next month even though we're not sure he'll *pass*.
6 This person teaches at a university. *lecturer*
7 This person trains a sports player or team. *coach*
8 This person teaches you how to do something, such as drive a car. *instructor*
9 This person has successfully completed a course at university. *graduate*
10 This person is studying at university. *undergraduate*

Fast finishers

Students write definitions for the words they didn't use in Exercise 1. They can read out their definitions to test the rest of the class when everyone has finished.

Answers

qualification: something such as a degree or a diploma that you get when you successfully finish a course of study

pupil: someone, especially a child, who goes to school or who has lessons in a particular subject

Refer students to the Vocabulary reference, page 162, for more information on topic vocabulary.

Phrasal verbs

2 1.08 Ask students to complete the exercise. Play the audio for students to listen and check their answers. Highlight that *to creep up on somebody* means to approach someone quietly and slowly, so that the person is suddenly surprised.

Answers/Audioscript

1 If you don't know a word, *look it up* in a dictionary. discover/find
2 I want to *set up* a computer-coding club at school. create
3 Alex *crept up behind* Jake while he was doing his homework and surprised him. approach
4 There's only five minutes left, so *hurry up*! increase (speed)
5 Laura *thought up* a ridiculous excuse about why she hadn't written her essay. create
6 When a student returns after being ill, they have to *catch up with* the rest of the class. approach
7 Go online and see what information you can *dig up* about the Romans for the class project. discover/find
8 I was going to do my presentation just on Antarctica, but I *ended up* doing it on the Arctic as well. finish/complete
9 *Speak up*, Simon! We can't hear you at the back. increase (volume)
10 Who's *used up* all the glue? There's none left! finish/complete

Refer students to the Vocabulary reference, page 162, for more information on phrasal verbs.

Extra support

Individually, students write personalised sentences with the phrasal verbs from Exercise 2. In pairs, they then read out their sentences without saying the phrasal verb (they could substitute this for a 'beep' sound) for their partner to guess.

Words + prepositions

3 1.09 Ask students to complete the exercise. Play the audio for students to listen and check their answers.

Answers/Audioscript

1 My brother's just *qualified as* a nurse and we're all really proud.
2 There's nothing *wrong with* deciding you don't want to go to university.
3 I'm going to quit the swimming team for a while as I have to *concentrate on* my studies.
4 Warren's *decided against* becoming a pilot and now wants to be a surgeon.
5 How *interested* are you *in* watching a documentary about archaeology?
6 We need to find someone who's *experienced in* teaching young children.
7 If you don't *pay attention to* anything I say, you're not going to learn anything!

8 All his explanation *succeeded in* doing was to confuse me further!
9 The new education laws were *criticised for* not *addressing* the problem of class sizes in secondary schools.
10 I'm so *bored of/with* doing homework – I can't wait to meet my friends afterwards.

Optional extension

Ask students if they find remembering word patterns like the ones in Exercise 3 easy or difficult.

In pairs or small groups, ask students to brainstorm ways of remembering them.

Elicit answers from different students around the class.

Suggested answers

Learn them by topic, personalise them, recycle and reuse them, draw pictures, test yourself, etc.

Refer students to the Vocabulary reference, page 163, for more information on word patterns.

Homework

Assign students Vocabulary exercises 1, 2 and 3 on pages 14–15 of their Workbook.

OWB

LISTENING

Multiple choice (extracts)

→ Student's Book, page 18 SB

Lesson aims

- Focus on multiple choice (extracts)
- Practise a multiple-choice (extracts) exam task

Lead-in

Play ***Back to the board***. Divide the class into two teams. Ask a volunteer from team A to sit with his/her back to the board, facing their team. Write words, phrases or sentences from the unit on the board one by one. Team A defines the word, phrase or sentence for the volunteer student to guess in one minute. After one minute, it is the other team's turn to define a word, and so on. The team that describes the most words in one minute wins the round.

1 In pairs or groups, students ask and answer the questions. Elicit answers from different students around the class.

Answers

Students' own answers

2 1.10 Play the audio for students to complete the exercise. Check their answers.

Answers

1 A **2** D **3** A **4** P **5** D

3 Ask students to complete the exercise and then compare in pairs before you check in open class.

Answers

Questions 1, 3, 6, 8

Extra support

Remind students that intonation usually falls in statements and rises in question tags that check information. Highlight the link between intonation and attitude. In pairs, ask students to first say the sentences as 'robots' and then try again, giving movement to their voices. Play the audio again, and stop after each phrase for students to repeat and compare.

OPTIMISE YOUR EXAM

Multiple choice (extracts)

Ask students to read the tips.

- In Exercise 3, students saw that they can work out from the questions what type of dialogue they are going to be listening to. If students know the key phrases we use to agree and disagree, they will be able to rapidly tune in when the speaker is discussing other people's ideas and decide if he/she agrees or disagrees with them. This skill is useful in listening exams, and raising students' awareness of how we indicate our opinion will also help them improve their performance in oral exams.
- Students are often tested on their ability to identify a speaker's opinion in listening exams. Intonation helps us emphasise significant points beyond words and syntax. In this lesson students work on how we can identify attitude by listening for changes in intonation, pace, volume and pitch, as well as listening carefully for words and phrases that identify opinions to back up the attitude they have identified.

Exam task

4 1.11 Play the track for students to listen and complete the exercise. Don't check answers at this stage, as students will listen again to check in Exercise 5.

Mixed ability

Ask students to exclude one of the options in each situation. Discuss students' reasons in open class before you play the track again. Don't give away the answers at this point. When you check the answers in Exercise 4, ask students to say which option they excluded on the first listening and if they were right.

5 1.11 Play the track again for students to check their answers to Exercise 4. In open class, discuss the specific clues that helped them choose them.

Answers

1 C (*You can't fault the instructor though. … No, not at all. She was great. Really kind, helpful and knowledgeable.*)

2 C (*I reckon you'll like their winter weekend drama course – it's just your thing. I think they even put on a show at the end.*)

3 B (*One thing's for sure – it's always been a lot easier in the past. … no doubt about that. This time last year they all came out with big smiles on their faces.*)

4 B (*… the children will be performing for free every Sunday evening for the next month in the town hall. It would be great if some of your listeners could come along and support.*)

5 A (*I wouldn't exactly say Dad taught me, but he really did encourage me to try to work it out for myself, and I'll never forget that.*)

6 C (*I'm really not convinced we'll get it all done in two evenings though. It's the whole year's notes. It's pages and pages! … No need to worry. I've got a plan.*)

7 B (*Well, we've now counted all the money we brought in, and you should all be very proud of yourselves as it's a fantastic £3,000 – far more than last year. So very, very well done everyone.*)

8 A (*I guess we need to have the exact costs before we ask them. … Yeah – let's get that tomorrow.*)

Optional extension

Ask students to choose a skill (e.g. juggling, mending a puncture on a bike, making an omelette, etc.) and write a simple set of instructions for a beginner on how to do it. Alternatively, using a smartphone or tablet, make a short film showing and describing what to do.

Homework

OWB

Assign students Listening exercises 1, 2, 3 and 4 on page 16 of their Workbook.

GRAMMAR 2

Tenses (2): present perfect simple, past perfect simple

→ Student's Book, page 19 SB

Lesson aims

- Understand the correct usage of the present perfect simple and past perfect simple
- Practise using the present perfect simple and the past perfect simple

Lead-in

Play ***Grammar tennis***. Write on the board the infinitive form of some verbs students have seen in the unit so far, e.g. *do, take, teach, be, make, sleep, become, have, get, fall,* etc. Divide the class into two teams, A and B.

Ask a volunteer from Team A to 'serve' one of the infinitives on the board to a student on Team B. This student must say the **past participle form** to win a point. If he/she gets it wrong, they get a second chance. If he/she still gets it wrong, elicit the correct form and write it on the board.

It is now Team B's turn to 'serve' and Team A's turn to respond to the service and give the **past simple form** of the same infinitive. Team A only has one chance. The first team to get five points is the winner.

Grammar in context

Ask students to complete the task. Refer them to the *Remember* box if they need help. Check answers in open class.

Remind students that they can find more information in the Grammar reference, Unit 2, page 150.

Answers

1 Because it's a completed action where what's important is the present result.

2 To show that the learning happened even further back in the past than the moment in the past when the speaker 'couldn't wait'.

Language note

Present perfect simple, past simple and past perfect simple

Both the present perfect simple and the past perfect simple talk about something that happened before a point in time (the reference point). In the present perfect simple, our reference point is the present. In the past perfect, our reference point is in the past.

Highlight the contracted form of *had* (*'d*). It is difficult for students to hear short forms, so they must listen carefully for *'d/hadn't* and pay attention to the context to be sure of the tense being used.

1 Ask students to complete the exercise. Students compare in pairs before you check in open class. Elicit the contracted forms of the verbs.

Answers

1 (has) decided, has just bought **2** had read **3** has ever failed **4** had not been, realised, (had) thought **5** have looked **6** (had) wanted, (has) changed

Extra support

Ask students to make negative and interrogative sentences in the present perfect simple, past simple or past perfect simple using some of the verbs in Exercise 1.

2 Ask students to complete the exercise. Have students check in pairs before you check their answers in open class.

Answers

1 ever **2** since **3** before **4** yet/already, just **5** yet **6** so **7** never **8** still

3 Ask students to complete the exercise. Check answers in open class.

Answers

1 have **2** had **3** ever **4** has **5** have **6** since **7** flown/sent/taken/carried/transported/etc. **8** had

Optional extension

Ask students to write two true sentences and one false sentence about themselves using the tenses in this lesson. In pairs or small groups, students read out their sentences for their partner to guess which sentences are true or false.

Mixed ability

Give less confident students the answers in a jumbled order to help them complete the exercise (*ever, has, since, flown, had × 2, have × 2*).

Ask stronger students to write two comprehension questions. They can read them out to test other students' understanding of the text once everyone has finished the exercise.

THINK | RESEARCH | CULTURE | **LEARN** | ME

In pairs or small groups, students discuss the questions. Elicit answers in open class.

Homework OWB

Assign students Grammar 2 exercises 1 and 2 on page 15 of their Workbook.

SPEAKING
Collaborative task

→ Student's Book, page 20 SB

Lesson aims

- Focus on agreeing and disagreeing
- Practise doing a collaborative task

The *Talk2Me* video in this unit focuses on school trips. People talk about school trips and what they can learn from going on them. Students answer some comprehension questions and then listen out for phrases to express agreement and disagreement. The video can be used in one of two ways:

Flipped classroom

Flipped classroom option

Using this approach, students watch the video and complete the exercises for homework. This prepares students for the speaking lesson by introducing them to the topic and the key phrases to use in the exam task. Teachers who use this method will find they have more class time to spend on activating the target language and developing fluency for the final task.

***Talk2Me* worksheet**

Ask students to also complete the *Talk2Me* worksheet on the Resource Centre for more detailed comprehension exercises and more practice of the key phrases.

Classroom option

1 Ask students to spend a minute or two reading the questions. Play the *Talk2Me* video for students to complete the exercise. Play the video again, if necessary, before checking their answers.

2 Play the *Talk2Me* video again, so students circle the phrases in the *Phrase expert* box. Pause the video from time to time if necessary. Check answers in open class.

***Talk2Me* worksheet**

Ask students to also complete the *Talk2Me* worksheet on the Resource Centre for more detailed comprehension exercises and more practice of the key phrases.

Answers

The transcript and answer key for the *Talk2Me* video exercises and Worksheet can be found on the Teacher's Resource Centre.

Lead-in

In pairs, students play ***Just a minute***. They speak for 60 seconds about the photo, trying not to hesitate, repeat any content words or deviate from the subject. Their partner times them. They then swap roles. In a less confident class, elicit vocabulary and expressions first to help them.

3 In pairs or groups, students ask and answer the questions. Elicit answers from different students around the class.

Answers

Students' own answers

4 Individually, students make notes before they complete the task in pairs or as a group. Elicit advantages from different students around the class.

Answers

Students' own answers

Mixed ability

In a less confident class, brainstorm some advantages for each option in open class and write them on the board. Feed in some interesting expressions and ideas for more advanced students to use, e.g. *team-building, make learning fun, improve self-confidence, understand other perspectives, provide cultural experiences you might not otherwise have, adventure, leadership, trust, respect, self-confidence, self-esteem skills to deal with risks*, etc.

Cultural note

School trips provide a great opportunity for students to face a range of challenges that can contribute significantly to their personal development. School trips can also make a major contribution to the acquisition of knowledge; students can study the natural and man-made world, the present and past, science and arts, language and music and new sports.

5 Ask students to complete the exercise. Check answers in open class.

Answers

2 Neither/Nor **3** don't **4** point **5** suppose **6** So

OPTIMISE YOUR EXAM

Collaborative task

Ask students to read the tips.

- Remind students that in many official oral exams, examiners give candidates marks for interactive communication, e.g. the ability to use strategies, such as agreeing and disagreeing, to keep the conversation going.
- Emphasise that it is important for students to take turns in a speaking exam. They will lose marks if they dominate or interrupt their partner in a discussion. A good response will show that the speaker has listened to and respects the arguments offered by their partner(s). Remind students to attack the argument, not the person, and not to take personally the fact that someone is arguing against them.

Exam task

6 In pairs, students complete the exercise. Set a two-minute time limit. Remind students to use phrases for making suggestions from the *Phrase expert* box.

Walk round, monitoring students for good use of language and errors to go over at the end of the activity. Write any errors on the board and go through them with students, eliciting corrections from them where possible.

Extra support

Model this activity first with a pair of confident students in open class. Introduce key expressions such as *What do you think? What about you? I like your idea of … because … What you said about … is really interesting.*

7 In pairs, students complete the task. Set a one-minute time limit. Elicit the decisions students reached from different pairs around the class.

Extra support

Elicit the key steps and useful phrases students can use when they have to reach a decision.

Define the issues – *Well, we have to talk about … so …*

Generate options – *What about …? How about …?*

Expand your ideas – *Yes, because …*

Look for the common ground – *Do we agree that …?*

Disagree on one thing – *I don't agree with you there.*

Reach a decision – *So, in the end, let's say …*

Optional extension

In class or for homework, students write about a school trip they have been on and say what they enjoyed. Encourage them to say what they think they learnt on the trip. Alternatively, students could plan a trip they would like to go on.

SAY IT RIGHT

Stress in phrases for agreeing and disagreeing TRC

For the *Say it right* pronunciation activity and instructions, go to the Teacher's Resource Centre.

Homework

OWB

Assign students Speaking exercises 1 and 2 on page 17 of their Workbook.

USE OF ENGLISH

Word formation | Sentence transformation

→ Student's Book, page 21 SB

Lesson aims

- Focus on word formation and practise a word-formation exam task
- Focus on sentence transformation and practise a sentence-transformation task

Lead-in

Play ***Noughts and crosses***. Draw a large 3 by 3 grid on the board. Number the boxes 1 to 9 and write time expressions (e.g. *already, yet, before, since, ever, never, just, still, so far*) in the boxes.

Divide the class into two teams, X and O. Flip a coin to see which team goes first.

In order for the team to receive the X or the O for the box they have chosen, they must make a correct sentence using the time expressions.

Alternate between the teams until one team has a line of three Xs or Os, or it is a draw.

1 Ask students to complete the exercise. Elicit answers from different students around the class.

Answers

1 difficult **2** champion, relate **3** success

Language note

Suffixes are commonly used to make nouns from adjectives and verbs. Elicit common suffixes in English, e.g. *-ment, -ity, -ness, -ance, -ence, -ship, -al, -th, -ent, -ive, -ous, -less*. Point out that students can guess the correct word by adding various prefixes and suffixes until they get something that sounds right and obeys the rules of word formation. Often, while they are doing this, they find the one that sounds right and suddenly realise that they were familiar with it after all. Highlight that the suffix often causes a spelling change to the original word.

OPTIMISE YOUR EXAM

Word formation

Ask students to read the tip.

- Suffixes are often tested in key word transformation tasks such as Exercise 2 in this lesson. Remind students that there are usually three or four conversions from verb to noun and at least one negative in this type of task.
- Remind students to read through the whole text again with their answers completed to make sure it makes sense and sounds correct. The type of mistake they will often pick up at this point is not changing words to the negative to fit in with the meaning of the text. By reading the whole text they will see that it is grammatically correct but it doesn't make sense in the context.

Exam task

2 Ask students to complete the exercise. Have students compare in pairs before you elicit answers in open class.

Answers
1 difficulty/difficulties **2** competitive **3** championships **4** mathematical **5** successfully **6** information **7** unbelievable **8** relationship

Refer students to the Vocabulary reference, page 163, for more information on word formation.

3 Ask students to complete the exercise. Check answers in open class.

Answers
1 1 (negative form)
2 5 (because the first sentence has the idea of '*become*', it's *get used to* not *be used to*)

OPTIMISE YOUR EXAM

Sentence transformation

Ask students to read the tip.

- Remind students that each sentence transformation question is marked in two halves (one point each half) and they can get a point in the exam for getting a single word correct. Encourage them to always try every question.
- Students will practise the type of task in this lesson many more times during the course.

Exam task

4 Ask students to complete the exercise. Check their answers.

Answers
1 didn't / did not usually use to **2** ended up getting/with **3** hasn't / has not taken exams for **4** was set up **5** get/become used to speaking **6** succeeded in remembering

Extra support

Check the answers to Exercise 4. Divide the class into A and B pairs, mixing up higher and lower level students. Tell Student A to read out the first sentences in 1–6 and say the word given. Student B tries to formulate the second sentence, without looking at their notes. If the answer is correct, Student B continues. If they make a mistake, Student A has a turn. However, Student B now reads out the second sentence in 1–6.

Student A must start again from question 1, but this time they can use their memory as well as logic. When Student A makes a mistake, Student B can try again, also starting from 1. The aim of the game is for both students to go through every sentence transformation in one go without making any mistakes.

THINK | RESEARCH | CULTURE | LEARN | ME

If you have access to the internet, students can research information in class. Alternatively, they could prepare this for homework and present their information at the start of the next lesson.

Homework

OWB

Assign students Use of English exercises 1, 2, 3 and 4 on page 17 of their Workbook.

WRITING
An essay

→ Student's Book, pages 22–23 SB

Lesson aims

- Focus on language in an essay
- Plan and write an opinion essay

Lead-in

Write these words on the board:

Money management / Shopping for food / Serving meals / Cleaning the house / Operating household appliances / Washing clothes / Painting and household repairs / Car maintenance / Gardening.

In pairs, students discuss how well prepared they are for these real-life tasks. Ask them to rate themselves from 1 to 10 in each area.

Elicit the areas they feel they are best/worst prepared for from students around the class.

1 In pairs or as a group, students answer the questions. Elicit answers in open class.

Answers
Students' own answers

2 Students complete the exercise. Elicit answers from different students around the class. Accept all sensible suggestions.

Suggested answers

do not make successful teachers

are not old enough to teach people things

are too young and inexperienced to teach others

3 Ask students to complete the exercise. Check answers in open class.

Answers

Students should tick: **2** I would argue that **3** … it seems to me that **4** In my view, **7** I disagree with **8** In my experience,

4 In pairs or groups, students complete the exercise. Walk round, monitoring students and helping them if necessary. Elicit answers in open class and accept all sensible suggestions.

Suggested answers

main point:	reason and/or example given to justify it:
teenagers are good at teaching	The writer says some people think *teenagers are too young and inexperienced*, but he/she argues that teenagers can teach many different things.
how to use modern technology	The writer's own parents often ask him/her for help and advice about smartphones, computers, tablets and apps / teenagers understand new gadgets almost instantly – and can teach others how to use them.
green issues	The writer's friends understand green issues more than their parents, and are often good at persuading them to change their ways, for instance with recycling.
particular interests or skills	The writer's sister loves fashion and often helps their dad choose stylish clothes.

OPTIMISE YOUR EXAM

An essay

Ask students to read the tips.

- Tell students that they're going to look at a typical writing exam task and practise agreeing or disagreeing with a statement. Point out to students that they should assume that whoever reads their essay has no idea about the topic. They should talk about possible opinions on the subject and give examples before they give a more personal opinion.
- Effective organisation and cohesion are important features of a successful essay and will help students score higher marks. In Exercise 3, students worked on a wide variety of linking words and phrases for giving examples. This will help them show clear and logical relationships between their arguments and examples in their writing.

For more information on writing an essay, refer students to the Writing reference, page 174.

▾ Exam task

5 Ask students to complete the exercise. Elicit answers from different students around the class.

Extra support

First discuss the questions after the task in Exercise 5 in open class. Elicit explanations and ask them to justify their answers. Encourage students to use some of the phrases in Exercise 3. Write some key words and expressions on the board that less confident students can refer back to when they write their essay.

6 Plan Ask students to complete the paragraph plan based on their discussion in Exercise 5. You may want to look at students' plans, if possible, to check them and give advice and suggestions for improvement before students take the next step.

7 Write Ask students to write their essay in an appropriate style in 140–190 words. Depending on time, it may be a good idea to set this and the subsequent checklist exercise for homework.

8 Check Ask students to complete the checklist before they hand in their essay.

Optional extension

Students swap essays and give marks from 1 (low) to 5 (high) for four different areas typically used for marking writing exams.

1 Content / task achievement – meaning properly answering the question.

2 Communicative achievement – successfully communicating ideas at the right level of formality.

3 Organisation – overall organisation and linking together of sentences and paragraphs.

4 Language – level and accuracy of grammar and vocabulary.

Homework OWB

Assign students Writing exercises 1, 2, 3 and 4 on page 18 of their Workbook and Progress check 2 on page 19.

Answers PROGRESS CHECK Units 1–2

Exercise 1
1 appearance **2** success **3** competitions **4** championship(s) **5** popularity **6** pleasure **7** believe **8** impressive

Exercise 2
1 took **2** makes **3** did / have done / 've done **4** has taken / 's taken **5** had done

Exercise 3
1 d **2** f **3** a **4** b **5** e

Exercise 4
1 over **2** up **3** setting **4** out **5** up **6** lie **7** catch

Exercise 5
1 to **2** for **3** as **4** with **5** on **6** against **7** at/in **8** in

Exercise 6
1 none **2** any **3** little **4** all **5** either

Exercise 7
1 were only a few **2** to get/become used to living **3** second time I had been / second time I'd been **4** in the existence of **5** make an effort **6** come up with

3 Invent and innovate

UNIT AIMS

Exam preparation in Unit 3:

- scan a science article to find specific information
- predict alternative ways of saying the same thing
- talk about similarities and differences between photos
- understand how countable and uncountable nouns are formed and use them in a word-formation exercise
- add suffixes and use them in a word-formation exercise
- make recommendations for a target audience in a review

TEACHER'S PRESENTATION KIT

- *Talk2Me* videos
- Speaking test videos
- Class and Workbook audio
- Workbook pages and answer key

UNIT OVERVIEW

Student's Book / Digital Student's Book (SB)		Workbook / Online Workbook (OWB)
LESSON / EXAM TASK	**EXAM SKILLS / LANGUAGE FOCUS**	**CONSOLIDATION**
Reading **Multiple matching**	Scanning A science article	Workbook, pp 20–21, Exercises 1, 2, 3 Unit 3, Reading, Exercises 1, 2, 3
Grammar 1	Tenses (3): continuous tenses	Workbook, p 22, Exercises 1, 2, 3 Unit 3, Grammar 1, Exercises 1, 2, 3
Vocabulary	Words connected with *manufacturing* and *tools* Phrasal verbs Collocations with *top* and *high*	Workbook, pp 22–23, Exercises 1, 2, 3 Unit 3, Vocabulary, Exercises 1, 2, 3
Listening **Multiple matching**	Listening for opinion and attitude (1)	Workbook, p 24, Exercises 1, 2, 3 Unit 3, Listening, Exercises 1, 2, 3
Grammar 2	Comparatives and superlatives	Workbook, p 23, Exercises 1, 2, 3 Unit 3, Grammar 2, Exercises 1, 2, 3
Speaking **Photo task**	Comparing and contrasting	Workbook, p 24, Exercises 1, 2 Unit 3, Speaking, Exercises 1, 2
Use of English **Word formation** **Multiple-choice cloze**	Countable and uncountable nouns Suffixes Prepositions	Workbook, p 25, Exercises 1, 2, 3 Unit 3, Use of English, Exercises 1, 2, 3
Writing **A review**	Making recommendations	Workbook, p 26, Exercises 1, 2, 3 Unit 3, Writing, Exercises 1, 2, 3
		Workbook, p 27, Progress check and Cumulative progress Progress check and Cumulative progress

Additional material

PRESENTATION KIT	TEACHER'S / STUDENT'S RESOURCE CENTRE (RC)	TEST GENERATOR
Talk2Me video *It's far better than …*	**Unit 3 worksheets:** *Optimise your grammar* (Standard and Higher), *Optimise your vocabulary* (Standard and Higher), *Talk2Me* video, *Say it right* **Units 3–4 worksheets:** CLIL, Culture, Everyday English (TRC only), Grammar communication (TRC only)	Unit Test 3 (Standard and Higher)

READING
Multiple matching | A science article

→ Student's Book, pages 26–27

Lesson aims

- Focus on multiple matching
- Practise a multiple-matching exam task

Lead-in

Elicit the meaning of the unit title ***Invent and innovate*** and ask students if they know the idiom *Necessity is the mother of invention* – an English-language proverb that means that the primary driving force for most new inventions is a need, e.g. if someone really needs to do something, they will find a way of doing it. Ask students what they think the lesson is going to be about (*science and technology*).

1 In pairs or groups, students ask and answer the questions. Elicit answers in open class and try to develop a class discussion on why these inventions are important, who invented them and what would life be like without them.

Answers

Students' own answers

2 Ask students to complete the exercise as quickly as possible. Check answers in open class.

Answers

1 Heat power **2** A new way to get medicine **3** A new way to speak **4** Better protection

3 Ask students to complete the exercise. Time this activity (two minutes) and give updates, e.g. *One minute to go … Only thirty seconds left.* Check answers in open class and elicit more information if the idea was mentioned.

Answers

1 Yes (*The inspiration for the invention came from a friend in the Philippines, who found it difficult to do homework in the evening because they didn't have electricity at home. Ann has described her eureka moment: 'I thought, why not body heat? We have so much heat radiating out of us and it's being wasted.'*)

2 No

3 No

4 Yes (*… as 16-year-old Ryan Beck … recognised while he was watching a particularly vicious game of American football. It was this particular game which inspired him to develop a safer and stronger kind of helmet, offering greater protection to the part of the brain called the 'temporal lobe' in the case of a head-on collision …*)

OPTIMISE YOUR **EXAM**

Multiple matching

Ask students to read the tips.

- Scanning is a strategy for speed reading in order to find specific information in the text. Students practised this technique in Exercises 2 and 3. Elicit situations where students need to find a particular piece of information quickly within a large amount of text (e.g. *when they look up words in a dictionary, a sports score in a newspaper, use a train or bus timetable,* etc.).
- Remind students that often exact word matches are a trap – if a key word in the text is exactly the same as the word in the question, students should be careful. It's almost certainly not the answer. They should also be careful of partial matches and find a sentence in the text that matches **all** the key words.
- Highlight that in this type of exam task, the questions and texts are not necessarily in the same order.

▾ Exam task

4 1.12 **Note: The reading text is also available on the audio CD. You may want to have students listen and read the text before doing the exam task.**

Ask students to complete the exercise. Check answers in open class and elicit evidence for their answers. This helps train students to check their choices carefully.

Answers

1 B (*While receiving her IV (intravenous) medicine, Kylie had to push a heavy metal pole around. This held the IV bag, and had wires dangling which were easy to trip over. Now recovering from her ordeal, Kylie wants to make life easier for children in a similar situation.*)

2 C (*He's under no illusions how beneficial this could be, describing it as having 'the potential to change the world'.*)

3 B (*Her design has won praise from medical practitioners and patients.*)

4 D (*… as 16-year-old Ryan Beck recognised while watching a particularly vicious game of American football.*)

5 A (*It then took months of hard work designing and fine-tuning the torch before she had a working model.*)

6 C (*Users breathe into a microphone, essentially creating dots and dashes, as in Morse Code.*)

7 C (*Arsh believes his system is three times faster than existing devices which rely on tracking eye movement, and is much more affordable.*)

8 A (*… which won her a prestigious award at the Google Science Fair.*)

9 D (*… a safer and stronger kind of helmet, offering greater protection to the part of the brain called the 'temporal lobe' in the case of a head-on collision …*)

10 A (*The inspiration for the invention came from a friend in the Philippines, who found it difficult to do homework in the evening because they didn't have electricity at home.*)

Extra support

In a less confident class, ask students to underline the key words in each question. This will help them identify synonyms in the text.

5 Ask students to complete the exercise. Elicit definitions from different students around the class.

Answers

bulky (adj): too big to be carried or stored easily

converts (v): changes from one system to another or makes something do this

collision (n): an accident in which a person that is moving crashes into something

dangling (v): hanging or swinging without anything stopping it

eureka moment (n): the moment when you suddenly have a great idea, or find the answer to a problem

fine-tuning (v): making small changes to something in order to make it as good or as effective as possible

ground-breaking (adj): using new methods, or achieving new results

impact (n): an effect, or an influence

ordeal (n): an extremely unpleasant experience, especially one that lasts for a long time

patenting (v): applying for an official document that gives someone who has invented something the legal right to make or sell that invention for a particular period of time, and prevents anyone else from doing so

potential (n): the possibility to develop or achieve something in the future

THINK | RESEARCH | CULTURE | LEARN | ME

In pairs or small groups, students discuss the questions. Elicit answers in open class.

Cultural note

The Google Science Fair is an online science competition sponsored by Google, Lego, Virgin Galactic, *National Geographic* and *Scientific American*. The competition is open to 13 to 18-year-old students around the globe, who formulate a hypothesis, perform an experiment and present their results. Prizes are awarded to three finalists. The grand prize includes a *National Geographic* trip to the Galapagos Islands, a US$50,000 scholarship, and an 'experience' at a sponsoring organisation.

Optional extension

Have a ***Balloon debate***. In small groups, students each choose one of the best inventions of the last 50 years. Tell them they are in a hot-air balloon which is losing height rapidly and will soon crash because it is too heavy. They have to decide which student to throw over the side (i.e. which invention is the least important).

Give students time to prepare their case as to why they must stay in the balloon.

Each student speaks for one minute and then the group votes.

This continues until only one student is left in the balloon.

Homework

Assign students Reading exercises 1, 2 and 3 on pages 20–21 of their Workbook.

OWB

GRAMMAR 1

Tenses (3): continuous tenses

→ Student's Book, page 28 SB

Lesson aims

- Understand the correct usage of continuous tenses
- Practise using continuous tenses

Lead-in

Play ***Hangman*** with some of the words from the Reading lesson.

Suggested words: *gadget, prestigious, scientist, lightweight, helmet, artificial, affordable, beneficial.*

Grammar in context

Ask students to complete the task. Refer them to the *Remember* box if they need help. Check answers in open class.

Point out to students that *while* expresses the idea of *during that time*. We use it mainly to talk about things that happen simultaneously.

Remind students that they can find more information in the Grammar reference, Unit 3, page 150.

Answers

1 to describe an unfinished action

2 to describe a situation in progress at a particular moment

Language note

Remind students that there is often very little difference between the present perfect simple and the present perfect continuous, e.g. *I've lived here for five years* and *I've been living here for five years.* Both tenses show a connection to the present. However, we use the present perfect continuous when we want to emphasise the process and duration of an action and say how long something has been happening up to now. If the action is very short, we cannot use the continuous form.

Point out that we often use adverbs like *'forever'* or *'constantly'* (as well as *'always'*) when we use the present continuous for annoying habits.

1 Ask students to complete the exercise. They compare in pairs before you check in open class.

Highlight the past perfect continuous in question 6. We use the past perfect continuous in the same way as the present perfect continuous, but with reference to a time earlier than 'before now'. As with the present perfect continuous, we are more interested in the process.

Answers

1 ✓

2 Have you been running? (*the present perfect continuous for an action continuing up to the present moment*)

3 have been studying (*the present perfect continuous for a situation continuing over a period of time up to the present*)

4 was always playing (*the continuous form is used to indicate an annoying habit*)

5 are creating (*the present continuous for an action in progress at the present moment*)

6 ✓

Extra support

Ask students to make negative and interrogative sentences with four continuous tenses (present continuous, past continuous, present perfect continuous and past perfect continuous).

2 Ask students to complete the exercise. Check their answers in open class.

Answers

1 have **2** had **3** was **4** have **5** guides **6** have **7** have **8** are

3 Ask students to complete the exercise. Check answers in open class.

Answers

1 A **2** B **3** C **4** B **5** B **6** B **7** C

Fast finishers

Ask fast finishers to write one or two comprehension questions on the text in Exercise 3 to ask the class when everyone has finished.

Optional extension

In pairs or small groups, students find out some interesting developments in the world of robotics and give their own opinion. If you have access to the internet, students can research information in class. Alternatively, they could prepare this for homework and present their information at the start of the next lesson.

Homework OWB

Assign students Grammar 1 exercises 1, 2 and 3 on page 22 of their Workbook.

VOCABULARY

Topic vocabulary | Phrasal verbs | Collocations

→ Student's Book, page 29 SB

Lesson aims

- Understand the correct usage of:
  - words connected with manufacturing and tools
  - phrasal verbs
  - collocations with *top* and *high*

Lead-in

Write these jumbled sentences on the board and ask students to reorder them:

you / surfing / Were / the / night / internet / last / ?
talking / Is / constantly / in / someone / loudly / class / ?
it / the / raining/ before / started / class / been / Had / ?
long / studying / you / English / have / How / been / ?
wearing / the / clothes / you / same / Are / yesterday / as / ?

In pairs, students ask and answer the questions.

Answers

Were you surfing the internet last night? Is someone constantly talking loudly in class? Had it been raining before the class started? How long have you been studying English? Are you wearing the same clothes as yesterday?

Words connected with *manufacturing* and *tools*

1 1.13 Ask students to complete the exercise. Play the audio for students to listen and check their answers. Elicit explanations for each word and check their pronunciation.

Answers/Audioscript

1 Do you know who first *discovered* that magnetism and electricity are connected?
2 How much energy does a solar panel *generate*?
3 The bikes are *manufactured* in a factory in Taiwan and then shipped to Europe.
4 We had a competition to see who could *create* the best app.
5 It's a good idea, but you need to *develop* the product further before you can sell it.
6 I'd love someone to *invent* an app that did all your homework for you.

2 1.14 Ask students to complete the exercise. Check answers in open class.

Answers/Audioscript

1 The plane is powered by four enormous jet *engines*.
2 The bikes used in the city's cycle hire scheme are powered by an electric *motor*.
3 Oh no! My bottle of water is stuck inside the vending *machine*.
4 Can you pass me the *remote control*? I want to change the channel.
5 The *tool* box had a hammer, a screwdriver and a saw for doing jobs around the house.
6 The company manufactures a number of kitchen *appliances*, including fridges and cookers.

Refer students to the Vocabulary reference, page 163, for more information on topic vocabulary.

Phrasal verbs

3 1.15 Ask students to complete the exercise. Play the audio for students to listen and check their answers.

Answers/Audioscript

1 I wasn't able *to figure out* how the app worked at first, but now I've got it.
2 The machine won't work if you don't *plug it in* first!
3 Physicists *are looking into* the source of the radiation.
4 The project's *coming on* nicely – I'm very optimistic.
5 A number of tests *are carried out* on the equipment to check that it's safe to use.
6 Who *came up with* such a brilliant idea first?

Extra support

Individually, students write personalised sentences with the phrasal verbs from Exercise 3. In pairs, they then read out their sentences without saying the phrasal verb (they could substitute this for a 'beep' sound) for their partner to guess.

Language note

There are five types of phrasal verb:

Intransitive (with no object), e.g. *You're driving too fast – can you slow down?*

Transitive verbs whose object is either after the verb or after the particle, e.g. *I think I'll put my jacket on.* / *I think I'll put on my jacket.* If the object is a pronoun, the object must come between the verb and the particle, e.g. *I think I'll put it on.* (not *I think I'll put on it.*)

Transitive verbs whose object must always come between the verb and the particle, e.g. *Its excellent results set the school apart from others in the area.*

Transitive verbs whose object must come after the particle, e.g. *He takes after his mother. Why do you put up with him?*

Verbs with two objects – one after the verb, the other after the particle, e.g. *They put their success down to good planning.*

Refer students to the Vocabulary reference, page 163, for more information on phrasal verbs.

Collocations with *top* and *high*

4 1.16 Ask students to complete the exercise. Play the audio for students to listen and check their answers.

Answers/Audioscript

1 Dan loves *high-tech* equipment and is always buying the latest gadgets.
2 This information's *top secret* so don't tell anyone what you've seen.
3 The Nobel Prizes in physics and chemistry are two of the *top awards* in science.
4 The engine's very *high-powered*, but extremely quiet.
5 The car has a *top speed* of about 200 km/h, but you can't drive at *high speed* on the roads round here!
6 My dad's company designs *high-performance* software for NASA's spacecraft.
7 I love watching movies on our new *high-definition* TV.
8 It's *high time* I got my invention manufactured and sold – in fact, it's now a *top/high priority.*

Optional extension

In pairs, students take it in turns to ask each other what gadgets and devices they have at home and which ones they couldn't live without.

Refer students to the Vocabulary reference, page 163, for more information on collocations.

Homework OWB

Assign students Vocabulary exercises 1, 2 and 3 on pages 22–23 of their Workbook.

LISTENING
Multiple matching

→ Student's Book, page 30 SB

Lesson aims

- Focus on multiple matching
- Practise a multiple-matching exam task

Lead-in

Play ***First to five*** to revise vocabulary from the unit. Say different categories (e.g. technology, collocations with *top* and *high,* inventions of the last 50 years, famous inventors, words connected to *manufacturing* and *tools*).

Small groups compete to think of five words for each one. When they have five, they shout 'First to five'. Check their words, giving one point for each correct answer. The group with the most points wins.

1 In pairs, students ask and answer the questions. Elicit answers from different students around the class. If possible, open this out into a class discussion and invite students to try to persuade their classmates to invest in their (imaginary) invention.

Suggested answers

1 Have a good business plan, negotiate well, prepare your pitch, do market research beforehand, etc.

2 The idea or product has a clear target market, the entrepreneur or inventor is well-prepared and has field-tested the product, etc.

2 1.17 Play the track for students to listen and complete the task. Check their answers.

Answers

1 F **2** F **3** T **4** F **5** T **6** F

3 1.17 Play the track again for students to complete the exercise. Ask students to compare in pairs before you check in open class.

Answers

1 sure **2** surprised **3** keen, appeal **4** tend **5** wonder **6** imagine

4 Ask students to complete the exercise. Check their answers and elicit other ways to say the same ideas. Accept all sensible suggestions.

Suggested answers

1 A (*how simple/straightforward it is to use*)

2 H (*it's handy, light, compact*)

3 F (*the product range can be developed*)

4 D (*it's economical*)

5 E (*find new markets*)

6 G (*it's multi-purpose*)

7 C (*it's made from high-standard materials*)

8 B (*its presentation*)

OPTIMISE YOUR **EXAM**

Multiple matching

Ask students to read the tips.

- If students predict the sort of things they are going to hear in the listening test, they can reduce the amount they need to listen out for during the test. Students usually have 30 seconds before the first listening to think of alternative ways of saying the same thing.
- Students find this type of task difficult because there are a lot of distractors, and students need a wide range of vocabulary to be able to deal with the answers. It is important to spend time analysing which key words and phrases helped them decide on their answers and why they got things wrong. Students will work on this intensively in Exercise 6.
- Remind students that they must only put one final answer – if they leave two answers, both will count as zero. Highlight that it is best to use CAPITAL letters and that they don't lose points for incorrect answers.

▾ Exam task

5 1.18 Play the track for students to listen and complete the exercise. Don't check answers at this stage, as students will listen again to check in Exercise 6.

6 1.18 Play the track again for students to listen and check their answers to Exercise 5. Elicit answers in open class and discuss the specific clues that helped them choose them.

Answers

1 F (*What really swings it for me is how you can take this idea and widen its appeal for people on holiday, different industries, even kids at school. … it wouldn't be difficult to adapt. So, I think the potential is huge*)

2 C (*I'm impressed with … how you've only used the very best plastic and metal putting this device together*)

3 A (*What I would say though is that operating it really is very simple indeed. And that I think gives you an edge.*)

4 G (*every single feature you've included does the job that it's supposed to do – and they're all important jobs at that.*)

5 D (*And I don't mean it's too expensive. I don't think it is. Quite the opposite, in fact. I'd say your pricing's spot on. Very reasonable.*)

Extra support

Play the track again for students to note down the distracting information in this task. You could provide students with an audioscript of the listening and ask them to underline the distractors. This is useful in helping students understand how listening tests are constructed and also helps them become aware of how different spoken and written forms are.

THINK | RESEARCH | CULTURE | LEARN | ME

In pairs, students complete the task. Elicit ideas in open class.

Optional extension

Students work in groups to come up with their own inventions and prepare pitches. Set a time limit for this. Tell the class there is a £1 million investment for the best invention. Each group pitches their idea and answers questions from the class. The class then votes on the best idea.

Homework OWB

Assign students Listening exercises 1, 2 and 3 on page 24 of their Workbook.

GRAMMAR 2
Comparatives and superlatives

→ Student's Book, page 31 SB

Lesson aims

- Understand the correct usage of comparatives and superlatives
- Practise using comparatives and superlatives

Lead-in

Play ***Twenty questions.*** Students have to guess the name of a technological object, e.g. a laptop computer, by asking you up to 20 *yes/no* questions. A *yes* answer earns the questioner the chance to ask another question; a *no* answer means the next student asks a question. If students don't guess the object after 20 questions, give them the answer.

Grammar in context

Ask students to complete the task. Refer them to the *Remember* box if they need help. Check answers in open class.

Remind students that they can find more information in the Grammar reference, Unit 3, page 151.

Answers

1 *I wonder if your product would be better if it was more portable.* (comparison: the current version of the product and a different version of the product)

2 *Invest in Me! is a great programme to watch, but I'm not sure that it's the best way of finding businesses to invest in.* (comparison: *Invest in Me!* and other ways of finding businesses to invest in)

Extra support

In less confident classes, draw this table on the board without the rules/answers and ask them to complete the comparative and superlative adjectives and elicit what the rules are. Elicit another adjective for each group.

Adjective	Comparative	Superlative
long	longer	the longest
One-syllable adjectives, add *-er* to make the comparative and *-est* to make the superlative, e.g. *tall*		
big	bigger	the biggest
One-syllable adjectives ending in vowel and consonant, double the last consonant, e.g. *thin*		
friendly	friendlier	the friendliest
An adjective ending in *–y*, replace the *y* with *i*, e.g. *tidy*		
ambitious	more ambitious	the most ambitious
Three-syllable and more adjectives, add *more* to make the comparative and *most* to make the superlative, e.g. *hard-working*		
bad little (determiner)	worse less	the worst the least
Irregular comparative and superlative forms, e.g. *far*		

Language note

Comparatives and superlatives

Highlight that if we want to talk about a quality which is smaller in an amount relative to others, we use the forms *less* (the opposite of the comparative *more*) and *least* (the opposite of the superlative *most*). *Less* is used to indicate that something or someone does not have as much of a particular quality as something or someone else, e.g. *this sofa is less comfortable than the other one. The least* is used to indicate that something or someone has less of a quality than any other person or thing of its kind, e.g. *the least expensive way to travel is by coach.*

1 Ask students to complete the exercise. Check answers in open class.

Answers

1 slower than **2** the latest **3** the most useful **4** the least expensive **5** more difficult **6** the worst **7** further

2 Ask students to complete the exercise. Have them check in pairs before you check their answers in open class.

Answers

1 best idea I have ever **2** is much cooler than **3** the most talented **4** were less successful than / were not as successful as **5** works as fast as

Mixed ability

Check the answers to Exercise 2. Divide the class into A and B pairs, mixing up higher and lower level students. Tell Student A to read out the first sentences in 1–5 and the sentence prompt. Student B tries to formulate the second sentence without looking at their notes. If the answer is correct, Student B continues. If they make a mistake, Student A has a turn, starting again from sentence 1. The aim of the game is for both students to go through all the sentence transformations in one go without making any mistakes.

3 Ask students to complete the exercise. Check answers in open class.

Answers

1 the latest **2** simpler **3** poorer / the poorest **4** smaller than **5** wider **6** longer than **7** healthier **8** better

Fast finishers

Ask fast finishers to write one or two comprehension questions on the text in Exercise 3 to ask the class when everyone has finished.

Optional extension

In pairs or small groups, ask students to discuss what they think of *The Shoe That Grows*. Ask them to list why low-tech solutions to issues in the developing world are important.

Homework OWB

Assign students Grammar 2 exercises 1, 2 and 3 on page 23 of their Workbook.

SPEAKING

Photo task

→ Student's Book, page 32 SB

Lesson aims

- Talk about the similarities and differences between photos
- Practise doing a photo task

The *Talk2Me* video in this unit focuses on gadgets and technology. People talk about gadgets at home and what advantages and disadvantages they have. Students answer some comprehension questions and then listen out for phrases to compare photographs. The video can be used in one of two ways:

Flipped classroom

Flipped classroom option

Using this approach, students watch the video and complete the exercises for homework. This prepares students for the speaking lesson by introducing them to the topic and the key phrases to use in the exam task. Teachers who use this method will find they have more class time to spend on activating the target language and developing fluency for the final task.

***Talk2Me* worksheet**

Ask students to also complete the *Talk2Me* worksheet on the Resource Centre for more detailed comprehension exercises and more practice of the key phrases.

Classroom option

1 Ask students to spend a minute or two reading the questions. Play the *Talk2Me* video for students to complete the exercise. Play the video again, if necessary, before checking their answers.

2 Play the *Talk2Me* video again, so students number the phrases in the *Phrase expert* box. Pause the video from time to time if necessary. Check answers in open class.

Talk2Me worksheet

Ask students to also complete the *Talk2Me* worksheet on the Resource Centre for more detailed comprehension exercises and more practice of the key phrases.

Answers

The transcript and answer key for the *Talk2Me* video exercises and Worksheet can be found on the Teacher's Resource Centre.

Language note

In the *Phrase expert* box, students see *while* and *whereas*, connectors that link two ideas that contrast with, but do not contradict, each other.

Lead-in

Play ***Noughts and crosses***. Draw a large 3 by 3 grid on the board. Number the boxes 1 to 9 and write time words from the previous lesson in the boxes (e.g. *wider, longer, healthier, better, worst, poorest, most, much, less*).

Divide the class into two teams, X and O. Flip a coin to see who goes first.

In order for the team to receive the X or the O for the box they have chosen, they must make a correct sentence using *'than'* or *'as'*.

Alternate between the teams until one team has a line of 3 Xs or Os, or it is a draw.

3 In pairs or small groups, students discuss the questions. Elicit answers from different students around the class.

Answers

Students' own answers

Optional extension

Open a class discussion on how late students should stay up and how much time they should spend on their mobile phones.

4 Ask students to complete the exercise. Check answers in open class.

Answers

1 far **2** as, as **3** whereas/while **4** (far) less **5** (far) less

5 In pairs, students complete the exercise. Elicit descriptions from students around the class.

Suggested answers

	PHOTO A	PHOTO B
Briefly describe the photos you are about to compare	In the first photo, I can see a group of teenagers playing a game on a games console.	In the second photo, I can see a few friends who are sitting together in a café. Each one is doing something on their own mobile phone and they are ignoring the other people in the group.
Are there any similarities between the photos?	Both photos show groups of teenagers in social situations.	In both photos, they are in relaxing situations. It could be holiday time or at the weekend.
Are there any differences between the photos?	One key difference is that in the first photo, they are doing an activity together **whereas** in the second photo, everyone is doing their own thing. Another difference is that the teenagers are having fun spending time as a group in the first photo **while** I think the other group are having a **more stressful time**.	In the first photo, the friends look happy and excited because they are playing a game. **However**, in the second photo, the teenagers don't look **as** happy **as** in the first photo. I think the teenagers are having a **better** time in the first photo.
How do you think the people might feel? Think of adjectives to describe feelings	relaxed, happy, excited	busy, stressful

Mixed ability

Elicit students' descriptions and write simple, correct sentences on the board and introduce interesting expressions for more advanced students. Keep this language on the board for students to refer to in Exercise 6.

OPTIMISE YOUR EXAM

Photo task

Ask students to read the tips.

- In this task, they should focus on talking about similarities and differences in the two photos. It is important that students understand that minor details are irrelevant here and they do not have to actually describe the photos.
- Point out to students that the language of comparison is one way of extending your answer.
- Students often lose marks in this section because they use the present simple when the present continuous would be more natural. This is an area where students can impress the examiner.

Exam task

6 In pairs, students complete the task. Remind students that strict timing is vital in an exam and tell them to time each other. Ask students to use their notes from Exercise 5 and the words and phrases in the *Phrase expert* box.

Walk round and monitor students, noting down errors and good use of language to go over in a feedback session at the end of the activity. Go through any errors you noted down on the board with students, eliciting corrections from them where possible. Students could then repeat this activity after the class feedback with another pair to try and improve their performance.

Optional extension

Students could listen and mark each other using this checklist. Write it on the board and ask students to copy it into their notebooks. This will help them give informative and directive feedback.

Did my partner use language from the Phrase expert *box? Yes/No*

Did my partner use the present continuous? Yes/No

Did my partner use expressions to express similarity and difference? Yes/No

Did my partner use interesting vocabulary, e.g. adjectives? Yes/No

Did my partner speak for a minute? Yes/No

SAY IT RIGHT

TRC

Stress in comparatives

For the *Say it right* pronunciation activity and instructions, go to the Teacher's Resource Centre.

Homework

OWB

Assign students Speaking exercises 1 and 2 on page 24 of their Workbook.

USE OF ENGLISH

Word formation | Multiple-choice cloze

→ Student's Book, page 33

SB

Lesson aims

- Focus on word formation and practise a word-formation exam task
- Focus on multiple-choice cloze and practise a multiple-choice cloze exam task

Lead-in

Write these words on the board:

English/Chinese, Russia, fast food / fruit and vegetables, football/basketball, Michael Jackson, Game of Thrones

Go round the class asking students to make comparative or superlative sentences, using some of the words on the board.

1 Ask students to complete the exercise. Elicit answers from different students around the class.

Answers

1 solve (solution), explore (exploration), create (creation)

2 science (scientist), solve (solver – note: this is not commonly used), explore (explorer), achieve (achiever), create (creator), discover (discoverer)

3 science (scientifically), create (creatively), simple (simply), fortunate (fortunately, unfortunately)

OPTIMISE YOUR EXAM

Word formation

Ask students to read the tip.

- Remind students that if they see a word ending in a suffix such as *-ment*, *-ity* or *-ness* it is likely to be a noun.
- Often, the suffix causes a spelling change to the original word, e.g.
  *beau**ty**, du**ty** + -ful → beau**ti**ful, du**ti**ful*
  *heav**y**, read**y** + -ness → heav**i**ness, read**i**ness*
  *ab**le**, possib**le** + -ity → ab**ility**, possib**ility***
  *permi**t**, omi**t** + -ion → permi**ss**ion, omi**ss**ion*

Exam task

2 Ask students to complete the exercise. Ask them to compare in pairs before you elicit answers in open class.

Answers

1 scientists **2** solutions **3** exploration **4** achievement **5** creative **6** discovery **7** simply **8** unfortunately

Refer students to the Vocabulary reference, page 163, for more information on word formation.

3 Ask students to complete the exercise. Check answers in open class.

Answers

2, 5

OPTIMISE YOUR EXAM

Multiple-choice cloze

Ask students to read the tip.

- Remind students that even if they don't know the answer, they can develop their intuition by saying the options to themselves. If one sounds right, they should go for it.
- Remind students to read through the completed task to make sure it makes sense with all the words in place.

Exam task

4 Ask students to complete the exercise. Check their answers.

Answers

1 B **2** A **3** D **4** D **5** C **6** A **7** B **8** B

Homework OWB
Assign students Use of English exercises 1, 2 and 3 on page 25 of their Workbook.

WRITING
A review

→ Student's Book, pages 34–35 SB

Lesson aims

- Focus on language in a review
- Plan and write a review of a product

Lead-in

Write these jumbled words for electronic gadgets on the board and ask students to reorder them:
ltaidig drcoeacmr, hepoehnsad, ksed mlpa, rahi sheerartsgnit, leswesir arekeps, patolp
You could set a time limit and ask students to race against each other in small groups or pairs.

Answers
digital camcorder, headphones, desk lamp, hair straighteners, wireless speaker, laptop

1 In pairs or as a group, students answer the questions. Elicit answers in open class and develop a discussion about why they would choose a particular product and how they conduct their research (e.g. YouTube and Vimeo reviews, Facebook posts, tweets, comparing reviews, etc.).

Answers
Students' own answers

2 Elicit from students the purpose of a review (to give factual information about the subject and, secondly, to give an opinion about it which will help the reader/viewer to decide whether to buy the product, go to the restaurant, watch the film, etc.).

Ask students to complete the exercise. Elicit answers from different students around the class.

Answers
1 the camera, because it captures a lot of detail, especially in low light **2** the size/width, because it starts to feel uncomfortable after a while **3** people who like to take a lot of photographs

3 Ask students to complete the exercise. Check answers in open class.

Answers
1 … it's not all good news. **2** … the advantages. **3** There is a downside … **4** On the whole, … **5** It's particularly suitable for …

4 Ask students to complete the exercise. Elicit answers in open class.

Suggested answers
1 a small laptop / a tablet **2** an action video camera **3** an e-reader **4** an MP3 player / a portable music player **5** a GPS / a satnav

5 In pairs or groups, students complete the exercise. Elicit answers in open class.

Answers
1 I'm happy to recommend this device for people who need to work when they are travelling.
2 I would recommend it for people who lead an active lifestyle.
3 This device is suitable for anyone who travels and likes reading.
4 People who are interested in music will find this device very interesting and easy to use.
5 This device is ideal for drivers who like to know where they are at a glance.

OPTIMISE YOUR EXAM

A review

Ask students to read the tips.

- As with any kind of writing, students need to start by identifying their audience, e.g. an interested but not entirely knowledgeable audience or a more specialised audience who are already aware of the general trends. Reviews can adopt a friendly, informal style and they should follow a typical structure for a review – **Inform, Describe, Analyse, Recommend**.
- Highlight how the writer in Exercise 2 states his/her personal experience and level of expertise with the gadget to set the expectations throughout the review.

For more information on writing reviews, refer students to the Writing reference, page 170.

▼ Exam task

6 Ask students to complete the exercise.

7 **Plan** Ask students to complete the paragraph plan using their notes from Exercise 6. You may want to look at students' plans, if possible, to check them and give advice and suggestions for improvement before students take the next step.

8 **Write** Students write their review in an appropriate style in 140–190 words. Depending on time, it may be a good idea to set this and the subsequent checklist exercise for homework.

9 **Check** Students complete the checklist before they hand in their review.

Homework OWB
Assign students Writing exercises 1, 2 and 3 on page 26 of their Workbook and Progress check 3 on page 27.

4 Crime doesn't pay

UNIT AIMS

Exam preparation in Unit 4:

- understand and use different reading techniques to answer questions about a news article
- listen for key information
- ask for and give an opinion in a discussion
- use context to form words in a word-formation exercise
- understand and use phrasal verbs in sentence transformations
- use formal language in a letter

TEACHER'S PRESENTATION KIT

- *Talk2Me* videos
- Speaking test videos
- Class and Workbook audio
- Workbook pages and answer key

UNIT OVERVIEW

Student's Book / Digital Student's Book SB		Workbook / Online Workbook OWB
LESSON / EXAM TASK	EXAM SKILLS / LANGUAGE FOCUS	CONSOLIDATION
Reading **Questions with short answers**	Identifying synonyms (1) A news article	Workbook, pp 28–29, Exercises 1, 2, 3 Unit 4, Reading, Exercises 1, 2, 3
Grammar 1	Tenses (4): the future	Workbook, p 30, Exercises 1, 2, 3 Unit 4, Grammar 1, Exercises 1, 2, 3
Vocabulary	Words connected with *law* and *order* Phrasal verbs Collocations with *crime*	Workbook, pp 30–31, Exercises 1, 2, 3 Unit 4, Vocabulary, Exercises 1, 2, 3
Listening **True/false**	Listening for synonyms (1)	Workbook, p 32, Exercises 1, 2, 3 Unit 4, Listening, Exercises 1, 2, 3
Grammar 2	Conditionals (1): zero and first conditionals	Workbook, p 31, Exercises 1, 2 Unit 4, Grammar 2, Exercises 1, 2
Speaking **Discussion**	Expressing and justifying opinions	Workbook, pp 32–33, Exercises 1, 2, 3, 4 Unit 4, Speaking, Exercises 1, 2, 3, 4
Use of English **Word formation** **Sentence transformation**	Context Phrasal verbs	Workbook, p 33, Exercises 1, 2 Unit 4, Use of English, Exercises 1, 2
Writing **A letter / An email**	Giving reasons and examples (1)	Workbook, p 34, Exercises 1, 2, 3, 4 Unit 4, Writing, Exercises 1, 2, 3, 4
Progress check	Check language progress for Units 3 and 4	Workbook, p 35, Progress check and Cumulative progress Progress check and Cumulative progress

Additional material

PRESENTATION KIT	TEACHER'S / STUDENT'S RESOURCE CENTRE RC	TEST GENERATOR
Talk2Me video *To my mind ...*	**Unit 4 worksheets:** *Optimise your grammar* (Standard and Higher), *Optimise your vocabulary* (Standard and Higher), *Talk2Me* video, *Say it right* **Units 3–4 worksheets:** CLIL, Culture, Everyday English (TRC only), Grammar communication (TRC only)	Unit Test 4 (Standard and Higher) Progress Test (Standard and Higher)

READING

Questions with short answers | A news article

→ Student's Book, pages 36–37 SB

Lesson aims

- Focus on questions with short answers
- Practise a short-answers exam task

Lead-in

Ask students to read the unit title ***Crime doesn't pay*** and elicit the meaning. (*There's never an advantage to committing a crime.*) Encourage discussion about the title and its meaning, to elicit some different views from students. Focus students' attention on the photo and ask students what they think the lesson is going to be about (*crime and social problems*).

1 In pairs or groups, students ask and answer the questions. Elicit answers in open class and try to develop a class discussion on different kinds of crime and ways to prevent crime.

Suggested answers

1 theft, burglary (to commit a burglary you must enter a structure or dwelling with the intent to commit a crime within it), robbery (like theft but a robbery is taking something *from a person* and using force, or the threat of force, to do it), speeding, cybercrime, murder, arson, shoplifting, fraud, etc.

2 Police surveillance, fingerprint matching (pattern recognition), CCTV, neighbourhood watch, etc.

Language note

Robbery and burglary are both crimes that involve theft and it is the circumstances that surround each that defines their differences. We talk about burglary when someone enters a building with the intention of committing a crime within it. Robbery means taking something *from a person* and using force, or the threat of force, to do it.

The verbs *rob* and *steal* both mean 'take something from someone without permission' but *rob* focuses on the place or person from which the thing is taken, e.g. *The gang robbed seven banks over a period of six months, but were finally caught. Steal* focuses on the thing that is taken, e.g. *My computer was stolen from my desk last week.*

We don't usually say *rob* + object stolen, e.g. ~~*My purse was robbed*~~. *My purse was stolen.*

2 Ask students to complete the exercise quickly. Time this activity (two minutes) and give updates, e.g. *One minute to go … Only thirty seconds left.* Check answers in open class.

Answers

Paragraph 1: an intriguing experiment **Paragraph 2:** public versus private behaviour **Paragraph 3:** an improvement to a system **Paragraph 4:** forms of social pressure **Paragraph 5:** not an isolated example **Paragraph 6:** moving the problem elsewhere

3 Ask students to complete the exercise.

Answers

1 a and b **2** a and b **3** a and c **4** a and b **5** b and c

OPTIMISE YOUR EXAM

Questions with short answers

Ask students to read the tips.

- Highlight to students that for this type of exam question, they need to follow a general reading technique: skim the questions, identify key words, scan the text, read carefully and then choose answers carefully.
- Point out that the questions in this type of task are in the same order as they appear in the text.
- Remind students that when they find the part of the text with the answer, they must then decide how to express it in four words or less. Major examination boards who use this task type accept that numbers can be written using figures or words. Contracted words are not tested and hyphenated words count as single words. Exercise 4 will allow them to practise this exam technique.

▼ Exam task

4 1.19 **Note: The reading text is also available on the audio CD. You may want to have students listen and read the text before doing the exam task.**

Ask students to complete the exercise. Check answers in open class and elicit the key sentences that helped them decide on their answers.

Elicit what students think of the bicycle experiment. Ask them where they might put a similar poster in their school to help with a problem.

Answers

1 honest and trustworthy (*People generally prefer to be seen as …*)

2 approval and disapproval (*Throughout history, people in communities have been regulated through …*)

3 eyes of a predator / eyes on wings (*… and so deter birds from eating the butterflies*)

4 shoplifting / shoplifting offences (*supermarkets place a cardboard cut-out figure in certain parts of the store …*)

5 it increased by 63% (*… but had been relocated to other parts of the campus*)

Fast finishers

Write these definitions on the board for students to match to words and phrases in the text.

1 *a sudden increase in the number of crimes committed in a particular area*

2 *not seen or perceived*

3 *a condition of disgrace or dishonour*

4 *looking directly and fixedly*

5 *stealing something from a shop*

6 *a grouping of things in the same category*

Answers

1 crime wave **2** unobserved **3** shame **4** staring **5** shoplifting **6** range

5 Ask students to complete the exercise. Check their answers and elicit definitions from different students around the class.

Answers

1 deter (*make someone decide not to do something*)

2 community (*the people who live in an area*)

3 instinct (*a natural tendency to behave in a particular way*)

4 predator (*an animal that kills and eats other animals*)

5 confirm (*prove that something is true*)

6 take precautions (*do something to protect people or things against possible harm or trouble*)

7 CCTV (*closed-circuit television*)

8 crime rate (*the number of crimes that people commit*)

Mixed ability

Supply less confident students with two options for each answer (**1** *deter/decide*, **2** *crime/community*, **3** *instinct/idea*, **4** *predator/precaution*, **5** *confirm/cause*, **6** *take precautions / tell people*, **7** *CCTV/CTCV*, **8** *crime rate / cut-out*). Students who finish early can think of two comprehension questions based on the text. They can read them out to test the class when everyone has finished.

Optional extension 1.19

Play the recorded text and ask students to underline all the words related to crime. Do a feedback session in open class and ask students to share items they underlined. Explain the meaning of any difficult vocabulary.

Answers

prevent crime, thieves, stealing, crime wave, crime prevention measures, theft, incidents, take precautions, CCTV cameras, tackle crime, police officer, criminals, shoplifting offences, speed camera warnings, crime rate

Homework

OWB

Assign students Reading exercises 1, 2 and 3 on pages 28–29 of their Workbook.

GRAMMAR 1

Tenses (4): the future

→ Student's Book, page 38 SB

Lesson aims

- Understand the correct usage of future tenses
- Practise using future tenses

Lead-in

Write the following on the board:

My arrangements for this evening.

My intentions for the rest of the year.

My predictions about crime in the future.

Ask different students to talk for a minute about each topic and make sure they are clear about the difference between arrangements, intentions and predictions.

Grammar in context

Future forms are tested in all parts of exams at this level and they are one of the most common grammatical topics covered in the Use of English exam.

Ask students to complete the task. Refer them to the *Remember* box if they need help. Check answers in open class.

Remind students that they can find more information in the Grammar reference, Unit 4, page 151.

Answers

1 Yes (it perhaps makes it a little more formal).

2 No, because it's not an arrangement.

3 No, because we don't use *will* after time words such as *when*.

Extra support

In pairs, ask students to make sentences similar to the examples for each point in the Remember box. Ask students to read out their sentences in open class. If appropriate, ask students to come up and write them on the board and discuss as a class if they are correct. Encourage them to make questions and negative sentences from their examples.

Language note

In English, we can use a variety of future forms to express different shades of meaning. We cannot be certain about what happens in the future so the choice of future form depends on the speaker's intention or mood.

Elicit the negative short form of *shall* (*shan't*). Point out that *shall* is restricted to first-person pronouns (*I* and *we*).

We use the present continuous to talk about future arrangements or plans that have been confirmed. This is often called the 'diary form' because you can use it for anything written in your diary. Fixed arrangements can also use *be going to*, but the present continuous is more common.

Remind students that *be going to* is generally found in informal spoken English. *Be going to* constructions often imply an intention and an expectation that the intention will be carried out.

Point out to students that we use the present simple to talk about a future event that is part of a timetable or routine in the future. These sentences usually contain words such as *to be, open, close, begin, start, end, finish, arrive, come, leave, return*.

1 Ask students to complete the exercise. Ask them to compare in pairs before you check answers in open class. Highlight the irregular question tag for *shall* in question 4.

Answers

1 ✓

2 'm going to study (we can't use the present continuous because it's an intention, not an arrangement)

3 he's going to steal (we usually use *be going to* when there's present evidence)

4 ✓

5 won't drive (we usually use *will not* or *won't* for refusals, although *'m not going to drive* is not incorrect)

6 Shall I check (we use *shall* for offers)

2 Ask students to complete the exercise. Check answers in open class. Highlight that the order of the clauses is interchangeable.

Answers

1 We'll call you once we find the thief.

2 We'll call you the moment we find the thief.

3 We'll call you as soon as we find the thief.

4 We won't call you until we find the thief.

Language note

Remind students that we can use *be going to* instead of *will* in the future continuous, the future perfect simple and the future perfect continuous, e.g. *I will be working. / I'm going to be working.* Unlike in the future simple, in these tenses the meaning is fairly interchangeable.

Highlight that we can also substitute modal verbs for *will*, e.g. *She may be waiting. / She may have waited. / She may have been waiting.*

We often use the future continuous to talk about what we assume is or will be happening at a particular moment, e.g. *She'll be having dinner by the time I get home.*

We often use the future perfect with *by* or *in*: *I think we will have landed on Mars by the year 2030. / I'll have finished in a while, then you can use the computer.*

By means 'not later than a particular time' and *in* means 'within a period of time', e.g. when we don't know exactly when something will finish.

The future perfect continuous is like the future perfect simple, but it expresses longer actions or states extending up to some specific event or time in the future.

Extra support

In small groups, have students write predictions about people they know, using each of the future tenses, e.g. *[Name] will have been studying the violin for ten years in 2020. / [Name] will be studying at university in three years' time.* Walk round, monitoring students and helping them where necessary.

3 Ask students to complete the exercise. Check answers in open class.

Answers

1 will have seen

2 is coming / is going to come

3 will be watching / will watch / are going to watch / are watching

4 will already have finished

5 are going to survive / will be surviving / will survive

6 won't do / aren't going to do / won't be doing

7 won't be / isn't going to be

8 will have been watching / will have watched

Fast finishers

Ask fast finishers to write one or two comprehension questions on the text in Exercise 3 to ask the class when everyone has finished.

Homework OWB

Assign students Grammar 1 exercises 1, 2 and 3 on page 30 of their Workbook.

VOCABULARY

Topic vocabulary | Phrasal verbs | Collocations

→ Student's Book, page 39 SB

Lesson aims

- Understand the correct usage of:
  - words connected with law and order
  - phrasal verbs
  - collocations with *crime*

Lead-in

Put key words from this lesson up on the board in a circle, rather than a list. Pre-teach the meaning where necessary.

Divide the class into small groups and give them a time limit of three minutes to come up with a short story that incorporates all or most of the words.

Ask groups to present their story to the class and vote on the best one.

Suggested words: *crime, prison, police station, armed robbers, CCTV, bank, cash, evidence.*

Words connected with *law* and *order*

1 1.20 Ask students to complete the exercise. Play the audio for students to listen and check their answers.

Answers/Audioscript

The *justice* system in the UK plays an important role in society. When the *victim* of a crime reports it to the police, the police must decide if there is enough *evidence* to charge someone with that crime. If there is, then it may lead to a *trial*. In serious cases, a *jury* (which consists of 12 ordinary citizens) decides whether the *accused* is *guilty* or not. Depending on this *verdict*, a *judge* then either releases the defendant or sentences them. This could mean *imprisonment* for a certain length of time, or a *fine*, or both.

Optional extension

Brainstorm famous criminals in history (e.g. *Al Capone, Billy the Kid, Jack the Ripper, Ned Kelly, Lee Harvey Oswald*). In pairs, students choose a famous criminal and write sentences, using as many words as they can from the box in Exercise 1. Set a five-minute time limit. In small groups, students can then read out their sentences without saying the name of the famous criminal for other students to guess who it is.

Refer students to the Vocabulary reference, page 163, for more information on topic vocabulary.

Phrasal verbs

2 1.21 Ask students to complete the exercise. Play the audio for students to listen and check their answers.

Answers/Audioscript

1 When her photo appeared on the internet, the thief decided to go to the police station and turn herself in. ✓

2 Armed robbers held the bank *up* and stole thousands of pounds in cash.

3 Police are appealing for members of the public who have any information about the crime to come forward. ✓

4 The guilty man was lucky to be let *off* with just a fine.

5 After escaping from prison, she made for the coast where she could hide. ✓

6 'You'll never get *away* with this!' I shouted after the thief.

7 Police are looking for two men who beat up a young man and stole his phone. ✓

8 The burglars obviously broke *in* through the window and then stole the car keys.

Language note

Highlight that the phrasal verbs in questions 1, 2, 4 and 7 are examples of separable phrasal verbs. They are *transitive* (they have an object). Most phrasal verbs are this type. Remind students that when the direct object is a pronoun, it must go between the verb and the particle, as in question 1.

Point out that questions 3, 5 and 8 are examples of non-separable phrasal verbs. Questions 3 and 8 are *intransitive* (they don't have an object) and you can't separate the two parts of the verb, while question 5 is a *transitive* verb whose object must come after the particle.

Highlight that question 6 is an example of a three-part verb. They have an adverb and a preposition followed by a direct object. You can't separate the parts of the phrasal verb.

Mixed ability

Write these definitions on the board.

1 *hurt someone by hitting or kicking them many times*

2 *move towards a place*

3 *steal from a person, business or vehicle by threatening them with a gun or other weapon*

4 *manage to do something bad without being punished or criticised for it*

5 *offer help or information*

6 *tell the police about somebody*

7 *enter a building by force, especially to steal things*

8 *allow someone not to do something that they were expecting to have to do*

Ask less confident students to match them to the phrasal verbs in Exercise 2. Have more confident students write an original sentence using each of the phrasal verbs in their notebooks.

Answers

1 beat up **2** make for **3** hold up **4** get away with
5 come forward **6** turn in **7** break in **8** let off

Refer students to the Vocabulary reference, page 164, for more information on phrasal verbs.

Collocations with *crime*

3 1.22 Ask students to complete the exercise. Play the audio for students to listen and check their answers.

Answers/Audioscript

1 crime lab: a place where forensic scientists analyse evidence

2 organised crime: crime controlled by a powerful secret organisation

3 crime wave: a sudden increase in the amount of crime in an area

4 hate crime: an attack against a person because of their race, religion, etc.

5 crime scene: the place where a crime has been committed

6 youth crime: crime committed by young people

7 petty crime: a crime that is not very serious

8 crime rate: the amount of crime in an area

9 crime prevention: measures to deter criminal activity

4 Ask students to complete the exercise. Check their answers.

Answers

1 crime lab **2** youth crime **3** crime rate **4** petty crime
5 crime prevention **6** crime wave **7** crime scene
8 organised crime **9** hate crime

Optional extension

Taboo: In pairs, students test each other on the vocabulary in Exercise 4. Write the phrases from Exercise 4 on the board and tell students to close their books. Student A describes as many words as possible in 90 seconds without actually saying them or using their native language. After 90 seconds, stop students or sound a buzzer. Ask them to count how many words their partner successfully guessed and then swap roles. The student with the most words is the winner.

Refer students to the Vocabulary reference, page 164, for more information on collocations.

THINK | RESEARCH | CULTURE | LEARN | ME

In pairs or small groups, students discuss the questions. Elicit ideas in open class.

Homework

Assign students Vocabulary exercises 1, 2 and 3 on pages 30–31 of their Workbook.

OWB

LISTENING
True/false

→ Student's Book, page 40 SB

Lesson aims

- Focus on true or false statements
- Practise a true/false exam task

Lead-in

Play **Hangman** with target vocabulary from the unit.

Suggested words: *guilty, criminal, burglary, thieves, episodes, accused, evidence, imprisonment, judge, verdict.*

1 In pairs, students ask and answer the questions. Elicit answers from different students around the class.

Suggested answers

1 The person in the photo is dressed as an old-fashioned detective. They're wearing a hat like Sherlock Holmes, called a deerstalker, and they're holding a magnifying glass. There is also a magnified fingerprint, and some crime scene tape with a body outline on the ground behind the 'detective'.

2 Students' own answers

2 Ask students to complete the exercise. Have students compare in pairs before you check in open class.

Answers

1 b **2** a **3** a **4** b **5** a **6** a

3 Ask students to complete the exercise. Check in open class.

Answers

1 intelligent **2** unusual theories **3** wish **4** crime stories **5** the real world **6** enjoy **7** responsible for **8** chance

OPTIMISE YOUR EXAM

True/false

Ask students to read the tips.

- Sometimes the answers are common sense. Remind students to trust their intuition and, before they listen, predict if the sentences are true or false. They then listen to confirm.
- It can also help students listen for the right information if they try changing the sentence into a question. For example, change the sentence *The events Serena puts on were first organised by writers of crime stories.* to a question: *Were the events Serena puts on first organised by writers of crime stories?* Students then listen for key information to confirm answers.
- Highlight to students that key information is usually stressed (this means we say words louder, for longer and at a higher pitch).
- Remind them to always answer all the questions. They have a 50% chance of being right!

Exam task

4 1.23 Play the track for students to listen and complete the exercise. Don't check answers at this stage, as students will listen again to check in Exercise 5.

Extra support

In a less confident class, provide students with the audioscript for this listening task and ask them to underline the specific clues that helped them decide on their answers.

5 1.23 Play the track again for students to listen and check their answers to Exercise 4. Elicit answers in open class and discuss the specific clues that helped them choose them.

Answers

1 F (*… writers such as Agatha Christie wrote novels about crimes that took place in large country houses. She doesn't say they put on mystery weekend events*)

2 T (*The guests arrive … When they come down to dinner, they learn that there has been a crime and no-one is allowed to leave the hotel.*)

3 T (*… the guests have to collect evidence … Finally, they are asked who they think is guilty of the crime, and the mystery is solved*)

4 T (*… whole families come along, enjoy working together and get involved in the mystery weekends*)

5 T (*If you work out the solution, you get a lot of satisfaction from it.*)

6 F (*… we have a very deep desire to see justice done …*)

7 T (*Often, it's the crazy ideas that help you find the solution*)

8 T (*… events such as these give you the chance to get away to a time and place that seems simpler than today*)

THINK | RESEARCH | CULTURE | LEARN | ME

In pairs or small groups, students discuss the questions. Elicit ideas in open class.

Optional extension

Give students more time to plan and present their mystery party. Write some more prompt questions on the board: *How many guests would you invite? What would the venue be? How would you create an atmosphere? Is there a prize for the winner? Would you provide food and drinks? How long would it go on for?*

Set a time limit for this. Each group presents their ideas and answers questions from the class. The class then votes on the best mystery party.

Cultural note

The first mystery game was known as *Jury Box* and it was popular in the United States in the 1930s. It is considered a predecessor to modern mystery games and role-playing games.

Cluedo (or *Clue* in the US) was the first mystery board game. It was released in 1948 and has continued to be popular.

The earliest mention of role-playing mystery games in their present format was in the 1980s.

Homework

OWB

Assign students Listening exercises 1, 2 and 3 on page 32 of their Workbook.

GRAMMAR 2

Conditionals (1): zero and first conditionals

→ Student's Book, page 41 SB

Lesson aims

- Understand the correct usage of zero and first conditionals
- Practise using zero and first conditionals

Lead-in

Elicit students' favourite films, TV series and novels about crime and crime fighting, and what they like about them.

Grammar in context

Ask students to complete the task. Refer them to the *Remember* box if they need help. Check answers in open class.

Remind students that they can find more information in the Grammar reference, Unit 4, page 152.

Answers

1 zero conditional

2 a general truth

3 It would be describing one specific occasion in the future, rather than a general truth.

Extra support

In pairs, ask students to make sentences similar to the examples for each point in the Remember box. Ask students to read out their sentences in open class. If appropriate, ask students to come up and write them on the board.

Language note

Although students will come across conditionals in all parts of an exam at this level, they are very likely to be formally tested on their knowledge in sentence transformations.

The clause without *if* is the main clause of the sentence, while the *if* clause is subordinate. The order of the two clauses is generally not that important to the meaning of the sentence, so we can switch the *if* clause to the end of the sentence if we want to.

Remind students we can also use *when* instead of *if*. *When* means a time, often an expected time of completion and *if* conveys conditionality.

When you pass the exam (= you know you are going to pass the exam), *you will get a certificate.*

If you pass the exam (= you don't know you are going to pass the exam), *you will get a certificate.* (the result)

The future tense can have other forms, of course, besides the usual *will*, e.g. *be going to* or modals, e.g. *might* or *could* (*We might/could go to the cinema if it rains*).

1 Ask students to complete the exercise. Check their answers in open class.

Answers

1 enjoy **2** if **3** in case **4** watch **5** I'll watch **6** you

2 Point out to students that these are all examples of the kind of things we hear in crime programmes and films. Ask students to complete the exercise. Have students check in pairs before you check answers in open class.

Answers

1 Provided (that) you do what I say, you won't get hurt! / You won't get hurt provided you do what I say!

2 I'll let them go as long as you give me a helicopter and a million dollars. / As long as you give me a helicopter and a million dollars, I'll let them go.

3 We can't arrest him unless we're sure he did it. / Unless we're sure he did it, we can't arrest him.

4 I'll come with you in case there's trouble. / In case there's trouble, I'll come with you.

5 I'm not letting the President in if we're not certain it's safe. / If we're not certain it's safe, I'm not letting the President in.

6 So long as you understand the danger involved, go ahead. / Go ahead, so long as you understand the danger involved.

3 Ask students to complete the exercise. Walk round, monitoring students and helping them with vocabulary if necessary.

Answers

Students' own answers

SAY IT RIGHT

Intonation in conditionals TRC

For the *Say it right* pronunciation activity and instructions, go to the Teacher's Resource Centre.

Optional extension

Ask students to do a class survey to find out their classmates' opinions of crime programmes, films and novels. Ask them to find out which is the most popular crime programme or film.

Homework OWB

Assign students Grammar 2 exercises 1 and 2 on page 31 of their Workbook.

SPEAKING

Discussion

→ Student's Book, page 42 SB

Lesson aims

- Focus on asking for and giving opinions
- Practise having a discussion

The *Talk2Me* video in this unit focuses on crimes and punishments. People talk about different crimes and punishments and suggest ways to tackle crime. Students answer some comprehension questions and then listen out for phrases to ask for and give opinions. The video can be used in one of two ways:

Flipped classroom

Flipped classroom option

Using this approach, students watch the video and complete the exercises for homework. This prepares students for the speaking lesson by introducing them to the topic and the key phrases to use in the exam task. Teachers who use this method will find they have more class time to spend on activating the target language and developing fluency for the final task.

***Talk2Me* worksheet**

Ask students to also complete the *Talk2Me* worksheet on the Resource Centre for more detailed comprehension exercises and more practice of the key phrases.

Classroom option

1 Ask students to spend a minute or two reading the questions. Play the *Talk2Me* video for students to complete the exercise. Play the video again, if necessary, before checking their answers.

2 Play the *Talk2Me* video again, so students write the name of the person who says the expressions in the *Phrase expert* box. Pause the video from time to time if necessary. Check answers in open class.

***Talk2Me* worksheet**

Ask students to also complete the *Talk2Me* worksheet on the Resource Centre for more detailed comprehension exercises and more practice of the key phrases.

Answers

The transcript and answer key for the *Talk2Me* video exercises and Worksheet can be found on the Teacher's Resource Centre.

Lead-in

Write these crime-related verbs on the board:
burgle, detect, investigate, murder, shoplift, thieve

In pairs, students race to think of as many nouns (thing) and nouns (person) as they can in a three-minute time limit. Stop the class and ask students to count up their words to see who the winner is. Elicit words from around the class and ask students to come up and write them on the board, if appropriate.

Answers

Verbs	Nouns (thing)	Nouns (person)
burgle	burglary	burglar
detect	detection	detective
investigate	investigation	investigator
murder	murder	murderer
shoplift	shoplifting	shoplifter
thieve	theft	thief

3 In pairs or small groups, students complete the task. Elicit answers from different students around the class.

Suggested answers

1 In Photo A someone is shoplifting.
Punishment depends on how expensive the goods are and if it is the first time or if the shoplifter is a repeat offender. Punishment could include paying a premium for stolen goods / parents take away mobile phone and video games / community service or a fine / be taken out of school / sent to an alternative education centre / get a criminal record / go to prison.

2 In Photo B someone is committing a cybercrime.
Punishments should reflect the severity of the crime. Punishment could include community service or a fine / be taken out of school / sent to an alternative education centre / get a criminal record / go to prison.

4 Ask students to complete the exercise. Encourage them to use phrases from the *Phrase expert* box. Check answers in open class and elicit reasons and examples.

Answers

Students' own answers

5 Ask students to complete the exercise. Have students compare their answers in pairs before you check in open class.

Answers

1 think, Personally **2** opinion, my mind **3** matters **4** agree, As I **5** hard to

OPTIMISE YOUR EXAM

A discussion

Ask students to read the tips.

- Point out to students that asking for and giving credit to others' opinions will earn them marks for Interactive Communication, one of the four marking criteria in many oral examinations.
- Remind them that they don't have to think of complex questions; 'standard' questions like '*What do you think about that? / What about you?*' are good enough.

▾ Exam task

6 In threes, students complete the task. Ask students to use their notes from Exercise 5 and the words and phrases in the *Phrase expert* box.

Walk round and monitor students, noting down errors and good use of language to go over in a feedback session at the end of the activity. Go through any errors you noted down on the board with students, eliciting corrections from them where possible.

Mixed ability

Ask examiners to listen and use this checklist to help them make notes on the candidates' discussion.

Did Students A & B ask for their partner's opinion?
Did Students A & B respond to their partner's comments?
Did they take turns to speak?
Did Students A & B use different expressions to give their opinions?
Did Students A & B try to keep the discussion going?

If weaker students take the role of examiner in the first round, the pressure is taken off them to produce language spontaneously, but they can prepare something to say at the end, which will provide a sense of achievement. After the discussion, ask examiners to give feedback to the pair.

Homework

OWB

Assign students Speaking exercises 1, 2, 3 and 4 on pages 32–33 of their Workbook.

USE OF ENGLISH

Word formation | Sentence transformation

→ Student's Book, page 43 SB

Lesson aims

- Focus on word formation and practise a word-formation exam task
- Focus on sentence transformation and practise a sentence-transformation exam task

Lead-in

Divide the students into two teams. Call out letters randomly (don't use the letter *X*) and ask teams to think of a word they've learnt so far which begins with that letter. Students put up their hand if they know a word. Choose the first student who puts their hand up and ask him/her to say the word. If it is correct, their team gets a point. Play for a set time. At the end, the team with the most points wins.

1 Ask students to complete the exercise. Elicit answers from different students around the class.

Answers

1 'shock' could be a verb or a noun; shocking (adj), shocked (adj), shockingly (adv)

2 verbs: prevent, understand, burgle, grow, satisfy

nouns from those words: prevention, understanding, misunderstanding, burglary, burglar, growth, grower, satisfaction, dissatisfaction

3 young (youth), grow (growth)

OPTIMISE YOUR EXAM

Word formation

Ask students to read the tip.

- Remind students to look at the word they have to change and think of words that are in the same word family.
- Emphasise the importance of good spelling as this is a common way for students to lose marks in this kind of exam task.

Exam task

2 Ask students to complete the exercise. They compare in pairs before you elicit answers in open class.

Answers

1 prevention **2** understanding **3** burglary/burglaries **4** vandalism **5** youth **6** shocking **7** growing **8** satisfying

Refer students to the Vocabulary reference, page 164, for more information on word formation.

3 Ask students to complete the exercise. Check answers in open class.

Answers

1 1, 2, 4 **2** 3, 5

OPTIMISE YOUR EXAM

Sentence transformation

Ask students to read the tip.

- Point out to students that this exam task has a special scoring system and it's possible to get 50% in this section without getting any of the questions 100% correct. They should try to answer every question as even incomplete answers can get points.
- Students are likely to find this type of task includes conditionals, *wish*, passives, reported speech, present perfect / simple past, (past) modals, *(not) as … as*, unless and *so/such*.
- In some major exams, sentence transformation questions are worth a lot of marks and it is worthwhile spending time in class on this type of task. In the following exercise, students will work intensively on this type of exam question.

Exam task

4 Ask students to complete the exercise. Check their answers.

Answers

1 are given privileges provided (that) **2** unless the jury are convinced **3** was let off with / got off with **4** as long as **5** got away with the robbery **6** as soon as they finish

Mixed ability

Check the answers to Exercise 4. Divide the class into A and B pairs, mixing up higher and lower level students. Tell Student A to read out the first sentences in 1–6 and the given word. Student B tries to formulate the second sentence without looking at their notes. If the answer is correct, Student B continues. If they make a mistake, Student A has a turn, starting again from sentence 1. The aim of the game is for both students to go through all the sentence transformations in one go without making any mistakes.

Homework

OWB

Assign students Use of English exercises 1 and 2 on page 33 of their Workbook.

WRITING
A letter / An email

→ Student's Book, pages 44–45 SB

Lesson aims

- Focus on language in a letter or an email
- Plan and write a formal letter

Lead-in

Go round the class asking students to tell you either one formal or one informal word or phrase used to begin or end an email.

1 In pairs or as a group, students answer the questions. Elicit answers in open class.

Answers
Students' own answers

2 Ask students to complete the exercise. Elicit answers from different students around the class.

Answers
1 b **2** b **3** a **4** a

3 Ask students to complete the exercise. Check answers in open class. Accept all grammatically correct suggestions.

Suggested answers
1 We need places for graffiti, for example certain walls at school or in parks. **2** We need places for graffiti, for instance certain walls at school or in parks. **3** We need places for graffiti, such as certain walls at school or in parks. **4** They should be punished, as we can't allow them to make people suffer. **5** They should be punished, since we can't allow them to make people suffer. **6** They should be punished because we can't allow them to make people suffer. **7** We can't allow them to make people suffer. Because of this, they should be punished.

OPTIMISE YOUR EXAM

A letter / An email

Ask students to read the tips.

- Before students start writing a text in an exam, they should ask themselves *What is the level of familiarity between me and my reader?* The answer will determine the layout of their text, its style, language and level of formality, which should remain consistent.
- Elicit key features of informal language (phrasal verbs, contractions, question tags, simpler sentence structure, connectors that are more specific to spoken language, e.g. *Well…, By the way …, Anyway …, Actually …,* etc.) and formal language (sentences tend to be more complex, no contractions, word choice is more precise, etc.)

For more information on writing formal letters/emails, refer students to the Writing reference, page 172.

Exam task

4 Ask students to complete the exercise.

Mixed ability

In open class, elicit students' opinions about the suggestion and write the arguments for and against banning mobile phones and money on the board. Write some key words and expressions on the board that less confident students can refer back to when they write their letter, e.g.

For: mobile phones are the most common item to be stolen, you don't need money at school, carrying around expensive gadgets and money makes students potential targets for thieves

Against: additional security before, during and after school hours, school activities connected to mobile use, need money for lunch and after school

Brainstorm ideas for the best ways to prevent crime in open class and feed in some interesting ideas and some language for more advanced students.

5 **Plan** Ask students to complete the paragraph plan using their notes from Exercise 4. You may want to look at students' plans, if possible, to check them and give advice and suggestions for improvement before students take the next step.

6 **Write** Ask students to write their letter in an appropriate style in 140–190 words. Depending on time, it may be a good idea to set this and the subsequent checklist exercise for homework.

7 **Check** Students complete the checklist before they hand in their letter.

Homework OWB

Assign students Writing exercises 1, 2, 3 and 4 on page 34 of their Workbook and Progress check 4 on page 35.

Answers PROGRESS CHECK Units 3–4

Exercise 1
1 invention **2** growing **3** prevention **4** solution **5** evidence **6** burglar **7** guilty **8** creatively

Exercise 2
1 the worst **2** not as innovative as / less innovative than **3** the cleverest **4** the least enjoyable **5** (the) furthest/farthest

Exercise 3
1 out **2** up **3** get **4** looking **5** in

Exercise 4
1 tell **2** was writing **3** will be lying **4** will have saved **5** have you been doing / were you doing **6** lands **7** Are you doing **8** will have been studying **9** will you do / are you going to do **10** will have finished

Exercise 5
1 a **2** a **3** c **4** b **5** b **6** a **7** c **8** b **9** b **10** a

Exercise 6
1 unless we have **2** have been working for over **3** more expensive than any (other/others) **4** came up with / thought up **5** figure out who **6** as soon as they try

5 You win some, you lose some

UNIT AIMS

Exam preparation in Unit 5:

- understand the main ideas of paragraphs in an online article
- recognise distractors in an interview
- speculate in a photo task
- use prefixes and suffixes for word formation
- use fixed expressions in an open-cloze exercise
- use formal language in an email

TEACHER'S PRESENTATION KIT

- *Talk2Me* videos
- Speaking test videos
- Class and Workbook audio
- Workbook pages and answer key

UNIT OVERVIEW

Student's Book / Digital Student's Book SB		Workbook / Online Workbook OWB
LESSON / EXAM TASK	**EXAM SKILLS / LANGUAGE FOCUS**	**CONSOLIDATION**
Reading **Gapped text**	Understanding text logic An online article	Workbook, pp 36–37, Exercises 1, 2, 3, 4 Unit 5, Reading, Exercises 1, 2, 3, 4
Grammar 1	Modals (1): ability, permission, advice/criticism, obligation	Workbook, p 38, Exercises 1, 2, 3 Unit 5, Grammar 1, Exercises 1, 2, 3
Vocabulary	Words connected with *sports* Phrasal verbs Words + prepositions	Workbook, pp 38–39, Exercises 1, 2, 3 Unit 5, Vocabulary, Exercises 1, 2, 3
Listening **Multiple choice (single extract)**	Listening for relevant information	Workbook, p 40, Exercises 1, 2 Unit 5, Listening, Exercises 1, 2
Grammar 2	Modals (2): degrees of certainty	Workbook, p 39, Exercises 1, 2 Unit 5, Grammar 2, Exercises 1, 2
Speaking **Photo task**	Speculating about a situation	Workbook, pp 40–41, Exercises 1, 2, 3 Unit 5, Speaking, Exercises 1, 2, 3
Use of English **Word formation** **Open cloze**	Prefixes and suffixes Set phrases and idioms	Workbook, p 41, Exercises 1, 2 Unit 5, Use of English, Exercises 1, 2
Writing **A letter / An email**	Formality (1)	Workbook, p 42, Exercises 1, 2, 3, 4 Unit 5, Writing, Exercises 1, 2, 3, 4
		Workbook, p 43, Progress check and Cumulative progress Progress check and Cumulative progress

Additional material

PRESENTATION KIT	TEACHER'S / STUDENT'S RESOURCE CENTRE RC	TEST GENERATOR
Talk2Me video *They seem to be …*	**Unit 5 worksheets:** *Optimise your grammar* (Standard and Higher), *Optimise your vocabulary* (Standard and Higher), *Talk2Me* video, *Say it right* **Units 5–6 worksheets:** CLIL, Culture, Everyday English (TRC only), Grammar communication (TRC only)	Unit Test 5 (Standard and Higher)

READING
Gapped text | An online article

→ Student's Book, pages 48–49 SB

Lesson aims

- Focus on gapped text
- Practise a gapped-text exam task

Lead-in

Ask students to read unit title ***You win some, you lose some*** and elicit the meaning (*you cannot always succeed – we say this when someone hasn't succeeded, to encourage them to try again*).

Elicit other ways of expressing sympathy, e.g. *too bad, bad/tough/hard luck, what a shame*. Focus students' attention on the photo and ask students what they think the lesson is going to be about (*sports and games*).

1 In pairs or groups, students ask and answer the questions. Elicit answers in open class and try to develop a class discussion.

Suggested answers

1 Students' own answers

2 Forward thinking, strategic planning, leadership, socialisation, hand-eye coordination, peripheral vision, visual acuity, brain functionality, sympathy and empathy, cognitive flexibility, etc.

2 Ask students to complete the exercise quickly. Time this activity (two minutes) and give updates, e.g. *One minute to go … Only thirty seconds left*. Check answers in open class.

Answers

A 3 **B** 7 **C** 1 **D** 6 **E** 4 **F** 2 **G** 5

3 Ask students to complete the exercise. Check answers in open class.

Answers

1 Yes **2** No **3** Yes **4** No **5** No **6** Yes **7** No

Fast finishers

Ask students to read out the idea mentioned in the text if they say *Yes* and to express the idea of each paragraph if they write *No*.

Answers

1 Some parents still believe that playing video games is bad for you.

2 Computer skills help us meet challenges in our daily lives.

3 … help us to develop problem-solving skills. Some games help develop patience and perseverance skills.

4 Players can make mistakes in the virtual world and assess the consequences.

5 StarCraft helped Sylvia improve her life skills, particularly planning ahead and thinking strategically.

6 I wasn't allowed to play games online for six months.

7 A not-for-profit organisation, Makerspace, has developed an educational programme where students play video games in class to develop life skills.

4 Ask students to complete the exercise. Check answers in open class.

Answers

1 G **2** B **3** E **4** C **5** A **6** D **7** F

Extra support

Go over the answers and ask students to find the synonyms and clues that helped them match each sentence with an idea.

Answers

1 difficulties – obstacles, resolve – solution

2 reliable – trust

3 practical – effectively, work

4 protect yourself – give out personal information

5 better decisions – informed choices, real life – real world

6 skilful – master

7 combination of skills – life skills, computer skills, future – future career

OPTIMISE YOUR EXAM

Gapped text

Ask students to read the tips.

- Remind students that some gaps can be filled by referring just to the immediate phrase or sentence, but others will require understanding of the whole paragraph. In reading exams, often the answer required for the space is dependent on a word or reference many words before or after it.
- Highlight that looking carefully at clues such as pronouns, linkers and vocabulary related to the theme will help students choose answers which fit grammatically and logically in the gap.

▼ Exam task

5 1.24 **Note: The reading text is also available on the audio CD. You may want to have students listen and read the text before doing the exam task.**

Ask students to complete the exercise. Play the audio for students to listen and check their answers. Check answers in open class.

Follow up this activity by asking students how important it is to have awareness training about the danger of video games. Ask students if their parents should restrict the time they spend playing video games or other online activities. Try to open a class discussion.

Answers

1 D **2** G **3** A **4** E **5** C **6** F

6 Ask students to complete the exercise. Elicit answers from different students around the class.

Answers

achievement (n): the fact of achieving or succeeding at things in general, by being determined or working hard

acquire (v): obtain

carry out (phr v): perform, conduct

expose (v): provide someone with the opportunity to experience new ideas, activities, etc. so that they can learn about them

motor skills (n): coordination of muscles

running up (phr v): if you run up a bill or a debt, you do things that cause you to owe a large amount of money

staring (v): looking at someone or something very directly for a long time

Optional extension 1.24

Play the recorded text and ask students to underline the life skills mentioned in the text. Do a feedback session in open class and ask students to share items they underlined and say why they think they are important in today's world.

Answers

computer skills, social skills, problem-solving skills, confidence, patience, perseverance, overcoming difficulties, making decisions, learning how to budget, plan ahead, think strategically, planning skills, memory, motor skills

Cultural note

StarCraft is a military science-fiction media franchise created by Chris Metzen and James Phinney, and owned by Blizzard Entertainment. The series centres on a galactic struggle for dominance between four species in a distant part of the Milky Way galaxy at the beginning of the 26th century. It has been praised as one of the best strategy games of its time.

The Sims is a life-simulation video-game series, developed by EA Maxis and published by Electronic Arts. It is one of the best selling video games series of all time. The player creates virtual people, called 'Sims', places them in houses and helps direct their moods and satisfy their desires.

Minecraft was developed by Markus 'Notch' Persson. The game revolves around breaking and placing blocks. The game world is composed of rough 3D objects, mainly cubes, arranged in a fixed grid pattern and representing different materials, such as dirt, stone, various ores, water, lava, tree trunks, etc. The game has no specific objectives for the player to accomplish so there is freedom for the player to choose how to play the game.

Homework

OWB

Assign students Reading exercises 1, 2, 3 and 4 on pages 36–37 of their Workbook.

GRAMMAR 1

Modals (1): ability, permission, advice/criticism, obligation

→ Student's Book, page 50 SB

Lesson aims

- Understand the correct usage of modals for ability, permission, advice/criticism and obligation
- Practise using modals for ability, permission, advice/criticism and obligation

Lead-in

Put students in pairs to play ***Hangman*** with vocabulary from the reading text in the previous lesson.

Grammar in context

Ask students to complete the task. Refer them to the *Remember* box if they need help. Check answers in open class.

Ask students to think of personalised sentences using the modals in the box. Elicit a few examples around the class.

Remind students that they can find more information in the Grammar reference, Unit 5, page 153.

Answers

1 obligation **2** ability **3** permission

Language note

Many modal verbs don't have a past tense form (exception: *can – could*) or a past participle and students need to know the substitutes to use for these modal verbs when required, e.g. *can – to be able to (I can play / I was able to play / I will be able to play . . .), must – have to (I must go / I had to go / I will have to go), may – be allowed to (I may go / I was allowed to go / I will be allowed to go).*

Remind students that the negative of *must* is not the same as *don't have to.*

mustn't do something = It's necessary not to do it.

You mustn't play with matches.

don't have to do something = You don't need to do it but if you want, you can.

You don't have to go to the party if you don't want to.

Draw students' attention to the silent letter *l* in *should* and the silent *t* in *mustn't*. Drill the pronunciation of these two forms.

Ought/oughtn't to can be used in the same way as *should/ shouldn't* but *should* is more common, especially in negatives and questions.

1 Ask students to complete the exercise. Ask them to compare in pairs before you check answers in open class.

Answers

1 be able to play **2** should not have lost **3** could have won
4 is allowed to watch **5** ought to try **6** must register
7 didn't have to

Extra support

In class feedback, ask students to comment on what each modal expresses.

Answers

1 future ability **2** past criticism **3** past possibility
4 present permission **5** present advice **6** present obligation
7 past lack of obligation

2 Ask students to complete the exercise. Check answers in open class and accept all sensible suggestions.

Suggested answers

1 You don't have to read aloud all the rules but you can if you want.

2 You needn't have brought a racket for me, but thanks anyway.

3 I hope you will be able/allowed to play next Saturday.

4 The referee shouldn't have stopped the game at that point.

5 A player must not pick up and carry the ball. / You are not allowed to pick up and carry the ball. / Picking up the ball and carrying it are not allowed. / A player is not allowed to pick up and carry the ball.

3 Ask students to complete the exercise. Check answers in open class and accept all sensible suggestions.

Suggested answers

1 don't have/need **2** can't **3** have/need to / have got to / must / should / ought to **4** have (done) **5** shouldn't be **6** shouldn't / ought not to **7** can't **8** be able

Mixed ability

Give less confident students a limited set of answers in a jumbled order (*be able, must, have done, can't, shouldn't be, shouldn't, can't, don't have*).

Tell more confident students how many answers are possible for each gap (Q1: two, Q2: one, Q3: six, Q4: one, Q5: one, Q6: two, Q7: one, Q8: one) and ask them to think of them all.

Fast finishers

Ask fast finishers to write one or two comprehension questions on the text in Exercise 3 to ask the class when everyone has finished.

THINK | RESEARCH | CULTURE | LEARN | ME

Ask students to complete the task individually, then to compare their reasons in pairs. Elicit answers in open class.

Homework OWB

Assign students Grammar 1 exercises 1, 2 and 3 on page 38 of their Workbook.

VOCABULARY

Topic vocabulary | Phrasal verbs | Word patterns

→ Student's Book, page 51 SB

Lesson aims

- Understand the correct usage of:
  - words connected with sports
  - phrasal verbs
  - words + prepositions

Lead-in

Write these verbs on the board: *play, do* and *go.*

Point to the words at random and invite students to suggest a collocation using the word.

Words connected with *sports*

1 1.25 Ask students to complete the exercise. Play the audio for students to listen and check their answers.

Answers/Audioscript

1 football field/pitch **2** boxing ring **3** golf course **4** ice skating rink
5 motor racing track **6** tennis court

2 1.26 Ask students to complete the exercise. Play the audio for students to listen and check their answers.

Answers/Audioscript

1 A person who watches a sports match in a stadium: *spectator*
A *viewer* watches on TV.

2 A person taking part in a race: *competitor*
Your *opponent* is a person you are competing against.

3 A judge in a tennis or cricket match: *umpire*
A *referee* is the judge in a football or basketball match, for example.

4 A piece of equipment used in squash: *racket*
A *cue* is a piece of equipment used in snooker, pool or billiards.

5 Hockey players play with this: *stick*
A *bat* is a piece of equipment used by baseball or cricket players, for example.

6 This is used in fishing: *rod*
A *ball* is used in many sports, for example, football or tennis.

3 1.27 Ask students to complete the exercise. Play the audio for students to listen and check their answers.

Answers/Audioscript

1 We've just got one more team to *beat* and we're in the final!

2 Who *scored* the final goal, do you know?

3 Both teams scored the same number of points, so they *drew* the first game.

4 Two runners reached the line at the same time, so it was difficult to see who'd actually *won.*

Refer students to the Vocabulary reference, page 164, for more information on topic vocabulary.

Phrasal verbs

4 1.28 Ask students to complete the exercise. Play the audio for students to listen and check their answers.

Answers/Audioscript

1 Dom really stands out in that team – he's far better than all the others. *be visible*

2 We got through to the semi-final, but then we were knocked out. *leave*

3 Hey! Check out this new fitness app. It's brilliant! *look and see*

4 Mind out – you're about to start walking on the golf course. *pay attention*

5 Caroline's had to pull out of the match on Saturday because of an injury. *leave*

6 He stuck out as the weak player in the team. *be visible*

7 Listen out for the whistle – it's a sign that the match has finished. *pay attention*

8 I can't make out which horse is in the lead – can you? *look and see*

Language note

Point out to students that sometimes they can understand the phrasal verb by looking at the particle (the second word). The particle *out* can sometimes mean 'removed' or 'disappeared'. The phrasal verbs *knock out* and *pull out* have this meaning. It is sometimes also used (as in verbs like *check out, listen out, make out*) to suggest the idea of discovering information by means of a thorough search.

Optional extension

Ask students to write personalised sentences for the phrasal verbs in Exercise 4.

Refer students to the Vocabulary reference, page 164, for more information on phrasal verbs.

Words + prepositions

5 1.29 Ask students to complete the exercise. Play the audio for students to listen and check their answers.

Answers/Audioscript

1 A string of injuries *prevented* her *from participating in* the squash championship.

2 No, I've never *cheated at* pool or snooker!

3 I'm really *anxious about* the hockey game tomorrow as it's so important.

4 He was *banned from* professional cricket for 10 years after failing a drug test.

5 The sports kit *consists of* a yellow shirt, blue shorts and white socks.

6 What's the *difference between* tennis and badminton?

7 Our baseball coach *insists on* us staying in the night before a big match.

8 It's not always easy for new players to *adjust to* being in a professional team, and many of them *benefit from* getting financial and media advice.

Optional extension

Ask students to write two true sentences and one false sentence about themselves using words and prepositions from Exercise 5. In pairs or small groups, students read out their sentences for their partner to guess which sentences are true or false.

Refer students to the Vocabulary reference, page 164, for more information on word patterns.

SAY IT RIGHT

Stress in phrasal verbs (2) TRC

For the *Say it right* pronunciation activity and instructions, go to the Teacher's Resource Centre.

THINK | RESEARCH | CULTURE | LEARN | **ME**

In pairs or small groups, students discuss the questions. Elicit ideas in open class.

Homework OWB

Assign students Vocabulary exercises 1, 2 and 3 on pages 38–39 of their Workbook.

LISTENING
Multiple choice (single extract)

→ Student's Book, page 52 SB

Lesson aims

- Focus on multiple choice (single extract)
- Practise a multiple-choice (single extract) exam task

Lead-in

Have a class discussion about sport. Elicit opinions from students, but tell them they must use a word or phrase from the previous lesson in their sentence.

1 In pairs or as a group, students ask and answer the questions. Elicit answers from different students around the class and accept all sensible suggestions.

Suggested answers

1 Because men and women are both superior in different ways. Physically, males tend to be stronger and faster. Females tend to be more agile and flexible, and have more physical coordination. However, there are some mixed teams that work well, e.g. tennis, badminton and table tennis. It is also a carry-over from a time when it was thought unseemly for women to compete against men.

2 Students' own answers

2 1.30 Play the track for students to complete the exercise. Have students compare in pairs before you check answers in open class.

Answers
All six ideas should be ticked.

Fast finishers

In pairs, ask students to match the synonyms and similar phrases in the ideas in questions 1–3 in Exercise 2 and question 1 in Exercise 4. Elicit answers in open class.

Answers
1 doing well – successful **2** good role model – help and teach
3 remarkable – unusual

3 Ask students to complete the exercise. Check in open class.

Answers
All of them

OPTIMISE YOUR EXAM

Multiple choice (single extract)

Ask students to read the tips.

- It is common that aspects of all the multiple choice options will be mentioned in the audio to distract listeners in this task. Often the first information you hear sounds as if it could be the answer to the question but in fact is not. This information matches one of the answers, but does not fit the criterion given in the question – the person could be talking about last week, say, when the question asks about next week. The correct information usually, but not always, comes directly before or afterwards.
- Remind students that it is important to spend time analysing which key words and phrases helped them decide on their answers and why they got things wrong.
- Remind them to always answer all the questions. They have a 33% chance of being right!

Exam task

4 1.31 Play the track for students to listen and complete the exercise. Don't check answers at this stage, as students will listen again to check in Exercise 5.

Mixed ability

Ask students to exclude one of the options in each situation. Discuss students' reasons in open class before you play the track again. Don't give away the answers at this point. When you check the answers in Exercise 5, ask students to say which option they excluded on the first listening and if they were right.

5 1.31 Play the track again for students to listen and check their answers to Exercise 4. Elicit answers in open class and discuss the specific clues that helped them choose them.

Answers
1 B (*... the main reason we asked you here today is to talk about some of the exciting changes that have happened to your team in the last couple of years*)
2 A (*two years ago ... We'd often kick a ball around together in the garden ...*)
3 C (*last year – we kept the teams separate ...*)
4 B (*but some of our parents tried to talk us out of it ...*)
5 B (*where we usually play – Eastbrook football field – there aren't any changing rooms anyway ...*)
6 A (*I think they're looking at us and seriously considering it now ...*)
7 C (*I really hope there will be ... I can't see any reason at all why it couldn't be a girl ...*)

Extra support

Play the track again for students to note down the distracting information in the incorrect options for each question. You could provide students with a transcript of the listening and ask them to underline the distractors. This is useful in helping students understand how listening tests are constructed and also helps them become aware of how different spoken and written forms are.

Suggested answers
1 The extract starts by the interviewer giving possible reasons why she could have invited her guest to distract listeners: I could have invited you in because your team's doing rather well this season, or perhaps because as captain you're a very good role model for other teenagers
2 Adam explains how they played in separate teams: I was in the Eastbrook under-16s boys' team, and my sister Rachel was in the girls' team. He also talks about the fact that they do PE together but not football – we do PE together at school, so why not football too?
3 Adam talks about how well the girls play but he doesn't say they are better than last year: *I'd been a bit worried that the* boys would beat the girls every match but fortunately they were far too good for that
4 Adam talks about how his teammates thought it was a good idea: well, actually, I don't think any of the actual players – boys or girls – thought it was a bad idea. I can't remember anyone saying we shouldn't try it
5 Adam says what people do because there are no changing rooms, he doesn't say they prefer it: At the end of a game, you put your tracksuit on, go home and have a shower at home.
6 Adam says there aren't many: No, not many! In this part of the dialogue he also says We don't care – as long as they don't care! This is distracting because it sounds as if he is not optimistic.
7 Adam uses a double negative to talk about next year's captain to distract listeners: *I can't see any reason at all why it couldn't be a girl.*

THINK | RESEARCH | CULTURE | LEARN | ME

In pairs or small groups, students discuss the questions. Elicit ideas in open class.

Homework OWB
Assign students Listening exercises 1 and 2 on page 40 of their Workbook.

GRAMMAR 2
Modals (2): degrees of certainty

→ Student's Book, page 53 SB

Lesson aims

- Understand the correct usage of modals expressing degrees of certainty
- Practise using modals to express degrees of certainty

Lead-in

In pairs, students try to think of one sport-related word for each letter of the alphabet (except x, y and z).

Suggested answers

archery, badminton, championship, diving, equipment, field, golf, hockey, ice skating, judo, karate, league, motor-racing, net, opponent, play, quarterback, referee, squash, tennis, umpire, viewer, win

Grammar in context

Ask students to complete the task. Refer them to the *Remember* box if they need help. Check answers in open class.

Remind students that they can find more information in the Grammar reference, Unit 5, page 153.

Answers

1 can't **2** must have

Language note

Remind students that we use *could, may* and *might* (and the past forms *could have, may have* and *might have*) when there is 50% possibility that something is or will be true. Elicit the negative forms – *may not, may not have, might not, might not have*. Point out that we cannot use the negative form *could not* when there is a 50% possibility that something isn't true.

We use *must* when we are 90%+ certain something is true (past form *must have*).

We use *can't* when we are 90%+ certain that something isn't true (past form *can't have*).

When we are speculating and making deductions, the opposite of *must* is *can't*.

1 Ask students to complete the exercise. Check their answers in open class and accept all sensible suggestions.

Suggested answers

1 It might be fun to play.
2 It shouldn't be too expensive.
3 You must download the game.
4 You can't play it without a mobile phone.

2 Ask students to complete the exercise. Have students compare in pairs before you check answers in open class.

Answers

1 be checking the football scores **2** be working **3** like the game **4** have trained harder **5** save the final game **6** be cheating

Extra Support

Supply less confident students with two options for each answer (**1** *have checked / be checking*, **2** *be working / have worked*, **3** *have liked / like*, **4** *train harder / have trained harder*, **5** *have saved / save the final game*, **6** *cheat / be cheating*).

3 Ask students to complete the exercise. Check answers in open class and accept all sensible suggestions.

Suggested answers

2 can't/couldn't have known **3** must have started **4** should have done / ought to have done **5** could have got **6** must have made **7** must have been **8** may/might/could have enjoyed

Fast finishers

Ask fast finishers to write one or two comprehension questions on the text in Exercise 3 to ask the class when everyone has finished.

Optional extension

Write these sentences on the board:

She failed her exam. He is driving an Aston Martin. He's had a crash. She's crying. He looks great. Her English has really improved.

Ask students to think about the situations and write at least two sentences about each one using *must have, might have* and *can't have*.

THINK | RESEARCH | CULTURE | LEARN | ME

Ask students to complete the task in pairs or small groups. Elicit ideas in open class.

Homework OWB

Assign students Grammar 2 exercises 1 and 2 on page 39 of their Workbook.

SPEAKING
Photo task

→ Student's Book, page 54 SB

Lesson aims

- Focus on speculating about a situation
- Practise talking about photos

The *Talk2Me* video in this unit focuses on speculating about people and situations in photographs: who the people are, what they are doing, what has happened, what is going to happen next. Students answer questions and then listen out for useful phrases to speculate and express possibility. The video can be used in one of two ways:

Flipped classroom

Flipped classroom option

Using this approach, students watch the video and complete the exercises for homework. This prepares students for the speaking lesson by introducing them to the topic and the key phrases to use in the exam task. Teachers who use this method will find they have more class time to spend on activating the target language and developing fluency for the final task.

***Talk2Me* worksheet**

Ask students to also complete the *Talk2Me* worksheet on the Resource Centre for more detailed comprehension exercises and more practice of the key phrases.

Classroom option

1 Ask students to spend a minute or two reading the questions. Play the *Talk2Me* video for students to complete the exercise. Play the video again, if necessary, before checking their answers.

2 Play the *Talk2Me* video again, so students circle the words and phrases in the *Phrase expert* box. Pause the video from time to time if necessary. Check answers in open class.

***Talk2Me* worksheet**

Ask students to also complete the *Talk2Me* worksheet on the Resource Centre for more detailed comprehension exercises and more practice of the key phrases.

Answers

The transcript and answer key for the *Talk2Me* video exercises and Worksheet can be found on the Teacher's Resource Centre.

Lead-in

Write the following anagrams on the board. Students find the sports-related phrases.

rugae thiw a freeeer, niw a tcamh, eb jrudnie, ndes fof a arylpe, cehegnir dcorw, lebatcere a citoyvr, hosw a lloyew rdac

Answers

argue with a referee, win a match, be injured, send off a player, cheering crowd, celebrate a victory, show a yellow card

3 In pairs, students complete the task. Encourage students to use phrases from the *Phrase expert* box. Elicit ideas from different students around the class.

Answers

Students' own answers

4 Ask students to complete the exercise. Check answers in open class.

Answers

1 might **2** talking **3** looks **4** have been **5** can't **6** must

5 Individually, students complete the exercise. Remind students to use phrases for speculating from the *Phrase expert* box. Walk round, helping students with vocabulary where necessary.

Suggested answers

	Photo A	Photo B
What is this a photo of?	It looks as if there is a team celebrating. They each have a medal and seem to be cheering.	It may be a game. It looks as if a player is being shown a red card.
Where was the photo taken?	It could be next to a lake.	It might be on a football pitch during a match.
What could the people be doing?	They could be celebrating.	They could be arguing with the referee.
What could have just happened?	They may have been in a rowing race and they have just won it and they are now celebrating.	The player might have broken the rules and he is being shown a red card.
What might they do next?	The team might meet up with families and friends because they want to celebrate with them.	The referee might change his mind and let the player stay on the field.
How do you think the people might be feeling?	They seem to be really happy.	The players look upset. The manager might be angry because he doesn't agree with the referee.

Mixed ability

Brainstorm ideas and help students complete the table. Feed in useful sentences (see Suggested answers in Exercise 5) and add some advanced vocabulary for higher level students to use in the following task.

OPTIMISE YOUR EXAM

Photo task

Ask students to read the tips.

- Students sometimes cannot be 100% sure of what is happening in a photo or a picture. Encourage students to use their imagination and say what they think is happening. Highlight that they will not lose any points if they speculate and they will even gain points if they use appropriate language for guessing.
- It is helpful for students to learn off by heart a good opening sentence for this task, e.g. *Both photos show ______ but there are some clear differences.* They can personalise this sentence.

Exam task

6 In pairs or groups of three, students complete the task. Ask students to use their notes from Exercise 5 and the words and phrases in the *Phrase expert* box. Walk round and monitor students, noting down errors and good use of language to go over in a feedback session at the end of the activity.

Homework

OWB

Assign students Speaking exercises 1, 2 and 3 on pages 40–41 of their Workbook.

USE OF ENGLISH

Word formation | Open cloze

→ Student's Book, page 55 SB

Lesson aims

- Focus on word formation and practise a word-formation exam task
- Focus on open cloze and practise an open-cloze exam task

Lead-in

Write this riddle on the board: *Jack and Jill are in the living room dead on the floor. They are surrounded by glass and water. How did they die?*

Write *can't, may, might, could, must* on the board and ask students to use these words to speculate about what might have happened to Jack and Jill, e.g. *They might have been burgled. / They may have cut themselves on the glass.*

Answer

Jack and Jill are goldfish. A cat came through the window and the bowl smashed on the floor.

1 Ask students to complete the exercise. Elicit answers from different students around the class.

Answers

1 argue (argument), develop (development) **2** long (length) **3** swim (swimming, swimmer), win (winner, winnings)

OPTIMISE YOUR EXAM

Word formation

Ask students to read the tip.

- Point out that students can guess the answer by adding various prefixes and suffixes until they get something that sounds right and obeys the rules of word formation. Often, while they are doing this, they find the one that sounds right and suddenly realise that they were familiar with it after all. If they don't know the correct answer, they should always make a guess.
- Highlight that a suffix often causes a spelling change to the original word.

Exam task

2 Ask students to complete the exercise. Ask them to compare in pairs before you elicit answers in open class.

Answers

1 swimmers **2** competitions **3** winner **4** lengths **5** failure **6** anxiety **7** arguments **8** development

Refer students to the Vocabulary reference, page 164, for more information on word formation.

3 Ask students to complete the exercise. Check answers in open class.

Answers

1 2, 5 **2** 1, 3, 4, 6, 7

OPTIMISE YOUR EXAM

Open cloze

Ask students to read the tips.

- Point out to students that they can expect to be tested on many different things in gapped texts, but most of the gaps are usually grammatical words, not topic vocabulary. Students should look out for fixed expressions, dependent prepositions after certain words, and linking words and phrases.
- Highlight that the word they choose must make sense in the context of the text as a whole. When they have finished, students should read through the text again with their answers in place to check that it makes sense.

Exam task

4 Ask students to complete the exercise. Check their answers.

Answers

1 about **2** have **3** on **4** from **5** must/might/may/could **6** from **7** back **8** when/if

Mixed ability

Supply less confident students with two options for each answer (***1*** *about/of* ***2*** *have/be* ***3*** *on/that* ***4*** *from/have* ***5*** *must/can't* ***6*** *from/of* ***7*** *back/forward* ***8*** *when/unless*). Students who finish early can think of two comprehension questions based on the text. They can read them out to test the class when everyone has finished.

THINK | RESEARCH | CULTURE | LEARN | ME

In pairs or small groups, students discuss the questions. Elicit ideas in open class.

Homework

OWB

Assign students Use of English exercises 1 and 2 on page 41 of their Workbook.

WRITING
A letter / An email

→ Student's Book, pages 56–57 SB

Lesson aims

- Focus on language in a letter or an email
- Plan and write a formal email

Lead-in

Play ***Hangman*** with some of the words from the unit.

Suggested words: *opponent, golf, referee, swimmer, competition, injury, match, team.*

1 Focus students' attention on the photo. In pairs or as a group, students answer the questions. Elicit answers in open class.

Answers

Students' own answers

2 Ask students to complete the exercise. Elicit answers from different students around the class. Accept all sensible suggestions.

Suggested answers

1 at Alison's school

2 suggestions regarding this year's Sports Day

3 (1) there should be some competitive sports, with prizes (2) there should be a greater variety of sports, including novelty sports such as three-legged races (3) hold it at the weekend

4 (1) nothing wrong with competitive sports, and most students at the school support them (2) many students enjoy novelty sports, and it would be entertaining and fun (3) so more parents will be able to attend

3 Ask students to complete the exercise. Check answers in open class. Ask students to explain why some of the statements are false.

Answers

1 F (She probably writes in an informal, chatty style to her friends using contractions, phrasal verbs, colloquial expressions, exclamation marks, question tags, simple sentence structure, etc.) **2** T **3** T **4** T **5** F (The final paragraph is a polite close to her email that encourages the reader to write back.)

4 Students complete the exercise. Check answers in open class.

Answers

1 I am writing in response to **2** your request for **3** suggestions for **4** I would like to put forward **5** consider

OPTIMISE YOUR **EXAM**

A letter / An email

Ask students to read the tips.

- The aim of the writing exam is to establish that candidates can write in different styles (essays, reports, emails, articles, etc.) and that they understand the concept of register (the choice of vocabulary plus the style of writing – formal or informal).
- In formal writing, sentences tend to be more complex and word choice is more precise. We use it when writing essays for school, cover letters to apply for jobs, emails and letters at work to people we do not know well, reports, articles and legal documents.

For more information on writing formal letters/emails, refer students to the Writing reference, page 172.

▾ Exam task

5 Ask students to complete the exercise. Check answers in open class. Point out to students that the notice doesn't say they have to suggest equipment for more than one sport but that suggesting three items will allow them to write a good answer to the task.

Answers

1 Students' own answers **2** No **3** Yes

6 Ask students to complete the exercise. Check their answers.

Answers

Students' own answers

7 **Plan** Ask students to complete the paragraph plan using their notes from Exercise 6. You may want to look at students' plans, if possible, to check them and give advice and suggestions for improvement before students take the next step.

8 **Write** Ask students to write their email in an appropriate style in 140–190 words. Depending on time, it may be a good idea to set this and the subsequent checklist exercise for homework.

9 **Check** Ask students to complete the checklist before they hand in their email.

Homework OWB

Assign students Writing exercises 1, 2, 3 and 4 on page 42 of their Workbook and Progress check 5 on page 43.

6 Next steps

UNIT AIMS

Exam preparation in Unit 6:

- identify synonyms in an information leaflet
- predict missing information in a short talk
- make suggestions in a collaborative task
- understand when to add suffixes and when to use adverbs in a word-formation exercise
- understand and use idioms and collocations in a multiple-choice cloze exercise
- use informal language in a letter

TEACHER'S PRESENTATION KIT

- *Talk2Me* videos
- Speaking test videos
- Class and Workbook audio
- Workbook pages and answer key

UNIT OVERVIEW

Student's Book / Digital Student's Book SB		Workbook / Online Workbook OWB
LESSON / EXAM TASK	**EXAM SKILLS / LANGUAGE FOCUS**	**CONSOLIDATION**
Reading **True/false with explanation**	Identifying synonyms (2) An information leaflet	Workbook, pp 44–45, Exercises 1, 2, 3, 4 Unit 6, Reading, Exercises 1, 2, 3, 4
Grammar 1	Verb patterns (1): verb + infinitive/-*ing*	Workbook, p 46, Exercises 1, 2 Unit 6, Grammar 1, Exercises 1, 2
Vocabulary	Words connected with *the world of work* Phrasal verbs Collocations with *go* and *get*	Workbook, pp 46–47, Exercises 1, 2, 3 Unit 6, Vocabulary, Exercises 1, 2, 3
Listening **Sentence completion**	Avoiding unnecessary detail	Workbook, p 48, Exercises 1, 2, 3 Unit 6, Listening, Exercises 1, 2, 3
Grammar 2	Verb patterns (2): infinitives of purpose	Workbook, p 47, Exercises 1, 2 Unit 6, Grammar 2, Exercises 1, 2
Speaking **Collaborative task**	Making suggestions	Workbook, pp 48–49, Exercises 1, 2, 3 Unit 6, Speaking, Exercises 1, 2, 3
Use of English **Word formation** **Multiple-choice cloze**	Suffixes and adjectives Prepositions and collocations	Workbook, p 49, Exercises 1, 2, 3 Unit 6, Use of English, Exercises 1, 2, 3
Writing **A letter / An email**	Making suggestions	Workbook, p 50, Exercises 1, 2, 3, 4 Unit 6, Writing, Exercises 1, 2, 3, 4
Progress check	Check language progress for Units 5 and 6	Workbook, p 51, Progress check and Cumulative progress Progress check and Cumulative progress

Additional material

PRESENTATION KIT	TEACHER'S / STUDENT'S RESOURCE CENTRE RC	TEST GENERATOR
Talk2Me video *Shall we move on to ...?*	**Unit 6 worksheets:** *Optimise your grammar* (Standard and Higher), *Optimise your vocabulary* (Standard and Higher), *Talk2Me* video, *Say it right* **Units 5–6 worksheets:** CLIL, Culture, Everyday English (TRC only), Grammar communication (TRC only)	Unit Test 6 (Standard and Higher)

READING

True/false with explanation | An information leaflet

→ Student's Book, pages 58–59 SB

Lesson aims

- Focus on true or false statements with explanations
- Practise a true/false with explanation exam task

Lead-in

Ask students to read unit title ***Next steps*** and elicit the meaning (*the things you need to or plan to do next in order to achieve what you're aiming for*) and an example sentence, e.g. *I'm hoping to get a job in the music industry.* Next steps include finding a work experience opportunity and doing some more research. Focus students' attention on the photo and ask students what they think the lesson is going to be about (*work and careers*).

1 In pairs or groups, students ask and answer the questions. Elicit the meaning of *career path* (the way that you progress in your work, either in one job or in a series of jobs). Discuss students' opinions and ideas in open class and try to develop a class discussion on what types of careers interest students and why.

Answers

Students' own answers

2 Ask students to complete the exercise quickly. Time this activity (two minutes) and give updates, e.g. *One minute to go … Only thirty seconds left.* Check answers in open class.

Answers

The best summary is b.

3 Ask students to complete the exercise. Check answers in open class.

Answers

1 a **2** b **3** c **4** c **5** b **6** b

Fast finishers

Ask students to define the words and phrases in Exercise 3 that do not mean something similar to the others and say if each is a verb, noun or adjective.

Answers

1 *influences (n):* the effects that a person or thing has on someone's decisions, opinions or behaviour, or on the way something happens

2 *effects (n):* changes that are produced in one person or thing by another

3 *qualifications (n):* things such as degrees or a diplomas that you get when you successfully finish a course of study

4 *challenging (adj):* difficult to deal with or achieve

5 *avoid (v):* try to prevent something from happening

6 *affected (v):* changed or influenced by something else

OPTIMISE YOUR EXAM

True/false with explanation

Ask students to read the tips.

- Remind students that **True** means there is information in the text that agrees exactly with the statement in the question. Point out that they will almost certainly need to look for synonyms here and match meaning and not words.
- **False** means there is information in the text that is directly opposite to or contradicts the statement in the question. Highlight that students will also need to think about meaning here. Remind them to pay careful attention to 'little' words that qualify or change meaning such as: *some, all, often, occasionally.*

▾ Exam task

4 2.01 **Note: The reading text is also available on the audio CD. You may want to have students listen and read the text before doing the exam task.**

Ask students to complete the exercise. Check answers in open class.

Answers

1 T, It can be daunting **2** T, That choice may sometimes **3** T, Students who decide to **4** F, We all have talents **5** T, Consistently high marks indicate **6** F, Ali Moore's advice is **7** T, It may imply that **8** F, Consulting parents and other

Mixed ability

Break the text into chunks and give less confident students the option of only reading some of the text and answering fewer questions. If stronger students finish early, ask them to write a short summary of the text.

Optional extension

Try to open a class discussion in which students compare the education system in their country with that of the UK. Elicit when students in their country make key decisions and how those decisions affect their future lives and careers.

5 Ask students to complete the exercise. Check answers by eliciting definitions from different students around the class.

Answers

consistently (adv): in a way that doesn't change
criteria (n): the standards by which you judge something
daunting (adj): (something) that makes you worried because it might be difficult
fulfilling (adj): making you feel happy and satisfied
peer pressure (n): the strong influence of a group on someone to behave the same way
(personality) traits (n): qualities in someone's character
suit (v): be right for a person
the general public (n): ordinary people in society

Optional extension 2.01

Play the recorded text and ask students to underline all the words related to academia and the workplace. Have a feedback session in open class and ask students to share items they underlined. Explain the meaning of any difficult vocabulary.

Answers

Academia: school subjects, qualifications, GCSEs, teacher, A level subjects, university education, course, assessments, high marks, lessons, school day, future studies

Workplace: career, job, rewards, qualifications, careers adviser, vocational course, apprenticeship, employer, train, career path

Homework

Assign students Reading exercises 1, 2, 3 and 4 on pages 44–45 of their Workbook.

OWB

GRAMMAR 1

Verb patterns (1): verb + infinitive/*-ing*

→ Student's Book, page 60

SB

Lesson aims

- Understand the correct usage of verbs followed by the infinitive or *-ing* form
- Practise using verbs followed by the infinitive or *-ing* form

Lead-in

In small teams, students make as many words as they can from the words *WORK EXPERIENCE PLACEMENT* in three minutes. The team with the most words wins. Elicit what students think a work experience placement is (*working for a short time to get an idea of what the world of work is like*).

Suggested answers: *pen, apple, place, experiment, ace, cement, expert, rice, nice, entice, permanent, near, pear, ear, clear, app, exit, axe, train, plain, main, meat, neat, peat, pleat, pork, wire, won, cow*

Grammar in context

Ask students to complete the task. Refer them to the *Remember* box if they need help. Check answers in open class.

Ask students to think of personalised sentences using the verbs in the *Remember* box. Elicit a few examples around the class.

Remind students that they can find more information in the Grammar reference, Unit 6, page 154.

Answers

1 That might mean selecting school subjects that will lead to a fulfilling career.

2 They regret making the choices they've made and may *drop out of* the course or training.

3 … perhaps the lessons seem to be challenging because they come at the end of the school day.

4 This doesn't necessarily mean you should aim to become a language teacher or an actor.

Language note

verb + object + bare infinitive

Verbs that follow this pattern include most, but not all, of the modal verbs, the auxiliary verbs and the verbs of perception: *could, feel, hear, help, let, make, may, might, must, notice, see, shall, should, watch, will, would.*

Students are tested on common verb patterns in all the different sections of the main exams, especially in Use of English papers. Remind students that they can look up verb patterns for individual verbs in a good monolingual dictionary, such as the *Macmillan Dictionary* (www.macmillandictionary.com).

1 Ask students to complete the exercise. Ask them to compare their answers in pairs before you check them in open class.

Answers

verbs followed by infinitive: afford, agree, attempt, choose, hope, manage, offer, pretend, promise, want

verbs followed by *-ing*: admit, consider, deny, dislike, enjoy, fancy, imagine, involve, suggest

verbs followed by infinitive or *-ing*: begin, continue, hate, intend, like, love, mean, prefer, regret, try

2 Ask students to complete the exercise. Check answers in open class.

Answers

1 to enjoy **2** getting **3** working **4** to set **5** creating **6** preparing / to prepare **7** to inform

Extra support

Write these sentences on the board and elicit the change in meaning, depending on whether we use a gerund or an infinitive.

1 *He stopped to rest for a minute.*

2 *I remembered to go to the bank this morning.*

3 *She forgot seeing that film when she was a kid.*

4 *I regretted being late for the interview.*

Answers

1 *Stop* is normally used with a gerund. When *stop* is used with an infinitive, the infinitive takes on the meaning 'in order to'.

2 When *remember* is used with a gerund, it means 'to remember that you have done something.' When *remember* is used with an infinitive, it means 'to remember that you need to do something'. The sentence above means that he remembered that he needed to go to the bank that morning.

3 When *forget* is used with a gerund, it means 'to forget that you have done something'. The sentence above means that she saw the film when she was a kid, and that she has forgotten that fact. When *forget* is used with an infinitive, it means 'to forget that you need to do something'.

4 *Regret* is normally used with a gerund. *Regret* is sometimes used with infinitives such as to inform, e.g. *We regret to inform you* which means 'We wish we did not have to tell you (bad news).'

3 Ask students to complete the exercise. Check answers in open class.

Answers

1 working **2** to learn **3** working **4** looking **5** to find **6** to be **7** to prove **8** to show **9** feeling **10** studying / to study

Fast finishers

Ask fast finishers to write one or two comprehension questions on the text to ask the class when everyone has finished.

Optional extension

Ask students if young people do work experience in their country. Elicit where they think it would be interesting to do work experience. Develop a class discussion.

Homework OWB

Assign students Grammar 1 exercises 1 and 2 on page 46 of their Workbook.

VOCABULARY

Topic vocabulary | Phrasal verbs | Collocations

→ Student's Book, page 61 SB

Lesson aims

- Understand the correct usage of:
  - words connected with the world of work
  - phrasal verbs
  - collocations with *go* and *get*

Lead-in

In pairs, students try to think of one job for each letter of the alphabet.

Suggested answers

A – architect, B – builder, C – careers advisor, D – doctor, E – engineer, F – factory worker, G – grocer, H – historian, I – investigator, J – judge, K – karate instructor, L – lawyer, M – mechanic, N – novelist, O – ophthalmologist, P – photographer, Q – quantum physicist, R – receptionist, S – scientist, T – teacher, U – umpire, V – violinist, W – waiter, X – X-ray technician, Y – yachtsman, Z – zookeeper

Words connected with *the world of work*

1 2.02 Ask students to complete the exercise. Play the audio for students to listen and check their answers.

Answers/Audioscript

1 You do this when you formally state that you are leaving a job permanently. *resign*

2 You do this when you stop working because you are officially too old to work. *retire*

3 This is the fixed amount of money you get paid monthly or yearly. *salary*

4 This is a small amount of money you get for providing good service. *tip*

5 This is an extra payment some companies make, for example at Christmas. *bonus*

6 This is the amount of money you get according to how many hours or days you work. *wage*

7 You are this when you stop working to protest about pay or conditions in the workplace. *on strike*

8 You are this when you don't have a job. *unemployed*

9 You are this when you are away from work after the birth of a child. *on maternity/paternity leave*

10 You are this when you don't go to work because you are ill. *off sick*

Optional extension

Taboo: In pairs, students test each other on the vocabulary in Exercise 1. Write the words or phrases from Exercise 1 on the board and tell students to close their books. Student A describes as many words as possible in 90 seconds without actually saying it or using their native language. After 90 seconds, stop students or sound a buzzer. Ask them to count how many words their partner successfully guessed and then swap roles. The student with the most words is the winner.

Refer students to the Vocabulary reference, page 165, for more information on topic vocabulary.

Phrasal verbs

2 2.03 Ask students to complete the exercise. Play the audio for students to listen and check their answers.

Answers/Audioscript

1 The company is growing so they've decided to *take on* an extra hundred workers.

2 I'm really ambitious and will do whatever it takes to *get ahead* and be successful.

3 The receptionist *keyed in* my name and waited for my booking to come up on the screen.

4 One of the other waiters asked me to *fill in for* him while he made a call.

5 I joined the factory as an intern and *worked* my way *up* to being the team leader.

6 Don't work late so often – you don't want to *burn out* before you're 30!

Refer students to the Vocabulary reference, page 165, for more information on phrasal verbs.

3 Ask students to complete the exercise. Check answers in open class.

Suggested answers

1 Could you copy me in when you send the email, please?

2 I'm afraid we're going to have to lay off some of our workers.

Collocations with *go* and *get*

4 2.04 Ask students to complete each phrase. Point out to students that *get the sack* and *get fired* are synonyms.

Answers

1 get a placement **2** go bankrupt **3** get fired **4** go missing **5** get ready **6** get the sack **7** go abroad **8** go crazy **9** get lost **10** go quiet **11** get the impression **12** get upset

5 2.05 Explain to students that they are going to read a text about a girl's first day on a work experience placement. Elicit the meaning of *nightmare* and ask them to imagine why her first day was so terrible. Give students a minute to read the text to see if they are right.

Ask them to complete the email. Play the audio for students to listen and check their answers.

Answers/Audioscript

Hi Lee,

Well, the first day of my work experience is over! I told you I *got a placement* in an office, and maybe from my description you *got the impression* that it was my dream work experience placement. Well, today was a nightmare!

I was so excited when *I was getting ready* for work this morning. And guess what? I *got lost* on the way to the office! I ended up in completely the wrong building. I was late, and the manager *got upset* with me because I'd missed my induction meeting with the whole department. And then an important file *went missing* and it took me an hour to find it. After that, my head was all confused and I had so much to do that I thought I would *go crazy*! I didn't manage to do it all, and the manager wasn't happy.

So, I almost *got fired / got the sack* on my first day! Imagine that – losing your job before you've even started! Let's hope the rest of my work experience is better!

Mel

Optional extension

Ask students to write personalised sentences for the collocations with *go* and *get* that they didn't use in Exercise 4 (*go abroad, go bankrupt, go quiet*).

Refer students to the Vocabulary reference, page 165, for more information on collocations.

SAY IT RIGHT

Stress in phrasal verbs (3) TRC

For the *Say it right* pronunciation activity and instructions, go to the Teacher's Resource Centre.

THINK | RESEARCH | CULTURE | LEARN | ME

In pairs or small groups, students discuss the questions. Elicit ideas in open class.

Homework

OWB

Assign students Vocabulary exercises 1, 2 and 3 on pages 46–47 of their Workbook.

LISTENING
Sentence completion

→ Student's Book, page 62 SB

Lesson aims

- Focus on sentence completion
- Practise a sentence-completion exam task

Lead-in

In pairs, students play ***Just a minute***. They speak for 60 seconds about the photos on the page, trying not to hesitate, repeat any content words or deviate from the subject. Their partner times them. Students then swap roles.

1 In pairs or as a group, students discuss the questions. Elicit answers from different students around the class. Accept all sensible suggestions.

Answers

Students' own answers

2 2.06 Play the track for students to complete the exercise. Have students compare their answers in pairs before you check them in open class.

Answers

1 F **2** T **3** F **4** F **5** T

Extra support

Elicit the answers for the false statements.

Answers

1 She speaks to young people about their career options.

3 W stands for weaknesses.

4 O stands for opportunities.

3 Ask students to complete the exercise. Check answers in open class.

Answers

1 ~~is~~ a careers adviser

2 ~~such as~~ ability in maths

3 ~~played a lot of~~ video games

4 honest ~~with yourself~~

5 ✓

6 ~~number of~~ university places

4 Ask students to complete the exercise.

Answers

Students' own answers

OPTIMISE YOUR EXAM

Sentence completion

Ask students to read the tips.

- Remind students that they have thought about words and phrases that could be included in the listening in exercises 2 and 3. This should help them predict what type of information they are going to hear.
- This type of exercise is like a dictation. Remind students that they need to spell the words correctly to get marks in this type of exam task.
- 'Word-spotting' is an important skill; students need to listen out for a word, or words, in the audio material to help them identify exactly where the 'gap area' occurs. Then they need to listen carefully to what is said in that part of the audio to find the information that fills the gap.

▾ Exam task

5 2.06 Play the track for students to listen and complete the exercise. Check answers in open class.

Answers

1 (better) choices **2** tool **3** (school) subjects **4** make a list **5** determination **6** filling in forms **7** disadvantage **8** achieve your goal **9** vet **10** pilot

THINK | RESEARCH | CULTURE | LEARN | **ME**

Ask students to make their lists individually and then compare them in pairs. Then ask students to discuss the question in pairs or small groups.

Elicit ideas in open class.

Try to open a class discussion on what skills are useful for any job (e.g. a positive attitude, self-motivation, concentration, emotional intelligence, etc.).

Homework

OWB

Assign students Listening exercises 1, 2 and 3 on page 48 of their Workbook.

GRAMMAR 2
Verb patterns (2): infinitives of purpose

→ Student's Book, page 63 SB

Lesson aims

- Understand the correct usage of verb patterns
- Practise using verb patterns

Lead-in

Ask students to brainstorm vocabulary related to the world of work. Write *WORK* in the centre of the board, with circles around it with these subheadings: *Working conditions, Skills, Words to describe work, Occupations*. Write all students' suggestions on the board, in the appropriate circles.

Grammar in context

Ask students to complete the task. Refer them to the *Remember* box if they need help. Check answers in open class.

Remind students that they can find more information in the Grammar reference, Unit 6, page 154.

Answers

1 I give them information about different occupations <u>in order to help them make better choices</u>.

2 One tool that I use with young people t<u>o guide them in this area</u> is a SWOT analysis.

3 Sometimes I make myself busy with other work <u>so as not to do it</u>.

The three structures used are: *in order to*, full infinitive and *so as not to*.

Language note

If we use *in order to* or *so as to* it sounds a bit more formal and explicit than *to* by itself, but both are equally possible in spoken and written English. They both convey exactly the same meaning when expressing purpose.

In a construction where the reason for the action is expressed in the negative, the addition of *so as to* or *in order to* makes it easier for the other person to understand, e.g. *I carried the glass carefully so as not to drop it. / I carried the glass carefully in order not to drop it.*

In order to and *so as to* are more common before stative verbs like *be, have, know, appear, seem, understand*, e.g. *I talked to them about the job so as to understand what they do.*

1 Ask students to complete the exercise. Check answers in open class.

Answers

1 so as not to be

2 in order to take on / so as to take on

3 so as not to forget / in order not to forget

4 in order not to get

2 Draw students' attention to the photo and elicit what is happening (a teenager is being interviewed for a job in a restaurant). Elicit what sort of questions they expect the interviewer to ask. Ask students to skim read the dialogue to find out if they were right. Then ask students to complete the exercise. Have students check their answers in pairs before you check them in open class. Elicit from students if they think Ed does well at the job interview.

Answers

1 in **2** rather **3** prefer **4** than **5** had **6** would **7** to **8** as

No, Ed's interview is probably not successful.

Extra support

In pairs, students note down five mistakes Ed makes in the interview in Exercise 2. Elicit answers in open class and ask students to suggest what answers Ed should have given in the interview.

Answers

Ed makes these mistakes …

1 He talks about money too early.

2 He says he doesn't have the appropriate skills for the job.

3 He says he'd rather not work if he had the choice.

4 He admits that coming for the interview was his mum's idea.

5 He tells the manager that he will eat the restaurant's food while he is working.

Ed should have …

asked about the company, the working hours, the conditions (uniform? outside/inside? pay?), the company's expectations of him, possibilities of promotion, when he can start

THINK | RESEARCH | CULTURE | LEARN | ME

Discuss the question in open class. Then ask students to complete the task.

You could ask students to act out their dialogues in small groups and vote on the most successful interview.

Optional extension

Disappearing text: Write a short dialogue in open class using the manager's questions from Exercise 2 and students' own ideas for Ed's improved answers. Ask students to act out the dialogue in pairs. Then rub off a small part of it and ask pairs to swap roles and say the whole dialogue again. Gradually rub off more and more in bits and each time get the students to say the whole text.

Homework OWB

Assign students Grammar 2 exercises 1 and 2 on page 47 of their Workbook.

SPEAKING

Collaborative task

→ Student's Book, page 64 SB

Lesson aims

- Focus on making suggestions
- Practise a collaborative task

The *Talk2Me* video in this unit focuses on discussing jobs. People talk about the advantages and disadvantages of working part-time. Students answer some questions and then listen out for useful phrases to use in a discussion. The video can be used in one of two ways:

Flipped classroom

Flipped classroom option

Using this approach, students watch the video and complete the exercises for homework. This prepares students for the speaking lesson by introducing them to the topic and the key phrases to use in the exam task. Teachers who use this method will find they have more class time to spend on activating the target language and developing fluency for the final task.

Talk2Me worksheet

Ask students to also complete the *Talk2Me* worksheet on the Resource Centre for more detailed comprehension exercises and more practice of the key phrases.

Classroom option

1 Ask students to spend a minute or two reading the questions. Play the *Talk2Me* video for students to complete the exercise. Play the video again, if necessary, before checking their answers.

2 Play the *Talk2Me* video again, so students underline the phrases in the *Phrase expert* box. Pause the video from time to time if necessary. Check answers in open class.

Talk2Me worksheet

Ask students to also complete the *Talk2Me* worksheet on the Resource Centre for more detailed comprehension exercises and more practice of the key phrases.

Answers

The transcript and answer key for the *Talk2Me* video exercises and Worksheet can be found on the Teacher's Resource Centre.

Lead-in

Individually, ask students to rank from 1 (most important) to 10 (least important) the factors young people consider when choosing a job. Ask students to compare in pairs and compare their rankings before you discuss in open class.

3 In pairs or groups, students ask and answer the questions. Elicit ideas from different students around the class.

Answers

Students' own answers

Cultural note

A survey conducted by Endsleigh in 2015 indicated that eight out of ten UK students work part-time to help fund their studies. 14% also said that they had full-time jobs either during term time, holidays or both. More than half (57%) of students who work part-time spend their additional income on necessities – accommodation, textbooks, food and household bills.

Students who work part-time can begin networking with others in their chosen field. Forming professional relationships at this early stage can help students' chances of gaining employment after graduation.

4 In pairs, students make notes for each point. Elicit ideas from different students around the class.

Answers
Students' own answers.

5 Ask students to complete the exercise. Check answers in open class.

Answers
1 Let's **2** How **3** I'd suggest **4** Shall we **5** What about **6** Why

OPTIMISE YOUR EXAM

Collaborative task

Ask students to read the tips.

- Highlight that a conversation is a two-way exchange where students build off of what one another says. Actively listening to their partner will give them all the material they need to relate, ask relevant questions, and have an engaging discussion.
- Students who score high marks in this type of task use a wide variety of tenses, future forms and vocabulary appropriate to the level.
- Highlight that students will also achieve high marks in this type of task for answering the questions in an extended fashion and giving interesting personal details and justifying their opinions. Point out to students that asking for and making suggestions will also earn them marks for Interactive Communication, one of the four marking criteria in many official oral examinations.
- Remind students to respond to each other's suggestions with positive responses, e.g. *That's a good idea, Sounds like a good idea*, etc.

Exam task

6 In pairs, students complete the task. Set a two-minute time limit.Ask students to use their notes from Exercise 4 and the words and phrases in the *Phrase expert* box. Elicit a good opening line, e.g. *Shall we start with this point first – learning to manage money. I think that is an advantage of working part time. What do you think?*

Walk round and monitor students, noting down errors and good use of language to go over in a feedback session at the end of the activity.

7 In pairs, students complete the task. Elicit decisions from different students around the class. Try to open a class discussion on the most important factors to think about when getting a part-time job.

Homework OWB

Assign students Speaking exercises 1, 2 and 3 on pages 48–49 of their Workbook.

USE OF ENGLISH

Word formation | Multiple-choice cloze

→ Student's Book, page 65 SB

Lesson aims

- Focus on word formation and practise a word-formation exam task
- Focus on multiple-choice cloze and practise a multiple-choice cloze exam task

Lead-in

As a class, brainstorm the topic of volunteering. Elicit what types of volunteer jobs students know about and if they have ever done any voluntary work. Do they think it's a good idea to volunteer? What volunteer jobs would they like to do?

1 In pairs, students complete the exercise. Elicit answers from different students around the class.

Answers
1 Verbs: employ, volunteer, finance (the noun is the same as the verb), satisfy, vary
Nouns from these words: (un)employment, volunteering, finances, (dis)satisfaction, variety, variation
2 employer, employee (also possibly 'the unemployed')
3 neighbourly (showing a helpful attitude to neighbours), poorly (badly), friendly (pleasant and helpful)

OPTIMISE YOUR EXAM

Word formation

Ask students to read the tip.

- Suffixes are commonly used to make nouns from adjectives and verbs. Remind students that they have formally studied words ending in the suffixes *-nce, –ship, -ion* and *-ment* in previous units. They have also come across many of the other common suffixes during the course, e.g. *-al, -ial, -th, -ent, -ive, -ous, -less*.
- Adverbs are words that modify a verb. Remind students that one of the key features of adverbs is their ability to move around in a sentence. We highlight the adverb by fronting it in a sentence for emphasis and effect.

Exam task

2 Ask students to complete the exercise. Ask them to compare their answers in pairs before you check them in open class.

Answers
1 employment **2** voluntary **3** financial **4** satisfaction
5 variety **6** neighbourhood **7** poverty **8** friendships

Refer students to the Vocabulary reference, page 165, for more information on word formation.

Cultural note

There are currently more than 22 million people in Britain who work as volunteers for many different organisations. Having some form of voluntary work on your CV can often improve your chances of getting a job. According to a Time Bank/Reed survey of 200 leading UK businesses:

- 73 per cent of employers would employ a candidate with volunteer experience over one without;
- 94 per cent believe that volunteering adds to skills;
- 58 per cent say that voluntary work experience can often be more valuable than experience gained in paid employment.

Volunteering offers young people the chance to develop and learn new skills, improve team-working skills and the ability to work independently. It also provides the opportunity to meet new people from different backgrounds and make new friends and gives an insight into different working environments.

3 Ask students to complete the exercise. Check answers in open class.

Answers

1 6 **2** 8 **3** 1, 2, 3, 5, 8 **4** 4

OPTIMISE YOUR EXAM

Multiple-choice cloze

Ask students to read the tips.

- In an exam, students should always read the text for general understanding first.
- This type of exam task is a test of vocabulary rather than grammar, and students are often tested on their knowledge of idioms and collocations. It can be difficult to predict which idioms students will be tested on in this type of task. If students don't know the collocation, they should first think of words that are associated with the vocabulary in the phrase. They should then use their intuition by saying the options and if one sounds right, they should go for that one.

Exam task

4 Ask students to complete the exercise. Check answers in open class.

Answers

1 C **2** A **3** D **4** C **5** A **6** A **7** D **8** B

Mixed ability

Give less confident students the answers in a jumbled order to help them complete the exercise (*get, getting, impression, means, get, cope, suits, ahead*).

Ask stronger students to write two comprehension questions. They can read them out to test other students' understanding of the text once everyone has finished the exercise.

Homework

Assign students Use of English exercises 1, 2 and 3 on page 49 of their Workbook.

WRITING
A letter / An email

→ Student's Book, pages 66–67

Lesson aims

- Focus on language in a letter
- Plan and write an informal letter

Lead-in

Play ***Back to the board***. Divide the class into two teams. Ask a volunteer from team A to sit with his/her back to the board, facing their team. Choose words from the unit and write the words on the board one by one. Team A defines the word for the volunteer student to guess in one minute. After one minute, it is the other team's turn to define the word. The team that describes the most words in one minute wins the round.

Suggested words: *salary, unemployed, bankrupt, volunteer, neighbour, financial, placement.*

1 Focus students' attention on the photos. In pairs or as a group, students answer the questions. Elicit answers in open class.

Answers

1 Students' own answers

2 The photos show fruit-picking and babysitting or child-minding

Optional extension

In pairs, students play ***Just a minute***. They speak for 60 seconds about the photos on the page, trying not to hesitate, repeat any content words or deviate from the subject. Their partner times them. Students then swap roles.

2 Ask students to complete the exercise. Elicit answers from different students around the class. Accept all sensible suggestions.

Suggested answers

1 you learn about handling money / you gain a sense of independence

2 don't let it affect your schoolwork

3 working on a farm; because her friend likes animals

3 Ask students to complete the exercise. Check answers in open class.

Answers

1 Hi Carlos,

2 It was great to hear from you!

3 You said you're thinking about getting a weekend job

4 Another thing that [some of my friends] do is help out on local farms.

5 Hope that helps!

6 Love,

4 Students complete the exercise. Check answers in open class.

Answers

1 How about asking farmers in your area if they need any help?
2 What about asking farmers in your area if they need any help?
3 I suggest asking farmers in your area if they need any help.
4 You should ask farmers in your area if they need any help.
5 How about giving it a go to see if you like it?
6 What about giving it a go to see if you like it?
7 Why not give it a go to see if you like it?
8 You should give it a go to see if you like it.

OPTIMISE YOUR EXAM

A letter / An email

Ask students to read the tips.

- Highlight that in a writing exam, students are often asked to reply to an informal letter. It's a good idea for students to start their letter with a brief greeting, refer to the letter to which they are replying and even talk about what they've been doing recently. However, remind students the main part of their letter should be devoted to dealing with the specific task outlined.
- Students should make sure that their reply answers any questions in the letter they are replying to. It is important to cover all the points in order to get a good grade.
- Elicit other key features of informal language that students can use to show their examiner that they are confident writing in a conversational style:
  - phrasal verbs
  - informal vocabulary (e.g. *I guess …*)
  - contractions, but not abbreviated language
  - question tags
  - simpler sentence structures
  - connectors that are more specific to spoken language, e.g. *Well … / By the way … / Anyway … / Actually …*

For more information on writing informal letters/emails, refer students to the Writing reference, page 171.

▼ Exam task

5 Ask students to complete the exercise. Discuss answers in open class.

Answers

Students' own answers

Extra support

In open class, elicit ideas and ask students to justify their answers. Write some key words and expressions on the board that less confident students can refer back to when they write their letter.

6 Plan Ask students to complete the paragraph plan using their notes from Exercise 5. You may want to look at students' plans, if possible, to check them and give advice and suggestions for improvement before students take the next step.

7 Write Ask students to write their letter in an appropriate style in 140–190 words. Depending on time, it may be a good idea to set this and the subsequent checklist exercise for homework.

8 Check Ask students to complete the checklist before they hand in their letter.

Homework OWB

Assign students Writing exercises 1, 2, 3 and 4 on page 50 of their Workbook and Progress check 6 on page 51.

Answers PROGRESS CHECK Units 5–6

Exercise 1
1 competition **2** viewers **3** various **4** volunteers **5** financial **6** anxiety **7** winner **8** satisfaction

Exercise 2
1 get **2** going **3** got **4** has gone / 's gone **5** to get

Exercise 3
1 of **2** from **3** between **4** to **5** from

Exercise 4
1 be able to **2** don't have to **3** should **4** must **5** can't

Exercise 5
1 make **2** Check **3** pull **4** stand **5** Mind

Exercise 6
1 stay **2** to be **3** getting **4** to inform **5** to buy **6** taking **7** to ask **8** helping **9** to write **10** to drive

Exercise 7
1 fill in for her **2** on us doing **3** have/get the impression (that) **4** should not have been talking / shouldn't have been talking **5** am/'m not allowed to **6** would/'d rather you didn't / did not

7 Exploring art

UNIT AIMS

Exam preparation in Unit 7:

- understand overall structure and meaning of a news article
- understand the speaker's purpose in short extracts
- express preference and give reasons in a photo task
- use context to form words in a word-formation exercise
- understand sentence structure and apply in a sentence-transformation exercise
- create a good plot in a story

TEACHER'S PRESENTATION KIT

- *Talk2Me* videos
- Speaking test videos
- Class and Workbook audio
- Workbook pages and answer key

UNIT OVERVIEW

Student's Book / Digital Student's Book SB		Workbook / Online Workbook OWB
LESSON / EXAM TASK	**EXAM SKILLS / LANGUAGE FOCUS**	**CONSOLIDATION**
Reading **Gapped text**	Understanding implication A news article	Workbook, pp 52–53, Exercises 1, 2, 3 Unit 7, Reading, Exercises 1, 2, 3
Grammar 1	Pronouns	Workbook, p 54, Exercises 1, 2 Unit 7, Grammar 1, Exercises 1, 2
Vocabulary	Words connected with *the arts* Phrasal verbs Collocations from the art world	Workbook, pp 54–55, Exercises 1, 2, 3 Unit 7, Vocabulary, Exercises 1, 2, 3
Listening **Multiple choice**	Listening for purpose	Workbook, p 56, Exercises 1, 2, 3 Unit 7, Listening, Exercises 1, 2, 3
Grammar 2	Result clauses, connectors of contrast	Workbook, p 55, Exercises 1, 2 Unit 7, Grammar 2, Exercises 1, 2
Speaking **Photo task**	Expressing preference and giving reasons	Workbook, pp 56–57, Exercises 1, 2, 3 Unit 7, Speaking, Exercises 1, 2, 3
Use of English **Word formation** **Sentence transformation**	Context Sentence structure	Workbook, p 57, Exercises 1, 2, 3 Unit 7, Use of English, Exercises 1, 2, 3
Writing **A story**	Creating a good narrative	Workbook, p 58, Exercises 1, 2, 3, 4 Unit 7, Writing, Exercises 1, 2, 3, 4
		Workbook, p 59, Progress check and Cumulative progress Progress check and Cumulative progress

Additional material

PRESENTATION KIT	TEACHER'S / STUDENT'S RESOURCE CENTRE RC	TEST GENERATOR
Talk2Me video *If I had to choose …*	**Unit 7 worksheets:** *Optimise your grammar* (Standard and Higher), *Optimise your vocabulary* (Standard and Higher), *Talk2Me* video, *Say it right* **Units 7–8 worksheets:** CLIL, Culture, Everyday English (TRC only), Grammar communication (TRC only)	Unit Test 7 (Standard and Higher)

READING

Gapped text | A news article

→ Student's Book, pages 70–71

SB

Lesson aims

- Focus on gapped text
- Practise a gapped-text exam task

Lead-in

Write the unit title ***Exploring art*** on the board and elicit different art forms students have come across, e.g. *paintings, advertising, sculptures, murals, street performance, gardens, graffiti, music, film, television, theatre, poetry, dance, circus, photographs, literature, architecture, comedy, prints, graphics in a video game*. Focus students' attention on the photo and ask them what they think the lesson is going to be about (*the world of art*).

1 In pairs or groups, students answer the questions. Elicit answers in open class and try to develop a class discussion.

Suggested answers

1 Students' own answers

2 Students' own answers

3 It is open to the public, inspirational, brings cities alive and is a tourist attraction.

2 Ask students to complete the exercise quickly. Check answers in open class.

Answers

1 People can download a special app to interact with the sculpture and can use their smartphone torches to paint graffiti.

2 It exposes art to more people and people can interact with art and have a hands-on experience.

3 Lots of different types of people: teenagers, young children, adults.

4 In Sydney, Australia, people can see iconic buildings lit up. There is a symbol of hope installation in Japan (Kobe Lumiere), set up after the 1995 Great Hanshin earthquake. In Amsterdam people can take a trip along the canals.

3 In pairs, students discuss the question. Elicit opinions from different students around the class.

Answers

Students' own answers

4 Ask students to complete the exercise. Check answers in open class.

Answers

1 1 by, 4 to, 5 of **2** 3, it **3** 6, free **4** 2, they **5** litter (trash = US), sea

OPTIMISE YOUR EXAM

Gapped text

Ask students to read the tips.

- In this type of exam task, students should always read the title and the gapped text first in order to gain an overall idea of the structure and meaning of the text. Remind students to read the text again with their answers in place before making their final decision.
- In this task, students are tested on text structure, cohesion and coherence. They need to be able to follow the development of ideas through the text as a whole, using their understanding of cohesive devices, e.g. time expressions, exemplification, repetition, concordance of tenses, pronouns.

▾ Exam task

5 2.07 **Note: The reading text is also available on the audio CD. You may want to have students listen and read the text before doing the exam task.**

Ask students to complete the exercise. Check answers in open class. Elicit the grammatical clues and evidence in the text that helped them decide on their answers.

Answers

1 F (the preposition *by* often follows a passive structure)

2 G (the pronoun *they* refers to the collective noun *audience* – it can be plural or singular – and the sculpture has already been mentioned in the paragraph)

3 A (the pronoun *we* agrees with the subject in the sentence)

4 E (in this context, the preposition *to* fits with the verb *aim* – *aim to do something*)

5 B (the preposition *of* fits with the adjectival expression *to be aware of something*)

6 D (the conjunction *but* introduces different information – that it is free)

6 Ask students to complete the exercise. Elicit answers from different students around the class.

Answers

bumped into (phr v): met someone unexpectedly

captive (audience) (adj): unable to leave; people who need to be there for some other reason, so have to see the show

fulfilling (v): achieving something that you wanted to do

gazing (v): looking at something for a long time because it is so interesting

the backing of (phr): the help or support of

worth a visit (adj phr): there's a good reason for visiting it because it's enjoyable

Fast finishers

Ask students to make personalised sentences using the words and phrases in Exercise 6. When all the students have finished Exercise 6, they read them out to the rest of the class in a random order and say *beep* for the word or phrase for other students to guess.

THINK | **RESEARCH** | CULTURE | LEARN | ME

In groups, students complete the task.

Students could vote on which light festival they think sounds the most interesting.
Alternatively, students could exhibit their summaries in class. Prepare a set of quiz questions to have a class competition to find out the information about the different festivals. Students go round and read classmates' summaries in teams or in pairs.

Cultural note

One of the earliest expressions of street art was the **graffiti** on walls and on the sides of train carriages, done by **gangs** in the 1920s and 1930s in New York.

By the end of the 20th century, street art had evolved into complex interdisciplinary forms of artistic expression ranging from graffiti, stencils, prints and murals to large-scale paintings, street installations, and performance and video art. Street art became a ground for experimenting with different kinds of methodology and is now at the core of contemporary art. Some of the world's most influential urban artists include Banksy, Roa, Vhils, Keith Haring and Blu.

Homework

OWB

Assign students Reading exercises 1, 2 and 3 on pages 52–53 of their Workbook.

GRAMMAR 1
Pronouns

→ Student's Book, page 72 SB

Lesson aims

- Understand the correct usage of pronouns
- Practise using pronouns

Lead-in

Put students in pairs to play ***Hangman*** with vocabulary from the reading text in the previous lesson.

Grammar in context

Ask students to complete the task. Refer them to the *Remember* box if they need help. Check answers in open class.

Ask students to think of personalised sentences using the reflexive pronouns in the box. Elicit a few examples around the class.

Remind students that they can find more information in the Grammar reference, Unit 7, page 155.

Answers

1 ourselves **2** anyone **3** there's

1 Ask students to complete the exercise. Ask them to compare their answers in pairs before you check them in open class.

Answers

1 yourselves **2** myself **3** itself **4** themselves **5** ourselves

2 Ask students to complete the exercise. Check answers in open class.

Answers

Essential: 1, 3, 4 Emphasis: 2, 5

3 Ask students to read the information in the *Remember* box.

Ask students to complete the exercise. Check answers in open class.

Answers

1 ✓ **2** There **3** ✓ **4** one/them **5** anyone **6** there **7** somewhere

Language note

We use indefinite pronouns to refer to people or things without saying exactly who or what they are. We use pronouns ending in *-body* or *-one* for people, and pronouns ending in *-thing* for things. We use indefinite pronouns with *no-* as the subject in negative clauses (not pronouns with *any*), e.g. ~~*Anybody didn't come*~~ *Nobody came.*

We use *there* as a dummy subject with part of the verb *to be* followed by a noun phrase to introduce a new topic. We use a singular verb if the noun phrase is singular, e.g. *There's a huge captive audience.* and a plural verb if the noun phrase is plural, e.g. *There are more than a hundred people looking at the sculpture.*

4 Ask students to complete the exercise. Check answers in open class.

Answers

1 There **2** something **3** It **4** themselves **5** there **6** It **7** anything

Mixed ability

Give less confident students a limited set of answers (*anything, something, it × 2, themselves, there × 2*).

Ask fast finishers to write one or two comprehension questions on the text to ask the class when everyone has finished.

SAY IT RIGHT

TRC

Stress in reflexive pronouns

For the *Say it right* pronunciation activity and instructions, go to the Teacher's Resource Centre.

THINK | RESEARCH | **CULTURE** | LEARN | ME

In pairs or small groups, students complete the task. Encourage them to give extended answers. Elicit answers in open class.

Homework

Assign students Grammar 1 exercises 1 and 2 on page 54 of their Workbook.

VOCABULARY

Topic vocabulary | Phrasal verbs | Collocations

→ Student's Book, page 73

Lesson aims

- Understand the correct usage of:
  - words connected with the arts
  - phrasal verbs
  - collocations from the art world

Lead-in

Read the short poem below, *Job Responsibility* by Charles Osgood, to students. Read the poem twice – the first time students just listen, and the second time they make notes. Ask them to retell the story in pairs. Elicit the story from students around the class. Ask them what they think the moral of the story is (*taking responsibility*).

This is a story about four people named Everybody, Somebody, Anybody, and Nobody.

There was an important job to be done and Everybody was sure that Somebody would do it.

Anybody could have done it, but Nobody did it.

Somebody got angry because it was Everybody's job.

Everybody thought Anybody could do it, but Nobody realised that Everybody wouldn't do it.

It ended up that Everybody blamed Somebody when Nobody did what Anybody could have done.

Words connected with *the arts*

1 2.08 Ask students to complete the exercise. Play the audio for students to listen and check their answers.

Answers/Audioscript

1 A painting consisting of coloured lines, circles and squares: *abstract*
2 A very famous and important painting, e.g. Da Vinci's *Mona Lisa*, Van Gogh's *Sunflowers*: *masterpiece*
3 A picture in a children's book: *illustration*
4 The temporary construction where a film or TV show is made: *set*
5 The part of the theatre where actors perform in front of an audience: *stage*
6 Where artists create their work: *studio*
7 Pieces of art that have been arranged in a specific way to produce a particular effect: *installation*
8 An event when items are sold to people who offer the most money: *auction*
9 A public show where works of art and other things are displayed so people can go and see them: *exhibition*
10 This person directs the musicians in an orchestra: *conductor*
11 This person plans the movements performed by dancers: *choreographer*
12 This person plans and coordinates film projects: *producer*

Refer students to the Vocabulary reference, page 165, for more information on topic vocabulary.

Phrasal verbs

2 2.09 Ask students to complete the exercise. Play the audio for students to listen and check their answers.

Answers/Audioscript

1 I wasn't happy with the drawing, so I *tore* it *up* and started again.
2 The director said that we had to *edit out* the music from the scene because she didn't like it.
3 I didn't use to enjoy ballet at all, but it's *grown on* me recently.
4 I always *sketch out* a rough outline of the picture before I start the painting itself.
5 The local council's *drawing up* plans to build a new art gallery in the town centre.
6 As he was painting, you couldn't see what it was – then he turned it upside down and it *turned out* to be a self-portrait!

Refer students to the Vocabulary reference, page 165, for more information on phrasal verbs.

Collocations from the art world

3 2.10 Ask students to complete the exercise. Play the audio for students to listen and check their answers.

Answers/Audioscript

1 Writing a novel, play or song is difficult because you basically start with a blank *canvas*.
2 Our hotel seems quiet and organised to guests, but it's often very hectic behind the *scenes*.
3 When we go out, Sam always tries to take *centre stage*. She loves being the centre of attention!
4 Performing on stage and doing schoolwork is a very difficult *balancing act* for young actors.
5 Mrs Parker was a wonderful headteacher, so she'll be a difficult *act* to follow. I'm going to do my best, though.
6 Everyone in class played an important *part* in raising money for charity.

Language note

By developing a clear understanding of figurative language, students can further comprehend texts that contain metaphorical and lexical meanings beyond the literal level.

A metaphor is an expression that refers to something that it does not literally mean in order to suggest a similarity, e.g. *The inside of the car was a fridge*. The metaphor implies that the inside of the car was very cold.

We use metaphors to communicate a lot of meaning with just a word or a phrase. They can help listeners or readers better understand something about the object or idea to which the metaphor is being applied.

Metaphors do not use *as* or *like*. (Expressions using *as* and *like* are called similes.)

Refer students to the Vocabulary reference, page 165, for more information on collocations.

THINK | RESEARCH | CULTURE | LEARN | ME

In pairs or small groups, students discuss the question. Elicit ideas in open class.

Homework OWB

Assign students Vocabulary exercises 1, 2 and 3 on pages 54–55 of their Workbook.

LISTENING
Multiple choice

→ Student's Book, page 74 SB

Lesson aims

- Focus on multiple choice
- Practise a multiple-choice exam task

Lead-in

Ask students to brainstorm vocabulary related to the world of art. Write *ART* in the centre of the board, with circles around it with these subheadings: *Occupations; Places; Art; TV, film and theatre; Art forms*. Write all students' suggestions on the board, in the appropriate circles.

Suggested answers

Occupations: artist, choreographer, conductor, producer, dancer, actor, musician, director, etc.

Places: gallery, theatre, museum, studio, exhibition, auction, installation, etc.

Art: abstract, illustration, masterpiece, painting, drawing, sketch out, self-portrait, blank canvas, paintbrush, exhibits, etc.

TV, film and theatre: set, stage, studio, audience, show, scene, take centre stage, play a part, behind the scenes, etc.

Art forms: paintings, advertising, sculptures, murals, street performance, gardens, graffiti, music, film, television, theatre, poetry, dance, circus, photographs, literature, architecture, comedy, prints, graphics in a video game, etc.

1 In pairs or as a group, students ask and answer the questions. Elicit answers from different students around the class and accept all sensible suggestions.

Suggested answers

1 museum, art supplies shop, cinema, arts centre, art room at school, TV/radio arts programme, art magazine/website, etc.

2 to inform, to persuade, to ask for information, to agree, to disagree, to learn, to criticise, etc.

2 2.11 Play the track for students to listen and complete the exercise. Ask students to compare their answers in pairs before you check them in open class.

Answers

1 asking for help **2** describing a problem **3** giving advice
4 expressing surprise **5** complaining about something
6 making a suggestion

Extra support

Elicit the key phrases which helped students decide on their answers to Exercise 2.

Answers

Extract 1: *Can I ask your opinion?*
Extract 2: *Well, it's difficult … I'm not sure what I can do about it now.*
Extract 3: *I'd get a rubber … It's worth a try, I'd say.*
Extract 4: *I couldn't believe it.*
Extract 5: *I can't see anything at all! It's really annoying.*
Extract 6: *So, shall we do it on cave paintings, then?*

3 Elicit synonyms for the word *purpose* (*reason, intention, objective*). Ask students to complete the exercise. Check in open class.

Answers

6, 8

OPTIMISE YOUR EXAM

Multiple choice

Ask students to read the tips.

- It is important that students are aware of the speaker's purpose and choice of language. Highlight that if students know the key words and phrases associated with language functions (making a suggestion, advice, etc.) they will be able to rapidly tune into the listening text and focus on the ideas. This skill is useful in listening exams, and raising students' awareness of these typical structures will also help them improve their performance in oral exams.
- Remind students to think about possible paraphrasing – answers may be rephrased, reported by another person or summarised. Highlight that sometimes, however, the speaker does use exactly the same words that appear in the question. Point out to students that these are often distractors. They must select the correct answer, not the first one they hear.

▼ Exam task

4 2.12 Play the track for students to listen and complete the exercise. Don't check answers at this stage, as students will listen again to check in Exercise 5.

Mixed ability

Ask students to exclude one of the options in each situation. Discuss students' reasons in open class before you play the track again. Don't give away the answers at this point. When you check the answers in Exercise 4, ask students to say which option they excluded on the first listening and if they were right.

5 2.12 Play the track again for students to listen and check their answers to Exercise 4. Elicit answers in open class and discuss the specific clues that helped them choose them.

Answers

1 B (*I think that might make it lighter.*)

2 B (The extract goes into detail about her decision to buy a silver ring.)

3 A (Jez: *I'm not sure I can see what all the fuss is about* Megan: *You're too old-fashioned to understand modern art – that's your problem!*)

4 B (*It's got hundreds of different things you can make …*)

5 A (*it caused a scandal when people first heard about it … Despite these difficulties, Drogin exhibited in Paris.*)

6 C (*No, the tickets have got seat numbers on. Not everyone's come in yet. It could be that those tickets have been sold.*)

7 C (The extract describes her entry into the world of art: *… what got you into sculpture in the first place?*)

8 B (*It's quite difficult to write about cave paintings without including pictures of them … Yeah, that's true. And we do have to write 500 words.*)

Extra support

Play the track again for students to look at Exercise 4 and listen for distractors.

Even if students think they know the answer to a question, they should also think about why the other answers are not correct. This will help them build good listening habits and become more aware of how distractors work in listening exams.

Suggested answers

1 Chloe asks Joel: *Do you think I should start again?* i.e. go and get another piece of paper (Option C), but Joel advises her not to: *That seems a bit extreme.* Joel also says: *You don't really have time, anyway,* which, if students are not listening carefully, sounds like he is telling her to ignore the mistake (Option A).

2 The woman does say there were a lot of people: *there were all these people, and so many things on display* (Option C), but she doesn't explain why. She says Matt didn't want to look through the catalogue: *I looked through it, but Matt didn't want to, really,* but she doesn't explain why he wasn't keen to be there (Option A).

3 Megan says: *I'm not even going to try and bother to change your mind,* and Jez agrees: *Absolutely!*, so there's no chance the man might appreciate the piece (Option B). Megan thinks the piece is both powerful and beautiful: *And the lights create an atmosphere of pain and suffering, and yet beauty at the same time. It's very powerful.* Jez seems to agree; he says *Right* (Option C), but he says it sarcastically. Point out how important it is to listen to the tone a speaker uses.

4 The shop assistant uses the word *interests* to ask about the teenager's hobbies (Option C): *Do you know if she has any specific interests – painting, photography, origami, those kinds of things?*

The customer talks about the price but doesn't say it was cheaper than she expected (Option A): Shop assistant: *14.99.* Customer: *That's great.*

5 The extract says: *Some people called … for the artist Drogin to be imprisoned.* But it doesn't say he went to prison (Option C). It talks about critics praising his painting, but this is after he first took it to Paris: *… it was there that critics began to recognise its greatness.* (Option B)

6 Greg says that person with the big hat is annoying: *I can't see anything at all! It's really annoying.* But he doesn't say moving will annoy other people (Option B). Greg doesn't want to swap places: *That won't help, will it? Then you won't be able to see,* but Charlotte suggests moving seats to where they can see: *Maybe we can move. There are some empty seats over there.* (Option A)

7 She talks about learning the techniques but doesn't explain them (Option A): *I started learning the techniques behind sculpture.* She says she loves Henry Moore's sculptures: *I've always been attracted to it,* but she doesn't compare herself to the artist (Option B).

8 The friends say what the teacher wants, but they don't say he wouldn't like it: *Mr Radley wants us mainly to write text, not paste in pictures.* (Option A) They don't say it's difficult to find pictures: *There's loads of stuff online about them.* (Option C)

THINK | RESEARCH | CULTURE | LEARN | ME

In pairs or small groups, students discuss the questions. Elicit ideas in open class.

Homework

OWB

Assign students Listening exercises 1, 2 and 3 on page 56 of their Workbook.

GRAMMAR 2

Result clauses, connectors of contrast

→ Student's Book, page 75 SB

Lesson aims

- Understand the correct usage of result clauses and connectors of contrast
- Practise using result clauses and connectors of contrast

Lead-in

Ask students to look at the different forms of art in this unit and choose their favourite. In pairs, students take it in turns to say which art form they like most and say why.

Grammar in context

Ask students to complete the task. Refer them to the *Remember* box if they need help. Check answers in open class.

Remind students that they can find more information in the Grammar reference, Unit 7, page 155.

Answers

1 so **2** too **3** enough **4** such

Language note

Highlight that *enough* means you have what you need, e.g. *We have enough food for everyone.* (Everyone has some food.) *Enough* is used in negative sentences to mean less than sufficient or less than necessary.

Enough can be replaced with *the* before a noun, e.g. *I don't have the money to go on holiday.*

Time or *room* can be used alone to mean *enough time* or *enough room*, e.g. *Is there room in your car for all of us? Do we have time to stop for a drink?*

1 Ask students to complete the exercise. Check answers in open class.

Answers

1 so **2** too **3** such an **4** enough visitors **5** knowledgeable enough **6** much too **7** such **8** much too much

Extra support

Ask students to match the sentences in Exercise 1 with the grammatical rules in the *Remember* box.

Answers

1 *so* + adjective **2** *too* + adverb **3** *such* + article + adjective + noun **4** *enough* + noun **5** adjective + *enough* **6** *much too* + adjective **7** *such* + adjective + noun **8** *much too* + adverb

2 Ask students to read the information in the *Remember* box. Ask them to complete the exercise. Ask students to compare their answers with a partner before checking them in open class.

Remind students that they can find more information in the Grammar reference, Unit 7, page 155.

Answers

1 Even though I got a new camera last month, I haven't taken any photos recently. / I haven't taken any photos recently even though I got a new camera last month.

2 In spite of getting a new camera last month, I haven't taken any photos recently. / I haven't taken any photos recently in spite of getting a new camera last month. / In spite of the fact (that) I got a new camera last month, I haven't taken any photos recently. / I haven't taken any photos recently in spite of the fact (that) I got a new camera last month.

3 I got a new camera last month. However, I haven't taken any photos recently. / I haven't, however, taken any photos recently. / I haven't taken any photos recently, however.

4 Although I got a new camera last month, I haven't taken any photos recently. / I haven't taken any photos recently although I got a new camera last month.

5 Despite getting a new camera last month, I haven't taken any photos recently. / I haven't taken any photos recently despite getting a new camera last month. / Despite the fact (that) I got a new camera last month, I haven't taken any photos recently. / I haven't taken any photos recently despite the fact (that) I got a new camera last month.

Language note

Remind students that we can use *in spite of* and *despite* with a subject and verb if we include the expression *the fact that*, e.g. *Despite / In spite of the fact that she studied all night, she didn't pass the exam.*

Although, *though* and *even though* are followed by a clause expressing contrary (opposite) information to the idea or situation expressed in the other clause. After *although/though*, we use a subject and a verb, e.g. *We enjoyed our holiday although it rained every day.* We use *even though* to give emphasis and it is followed by a subject and a verb, e.g. *Even though we were in a horrible hotel, we had a great time.*

Highlight to students that because these words have similar meanings but use different structures, they are very typically tested in sentence transformation tasks in Use of English exams.

3 Ask students to complete the exercise. Check answers in open class.

Answers

1 Even **2** However **3** being **4** however/though **5** too **6** enough **7** that **8** such

Mixed ability

Give less confident students the answers in a jumbled order (*being, however, though, even, such, too, that, enough*).

Ask fast finishers to write a question about the text. The questions can then be given to other early finishers to answer and then passed back to the original student for marking.

Homework OWB

Assign students Grammar 2 exercises 1 and 2 on page 55 of their Workbook.

SPEAKING
Photo task

→ Student's Book, page 76 SB

Lesson aims

- Focus on expressing preference and giving reasons
- Practise doing a photo task

The *Talk2Me* video in this unit focuses on types of music and what people prefer to listen to and where. Students answer some questions and then listen out for useful phrases to use when discussing preferences. The video can be used in one of two ways:

Flipped classroom

Flipped classroom option

Using this approach, students watch the video and complete the exercises for homework. This prepares students for the speaking lesson by introducing them to the topic and the key phrases to use in the exam task. Teachers who use this method will find they have more class time to spend on activating the target language and developing fluency for the final task.

***Talk2Me* worksheet**

Ask students to also complete the *Talk2Me* worksheet on the Resource Centre for more detailed comprehension exercises and more practice of the key phrases.

Classroom option

1 Ask students to spend a minute or two reading the questions. Play the *Talk2Me* video for students to complete the exercise. Play the video again, if necessary, before checking their answers.

2 Play the *Talk2Me* video again, so students write the names of the people who use the phrases in the *Phrase expert* box. Pause the video from time to time if necessary. Check answers in open class.

***Talk2Me* worksheet**

Ask students to also complete the *Talk2Me* worksheet on the Resource Centre for more detailed comprehension exercises and more practice of the key phrases.

Answers

The transcript and answer key for the *Talk2Me* video exercises and Worksheet can be found on the Teacher's Resource Centre.

Language note

Ask students what *'d* stands for in the sentences (*would*). Elicit the negative form of *I'd prefer* (*I'd prefer not to have*). Highlight the use of adverbs to add emphasis (*definitely/never*) and note the position of these adverbs in the phrases. Ask students to notice the word patterns for the phrase *I'd rather* and elicit the negative form. Remind them that *I'd rather* is followed by the bare infinitive.

Lead-in

Put students in pairs or groups of three or four. Ask them to think of the name of a band or a famous singer for each letter of the alphabet. Set a time limit of five minutes.

Suggested answers

AC/DC, Bon Jovi, Coldplay, Disturbed, Evanescence, Flaming Lips, Guns n Roses, Hot Hot Heat, Iggy Pop, Jesus and Mary Chain, Kinks, Linkin Park, Muse, Nonpoint, Otis Redding, Panic at the disco, Queen, Red Hot Chili Peppers, System of a down, Trivium, U2, Velvet Underground, Walls of Jericho, Xandria, Yeah Yeah Yeahs, ZZTop

3 In pairs or groups, students ask and answer the questions. Encourage students to use phrases from the *Phrase expert* box. Elicit preferences from different students around the class.

Answers

Students' own answers

4 Ask students to complete the exercise. Check answers in open class.

Answers

that's the reason why, if I had to choose, I'd rather, because

Optional extension

Write some options on the board for weekend activities. In pairs, students discuss their preferences and give reasons.

5 Ask students to complete the exercise. Have students compare in pairs before you elicit ideas in open class.

Suggested answers

	Photo A	Photo B
Describe what you can see briefly.	In this photo, I can see a small concert in a bar or a small club. There is a solo singer and some members of a band playing different instruments.	This photo shows an outdoor music festival. There is a musical performance happening on stage.
Similarities and differences	I think it's probably an intimate, indoor gig with a small audience.	In contrast, in this photo we can see a massive crowd and lots of lights. I think the music is probably very loud.
What might the people enjoy about being in these places?	I think people might enjoy being in a relaxed atmosphere. The music might be quite quiet so that people can talk as well as listen to the music.	I think people enjoy dancing and singing along at these concerts. There is probably a party atmosphere and everyone looks like they are having a great time.

OPTIMISE YOUR EXAM

Photo task

Ask students to read the tips.

- Remind students that if they can express preferences and give reasons for their choices in a natural and accurate way, they can improve their marks both for Interactive Communication and Grammar and Vocabulary. Point out that they should take careful note of the word patterns.
- Highlight some key expressions that are useful when discussing options, e.g. *Out of all of them, Personally, …*

Exam task

6 In pairs, students complete the task and time each other for one minute. Ask students to use their notes from Exercise 5 and the words and phrases in the *Phrase expert* box.

Walk round and monitor students, noting down errors and good use of language to go over in a feedback session at the end of the activity.

Extra support

Ask students to write their choices before doing this as a speaking activity and remind them that it is important for them to justify their choices.

7 In pairs, students complete the task and time each other for 30 seconds. Elicit decisions from different students around the class. Start a discussion about which place students prefer and why.

Homework

OWB

Assign students Speaking exercises 1, 2 and 3 on pages 56–57 of their Workbook.

USE OF ENGLISH

Word formation | Sentence transformation

→ Student's Book, page 77

Lesson aims

- Focus on word formation and practise a word-formation exam task
- Focus on sentence transformation and practise a sentence-transformation exam task

Lead-in

In pairs, students try to think of one art-related word for each letter of the alphabet (except q, x, y and z).

Suggested answers

abstract, brush, choreography, drawing, exhibit, film, graffiti, horizon, image, jazz, kitsch, literary, museum, naturalistic, orchestra, painting, realistic, stage, theatre, urban, video game, watercolour

1 Ask students to complete the exercise. Check by eliciting answers from different students around the class.

Answers

1 undoubtedly **2** beautifully, doubtfully **3** equipment

OPTIMISE YOUR EXAM

Word formation

Ask students to read the tips.

- Point out that in the examination, when students see the prompt word at the end of the line, they must not automatically write a related word they know well as the answer. They need to read the whole text first to decide what the word is. This type of task tests students' knowledge of the way words are formed in English, including the addition of prefixes and suffixes, the formation of compound words, 'internal changes' (*undoubt**ed**ly*) and the spelling rules associated with all these changes.
- Highlight that students can improve in this area if they try to divide long words into their stem/root, prefix and suffix when they are reading.

Refer students to the Vocabulary reference, page 165, for more information on word formation.

Language note

Normally, adverbs are formed by adding *-ly*, e.g. *quickly, dangerously*.

If an adjective ends in *-e*, we add *-ly* to form the adverb, e.g. *politely*.

If an adjective ends in *-le*, we remove the *e* and add **y**, e.g. *probably*.

If the adjective ends in *-l*, we simply add *-ly* and the adverb will then end in *-lly*, e.g. *beautifully, helpfully*.

▾ Exam task

2 Ask students to complete the exercise. Ask them to compare their answers in pairs before you check them in open class.

Answers

1 beautiful **2** easily **3** accessible **4** equipment **5** patiently **6** Undoubtedly/Doubtless **7** massively **8** attractions

3 Ask students to complete the exercise. Check answers in open class.

Answers

1 3 **2** 1 **3** 5

OPTIMISE YOUR EXAM

Sentence transformation

Ask students to read the tips.

- Remind students to always put the prompt word in their answer and not to change this word in any way.
- Point out that contractions, e.g. *I'm*, count as two words.
- If students get the answers wrong in Exercise 4, suggest that they can improve if they think of their own sentence using the same structure, to make sure they understand the meaning.

▾ Exam task

4 Ask students to complete the exercise. Check answers in open class.

Answers

1 such a lot of **2** in spite of it/its being **3** don't cut yourselves/yourself **4** not old enough **5** make do with **6** has been said

Mixed ability

Check the answers to Exercise 4. Divide the class into A and B pairs, mixing up higher and lower level students. Tell Student A to read out the first sentences in 1–6 and say the word given. Student B tries to formulate the second sentence, without looking at their notes. If the answer is correct, Student B continues. If they make a mistake, Student A has a turn. However, Student B now read out the second sentence in 1–6. Student A must start again from Question 1, but this time they can use their memory as well as logic. When Student A makes a mistake, Student B can try again, also starting from 1. The aim of the game is for both students to go through every sentence transformation in one go without making any mistakes.

Homework

OWB

Assign students Use of English exercises 1, 2 and 3 on page 57 of their Workbook.

WRITING
A story

→ Student's Book, pages 78–79 SB

Lesson aims

- Focus on language in a story
- Plan and write a story

Lead-in

Play ***Twenty questions***. Ask students to guess the name of a famous artist that you are thinking of by asking up to 20 *yes/no* questions. A *yes* answer earns the questioner the chance to ask another question; a *no* answer means the next student asks a question. If students don't guess the artist after 20 questions, give them the answer.

1 Focus students' attention on the photo. In pairs or as a group, students answer the questions. Elicit answers in open class.

Suggested answers

1 It's very valuable; it might be damaged if people touch it

2 Surveillance, alarms, CCTV cameras, security checks on bags and rucksacks, alarmed doors and windows, vibration sensors, inventory numbers, background checks on security staff, motion-sensitive cameras, etc.

2 Ask students to complete the exercise.

Answers

Students' own answers

3 Ask students to complete the exercise. Elicit answers in open class.

Suggested answers

Title – Yes, it's appropriate – but it could be made more exciting/suspenseful

Main characters – Mickey and Lou are the main characters. Yes, they're believable and interesting.

Setting – It's set in a hotel reception.

Plot – Two thieves are getting ready to steal a valuable vase from a famous art gallery. They are nervous but excited. They have been planning for this moment for a long time and the outcome is very important to their future – they could become very rich or they could go to jail if they are caught.

Suspense – Yes, the thieves are nervous – Mickey's heart is beating fast.

Emotions – Mickey is confident but nervous. They are both excited.

Ending – There is a sense of excitement and the reader wants to know what happens next in the story.

Tenses

Past simple: this is the main narrative tense

Past continuous: a situation in progress at a particular moment

Past perfect and past perfect continuous: for past situations that happened before the main narrative time

Present simple: direct speech

Language

It's fairly formal with elements of appropriate informality. The direct speech sounds authentic and realistic. There is a good variety of tenses and grammatical structures.

OPTIMISE YOUR EXAM

A story

Ask students to read the tips.

- Remind students that a good plot needs a problem that introduces conflict, danger or tension that must be resolved. Students can be inspired by narratives they have read, seen and heard in books and films. However, because there is usually a word limit (in this case 140–190 words), students have to keep the story plot simple and to the point – a few key events and characters is all students have space for.
- Highlight that the story includes the use of direct speech, e.g. *'Stop! Put your hands up in the air!'* This makes texts more interesting to read than a simple narrative of events, and including direct speech shows an examiner that you are confident with punctuation.

For more information on writing stories, refer students to the Writing reference, page 173.

▾ Exam task

4 Ask students to complete the exercise. Discuss answers in open class.

Answers

Students' own answers

5 Plan Ask students to complete the paragraph plan using their notes from Exercise 4. You may want to look at students' plans, if possible, to check them and give advice and suggestions for improvement before students take the next step.

Extra support

First discuss the questions after the task in Exercise 5 in open class. Elicit explanations and ask them to justify their answers. Encourage students to use some of the phrases in Exercise 3. Write some key words and expressions on the board that less confident students can refer back to when they write their story.

6 Write Ask students to write their story in an appropriate style in 140–190 words. Depending on time, it may be a good idea to set this and the subsequent checklist exercise for homework.

7 Check Ask students to complete the checklist before they hand in their story.

Homework OWB

Assign students Writing exercises 1, 2, 3 and 4 on page 58 of their Workbook and Progress check 7 on page 59.

8 The world around us

UNIT AIMS

Exam preparation in Unit 8:

- understand implication in a nature article
- predict alternative ways of saying the same thing
- develop a discussion and express opinions
- understand spelling changes and apply them in a word-formation exercise
- understand prepositions and use them in an open-cloze exercise
- give examples in an article

TEACHER'S PRESENTATION KIT

- *Talk2Me* videos
- Speaking test videos
- Class and Workbook audio
- Workbook pages and answer key

UNIT OVERVIEW

Student's Book / Digital Student's Book SB		Workbook / Online Workbook OWB
LESSON / EXAM TASK	**EXAM SKILLS / LANGUAGE FOCUS**	**CONSOLIDATION**
Reading **Multiple matching**	Understanding attitude and opinion A nature article	Workbook, pp 60–61, Exercises 1, 2, 3 Unit 8, Reading, Exercises 1, 2, 3
Grammar 1	Conditionals (2): second, third and mixed conditionals	Workbook, p 62, Exercises 1, 2, 3 Unit 8, Grammar 1, Exercises 1, 2, 3
Vocabulary	Words connected with *environmental issues* Phrasal verbs Words + prepositions	Workbook, p 63, Exercises 1, 2, 3 Unit 8, Vocabulary, Exercises 1, 2, 3
Listening **Multiple matching**	Predicting and anticipating	Workbook, p 64, Exercises 1, 2, 3 Unit 8, Listening, Exercises 1, 2, 3
Grammar 2	Unreal past and past wishes	Workbook, p 63, Exercises 1, 2 Unit 8, Grammar 2, Exercises 1, 2
Speaking **Discussion**	Qualifying your opinion	Workbook, pp 64–65, Exercises 1, 2 Unit 8, Speaking, Exercises 1, 2
Use of English **Word formation** **Open cloze**	Spelling changes Prepositions	Workbook, p 65, Exercises 1, 2, 3 Unit 8, Use of English, Exercises 1, 2, 3
Writing **An article**	Giving reasons and examples (2)	Workbook, p 66, Exercises 1, 2, 3, 4 Unit 8, Writing, Exercises 1, 2, 3, 4
Progress check	Check language progress for Units 7 and 8	Workbook, p 67, Progress check and Cumulative progress Progress check and Cumulative progress

Additional material

PRESENTATION KIT	TEACHER'S / STUDENT'S RESOURCE CENTRE RC	TEST GENERATOR
Talk2Me video *The reason I say this …*	**Unit 8 worksheets:** *Optimise your grammar* (Standard and Higher), *Optimise your vocabulary* (Standard and Higher), *Talk2Me* video, *Say it right* **Units 7–8 worksheets:** CLIL, Culture, Everyday English (TRC only), Grammar communication (TRC only)	Unit Test 8 (Standard and Higher) Progress Test (Standard and Higher)

READING
Multiple matching | A nature article

→ Student's Book, pages 80–81

Lesson aims
- Focus on multiple matching
- Practise a multiple-matching exam task

Lead-in
Write the unit title ***The world around us*** on the board and elicit what the title refers to (*all the things we see, hear and experience in our everyday lives*). Elicit ideas from different students about how they would personally describe the world around them. Ask what they feel the most significant things are. Focus students' attention on the photos on pages 80 and 81, and ask students what they think the lesson is going to be about (*nature and the environment*).

1 In pairs or groups, students answer the questions. Elicit answers in open class and try to develop a class discussion.

Answers
Students' own answers

2 Ask students to complete the exercise quickly. Check answers in open class.

Answers
A 4 **B** 1 **C** 3 **D** 5
2 is not needed.

Extra support
Elicit the key phrases in the texts that helped students decide on their answers.

Answers
A *If I'd known more about the history before going, I'd have got more out of it.*
C *It's vital that we explore ways in which our society can develop at the same time as preserving the spectacular natural resources we have.*
B *... the reef is something we have to preserve very carefully for future generations ... past mistakes and a changing climate mean that parts of the reef are struggling to recover.*
D *It gave us some insight into what their lives were like.*

3 Ask students to complete the exercise. Elicit answers from different students around the class.

Answers
1 I found it **2** Not surprisingly, **3** For me, To my mind, **4** my own view is that **5** There's no doubt that

OPTIMISE YOUR EXAM

Multiple matching
Ask students to read the tips.
- This type of task focuses on detail, opinion, specific information and implication (things that are implied or suggested in the text). Remind students to use paraphrasing of the ideas – retelling the information without changing the original idea – rather than individual words in the questions to help them identify the answer in the text.
- Remind students that often exact word matches are a trap. If a key word in the text is exactly the same as the word in the question, students should be careful. It's almost certainly not the answer. They should also be careful of partial matches and find sentences in the text that match **all** the key words.

▼ Exam task

4 2.13 **Note: The reading text is also available on the audio CD. You may want to have students listen and read the text before doing the exam task.**
Ask students to complete the exercise. Check answers in open class. Elicit the sentences in the texts that match the questions to help train students to check their choices carefully.

Answers
1 C (*To my mind, national parks are there not only for the conservation of wildlife, but to inspire us to lead better lives.*)
2 B (*The Great Barrier Reef has become one of the global symbols of just how fragile nature can be.*)
3 D (*... but my own view is that it's the ordinary aspects of everyday life that tell us a lot more.*)
4 A (*If I'd known more about the history before going, I'd have got more out of it.*)
5 B (*The diversity of life in the area is breathtaking!*)
6 D (*The park is also home to jaguars and other animals. ... It gave us some insight into what their lives were like.*)
7 A (*... it was a relief to go on a 'wild' tour, which takes you to some of the less-developed parts of the cave system.*)
8 D (*We often look at constructions and monuments and think they represent what a culture was like, but ... it's the ordinary aspects of everyday life that tell us a lot more.*)
9 B (*If we had done something like that years ago, the reef would be in a much better state now!*)
10 C (*... the struggle of the wildebeest to survive in dangerous conditions ... reminded me of the daily struggle to survive that many people in my country face.*)

5 Ask students to complete the exercise. Elicit definitions from different students around the class.

Answers

fragile (adj): easy to damage
insight (n): a chance to understand something or learn more about it
inspire (v): give someone the enthusiasm to do or create something
laid on (phr v): provided
minimise (v): reduce something harmful to the smallest amount or degree
preserve (v): take care of a place to prevent it from being harmed or destroyed
striking (adj): attracting your interest or attention because of some unusual feature
tedious (adj): boring and continuing for too long

Optional extension 2.13

Play the recorded text and ask students to underline the different adjectives in the text. Ask students to define the more difficult words, and highlight that if students use a wide range of more complex vocabulary when they write descriptions, they will earn higher marks in exams.

Answers

extensive, underground, impressive, incredible, tedious, national, wild, less-developed, small, real, early, local, wanted, fresh, epic, dangerous, daily, better, fantastic, natural, difficult, living, vital, spectacular, global, fragile, future, breathtaking, exciting, marine, human, different, stunning, past, changing, amazing, Mayan, major, awesome, striking, fascinating, ordinary, everyday

THINK | RESEARCH | **CULTURE** | LEARN | ME

Ask students to complete the task.

If you have access to the internet, students can research information in class. Alternatively, they could prepare this for homework and present their information at the start of the next lesson. Students can vote on which national park they would most like to visit.

Homework OWB

Assign students Reading exercises 1, 2 and 3 on pages 60–61 of their Workbook.

GRAMMAR 1
Conditionals (2): second, third and mixed conditionals

→ Student's Book, page 82 SB

Lesson aims

- Understand the correct usage of second, third and mixed conditionals
- Practise using second, third and mixed conditionals

Lead-in

Divide the class into two teams, A and B. Choose a word from the previous lesson and say it to Team A for them to spell it, letter by letter. If they spell the word correctly, they score one point. However, if at any point they say an incorrect letter, the part-word is handed over to Team B (and back again if they make an error). This continues until one team finishes the word and wins the point. The team with the most points wins the game.

Suggested words: *wealth, Serengeti, crocodiles, wildebeest, scenery, tedious, impressive, stunning, unfortunately, courts.*

Grammar in context

Ask students to complete the task. Refer them to the *Remember* box if they need help. Check the answer in open class.

Ask students to think of personalised sentences using the second, third and mixed conditionals. Elicit a few examples around the class.

Remind students that they can find more information in the Grammar reference, Unit 8, page 156.

Answers

Hypothetical events

1 Ask students to complete the exercise. Ask them to compare their answers in pairs before you check them in open class.

Answers

1 b **2** a **3** b **4** b **5** b **6** b

Extra support

Elicit the type of conditional in each sentence.

Answers

1 second conditional **2** third conditional **3** second conditional **4** second conditional **5** mixed conditional **6** third conditional

2 Ask students to complete the exercise. Check answers in open class. Accept all sensible suggestions.

Suggested answers

1 what would you do
2 what would you have done instead / what would you be doing instead
3 how would your life have been different / how would your life be different
4 what would you like to see
5 would you have started recycling years ago
6 what (animal) would you be

3 Ask students to complete the exercise. Check answers in open class.

Answers

1 wanted **2** would have survived **3** hadn't brought **4** would be **5** had been aware **6** wouldn't be **7** had seen **8** would have learnt **9** Had **10** wouldn't have been saved

Mixed ability

Give less confident students the answers in a jumbled order (*hadn't brought, would have learnt, wanted, wouldn't have been saved, would be, had been aware, wouldn't be, had seen, Had, would have survived*). Challenge more advanced students who finish early to write two or three comprehension questions on the text in Exercise 3. When everyone has finished, they can read them out to test the class.

Homework OWB

Assign students Grammar 1 exercises 1, 2 and 3 on page 62 of their Workbook.

VOCABULARY

Topic vocabulary | Phrasal verbs | Word patterns

→ Student's Book, page 83 SB

Lesson aims

- Understand the correct usage of:
  - words connected with environmental issues
  - phrasal verbs
  - words + prepositions

Lead-in

Draw a table on the board.

	What's going wrong?	What are the solutions?
oceans		
forests		
deserts		
animals		
weather		

In pairs, students complete the table. Students then change partners and share what they wrote. Elicit answers in open class.

Words connected with *environmental issues*

1 2.14 Ask students to complete the exercise. Play the audio for students to listen and check their answers.

Answers/Audioscript

1 global warming **2** climate change **3** greenhouse effect **4** toxic waste **5** carbon footprint **6** renewable energy **7** sustainable development **8** ozone layer

Refer students to the Vocabulary reference, page 166, for more information on topic vocabulary.

2 Ask students to complete the exercise. Check answers in open class.

Answers

1 climate change / global warming **2** carbon footprint **3** sustainable development **4** toxic waste **5** global warming **6** renewable energy **7** ozone layer **8** greenhouse effect

Extra support

Write *global warming* in the centre of the board. Elicit which are the problems and which are the solutions in Exercise 1 and write them on the board.

Play the audio from Exercise 1 again for students to note down the main stress in the phrases, i.e. which sound is longer, louder and is said more clearly with a change in pitch. Ask students to come up and mark the stress pattern on the board. Drill in open class.

Answers

glo̲bal wa̲rming (problem), cli̲mate cha̲nge (problem), gree̲nhouse effe̲ct (problem), to̲xic wa̲ste (problem), ca̲rbon foo̲tprint (problem), rene̲wable e̲nergy (solution), susta̲inable deve̲lopment (solution), o̲zone la̲yer

Phrasal verbs

3 2.15 Ask students to complete the exercise. Play the audio for students to listen and check their answers.

Answers/Audioscript

1 Some animal species *died out* due to human activities.

2 People *are calling for* urgent action on climate change.

3 Will we just keep using oil until it all *runs out*?

4 We all have a responsibility to help *clean up* our beaches.

5 If we're not careful, our actions are going to *wipe out* the wild elephant.

6 I think we should *do away with* cars that produce lots of pollution in city centres to protect the environment.

7 When we *chop down* trees, we remove the natural habitat of a number of species.

8 Don't just *throw away* your old bottles. Recycle them!

Extra support

Individually, students write personalised sentences with the phrasal verbs from Exercise 3. In pairs, they then read out their sentences without saying the phrasal verb (they could substitute this for a 'beep' sound) for their partner to guess.

Refer students to the Vocabulary reference, page 166, for more information on phrasal verbs.

Fast finishers

Ask students to say if the phrasal verbs are separable or non-separable.

Answers

Separable: 4, 5, 7, 8 Inseparable: 1, 2, 3, 6

Words + prepositions

4 2.16 Ask students to complete the exercise. Play the audio for students to listen and check their answers.

Answers/Audioscript

1 Water pollution can be *harmful to* fish and animals that live along the river.

2 The Sumatran rhino is *threatened by* hunters.

3 Without the ozone layer, we would be *exposed to* UV rays that can cause cancer.

4 Do you think we do enough to *protect* animals *from* illegal activity?

5 Which countries will be most *affected by* climate change?

6 Using drinking water to water the garden is a *waste of* natural resources!

Refer students to the Vocabulary reference, page 166, for more information on word patterns.

THINK | RESEARCH | CULTURE | **LEARN** | ME

Ask students to complete the task. Ask them to present what they have learnt in open class.

Homework OWB

Assign students Vocabulary exercises 1, 2 and 3 on page 63 of their Workbook.

LISTENING
Multiple matching

→ Student's Book, page 84 SB

Lesson aims

- Focus on multiple matching
- Practise a multiple-matching exam task

Lead-in

In pairs, students try to make the longest chain of sentences using the second conditional. Start with an example, such as *If I won the lottery, …* then ask a student to complete the sentence, e.g. *… I'd travel around the world*. Ask another student to continue, e.g. *If I travelled around the world, …* then point to another student to complete this sentence, e.g. *… I'd visit Australia*.

Write two more half sentences on the board for students to continue in pairs:

If I met my favourite film star, …

If I found €500 in the street, …

When students have finished, elicit some conditional chains from different pairs around the class.

1 In pairs or as a group, students ask and answer the questions. Elicit answers from different students around the class and accept all sensible suggestions.

Suggested answers

1 There is a photo of wind turbines and a photo of solar panels. They are sources of renewable energy.

2 Hydropower (wave power), geothermal energy (thermal energy made and stored in the earth), bioenergy (biomass from plants), etc.

2 Ask students to complete the exercise. Check answers in open class.

Answers

1 G **2** D **3** F **4** H

Extra support

Elicit the synonyms and related phrases that helped students decide on their answers.

Answers

1 grateful – G thankful

2 worried about – D concerns

3 energy, test – F energy, show that I knew

4 People didn't seem to know very much – H people needed to be educated

3 Ask students to complete the exercise. Elicit ideas in open class and accept any sensible answers.

Suggested answers

1 Statement A ('I loved it when I saw people following my suggestions.')

2 Statement B ('It was hard, but I was glad when I managed it.')

3 Statement C ('I was concerned that we might not have any effect.')

4 Statement E ('I did some things that I didn't think I was capable of doing.')

OPTIMISE YOUR EXAM

Multiple matching

Ask students to read the tips.

- In listening exams, where speech can be quite fast, this strategy helps students identify relevant points, reject irrelevant information and guess unknown words or phrases. Students usually have 30 seconds before the first listening to think of alternative ways of saying the same thing.
- Students often make the mistake of writing the first answer they hear. Remind them to listen for gist – the key words – the first time and build a general image in their mind of the opinion and attitude of the speakers. During the second listening, remind students that they should listen for any key words and synonyms and eliminate the three options they don't need.

▼ Exam task

4 2.17 Play the track for students to listen and complete the exercise. Don't check answers at this stage, as students will listen again to check in Exercise 5.

5 2.17 Play the track again for students to listen and check their answers to Exercise 4. Elicit answers in open class and discuss the specific clues that helped them choose them.

Answers

1 G (*The family I stayed with … really looked after me well and I was so grateful …*)

2 A (*It was really satisfying when the school governors agreed and the project went ahead.*)

3 E (*I learnt a lot about myself and what I'm capable of*)

4 B (*but I pushed myself and was really glad that I met the challenge.*)

5 H (*I wish more people knew about geothermal energy. If they were better informed … local people were largely ignorant …*)

Optional extension

Play the track again for students to listen and answer the following questions about the different projects in the audio in Exercise 4.

Where does the project take place? What does it involve?

Ask students to compare their answers in pairs before you elicit them in open class.

Suggested answers

1 Nepal, Plan small hydropower stations to meet the energy needs of local people

2 At school, Asked for ideas to make the school to go green. They suggested solar panels to provide heating and hot water by renewable energy.

3 Peru, WindAid builds wind turbines to provide clean energy to communities who have never had electricity.

4 Off the coast where the speaker lives, Explaining the advantages of building a wave energy farm

5 The north of England, Interviewing local people and finding out about their attitudes towards geothermal energy

THINK | RESEARCH | CULTURE | LEARN | ME

In pairs or small groups, students discuss the questions. Elicit ideas in open class.

Homework

Assign students Listening exercises 1, 2 and 3 on page 64 of their Workbook.

OWB

GRAMMAR 2
Unreal past and past wishes

→ Student's Book, page 85 SB

Lesson aims

- Understand the correct grammar to talk about the unreal past and past wishes
- Practise using the correct grammar to talk about the unreal past and past wishes

Lead-in

Ask students to brainstorm vocabulary related to the environment. Write *NATURE AND THE ENVIRONMENT* in the centre of the board, with circles around it with these subheadings: *Words related to animals*, *Environmental problems*, *Environmental solutions*, *Nature*. Write all students' suggestions on the board, in the appropriate circles.

Suggested answers

Words related to animals: dodo, wildebeest, crocodile, jaguar, species, extinct, wildlife, wild creatures, elephant, rhino, etc.

Environmental problems: global warming, climate change, greenhouse effect, toxic waste, carbon footprint, ozone layer, dangerous ultraviolet light, pollution, water pollution, UV rays, etc.

Environmental solutions: conservation, cultivation, renewable energy, sustainable development, wind power, wave power, recycle, etc.

Nature: reef, cave, rock formation, national park, natural resources, preserve, weather patterns, habitat, beach, etc.

Grammar in context

Ask students to complete the task. Refer them to the *Remember* box if they need help. Check answers in open class.

Remind students that they can find more information in the Grammar reference, Unit 8, page 157.

Answers

1 present **2** present **3** past

1 Ask students to complete the exercise. Check answers in open class.

Answers

1 stopped **2** had **3** burnt **4** had known **5** were/was **6** tried

2 Ask students to complete the exercise. Ask them to compare their answers in pairs before you check them in open class.

Answers

1 I'd rather you didn't throw your litter on the ground.
2 I wish I hadn't bought such a large motorbike.
3 It's high time we manufactured more electric cars in order to help the environment.
4 If I could wave a magic wand and solve climate change, I would.
5 It's (high) time people realised that we have to use more renewable energy.
6 Would you rather people took the threat to the environment more seriously?

Mixed ability

Check the answers to Exercise 2.

Divide the class into A and B pairs, mixing up higher and lower level students. Tell Student A to read out the first sentence in Exercise 2 and say the word given. Student B tries to reformulate the sentence, without looking at their notes.

If the answer is correct, Student A reads out the next question and Student B tries to reformulate the sentence.

If Student B makes a mistake, Student B reads out the questions, starting from question 1, and Student A tries to reformulate it.

When Student A makes a mistake, Student B can try again, starting from 1.

The aim of the game is for both students to complete all the sentence transformations in one go without making any mistakes.

3 Ask students to complete the exercise. Check answers in open class.

Answers

1 got **2** went **3** had **4** had started **5** could **6** thought **7** provided **8** faced

Fast finishers

Ask fast finishers to write one or two comprehension questions on the text in Exercise 3 to ask the class when everyone has finished.

THINK | RESEARCH | CULTURE | LEARN | ME

In pairs or small groups, students discuss the questions. Elicit ideas in open class.

Homework OWB

Assign students Grammar 2 exercises 1 and 2 on page 63 of their Workbook.

SPEAKING
Discussion

→ Student's Book, page 86 SB

Lesson aims

- Focus on developing a discussion and expressing opinions
- Practise having a discussion

The *Talk2Me* video in this unit focuses on environmental problems. People discuss how these problems can be prevented and who is responsible. Students answer some questions and then listen out for useful phrases for giving reasons and examples. The video can be used in one of two ways:

Flipped classroom

Flipped classroom option

Using this approach, students watch the video and complete the exercises for homework. This prepares students for the speaking lesson by introducing them to the topic and the key phrases to use in the exam task. Teachers who use this method will find they have more class time to spend on activating the target language and developing fluency for the final task.

***Talk2Me* worksheet**

Ask students to also complete the *Talk2Me* worksheet on the Resource Centre for more detailed comprehension exercises and more practice of the key phrases.

Classroom option

1 Ask students to spend a minute or two reading the questions. Play the *Talk2Me* video for students to complete the exercise. Play the video again, if necessary, before checking their answers.

2 Play the *Talk2Me* video again, so students tick the phrases in the *Phrase expert* box. Pause the video from time to time if necessary. Check answers in open class.

***Talk2Me* worksheet**

Ask students to also complete the *Talk2Me* worksheet on the Resource Centre for more detailed comprehension exercises and more practice of the key phrases.

Answers

The transcript and answer key for the *Talk2Me* video exercises and Worksheet can be found on the Teacher's Resource Centre.

Lead-in

Write these phrases related to the environment on the board. In pairs, students decide which one is the odd one out.

green – efficient – environmentally friendly – nature-friendly
to conserve – to threaten – to protect – to preserve
sustainable – economical – renewable – recyclable
Siberian tiger – African lion – American bison – Australian koala

Answers

efficient (all the others are synonyms of *eco-friendly*)

to threaten (all the others are related to protecting the environment)

economical (all the others avoid pollution and protect the environment)

koala (all the others are endangered species)

3 In pairs or groups, students ask and answer the questions. Elicit answers from different students around the class.

Answers

Students' own answers

4 Ask students to complete the exercise. Check answers in open class.

Answers

1 addition **2** Having **3** well **4** importantly **5** said **6** why

5 In pairs, students complete the exercise. Encourage them to use phrases from the *Phrase expert* box. Elicit ideas and opinions in open class.

Extra support

Ask students to write their choices before doing this as a speaking activity and remind them that it is important for them to develop their ideas by giving reasons or examples.

OPTIMISE YOUR EXAM

Discussion

Ask students to read the tips.

- Students can score points for their interactive skills if they add to what their partner has already said with expressions such as, *I like your idea of … because …* or *What you said about … is really interesting due to the fact that …* This will show the examiner that you are really listening to your partner and collaborating effectively. Elicit some examples they can remember for giving reasons and examples, e.g. *because, due to the fact that, The reason why … is, The reason for me never choosing X is …, so ….*
- Students can follow a simple format when discussing their opinions on a subject:
  Introduction – Expression of own opinion – Expression of a contrasting opinion (plus a statement of why this argument is different) – Conclusion. If they use words or phrases to signal a constrasting opinion, students help the examiner and their fellow candidate(s) follow their argument.

Exam task

6 In groups of three, students complete the task. Ask students to use the words and phrases in the *Phrase expert* box.

Walk round and monitor students, noting down errors and good use of language to go over in a feedback session at the end of the activity.

Mixed ability

Ask examiners to listen and use this checklist to help them make notes on the candidates' discussion.

Did Students A & B ask for their partner's opinion?
Did Students A & B respond to their partner's comments?
Did they take turns to speak?
Did Students A & B use different expressions to give their opinions?
Did Students A & B develop their ideas by giving reasons and examples?

If weaker students take the role of examiner in the first round, the pressure is taken off them to produce language spontaneously, but they can prepare something to say at the end, which will provide a sense of achievement. After the discussion, ask examiners to give feedback to the pair.

SAY IT RIGHT

Stress in opinion phrases

TRC

For the *Say it right* pronunciation activity and instructions, go to the Teacher's Resource Centre.

Homework

OWB

Assign students Speaking exercises 1 and 2 on pages 64–65 of their Workbook.

USE OF ENGLISH

Word formation | Open cloze

→ Student's Book, page 87

SB

Lesson aims

- Focus on word formation and practise a word-formation exam task
- Focus on open cloze and practise an open-cloze exam task

Lead-in

Play ***First to five*** to revise vocabulary from the unit. Say different word categories (e.g. types of renewable energy sources, animals, words connected with climate change, phrasal verbs connected to the environment). Small groups compete to think of five words or phrases for each one. When they have five, they shout 'First to five'. Check their words, giving one point for each correct answer. The group with the most points wins.

1 Ask students to complete the exercise. Check answers by asking different students around the class.

Answers

1 tradition (traditional), industry (industrial), benefit (beneficial), origin (original) **2** storm (stormy), live (alive)

OPTIMISE YOUR EXAM

Word formation

Ask students to read the tip.

- Encourage students to trust their feelings for the language and write the word that sounds instinctively correct. Students often lose marks because they change answers at the last moment.
- Highlight that it's good practice to go through this type of task asking themselves *What category of word?* and *Positive or negative?*. If students train themselves to always be thinking in these terms, it will make word formation tasks a lot easier for them.

Refer students to the Vocabulary reference, page 166, for more information on word formation.

Exam task

2 Ask students to complete the exercise. Ask them to compare their answers in pairs before you check them in open class.

Answers

1 traditional **2** extraordinary **3** stormy **4** industrial **5** significant **6** beneficial **7** originality **8** living

Optional extension

In pairs or small groups, students have three minutes to think of as many words as they can based on the words in Exercise 2. Remind them to use prefixes, suffixes, adverbs, different verb forms, etc. to form more words.

Stop the clock and ask students to count up their words. Ask the winning pair or group to write their words on the board.

Suggested answers

tradition(s): traditionally, traditional, traditionalist, traditionalism
ordinary: ordinarily, extraordinary, extraordinarily, ordinariness
storm(s): stormy, stormily, storms, storming
industry: industries, industrial, industrially, industrious
signify: signifies, signified, (in)significant, significance(s), (in)significantly, signifying
benefit(s): benefitted, beneficial, beneficially, benefitting, benefaction, benefactor
origin(s): originate, originated, (un)original, originally, originality, originating, originator
live(s): lived, life, lifeless, alive, living, outlive, relive, outliving, reliving, lively, liveliness

3 Ask students to complete the exercise. Check answers in open class.

Answers

1 3, 6 **2** 8 **3** 4, 5 **4** 1, 7

OPTIMISE YOUR EXAM

Open cloze

Ask students to read the tips.

- Prepositions are usually followed by objects in prepositional phrases. They can also be used to indicate time, place, frequency, duration, reason, manner, or to show contrast.
- Remind students to read the whole sentence. The answer required for the space may be dependent on a word or reference many words before or after it.
- Students should not leave the answer sheet blank for any question. If they don't know the correct answer, they should always make a guess.

Exam task

4 Ask students to complete the exercise. Check answers in open class.

Answers

1 would **2** carbon **3** for **4** to **5** by **6** away **7** could **8** time

Fast finishers

Ask fast finishers to write one or two comprehension questions on the text in Exercise 4 to ask the class when everyone has finished.

Homework

OWB

Assign students Use of English exercises 1, 2 and 3 on page 65 of their Workbook.

WRITING

An article

→ Student's Book, pages 88–89 SB

Lesson aims

- Focus on language for an article
- Plan and write an article

Lead-in

Write the word *ENVIRONMENTALIST* on the board. In pairs, students race to make as many words as they can from this word in three minutes. Their words should have three letters or more.

Suggested answers: *mental, mint, list, environment, viral, mean, meal, mist, vote, star, vine, vein, vision, venal, malt, melt, reel, real, rate, rote, ran, roam, role,* etc.

1 Focus students' attention on the photo. In pairs or as a group, students answer the questions. Elicit answers in open class.

Suggested answers

1 Children are cleaning up a beach with the help of an adult.

2 Students' own answers

2 Students complete the exercise. Check answers in open class.

Answers

1 by referring to their own experience (*If you're anything like me …*)

2 Two, *The first thing we should consider …*, *Another great way …*

3 *So, I would …*

3 Ask students to complete the exercise. Check answers in open class.

Answers

1 *For example,*

2 *This includes …*

Other phrases: *One example of this is …, for instance, such as, like*

4 Ask students to complete the exercise. Check answers in open class.

Answers

1 due to the fact that **2** as

Other phrases: because, because of, since

OPTIMISE YOUR EXAM

An article

Ask students to read the tips.

- Remind students that examples are used to illustrate and drive an argument and should offer detail and evidence. In Exercise 3, students looked at a variety of linking words and phrases for giving examples. This will help them show clear and logical relationships between their arguments and examples in their writing. Point out to students that a lack of transitions between examples, e.g. over-repetition of *for example*, will not gain them any points in a writing exam.
- Ask students to put themselves in the examiner's shoes. Ask them to imagine that they have 50 articles to mark and they are feeling a bit frustrated after having marked some boring texts. Elicit what will impress an examiner apart from good spelling, grammar and punctuation: *real-life examples, a great introduction, strong opening sentences that tell the reader what the paragraph is going to be about, clear and logical progression of ideas, good pronoun referencing (not repeating the same noun again and again), a conclusive ending*, etc.

For more information on writing articles, refer students to the Writing reference, page 169.

Exam task

5 Ask students to complete the exercise. Elicit ideas in open class.

Answers

Students' own answers

Extra support

Discuss students' answers in open class. Write some key words and expressions on the board that less confident students can refer back to when they write their article.

6 **Plan** Ask students to complete the paragraph plan using their notes from Exercise 5. You may want to look at students' plans, if possible, to check them and give advice and suggestions for improvement before students take the next step.

7 **Write** Ask students to write their article in an appropriate style in 140–190 words. Depending on time, it may be a good idea to set this and the subsequent checklist exercise for homework.

8 **Check** Ask students to complete the checklist before they hand in their article.

Homework OWB

Assign students Writing exercises 1, 2, 3 and 4 on page 66 of their Workbook and Progress check 8 on page 67.

Answers PROGRESS CHECK Units 7–8

Exercise 1

1 originally **2** extraordinary **3** equipment **4** accessible **5** patience **6** significantly **7** traditional **8** exhibition

Exercise 2

1 had told **2** found **3** took **4** invented **5** have happened **6** do / be doing **7** had listened **8** have passed **9** stopped **10** paid

Exercise 3

1 out **2** out **3** up **4** away **5** down **6** on **7** up **8** out **9** for **10** up

Exercise 4

1 <u>Even</u> – Even though / Although / Though **2** <u>enough old</u> – old enough **3** <u>somewhere</u> – anywhere **4** ✓ **5** <u>don't</u> – didn't **6** ✓ **7** ✓ **8** <u>me</u> – myself **9** <u>such</u> – so **10** <u>himself</u> – themselves

Exercise 5

1 die out because of / die out due to **2** she hadn't / had not let **3** such a hot day that / such hot weather that **4** harmful to **5** if you had not / hadn't arrived **6** (finally) turned out to be

9 A word to the wise

UNIT AIMS

Exam preparation in Unit 9:

- understand implication in a story extract
- listen for key information in an interview
- talk about personal experiences in an interview task
- understand and apply spelling changes in a word-formation exercise
- read for gist in a multiple-choice cloze exercise
- use adjectives and adverbs in a story

TEACHER'S PRESENTATION KIT

- *Talk2Me* videos
- Speaking test videos
- Class and Workbook audio
- Workbook pages and answer key

UNIT OVERVIEW

Student's Book / Digital Student's Book SB		Workbook / Online Workbook OWB
LESSON / EXAM TASK	**EXAM SKILLS / LANGUAGE FOCUS**	**CONSOLIDATION**
Reading **Multiple choice**	Understanding references (2) An extract from a novel	Workbook, pp 68–69, Exercises 1, 2, 3 Unit 9, Reading, Exercises 1, 2, 3
Grammar 1	The passive	Workbook, p 70, Exercises 1, 2 Unit 9, Grammar 1, Exercises 1, 2
Vocabulary	Words connected with *literature* Phrasal verbs Collocations with *say*, *speak* and *tell*	Workbook, pp 70–71, Exercises 1, 2, 3 Unit 9, Vocabulary, Exercises 1, 2, 3
Listening **True/false/not stated**	Recognising difference in meaning	Workbook, p 72, Exercises 1, 2 Unit 9, Listening, Exercises 1, 2
Grammar 2	The causative, direct and indirect objects	Workbook, p 71, Exercises 1, 2 Unit 9, Grammar 2, Exercises 1, 2
Speaking **Interview**	Talking about experiences	Workbook, pp 72–73, Exercises 1, 2 Unit 9, Speaking, Exercises 1, 2
Use of English **Word formation** **Multiple-choice cloze**	Spelling Reading for general understanding	Workbook, p 73, Exercises 1, 2 Unit 9, Use of English, Exercises 1, 2
Writing **A story**	Using descriptive language	Workbook, p 74, Exercises 1, 2, 3 Unit 9, Writing, Exercises 1, 2, 3
		Workbook, p 75, Progress check and Cumulative progress Progress check and Cumulative progress

Additional material

PRESENTATION KIT	TEACHER'S / STUDENT'S RESOURCE CENTRE RC	TEST GENERATOR
Talk2Me video *Looking back now …*	**Unit 9 worksheets:** *Optimise your grammar* (Standard and Higher), *Optimise your vocabulary* (Standard and Higher), *Talk2Me* video, *Say it right* **Units 9–10 worksheets:** CLIL, Culture, Everyday English (TRC only), Grammar communication (TRC only)	Unit Test 9 (Standard and Higher)

READING
Multiple choice | An extract from a novel

→ Student's Book, pages 92–93 SB

Lesson aims

- Focus on multiple choice
- Practise a multiple-choice exam task

Lead-in

Elicit the meaning of the word *wise* in the unit title and the difference between *intelligent* and *wise* (*intelligent* = having the ability to learn and understand things easily; *wise* = having or showing the ability to make good judgements, based on a deep understanding and experience of life). Elicit the meaning of the unit title ***A word to the wise***. (*You don't have to explain everything in full to a wise person. This expression is often used before a warning. e.g. A word to the wise, the new teacher doesn't like students who arrive late.*) Draw students' attention to the photo and ask them what they think the lesson is going to be about (*Language and culture / Literature*).

1 In pairs or as a group, students answer the questions. Elicit answers in open class and try to develop a class discussion.

Suggested answers

1 Students' own answers

2 (a) Advantages of reading books electronically: It is more convenient, you can carry many books with you, they are easy to buy, they are cheaper, you can adjust the size of the text and some e-books have links to further information, audio or video.

Disadvantages: you have to buy a reader and you need to recharge the battery.

(b) Advantages of reading books on paper: Paper books look and feel nice and you can exchange them with friends or resell them.

Disadvantages: they take up a lot of space in your house, some books are very heavy.

2 2.18 Ask students to read through the gapped sentences before you play the audio, so they can think about what type of word or phrase might be needed for each gap. Play the audio for students to complete the sentences. Play the audio a second time for them to check their answers. Ask students to compare their answers in pairs before you check them in open class.

Answers

1 *Vanity Fair* is a novel set in the **(early) 1800s** and it includes **romance** and **adventure**.

2 Amelia is kind but is also an **innocent** person. Her family is **rich** but Becky's family is **poor**. Becky is a *selfish* person.

3 Becky goes to **teach** and take care of Sir Pitt Crawley's daughters. She secretly marries Captain Rawdon Crawley who is Sir Pitt's **son**.

4 George Osborne is a family friend of the **Sedley** family and he likes **Amelia**.

5 The Sedleys lose all their **money**.

6 George's friend Dobbin encourages him to **marry** Amelia, but because she is now poor, George's father leaves him no **money** after his death.

3 Ask students to complete the exercise. Set a time limit of two minutes to encourage students to do this quickly. Check answers in open class.

Answers

1 isn't an easy person to comprehend **2** with borrowed money **3** wouldn't have contact with her nephew **4** unhappy

OPTIMISE YOUR EXAM

Multiple choice

Ask students to read the tips.

- Understanding implication is what we mean by 'reading between the lines', because the suggestion, rather than the actual words, carries the meaning. An inference is an implied meaning that is not directly stated but can be deduced from clues.
- Writers often imply information in texts: a point that makes us think and taps our imagination has a greater impact on us than one that is obviously stated.
- Remind students that after they have located the specific part of the text that relates to a question, they should read carefully **before** and **after** that part to look for clues that will help them deduce the meaning.

▾ Exam task

4 2.19 **Note: The reading text is also available on the audio CD. You may want to have students listen and read the text before doing the exam task.**

Ask students to complete the exercise. Check answers in open class and elicit the evidence.

Answers

1 B (*'Portrait of a large gentleman on an elephant!' he cried. 'Who will pay twenty guineas? Fifteen guineas? Five?'* As no-one offered money for the painting we can deduce that no-one wanted it.)

2 D (*What can he want with a piano? He can't play.*)

3 D (*Everything had been bought on credit.*)

4 B (*Miss Crawley was still refusing to see her nephew, but he had not given up hope. One day she would forgive him …*)

5 A (*Mr Sedley had bought a great deal of stock on the French stock market. Then Napoleon returned from Elba and the stockbroker lost all his money.*)

6 C (*Amelia knew that George Osborne had bought it [the piano] for her.*)

5 Ask students to complete the exercise. Check answers in open class.

Answers

a considerable amount (phr): a great deal
enormously (adv): extremely
good-natured (adj): kind
heartless (adj): cruel
presents (n): gifts
sad (adj): upset
savings (n): money you have saved
shouted (v): called
sweet (adj): having a gentle heart

Fast finishers

Ask students to think of more synonyms for the words in the box.

Answers

a considerable amount (phr): a lot, a large quantity
enormously (adv): very, by a large amount, a lot, greatly
good-natured (adj): friendly, nice, warm
heartless (adj): unkind, mean, insensitive, inconsiderate
sad (adj): unhappy
shouted (v): exclaimed, screamed, yelled, called out
sweet (adj): kind, gentle, sensitive, nice, empathetic

Cultural note

William Makepeace Thackeray was born in India in 1811. He was educated in boarding schools in England and went to the University of Cambridge. When he got married at the age of 25, he had to find a regular income, so he became a journalist. By 1840 he had achieved some fame with two travel books, but it was in 1847, when the classic novel *Vanity Fair* was published, that he began to experience great success and fortune.

Napoleon Bonaparte was a military general who became the emperor of France. As a general, he led several successful campaigns during the Revolutionary Wars and became known as a great commander. As Napoleon I, he was emperor from 1804 until 1814. After an unsuccessful campaign in Russia, he was sent into exile on the island of Elba. In March 1815, he escaped and went back to Paris, where he triumphantly returned to power. However, this was short-lived. He was defeated by Wellington at the Battle of Waterloo in June 1815 and sent to the island of St Helena. There he remained until his death in 1821.

Optional extension 2.19

Play the recorded text and ask students to underline words or phrases in the text that they don't fully understand. If dictionaries or internet access are available, let students research the vocabulary they have highlighted. Alternatively, this stage could be set as homework. Have a feedback session in open class and ask students to share some of the items they chose and to explain what they mean.

Optional extension

Write the following on the board: *Many books are turned into films. Some people say the book is always better than the film.*

Ask students to discuss the statement in open class. Invite them to think of examples where this is true or not and to decide whether they agree with the statement.

Homework

OWB

Assign students Reading exercises 1, 2 and 3 on pages 68–69 of their Workbook.

GRAMMAR 1
The passive

→ Student's Book, page 94 SB

Lesson aims

- Understand the correct usage of the passive
- Practise using the passive

Lead-in

In pairs, students write down as many answers as they can in one minute.

Books that have been written by J.K. Rowling

Songs that have been sung by Ed Sheeran

Films that have been directed by Steven Spielberg

After each minute, see which pair has the most answers. Check answers in open class, modelling the passive, e.g. *Was* The Lord of the Rings *written by J.K. Rowling?* to see how well students know the passive voice.

Grammar in context

Ask students to complete the task. Refer them to the *Remember* box if they need help. Check answers in open class.

Remind students that they can find more information in the Grammar reference, Unit 9, page 157.

Answers

1 sold **2** bought **3** been

1 Ask students to complete the exercise. Check answers in open class. Point out both possible answers in 1 and 2.

Answers

1 in/with **2** of/from **3** as **4** to **5** that

Fast finishers

Ask fast finishers to underline examples of the passive in the sentences.

Answers

1 'The roads <u>are covered with</u> (or 'in') snow!'
2 'What is this box <u>made of</u>?'
3 'He<u>'s been described</u> as the father of modern poetry,'
4 'This brilliant book <u>was given</u> to me by my best friend,'
5 'It<u>'s often said</u> that Shakespeare is the greatest playwright of all time,'

2 Ask students to complete the exercise. Check answers in open class.

Answers

1 used **2** Was **3** hasn't been translated **4** said

Optional extension

Students write the following on six pieces of paper: a song, the singer of the song, a film, the director of the film, a book, the writer of the book.

They put the pieces of paper with the people's names on in one envelope and the other pieces of paper in another envelope.

Students take it in turns to take a piece of paper from each envelope and try to make a true passive sentence, e.g. Feeling Happy *wasn't sung by Leonardo DiCaprio.*

If a student gets a matching pair and makes a correct passive sentence, they keep the pair.

3 Ask students to look at the photo. Elicit the meaning of the expression *poetry slam* or ask students to skim the text to find the meaning.

Ask students to complete the exercise. Ask them to compare their answers in pairs before you check them in open class.

Answers

1 were (first) performed **2** are organised **3** are performed **4** are judged **5** have been chosen / are chosen **6** is prohibited **7** has been taken up **8** is thought **9** be exposed **10** are awarded **11** have been uploaded

THINK | RESEARCH | CULTURE | LEARN | ME

In pairs or small groups, students discuss the questions. Elicit ideas in open class.

Optional extension

Bring in some short poems that teenagers might enjoy. You might choose classical poems or more modern urban ones that you can find on the internet, though the latter will need careful checking regarding the suitability of the content. Distribute one poem per pair of students. In pairs, students practise reading the poem before reading it to the class.

Homework

OWB

Assign students Grammar 1 exercises 1 and 2 on page 70 of their Workbook.

VOCABULARY

Topic vocabulary | Phrasal verbs | Collocations

→ Student's Book, page 95 SB

Lesson aims

- Understand the correct usage of:
  - words connected with literature
  - phrasal verbs
  - collocations with *say, speak* and *tell*

Lead-in

Play ***Board race***. Divide the board into two halves and the class into two teams. Students stand up in two lines in front of their halves of the board. Elicit from the class what a literary genre is (*a type or category of fictional writing*). The person at the front of each line writes a literary genre on their side of the board, passes the pen to the person behind them and goes to the back of the line. Students cannot repeat a category written by the other team.

This continues until you say 'Stop'. The team with the most correct words wins.

Possible answers

comic/graphic novel, crime/detective, fan fiction, fantasy, historical fiction, horror, legend, mystery, science fiction, short story, suspense, thriller, tragedy

Words connected with *literature*

1 2.20 Ask students to complete the exercise. Play the audio for students to listen and check their answers. Elicit explanations for each word and check their pronunciation.

Answers/Audioscript

Literary genres: crime fiction, fantasy, graphic novel, historical fiction, legend, romantic novel, science fiction, tragedy

Literary jobs: critic, editor, novelist, playwright

Refer students to the Vocabulary reference, page 166, for more information on topic vocabulary.

2 Ask students to complete the exercise. Elicit answers from different students around the class.

Answers

1 critic **2** graphic novel **3** novelist **4** legend **5** crime fiction **6** fantasy

3 Ask students to complete the exercise. Elicit answers from different students around the class.

Suggested answers

Literary genres: fan fiction, horror, mystery, short story, suspense, thriller

Literary jobs: writer, author, reporter, journalist, blogger

Fast finishers

Students put the literary jobs in categories according to the suffix. Students add two more jobs to each category.

Suggested answers

-er: writer, reporter, blogger, painter, gardener

-or: editor, author, decorator, actor

-ist: novelist, journalist, artist, biologist

Phrasal verbs

4 2.21 Ask students to complete the exercise. Play the audio for students to listen and check their answers.

Answers/Audioscript

1 It's helpful if you *read up about* the play before you go and see it.

2 We will *bring up* the subject of reading in the education forum next week.

3 I've *flicked through* the magazine briefly but I haven't read the articles in detail yet.

4 It's not always easy to *get* your point *across* clearly in a different language.

5 It's good to *talk through* problems with a close friend.

6 If anyone has any suggestions, please *put* them *forward* now.

7 Max is nice but he *goes on* a lot. He can't be quiet!

8 If you don't understand the instruction, let me *spell* it *out* to you.

Refer students to the Vocabulary reference, page 166, for more information on phrasal verbs.

Optional extension

In pairs, or as a group, ask students to discuss the meaning of each of the phrasal verbs in Exercise 4.

Elicit definitions of each phrasal verb from different students around the class. Ask which phrasal verb doesn't take an object (*go on*).

Answers

read up about something: get information on a particular subject by reading a lot about it

bring something up: start discussing a subject

flick through something: turn the pages of a book, magazine, newspaper, etc. quickly, looking at some of the pages for a very short time

get something across: make people understand something

talk through something: discuss a plan or a situation in a detailed way

put something forward: offer an idea, opinion, reason, etc., especially so that people can discuss it and make a decision

go on: talk so much that people become bored or annoyed

spell something out: say or explain something very clearly because someone has not understood something

Collocations with *say*, *speak* and *tell*

5 2.22 Ask students to complete the exercise. Play the audio for students to listen and check their answers.

Answers/Audioscript

1 tell a lie / the truth **2** say sorry **3** speak for yourself **4** tell a joke **5** speak your mind **6** tell a story **7** speak against or in favour of something **8** speak well/highly of someone **9** tell the difference between things **10** say hello/goodbye/goodnight **11** tell the time **12** tell someone a secret

Refer students to the Vocabulary reference, page 166, for more information on collocations.

THINK | RESEARCH | CULTURE | LEARN | **ME**

In pairs or small groups, students do the task. Elicit examples in open class.

Homework OWB

Assign students Vocabulary exercises 1, 2 and 3 on pages 70–71 of their Workbook.

LISTENING
True/false/not stated

→ Student's Book, page 96 SB

Lesson aims

- Focus on true, false or not stated statements
- Practise doing a true/false/not stated exam task

Lead-in

Play ***Twenty questions***. Ask students to guess a film or a book that you are thinking of by asking up to 20 *yes/no* questions. A *yes* answer earns the questioner the chance to ask another question; a *no* answer means the next student asks a question. If students don't guess the answer after 20 questions, give them the answer.

1 In pairs or as a group, students answer the questions. Elicit ideas from different students around the class.

Suggested answers

1 The language is Elvish and is featured in *The Lord of the Rings*, a trilogy of fantasy books written by J.R.R. Tolkien. It is spoken by the elves in the story and other characters who know it.

2 Students' own answers; Possible answers: Klingon, in the *Star Trek* films and television series, created by Marc Okrand; Nadsat slang, *A Clockwork Orange*, Anthony Burgess (1962); Dothraki, created by David J. Peterson for the TV series *Game of Thrones* (based on the novel series *A Song of Ice and Fire* by George R.R. Martin); Na'vi, the fictional language spoken by the Na'vi in *Avatar*, created by Paul Frommer.

Cultural note

The Lord of the Rings is one of the best-selling novels ever written, with more than 150 million copies sold. The story began as a sequel to Tolkien's earlier fantasy novel *The Hobbit* (1937), but eventually developed into a much larger work. It was published in three volumes: *The Fellowship of the Ring*, *The Two Towers* and *The Return of the King*. It was written in stages between 1937 and 1949, much of it during the Second World War.

2 Ask students to complete the exercise. Check answers in open class.

Answers

1 a F, **b** NS **2 a** F, **b** NS **3 a** NS, **b** F

3 Ask students to complete the exercise. Remind them to refer to the advice in the *Optimise your exam* box. Check answers in open class.

Answers

Students' own answers

OPTIMISE YOUR **EXAM**

True/false/not stated

Ask students to read the tips.

- In Exercise 3, students discussed how to distinguish *false* and *not stated* options. Remind students that information which is *true* is likely to use synonyms and paraphrasing of the wording in the given statements. Students should look out for words such as *all, never, most, main, the majority,* etc. If the statement says *all* and the speaker says *some* then the statement is false.
- Remind students that they should use the second listening to check all their answers carefully.

Exam task

4 2.23 Play the track for students to listen and complete the exercise. Don't check answers at this stage, as students will listen again to check in Exercise 5.

5 2.23 Play the track again for students to listen and check their answers to Exercise 4. In open class, discuss the specific clues that helped them choose their answers.

Answers

1 T (*And sometimes, in order to make it seem as believable as possible for the audience, authors go one step further, and create a whole new language for the characters from that place to use.*)

2 NS

3 T (*It's already got 4,000 words and its own language-learning app!*)

4 F (*Well, it was created for the* Star Trek *films in the 1980s.*)

5 T (*The result was a language that initially had around 1,500 words, and its own strict grammar and pronunciation rules. And since its initial invention, the Klingon vocabulary has doubled to about 3,000 words.*)

6 NS

7 F (*... a simplified version of English with all the feeling, beauty and passion removed, as well as many of the negative words.*)

8 F (*In fact, he invented over 1,700 words that are still in use today.*)

Mixed ability

Give students a copy of the audioscript. Ask less confident students to underline the parts of the text where the answers were either *true* or *false*. Ask higher-level students to select three new words or phrases, look them up in their dictionaries and write them up on the board, with definitions.

THINK | RESEARCH | CULTURE | LEARN | ME

In pairs or small groups, students discuss the questions. Elicit ideas in open class.

Homework OWB

Assign students Listening exercises 1 and 2 on page 72 of their Workbook.

GRAMMAR 2
The causative, direct and indirect objects

→ Student's Book, page 97 SB

Lesson aims

- Understand the correct usage of the causative, and direct and indirect objects
- Practise using the causative, and direct and indirect objects

Lead-in

Play ***Hangman*** with some of the words from the Vocabulary lesson.

Suggested words: *romantic novel, science fiction, graphic novel, historical fiction, tragedy, critic, editor, legend, novelist, fantasy.*

Grammar in context

Ask students to complete the task. Refer them to the *Remember* box if they need help. Check answers in open class.

Remind students that they can find more information in the Grammar reference, Unit 9, page 158.

Answers

1 had **2** published **3** by

Language note

The causative, direct and indirect objects

Draw students' attention to the difference between someone doing something for us and something happening to us. In the former, we usually organise the service ourselves and often we pay an expert to do it. In the latter, what happens to us is not desirable or controlled by us.

Point out that the causative *have/get something done* is similar to the passive in that the agent does not have to be stated but if it is, we use the preposition *by*, e.g. *I had my hair cut (by the hairdresser).*

1 Ask students to complete the exercise. Ask them to compare their answers in pairs before you check them in open class.

Answers

1 having/getting a book published

2 have/get their work edited by

3 have/get their autobiography written by

4 having/getting the job done by

5 have/get all the facts given to them

6 have/get their story told

7 Has the author actually had this book ghostwritten by / Did the author actually have/get this book ghostwritten by

2 Ask students to complete the exercise. Refer them to the *Remember* box if they need help. Ask students to compare their answers in pairs before you check them in open class.

Remind students that they can find more information in the Grammar reference, Unit 9, page 158.

Answers

1 Dad read the kids a bedtime story. **2** Allie ordered her brother a book online. **3** Phil told everyone a stupid joke. **4** –
5 The students weren't given the answers beforehand.

3 Ask students to complete the exercise. Ask them to discuss their answer in pairs before you check it in open class.

Answers

The verb *describe* doesn't take two objects. It is not possible to say *I'd like you to describe me the two photos.* Other common verbs that only take one object are: *need, take, attend, discuss, like, believe, join, use, enjoy, lose, say, want, expect, love, suggest.*

SAY IT RIGHT

Sentence stress in the passive

TRC

For the *Say it right* pronunciation activity and instructions, go to the Teacher's Resource Centre.

Homework

OWB

Assign students Grammar 2 exercises 1 and 2 on page 71 of their Workbook.

SPEAKING
Interview

→ Student's Book, page 98 SB

Lesson aims

- Focus on talking about experiences
- Answer personal questions

The *Talk2Me* video in this unit focuses on interviews. People talk about personal experiences and how they felt about those experiences. Students answer some comprehension questions and then listen out for phrases describing personal experiences, feelings and reactions. The video can be used in one of two ways:

Flipped classroom

Flipped classroom option

Using this approach, students watch the video and complete the exercises for homework. This prepares students for the speaking lesson by introducing them to the topic and the key phrases to use in the exam task. Teachers who use this method will find they have more class time to spend on activating the target language and developing fluency for the final task.

***Talk2Me* worksheet**

Ask students to also complete the *Talk2Me* worksheet on the Resource Centre for more detailed comprehension exercises and more practice of the key phrases.

Classroom option

1 Ask students to spend a minute or two reading the questions. Play the *Talk2Me* video for students to complete the exercise. Play the video again, if necessary, before checking their answers.

2 Play the *Talk2Me* video again, so students circle the phrases in the *Phrase expert* box. Pause the video from time to time if necessary. Check answers in open class.

***Talk2Me* worksheet**

Ask students to also complete the *Talk2Me* worksheet on the Resource Centre for more detailed comprehension exercises and more practice of the key phrases.

Answers

The transcript and answer key for the *Talk2Me* video exercises and Worksheet can be found on the Teacher's Resource Centre.

Language note

Remind students that if we don't know whether a person has had an experience or not, we always ask using the present perfect. Once we know that the experience has happened and is finished then we use the past simple to ask about details of the experience.

Lead-in

In pairs, students take turns to ask each other questions, using either the present perfect tense or the past simple tense.

3 In pairs or groups, students ask and answer the questions. Elicit answers from different students around the class.

Answers

Students' own answers

Extra support

Ask students to identify the adjectives and adverbs in the *Phrase expert* box and copy them in four columns. Check their answers then ask students to add more to the list.

Suggested answers

Positive adjectives: *excited, surprised* (other possibilities: *happy, glad, pleased*)

Negative adjectives: *nervous* (other possibilities: *worried, confused, anxious*)

Positive adverbs: *thankfully, happily* (other possibilities: *fortunately, luckily, amazingly*)

Negative adverbs: *sadly, unfortunately* (other possibilities: *unluckily, disappointingly*)

Language note

Remind students that the adverbs in the *Phrase expert* box are adverbs of viewpoint or opinion and express the attitude of the speaker. They usually appear at the beginning of a sentence. When written they are always followed by a comma.

4 Ask students to complete the exercise. Check answers in open class.

Answers

1 b **2** e **3** a **4** c **5** d

5 Ask students to make notes.

Extra support

Elicit from the class other experiences in addition to those listed in Exercise 5 and write them on the board. If the students haven't had the experiences listed in the exercise, they can replace them with one or more experiences from the board.

Suggested answers

comedy show, concert, magic show, football match, ballet performance.

OPTIMISE YOUR EXAM

Interview

Ask students to read the tips.

- Explain that answering questions about personal experiences is common in official speaking exams, especially where the student is speaking one-to-one with the examiner or as part of a discussion activity with another candidate.
- These kinds of questions often use the present perfect, e.g. *Have you ever travelled abroad?* so students should answer in this tense. However, remind the students that if they start talking about the details of a specific experience, they will use past tenses:
  Yes, I have travelled abroad last year. ✗
  Yes, I have. I went to Germany last year. ✓
- Explain that in this lesson students will practise these kinds of questions and learn some common everyday expressions that are useful for answering questions like these. Using past tenses and a range of adjectives and adverbs correctly will impress the examiners.
- For example, to the question *Have you tried an extreme sport?* a student could respond simply, e.g. *Yes, I have. I went bungee jumping last year*, or they could add more detail, e.g. *Yes, I have. I went bungee jumping last year. It was incredible. Fortunately, I had a great instructor and although I was nervous, he helped me relax. Looking back now I can't believe I did it!*

▾ Exam task

6 In pairs, students complete the task. Elicit interesting or surprising answers from different students around the class.

Extra support

Demonstrate the activity first by getting students to ask you the questions. This will provide model questions for the past simple prompts and give you the opportunity to demonstrate how students might incorporate the expressions from the *Phrase expert* box into their replies.

Optional extension

Students repeat the activity, asking questions about experiences of their own choice and using the prompts in Exercise 5 to get more information.

Homework

Assign students Speaking exercises 1 and 2 on pages 72–73 of their Workbook. OWB

USE OF ENGLISH

Word formation | Multiple-choice cloze

→ Student's Book, page 99 SB

Lesson aims

- Focus on word formation and practise a word-formation exam task
- Focus on multiple-choice cloze and practise a multiple-choice cloze exam task

Lead-in

Play ***Word tennis***. Students line up in two teams facing each other. Give a student a ball and a word (e.g. *able*). This student 'serves' the word to the other team by saying it out loud and throwing the ball to the other team. The player who catches the ball must change the form of the word (e.g. *disable*) and 'return' it by throwing the ball to a different member of the first team.

Play continues until a student produces a word that does not exist or hesitates for three seconds. The other team then scores a point.

Continue the game by giving other words.

1 Ask students to complete the exercise. Elicit answers from different students around the class.

Answers

1 able: adjective, lonely: adjective

2 vary: variation, variety, varieties, variable(s); know: knowledge; appear: (dis)appearance(s), (dis)appearing; speak: speech, speaker(s); surround: surroundings; think: thinker, thought(s), thinking

3 vary: various, (in)variable, varying, varied; know: knowledgeable, knowing, (un)known; appear: apparent, (dis)appearing, (un)apparent; speak: (un)spoken, unspeakable, speechless; surround: surrounding; think: thoughtless, thoughtful, (un)thinking

OPTIMISE YOUR EXAM

Word formation

Ask students to read the tip. Ask them to answer the question after completing Exercise 2.

- Tell students that they should check their spelling carefully when writing their answers.
- Remind students that they must use correct spelling in a word-formation exercise otherwise the answer is incorrect.
- Remind students that when they learn a new word they should write down all the verb forms, adjective forms (positive, negative, comparative and superlative) and noun forms (singular, plural and abstract).
- Encourage students to highlight words that have irregular spelling changes in their vocabulary notebooks.

Refer students to the Vocabulary reference, page 167, for more information on word formation.

Answers

4 the 'ea' changes (to 'a') **5** the 'ea' changes (to 'o') **7** the 'ink' changes (to 'ought')

Exam task

2 Ask students to complete the exercise. Ask them to compare their answers in pairs before you check them in open class.

Answers

1 ability **2** various **3** knowledge **4** apparently **5** spoken **6** surroundings **7** thoughts **8** loneliness

3 Ask students to complete the exercise. Ask them to compare their answers in pairs before you check them in open class.

Answers

1 1,6 **2** 5 **3** 2,8 **4** 3

OPTIMISE YOUR EXAM

Multiple-choice cloze

Ask students to read the tips.

- The title immediately tells the student what the text is about.
- Reading the whole text first helps students see how the paragraphs and sentences relate to each other. When reading, students may immediately have an idea of what word could fill the gap. If so, they should make a note of their idea which they can then check when they look at the options.
- If students are not sure what type of word (verb, noun, etc.) goes in the gap they could experiment with the verb *do* or the adjective *good* to test if these words make sense. If they don't, the required word is probably a noun or a preposition.

Exam task

4 Ask students to complete the exercise. Check answers by having different students read the text one sentence at a time, checking each answer as you go.

Answers

1 B **2** C **3** A **4** D **5** D **6** B **7** B **8** C

Fast finishers

Ask fast finishers to underline the interesting adjectives in the text. Ask students to write one sentence with each adjective about a book or film they know.

Suggested answers

extraordinary, debut, (non-)magical, outstanding, terrifying

Optional extension

Ask students to discuss whether they would like to read *The Catalyst* or not.

Homework

OWB

Assign students Use of English exercises 1 and 2 on page 73 of their Workbook.

WRITING

A story

→ Student's Book, pages 100–101 SB

Lesson aims

- Focus on language in a story
- Plan and write a story

Lead-in

Play ***Noughts and crosses***. Draw a large 3 by 3 grid on the board. Number the boxes 1 to 9 and write the following words in the boxes: *value, vary, know, appear, speak, think, lone, impress, ability.*

Divide the class into two teams, X and O. Flip a coin to see which team goes first.

In order for the team to receive the X or the O for the box they have chosen, they must change the word into an adjective.

Alternate between the teams until one team has a line of three Xs or Os, or it is a draw.

Possible answers

(in)valuable; (in)variable, varying; knowing, (un)known, knowledgeable; apparent; (un)spoken, unspeakable, speechless; thoughtless, thoughtful, (un)thinking; lonely, lonelier, loneliest; impressed, impressive; able, unable, disabled

1 In pairs or as a group, students answer the questions. Elicit answers in open class.

Suggested answers
1 nervous, afraid, scared, terrified **2** Students' own answers

2 Ask students to complete the exercise. Check answers in open class.

Suggested answers
1 Past simple: *The camp was miles away and Max was totally lost.* We use it to narrate the story.
Past continuous: *The sky was getting darker and the temperature was getting colder.* We use it to describe longer actions and background situations in progress at a certain time.
Past perfect: *He knew he'd taken the wrong turn around an hour ago.* We use it to go back to an earlier point in the story.
2 Adjectives: *dirty, heavy, darker, colder, cool, pale.*
Adverbs: *totally, rapidly.*
They bring the story to life and make it easier for the reader to picture the situation.
3 It invites the reader to think about what is going to happen and creates suspense.
4 Students' own answers

OPTIMISE YOUR EXAM

A story

Ask students to read the tips.

- Highlight how the writer grabs the reader's attention by quickly setting the scene and having the protagonist immediately facing a challenge: *... Max was totally lost. He had no idea where he was or where he was going.*
- A story usually has a beginning, middle and end.
- The beginning usually introduces the main characters, the setting, the time and the main conflict. The beginning also sets the tone of the story, whether it be suspense, comedy or romance.
- The middle often involves problems or complications which increase the tension. The main character will often have to make decisions which will determine the outcome of the story.
- The end is where the main conflict is resolved. The protagonist should be changed in some way by the events, e.g. by learning something or becoming a better person.
- Remind students that examiners will be looking for a range of narrative tenses and a wide variety of adjectives and adverbs. Above all, the story should be interesting and satisfy the reader.
- It is not always necessary to use direct speech but by doing so the student can demonstrate control of other tenses and structures.
- Remind students that if the writing task says ***must begin*** or ***end*** with a given sentence then the student must write those exact words at the beginning or end. Students must also include other elements if instructed to do so.

For more information on writing stories, refer students to the Writing reference, page 173.

Exam task

3 Ask students to complete the exercise. Elicit ideas in open class.

Answers
Students' own answers

Mixed ability

Mix higher and lower level students in pairs and ask them to work through the questions together, exchanging ideas.

Extra support

Put any useful vocabulary that emerges on the board to support students.

4 Plan Ask students to complete the paragraph plan using their notes from Exercise 3. You may want to look at students' plans, if possible, to check them and give advice and suggestions for improvement before students take the next step.

Mixed ability

Elicit students' ideas and put useful expressions and vocabulary on the board for less able students to use.

5 Write Ask students to write their story in an appropriate style in 140–190 words. Depending on time, it may be a good idea to set this and the subsequent checklist exercise for homework.

6 Check Ask students to complete the checklist before they hand in their story.

Homework OWB

Assign students Writing exercises 1, 2 and 3 on page 74 of their Workbook and Progress check 9 on page 75.

10 Spending power

UNIT AIMS

Exam preparation in Unit 10:

- understand the writer's purpose in an online article
- listen for words and phrases with similar meanings
- reach a decision in a collaborative task
- use common word endings in word formation
- form and use collocations
- write a strong introduction and conclusion in an essay

TEACHER'S PRESENTATION KIT

- *Talk2Me* videos
- Speaking test videos
- Class and Workbook audio
- Workbook pages and answer key

UNIT OVERVIEW

Student's Book / Digital Student's Book SB		Workbook / Online Workbook OWB
LESSON / EXAM TASK	**EXAM SKILLS / LANGUAGE FOCUS**	**CONSOLIDATION**
Reading **Multiple choice**	Understanding purpose An online article	Workbook, pp 76–77, Exercises 1, 2, 3 Unit 10, Reading, Exercises 1, 2, 3
Grammar 1	Relative clauses	Workbook, p 78, Exercises 1, 2, 3 Unit 10, Grammar 1, Exercises 1, 2, 3
Vocabulary	Words connected with *spending money* Phrasal verbs Collocations with *do*, *get*, *go* and *make*	Workbook, pp 78–79, Exercises 1, 2, 3 Unit 10, Vocabulary, Exercises 1, 2, 3
Listening **Multiple choice**	Understanding responses to questions	Workbook, p 80, Exercises 1, 2 Unit 10, Listening, Exercises 1, 2
Grammar 2	Participle clauses	Workbook, p 79, Exercises 1, 2 Unit 10, Grammar 2, Exercises 1, 2
Speaking **Collaborative task**	Reaching a decision	Workbook, pp 80–81, Exercises 1, 2 Unit 10, Speaking, Exercises 1, 2
Use of English **Word formation** **Open cloze**	Verb endings Collocations	Workbook, p 81, Exercises 1, 2, 3 Unit 10, Use of English, Exercises 1, 2, 3
Writing **An essay**	Introducing and concluding	Workbook, p 82, Exercises 1, 2, 3, 4, 5 Unit 10, Writing, Exercises 1, 2, 3, 4, 5
Progress check	Check language progress for Units 9 and 10	Workbook, p 83, Progress check and Cumulative progress Progress check and Cumulative progress

Additional material

PRESENTATION KIT	TEACHER'S / STUDENT'S RESOURCE CENTRE RC	TEST GENERATOR
Talk2Me video *To sum up …*	**Unit 10 worksheets:** *Optimise your grammar* (Standard and Higher), *Optimise your vocabulary* (Standard and Higher), *Talk2Me* video, *Say it right* **Units 9–10 worksheets:** CLIL, Culture, Everyday English (TRC only), Grammar communication (TRC only)	Unit Test 10 (Standard and Higher)

READING

Multiple choice | An online article

→ Student's Book, pages 102–103 SB

Lesson aims

- Focus on multiple choice
- Practise a multiple-choice exam task

Lead-in

Elicit the meaning of the unit title ***Spending power*** (*the extent to which people have money to buy goods and services*). Ask students to discuss how important spending power is in their country. Ask students what they think the lesson is going to be about (*money and consumerism*).

1 In pairs or as a group, students answer the questions. Elicit answers in open class and try to develop a class discussion on what or who has the biggest influence on their spending decisions.

Answers

Students' own answers

2 Ask students to complete the exercise. Check answers in open class. Remind students to underline the key words in the five points first and then scan each paragraph looking for those points. Check the meaning of *peer pressure* (*influence on people by people of a similar age, social status or group*).

Answers

a 5 **b** 4 **c** 2 **d** 1 **e** 3

3 Ask students to complete the exercise. Ask them to compare their answers in pairs before you check them in open class.

Answers

1 1, 6

2 surprisingly high

3 to show us how big the issue is

4 a way of achieving an aim

5 focus on a long-term goal, put together a budget, think carefully about how brands try to influence you, realise that not everything you see on social media is true

6 to give teens ways of avoiding peer pressure

Mixed ability

Break the text into chunks and give less confident students the option of only reading some of the text and answering fewer questions. If stronger students finish early, ask them to write a short summary of the text.

OPTIMISE YOUR EXAM

Multiple choice

Ask students to read the tips.

- Often in a multiple-choice reading exam, students are tested in one or two questions on their ability to deduce the writer's purpose, either for writing the text as a whole or for writing specific parts.
- Encourage students to think about the writer's purpose when they read any text. Why did the writer write this text? What is the purpose of each paragraph? Often the key to the writer's intentions is in the final paragraph.
- Ask students if they can think of any other purposes that are not mentioned in the tips (*to entertain, to sell, to compare, to evaluate*).
- Encourage students to make lists of words or expressions that express different purposes in their notebooks.

▼ Exam task

4 3.01 **Note: The reading text is also available on the audio CD. You may want to have students listen and read the text before doing the exam task.**

Ask students to complete exercise. Check in open class and elicit evidence for their answers.

Answers

1 A **2** D **3** C **4** A **5** B **6** C

Fast finishers

Ask students to find words in the text to match these definitions (*answers in brackets*).

the amount of money a person or organisation has to spend on something (*budget*)

something you buy (*purchase*)

get, obtain (*acquire*)

as well as (*on top of*)

Optional extension 3.01

Play the recorded text and ask students to underline all the words and expressions related to money.

Answers

spending decisions, buy, buying power, total spending, income, allowances, budget, household spending, purchase, paid, sell, save for, put away, spend, fixed amount (of money), save

Optional extension

Students discuss how they decide spending strategies in their families, such as where to eat, what groceries to buy and where to go on holiday.

5 Ask students to complete the exercise. Check answers in open class.

Answers

consult (v): ask for information or advice from someone who has special knowledge about a particular subject

dictating (v): influencing or controlling how something is done

genuine (adj): real, rather than pretended or false

membership (n): the fact of being a member of a club, organisation, or group

reinforces (v): makes (an idea, belief or feeling) stronger

status (n): someone's position in a group, profession or society, especially compared with other people

trend (n): a gradual change or development that produces a particular result

Extra support

Point out that students should always look around the word to see if the text actually defines the word, restates the word in another way, or provides a synonym or an antonym. Sometimes the text gives examples that help explain the word in question.

Homework

Assign students Reading exercises 1, 2 and 3 on pages 76–77 of their Workbook.

OWB

GRAMMAR 1
Relative clauses

→ Student's Book, page 104

SB

Lesson aims

- Understand the correct usage of relative clauses
- Practise using relative clauses

Lead-in

Play ***Back to the board***. Divide the class into two teams. Ask a volunteer from team A to sit with his/her back to the board, facing their team. Choose words from the previous lesson and write the words on the board one by one. Team A defines the word for the volunteer student to guess in one minute. After one minute, it is the other team's turn to define a word, and so on. The team that describes the most words in one minute wins the round.

Suggested words: *money, save, peer pressure, purchase, budget, income, spend, gadget, sell.*

Grammar in context

Ask students to complete the task. Refer them to the *Remember* box if they need help. Check answers in open class.

Remind students that they can find more information in the Grammar reference, Unit 10, page 158.

Answers

1 a **2** b **3** b

Optional extension

Students read the first paragraph of the text again and find examples of defining and non-defining relative clauses.

Answers

Non-defining: *In the USA, for example, **where** there are around 25.6 million teens,; Teen income from allowances and employment, **which** comes to over $90 billion, is only part of the story.*

Defining: *the total spending on products **which** are bought by and for teens is about $210 billion a year; It seems there's no area of household spending **that** teenagers don't exert an influence over.*

1 Ask students to complete the exercise. Refer them to the *Remember* box if they need help. Ask students to compare their answers in pairs before you check them in open class.

Answers

1 a **2** b **3** a **4** a

Fast finishers

Ask students to write *defining* or *non-defining* next to each correct sentence.

Ask students in which sentence the relative pronoun has been removed. (*Sentence 3*)

Answers

1 defining
2 non-defining
3 defining
4 defining

2 Ask students to complete the exercise. As you monitor, make sure students are focusing on the relative clauses. Ask students to compare their answers in pairs before you check them in open class.

Extra support

When monitoring, assist less confident students by showing them where some, or all, of the sentences are to be found so they have more time to rewrite them correctly.

Answers

1 *Essena O'Neil who is from Australia was an Instagram star.*
Essena O'Neil, who is from Australia, was an Instagram star.

2 *However, the people, who followed her, didn't know she was being paid.*
However, the people who followed her didn't know she was being paid.

3 *She described how the photos who she put online were heavily edited.*
She described how the photos (that/which) she put online were heavily edited.

4 *She deleted over 2,000 photos, that had appeared on her Instagram account.*
She deleted over 2,000 photos that had appeared on her Instagram account.

3 Ask students to complete the exercise. Check answers in open class.

Answers

The relative pronouns in bold could be left out of these sentences:
She also talked about products ***which*** *she was being paid to promote.*
She described how the photos ***that/which*** *she put online were heavily edited.*

SAY IT RIGHT

Intonation in relative clauses

For the *Say it right* pronunciation activity and instructions, go to the Teacher's Resource Centre. TRC

THINK | RESEARCH | CULTURE | LEARN | ME

In pairs or small groups, students discuss the questions. Elicit ideas in open class.

Homework

Assign students Grammar 1 exercises 1, 2 and 3 on page 78 of their Workbook. OWB

VOCABULARY

Topic vocabulary | Phrasal verbs | Collocations

→ Student's Book, page 105 SB

Lesson aims

- Understand the correct usage of:
  - words connected with spending money
  - phrasal verbs
  - collocations with *do, get, go* and *make*

Lead-in

Write these proverbs related to money on the board:
1 *The best things in life are free.*
2 *Money doesn't grow on trees.*
3 *Lend money and lose a friend.*

Students discuss the meaning of each expression and how much they agree with each one.

Answers

1 The most satisfying experiences do not cost any money.
2 You have to work to earn money.
3 You should not lend money to your friends; if you do, your friend may not repay the loan, which will affect your friendship.

Words connected with *spending money*

1 3.02 Ask students to complete the exercise. Play the audio for students to listen and check their answers.

Elicit explanations for each word and check the pronunciation of the following words: *receipt* /rɪ'siːt/ and *refund* /'riːfʌnd/.

Answers/Audioscript

Assistant: Could you come to the other *till*, please? Now, the total *bill* comes to £15, and that's with a 10% *discount*. How would you like to pay?

Customer: By *credit card*. Oh, wait. It's a new one and I've forgotten the *PIN*. I'll have to pay in *cash*. Luckily, I've just been to the *cashpoint*, so I've got enough.

Assistant: That's fine, thank you. And here's your *change* – £5 – and your *receipt*. Keep it, because it's also your guarantee. If anything goes wrong with the headphones, just bring them back and we'll exchange them or give you a *refund*.

Customer: Thank you.

Refer students to the Vocabulary reference, page 167, for more information on topic vocabulary.

Optional extension

When checking the answers, write them up on the board as follows:
Assistant: ***1*** *till* ***2*** *bill* ***3*** *discount*
Customer: ***4*** *credit card* ***5*** *PIN* ***6*** *cash* ***7*** *cashpoint*
Assistant: ***8*** *change* ***9*** *receipt* ***10*** *refund*

First, students act out the dialogue, reading it from their books. Then, closing their books, they try to recreate the dialogue using the prompts on the board.

Phrasal verbs

2 3.03 Ask students to complete the exercise. Play the audio for students to listen and check their answers.

Answers/Audioscript

1 If we *carry on* like this, we'll have no money left! *continue*
2 You need to *switch* the computer *on* and then enter your password. *start working*
3 Did you *decide on* the restaurant you want to eat at? *think about*
4 Why do you always *pick on* me when I haven't done anything? *treat badly*
5 I haven't *put* the heating *on* because we're trying to save money. *start working*
6 Don't *start on* me just because I forgot to bring any cash. *treat badly*
7 Let's just *press on* until we get the job done. *continue*
8 Let me *sleep on* the problem and I'll get back to you tomorrow. *think about*

Refer students to the Vocabulary reference, page 167, for more information on phrasal verbs.

3 Ask students to complete the exercise. Ask them to compare their answers in pairs before you check them in open class.

Answers

1 decide on **2** carry on **3** switch on / put on **4** Picking on
5 sleep on **6** carried on / pressed on

Extra support

If students have problems remembering phrasal verbs, get them to draw pictures which represent the phrasal verb, with the phrasal verb at the top and an example sentence at the bottom. Stick the pictures around the class.

Collocations with *do, get, go* and *make*

4 3.04 Ask students to complete the exercise. Play the audio for students to listen and check their answers.

Answers/Audioscript

1 I think she *makes a living* from the weekly vlogs on her YouTube channel.

2 They're a good company to *do business with.*

3 If a company *goes bankrupt*, it has to stop trading.

4 Jake *made a fortune* when he sold his vintage comics at the auction.

5 Whenever you *make a purchase* online, be careful of the risk of internet fraud.

6 These trainers were in the sale and I really *got a bargain*.

7 Nina sold some old DVDs online but *made a loss* as she got less than what she paid for them.

8 They announced that the bookshop *made a profit* last year!

Refer students to the Vocabulary reference, page 167, for more information on collocations.

THINK | RESEARCH | CULTURE | **LEARN** | ME

In pairs or small groups, students do the task and answer the question. Elicit answers in open class.

Homework OWB

Assign students Vocabulary exercises 1, 2 and 3 on pages 78–79 of their Workbook.

LISTENING
Multiple choice

→ Student's Book, page 106 SB

Lesson aims

- Focus on multiple choice
- Practise a multiple-choice exam task

Lead-in

In pairs, students make a list of words/phrases connected with spending money. Set a time limit of one minute. The pair with the most correct words/phrases at the end of the time wins.

1 In pairs or as a group, students ask and answer the questions. Elicit answers in open class and try to develop a class discussion on what problems having a lot of money can bring.

Answers

Students' own answers

2 Ask students to complete the exercise. Ask them to compare their answers in pairs before you check them in open class.

Answers

1 yes **2** yes **3** yes

3 In pairs, students answer the questions. Elicit ideas from different students around the class.

Suggested answer

The man is scuba-diving. He is looking for underwater treasure.

Extra support

Before students do Exercise 3, elicit vocabulary to describe the photo (e.g. *scuba-diving, torch, treasure, coins, broken pot*).

OPTIMISE YOUR EXAM

Multiple choice

Ask students to read the tips.

- Students are usually given some time to look at the questions before they listen. Tell them to use this time to focus on the questions, underlining any key words. As the questions are in order, students should pay attention to the question that is coming so they know when to stop looking at one question and focus on the next.
- Students should avoid 'word spotting', i.e. choosing an option because they hear one word contained in it. Instead, they should listen for the section which answers each question and choose the option which most closely represents the idea expressed.
- Point out to students that if they miss an answer, they should try not to worry but move quickly to the next question. They can use the second listening to listen for any answers they might have missed, as well as eliminating wrong answers.

Exam task

4 3.05 Play the track for students to listen and complete the exercise. Don't check answers at this stage, as students will listen again to check in Exercise 5.

5 3.05 Play the track again for students to listen and check their answers. In open class, discuss the specific clues that helped them choose their answers.

Answers

1 B (*The post, 'Lucky Finds', is really about the stories of people whose lives change very suddenly after finding something … ; more about how people react to this amazing luck …*)

2 C (*he called his friend Eric and asked him to help look for it … they did find some very old silver spoons, gold jewellery, and ancient coins.*)

3 C (*… under British law, buried treasure becomes the property of the state.*)

4 C (*Teri Horton went into a local second-hand shop to buy a friend of hers a gift. The painting was 'strange' and 'funny' but not beautiful.*)

5 A (*... her friend wasn't keen on it so Teri kept it for herself*)

6 B (*Some art experts came to look at the painting, but none of them was sure about it being genuine, The art world still isn't sure about Teri's painting*)

7 C (*... being sure he could make some money from it, he bought it.*)

Mixed ability

Give students a copy of the audioscript. Ask students who got some of the answers wrong to underline the distractors in the listening to help them understand more about the kind of traps examiners set. Students who got few or no answers wrong go through the audioscript finding words they don't know, looking them up in their dictionaries and writing them up on the board, with definitions.

Optional extension

In pairs or small groups, students share any stories about times when they or people they know have been lucky. Elicit the best stories in open class.

THINK | **RESEARCH** | CULTURE | LEARN | ME

If you have access to the internet, students can research information in class. Alternatively, they could prepare this for homework and present their information at the start of the next lesson.

Homework

OWB

Assign students Listening exercises 1 and 2 on page 80 of their Workbook.

GRAMMAR 2
Participle clauses

→ Student's Book, page 107 SB

Lesson aims

- Understand the correct usage of participle clauses
- Practise using participle clauses

Lead-in

Write this jumbled sentence on the board and ask students to work in pairs to reorder it:
car / James Bond / an / Aston Martin / The / by / was / used

Then repeat with this one:
wanted / it / car / I / Seeing / to / buy / the

Write the two sentences on the board and underline the participle. Ask students what type of words they are (*participles*). Elicit which one is the past participle (*used*) and which is the present participle (*Seeing*).

Answers

The car used by James Bond was an Aston Martin.

Seeing the car, I wanted to buy it.

Grammar in context

Ask students to complete the task. Refer them to the *Remember* box if they need help. Check answers in open class.

Remind students that they can find more information in the Grammar reference, Unit 10, page 159.

Answers

1 ~~By~~ thinking ~~that~~ it was funny, she decided to buy it there and then for $5.

2 ~~But~~ having bought it and ~~then~~ taken it home, her friend wasn't keen ...

1 Ask students to complete the exercise. Ask them to compare their answers in pairs before you check them in open class.

Answers

1 Someone **buying** a product has often been influenced by advertising **shown** on TV.

2 **Having read** about product placement, I wasn't surprised to see an iPhone **used** by a character in the movie.

3 **Having seen** the film, I decided to go out and buy the same jacket **worn** by the star.

4 **Having seen** how easily teens **exposed** to product placement respond to that kind of marketing, some people are worried.

Extra support

Check the answers to the first question in Exercise 1 before asking students to complete the rest.

Optional extension

Before doing Exercise 2, draw students' attention to the photo and ask them what they can see (*an example of product placement*).

Ask students if they can think of any other examples of product placement (e.g. *Fedex and Wilson football in* Castaway, *Nike in* Back to the Future, *Omega watch and Aston Martin in James Bond films*).

2 Ask students to complete the exercise. Check answers in open class.

Answers

1 *<u>While you are watching</u> TV today, you may well see your favourite character using a product you recognise.* (Watching / While watching)

2 *Shows <u>that are watched</u> by millions of people use product placement as a way of replacing traditional advertising.* (watched)

3 *<u>Because we are exposed</u> to traditional ads all day, we stop noticing them and ignore their messages.* (Being exposed)

4 *The idea with product placement is that <u>after you have seen</u> the character use a product, you will go out and buy that product yourself.* (having seen / after having seen / after seeing)

5 *<u>If it is used in moderation</u>, product placement seems to be a powerful marketing tool for all ages.* (Used in moderation / If used in moderation)

6 *However, <u>because they know</u> teens in particular want to copy characters they admire, businesses pay a lot of money to get their products into films and TV shows <u>which are aimed</u> at young people.* (knowing, aimed)

Extra support

When monitoring, assist less confident students by showing them where some, or all, of the clauses are to be found so they have more time to rewrite an appropriate participle clause.

THINK | RESEARCH | **CULTURE** | LEARN | ME

In pairs or small groups, students discuss the questions. Elicit ideas in open class.

Homework

OWB

Assign students Grammar 2 exercises 1 and 2 on page 79 of their Workbook.

SPEAKING

Collaborative task

→ Student's Book, page 108 SB

Lesson aims

- Focus on reaching a decision
- Practise a collaborative task

The *Talk2Me* video in this unit focuses on evaluating ways to raise money for good causes. People talk about different fundraising activities and decide which one is the best. Students answer some comprehension questions and then listen out for phrases for reaching a decision. The video can be used in one of two ways:

Flipped classroom

Flipped classroom option

Using this approach, students watch the video and complete the exercises for homework. This prepares students for the speaking lesson by introducing them to the topic and the key phrases to use in the exam task. Teachers who use this method will find they have more class time to spend on activating the target language and developing fluency for the final task.

***Talk2Me* worksheet**

Ask students to also complete the *Talk2Me* worksheet on the Resource Centre for more detailed comprehension exercises and more practice of the key phrases.

Classroom option

1 Ask students to spend a minute or two reading the questions. Play the *Talk2Me* video for students to complete the exercise. Play the video again, if necessary, before checking their answers.

2 Play the *Talk2Me* video again, so students complete the sentences with one word. Pause the video from time to time if necessary. Check answers in open class.

***Talk2Me* worksheet**

Ask students to also complete the *Talk2Me* worksheet on the Resource Centre for more detailed comprehension exercises and more practice of the key phrases.

Answers

The transcript and answer key for the *Talk2Me* video exercises and Worksheet can be found on the Teacher's Resource Centre.

Lead-in

Put the word *SPONSOR* on the board. Elicit from the class what it means as a verb (*to support a person, organisation, or activity by giving money*) and as a noun (*a person or company who supports a person/organisation or activity by giving money*). Elicit the names of companies that sponsor large sports events (*Coca-Cola, McDonalds, Nike*). Ask students if they wanted to raise money for a good cause, e.g. for poor people, how they would do it. Write one of the ideas on the board in this form.

People sponsored me €5 to clean their cars. I raised €100 for a children's charity.

Ask students if they have ever been sponsored to do something, how much they raised and what the money was for. Elicit sentences from the students following the model on the board.

3 Ask students to complete the exercise. Elicit answers from different students around the class.

Answers

1 a non-uniform day **2** a sponsored run **3** a student art exhibition **4** a cake sale **5** a talent show

Optional extension

In pairs, or small groups, students think of other ways of raising money for good causes.

Possible answers

People sponsoring you for each day you go without something, e.g. watching TV, using the mobile, etc.

Doing a sponsored swim or long walk.

Doing activities for parents/teachers/the public, e.g. washing cars or ironing clothes.

Organising an event, e.g. concert or school disco and collect money for entry.

Language note

Remind students that if they want to introduce different options with a verb, they need to use the gerund form (e.g. *having*).

Have a talent show is a good idea. ✗

***Having** a talent show is a good idea.* ✓

I think we should choose have a cake sale. ✗

*I think we should choose **having** a cake sale.* ✓

4 Ask students to complete the table. Elicit answers from different students around the class.

Extra support

Do the first example in open class and write the students' ideas on the board. This will help students with the phrasing of the remaining answers.

Suggested answers

A cake sale: Advantages: Many people like cakes. Cakes are easy to make. Disadvantages: You have to pay for the ingredients. You only have a limited time to sell them before they lose their quality.

A non-uniform day: Advantages: All students could participate. It's easy to organise. Disadvantages: Some school children don't wear uniforms.

A sponsored run: Advantages: It's easy to organise. People can sponsor an amount either for each kilometre or for completing the distance. Disadvantages: If it rains some people might not run. You need a place to run.

A student art exhibition: Advantages: People might pay a lot of money for an original piece of art. Disadvantages: You need to pay for paint and materials. It takes time and ability to produce good art.

A talent show: Advantages: Talent shows are very popular. Parents like watching their children perform. Disadvantages: It might be difficult to find people who want to perform. You need a place to perform and lots of seats.

OPTIMISE YOUR EXAM

Collaborative task

Ask students to read the tips.

- Remind students that in many official oral exams, candidates will be required to work towards a decision.
- It is important that students don't simply choose one of the options and stop talking!
- Remind students that they need to suggest an option to their partner and justify why they have chosen it. Their partner should respond and expand on the idea. Students should continue adding reasons and responding to each other until they can't think of any more or the examiner has told them to stop.
- If agreement is made and there is still time remaining, then students should consider the other options and justify why they are not suitable.
- Emphasise that it is important for students to keep talking until they are told to stop by the examiner.

Exam task

5 In pairs, students complete the task. Elicit interesting or surprising answers from different students around the class.

Extra support

Before students attempt the task, elicit ways that students might start the conversation. This could be done with a question or a statement.

Suggested answers

Questions: Would you like to start or shall I? Where shall we start? Can I start? What do you think about X?

Statements: Well, I think that … Let's start with X … Personally …

6 In pairs, ask students to complete the exercise. Time this activity (two minutes) and give updates, e.g. *One minute to go … Only thirty seconds left.*

Walk round and monitor students, noting down errors and good use of language to go over in a feedback session at the end of the activity. Go through any errors you noted down on the board with students, eliciting corrections from them where possible.

Optional extension

Finish the activity by eliciting ideas from the class and having a class discussion to decide on the most effective way and the method that would interest the biggest number of people.

Homework

Assign students Speaking exercises 1 and 2 on pages 80–81 of their Workbook. OWB

USE OF ENGLISH

Word formation | Open cloze

→ Student's Book, page 109 SB

Lesson aims

- Focus on word formation and practise a word-formation exam task
- Focus on open cloze and practise an open-cloze exam task

Lead-in

Write the word *able* on the board. In pairs, students have two minutes to write down as many words that they can form using *able* as the root word.

Suggested answers

Verbs: *enable, enables, enabled, disable, disables, disable*

Adjectives: *capable, incapable, unable, enabling, disabling*

Nouns: *ability, abilities, disability, disabilities, capability, capabilities*

Adverbs: *ably, capably*

(Note: there are thousands of words that end in *-able*, but *able* is not the root word.)

1 Ask students to complete the exercise. Elicit answers from different students around the class.

Answers

1 strong (strength), grow (growth)

2 desires, nations, nationality, nationalities, revolutions, strengths, supplies, economies, stimulation(s)

3 nationalise, revolutionise, economise

OPTIMISE YOUR EXAM

Word formation

Ask students to read the tips.

- Prompt them to think of more verbs with the endings *-ate*, *-ify* and *-ise*.

Refer students to the Vocabulary reference, page 167, for more information on word formation.

Exam task

2 Ask students to complete the exercise. Elicit answers from different students around the class.

Answers

1 desirable **2** national **3** revolutionise **4** strengthen **5** suppliers **6** economic **7** stimulate **8** growth

Optional extension

Ask students to discuss if they think having a currency for their city would be a good thing or not.

3 Ask students to complete the exercise. Elicit answers from different students around the class.

Answers

1 2, 6 **2** 1, 5 **3** 7 **4** 3, 4, 8

OPTIMISE YOUR EXAM

Open cloze

Ask students to read the tips.

- Encourage students to record collocations in their notebooks and review the most frequent ones, e.g. those with *make* and *do*.
- The only relative pronoun which is followed by a noun is *whose*. The others usually relate back to the last item before the relative pronoun, e.g. *the place where, the person who*, etc. Sometimes the relative pronoun relates to the whole of the preceding sentence, in which case *which* should be used, e.g. *Someone found my wallet, which was lucky as it was full of money*. Here, *which* refers to 'the fact that someone found my wallet'.

Exam task

4 Ask students to complete the exercise. Ask them to compare their answers in pairs before you check them in open class.

Answers

1 where **2** on **3** make/earn **4** make **5** who **6** on **7** Having **8** made

Mixed ability

Supply less confident students with two options for each answer: (**1** *which/where* **2** *off/on* **3** *make/do* **4** *win/make* **5** *and/who* **6** *with/on* **7** *When/Having* **8** *bought/made*). Students who finish early can write one or two comprehension questions based on the text in Exercise 4 to check students' understanding. When the class has finished, students read out their questions for the class to answer.

Optional extension

In pairs or small groups, students discuss the following questions.

How often do you or your family buy things online?

What type of things do you buy?

How do you protect yourself online?

Homework

OWB

Assign students Use of English exercises 1, 2 and 3 on page 81 of their Workbook.

WRITING

An essay

→ Student's Book, pages 110–111 SB

Lesson aims

- Focus on language in an essay
- Plan and write an opinion essay

Lead-in

Tell students to make two columns in their notebooks with the headings *MAKE* and *DO*.

Dictate the following words, allowing students time to write the words in one of the columns: *housework, a decision, the shopping, money, a mistake, a favour, a choice, the dishes, the beds, exercise, homework, a fortune, business, a purchase, a profit*.

Ask students to check their answers in pairs before you check them in open class.

Answers

Make: *a decision, money, a mistake, a choice, the beds, a fortune, a purchase, a profit*

Do: *housework, the shopping, a favour, the dishes, exercise, homework, business*

1 In pairs or as a group, students answer the questions. Elicit answers in open class.

Answers

Students' own answers

2 Ask students to complete the exercise. Ask them to compare their summaries in pairs before you check the answer in open class.

Suggested answer

The writer argues that teenagers should make their own spending decisions because that's the only way to learn how to make good decisions. They should be allowed to make mistakes so that they learn how to handle money, which they have to do throughout their lives.

Extra support

Tell students to work in pairs and agree on the writer's argument before they start writing their summary in Exercise 2.

3 Ask students to complete the exercise. Check answers in open class.

Answers

1 I would argue that … **2** Given that freedom, …
3 Having said that, … **4** They are certain to make …
5 In conclusion, … **6** I would like to emphasise that …

4 Ask students to complete the exercise. Check answers in open class.

Answers

The question of whether …; is a difficult one; I would argue that …

Fast finishers

Students repeat Exercise 4 with the other paragraphs.

Answers

Paragraph 2: *However, I don't see how …; I believe that …*
Paragraph 3: *Having said that, …; For instance, …*
Paragraph 4: *In conclusion, I would like to emphasise that …*

5 Ask students to complete the exercise. Check answers in open class.

Answers

1 C **2** I **3** C **4** I **5** I **6** C

OPTIMISE YOUR EXAM

An essay

Ask students to read the tips.

- Tell students that the introduction should introduce the topic clearly in an interesting way and give a brief outline of the issue, saying why it is important or why people have different opinions about it.
- The content paragraphs should build towards the conclusion, in which the writer's opinion is clearly stated.

For more information on writing essays, refer students to the Writing reference, page 174.

Exam task

6 Ask students to complete the exercise individually. Then ask them to discuss their ideas in pairs. Walk round, helping students and monitoring for accuracy.

Mixed ability

Mix less confident and more confident students in pairs and ask them to work through the questions together exchanging ideas. Elicit students' ideas and put any useful expressions and vocabulary that emerges on the board.

7 Plan Ask students to complete the paragraph plan using their notes from Exercise 6. You may want to look at students' plans, if possible, to check them and give advice and suggestions for improvement before students take the next step.

8 Write Ask students to write their essay in an appropriate style in 140–190 words. Depending on time, it may be a good idea to set this and the subsequent checklist exercise for homework.

9 Check Ask students to complete the checklist before they hand in their essay.

Homework OWB

Assign students Writing exercises 1, 2, 3, 4 and 5 on page 82 of their Workbook and Progress check 10 on page 83.

Answers PROGRESS CHECK Units 9–10

Exercise 1
1 international **2** strengthen **3** thought **4** variety **5** economic **6** growth **7** unable **8** desirable

Exercise 2
1 flicked **2** press **3** got **4** decide **5** sleep **6** carry **7** put **8** going

Exercise 3
1 tell **2** make **3** speak **4** told **5** does **6** speaks **7** got

Exercise 4
1 f **2** b **3** g **4** a **5** h **6** d **7** c **8** e

Exercise 5
1 ✓ **2** were had – had **3** estimate – estimated **4** ✓
5 must entered – must be entered **6** ✓ **7** was be given – was given

Exercise 6
1 given a discount by
2 to make a profit
3 get the poem translated by
4 book was published after / was not / wasn't published until
5 give you a refund
6 speak their mind

11 A long way from home

UNIT AIMS

Exam preparation in Unit 11:

- understand linking words/phrases in a travel article
- listen for synonyms and distractors in an interview
- answer questions promptly in an interview
- understand and apply spelling changes in a word-formation exercise
- understand and use correct structures in a sentence-transformation exercise
- use informal language in an email

TEACHER'S PRESENTATION KIT

- *Talk2Me* videos
- Speaking test videos
- Class and Workbook audio
- Workbook pages and answer key

UNIT OVERVIEW

Student's Book / Digital Student's Book SB		Workbook / Online Workbook OWB
LESSON / EXAM TASK	EXAM SKILLS / LANGUAGE FOCUS	CONSOLIDATION
Reading **Gapped text**	Understanding linking words/phrases A travel article	Workbook, pp 84–85, Exercises 1, 2, 3, 4 Unit 11, Reading, Exercises 1, 2, 3, 4
Grammar 1	Reported speech	Workbook, p 86, Exercises 1, 2, 3 Unit 11, Grammar 1, Exercises 1, 2, 3
Vocabulary	Words connected with *travelling* Phrasal verbs Words + prepositions	Workbook, pp 86–87, Exercises 1, 2, 3 Unit 11, Vocabulary, Exercises 1, 2, 3
Listening **Sentence completion**	Listening for synonyms (2)	Workbook, p 88, Exercises 1, 2 Unit 11, Listening, Exercises 1, 2
Grammar 2	Indirect questions	Workbook, p 87, Exercises 1, 2 Unit 11, Grammar 2, Exercises 1, 2
Speaking **Interview**	Answering questions promptly	Workbook, pp 88–89, Exercises 1, 2, 3 Unit 11, Speaking, Exercises 1, 2, 3
Use of English **Word formation** **Sentence transformation**	Spelling Sentence structure	Workbook, p 89, Exercises 1, 2, 3 Unit 11, Use of English, Exercises 1, 2, 3
Writing **A letter / An email**	Formality (2)	Workbook, p 90, Exercises 1, 2, 3, 4 Unit 11, Writing, Exercises 1, 2, 3, 4
		Workbook, p 91, Progress check and Cumulative progress Progress check and Cumulative progress

Additional material

PRESENTATION KIT	TEACHER'S / STUDENT'S RESOURCE CENTRE RC	TEST GENERATOR
Talk2Me video *It's hard to say, but ...*	**Unit 11 worksheets:** *Optimise your grammar* (Standard and Higher), *Optimise your vocabulary* (Standard and Higher), *Talk2Me* video, *Say it right* **Units 11–12 worksheets:** CLIL, Culture, Everyday English (TRC only), Grammar communication (TRC only)	Unit Test 11 (Standard and Higher)

READING

Gapped text | A travel article

→ Student's Book, pages 114–115 SB

Lesson aims

- Focus on gapped text
- Practise a gapped-text exam task

Lead-in

Ask students to look at the unit title ***A long way from home***, and ask them what they think the lesson is going to be about (*travel and tourism*). Ask them to think how far away they would have to be before they would consider themselves a long way from home.

Draw students' attention to the photo and ask if anyone knows what it is and where it is. (*The Giant's Causeway, County Antrim, Northern Ireland.*)

Cultural note

The Giant's Causeway is an area of about 40,000 interlocking, hexagonal, basalt columns, resulting from an ancient volcanic eruption. It is both a UNESCO World Heritage Site and a national nature reserve. According to legend, an Irish giant, Finn MacCool, was challenged to a fight by Benandonner, a Scottish giant. Finn built the causeway so he could get to Scotland without getting his feet wet. One version of the story says that Finn defeated Benandonner; however, another more curious version tells that when Finn saw that Benandonner was much bigger than him he ran back to Ireland. Benandonner crossed the causeway looking for Finn. He arrived at Finn's house where Finn's wife, Oonagh, had disguised Finn as a baby. When Benandonner saw the baby, he was afraid that the father, Finn, must be enormous. Benandonner, terrified, ran back to Scotland destroying the causeway so that Finn could not follow. In fact, in a part of Scotland there are identical basalt columns, which give popularity to this legend.

1 In pairs or groups, students answer the questions. Elicit answers in open class and try to develop a class discussion about the topic.

Answers

Students' own answers

2 Ask students to complete the exercise. Ask them to compare their answers in pairs before you check them in open class.

Answers

1 $75

2 at least £50 million over a period of five years

3 around 80%

4 Nearly a thousand full-time jobs and many part-time jobs

5 New Zealand, Spain (Seville, Girona, Peñiscola), Croatia (Dubrovnik), Northern Ireland (Belfast, Giant's Causeway), UK (the Wye Valley, Forest of Dean), Republic of Ireland (Skellig Michael Island).

6 working as extras, working for film and series tour companies, carpenters building film sets, jobs in hotels

3 Ask students to complete the exercise. Check answers in open class.

Answers

1 due to, Consequently, So, As a result **2** What's more, Besides **3** Although, However **4** of course **5** thankfully

OPTIMISE YOUR EXAM

Gapped text

Ask students to read the tips.

- Remind students that in a gapped-text reading exam they should look for linking words which come just before or after a gapped sentence. For example, *However* and *So* in the text.
- Encourage students to think about what they know about the information in the gaps because of the meaning of the linking words which precede or follow them. For example, in the exam task in Exercise 4, the information in gap 4 must contrast with the information that appears after *However*, while the information in gap 5 is a cause of the information that appears after *So*.
- Remind students that they can complete the answers in a gapped text in any order, and so they should do the easiest ones first and leave the most difficult ones until the end.
- Remind students that when they have selected an answer for all the gaps, they should read through the text to confirm the information before and after the gap makes sense.

Exam task

4 3.06 **Note: The reading text is also available on the audio CD. You may want to have students listen and read the text before doing the exam task.**

Ask students to complete the exercise. Have students compare in pairs before you check in open class. Ask students to explain their evidence.

Answers

1 E (All of these places *follow logically from real-life locations in Seville, Girona and Peñíscola.*)

2 B (*Options B and F both include a pronoun* (he) *and a reference to getting a part* (an extra). *However, option F suggests he moved on which is not consistent with the information after the gap …* he was still living there.)

3 G (*Northern Ireland and the same series are consistent with Giant's Causeway and Game of Thrones. Also fans … coming in their hordes matches option G.*)

4 A (*The information after* However *is positive* (opportunity … had changed his life)*; therefore, the information before the gap should be negative. Options A, B and F all contain negative information about a man, but A is the only one which introduces the man using the proper noun* Brendan. *Also, the fact that Brendan had been unemployed for three years would justify the phrase* had changed his life *when he found work as a carpenter.*)

5 D (*Students should be looking for information in one of the options that cause a lot more filming over here in the future. Option D is the only option which suggests a cause of more filming (options C and G suggest results). Also, the adverb* here *is used in both option D and the sentence after the gap, providing cohesion.*)

6 C (*Option C and the sentence following the gap are in the past. The pronoun* this *refers back to £140 million.*)

Extra support

Remind students that certain words, e.g. *this, that, these, those,* and pronouns in a gapped sentence or following a gap, 'point' directly at something in the previous sentence.

Ask students to find examples in the options A–G, as well as any other words that signal backwards. (Option B: pronoun *he*. Option D: *here* (referring to a place previously mentioned). Option E: *these places*. Option F: pronoun *he*. Option G: *also*.

5 Ask students to complete the exercise. Check answers in open class.

Answers

a trail (n): a path through the countryside

booming (v): if a country, region, or industry is booming, it is experiencing a period of economic success, with a lot of trade and business activity

big draws (noun phr): events or performers that a lot of people will come to see

fed up with (phr v): annoyed or bored with something that you feel you have accepted for too long

hordes (n): large numbers of people

windswept (adj): a windswept place has a lot of wind and not many buildings or trees to protect it

Homework OWB

Assign students Reading exercises 1, 2, 3 and 4 on pages 84–85 of their Workbook.

GRAMMAR 1
Reported speech

→ Student's Book, page 116 SB

Lesson aims

- Understand the correct usage of reported speech
- Practise using reported speech

Lead-in

Play ***Twenty questions***. In groups of three or four, one student thinks of a film or TV series and the other students take turns trying to guess it by asking up to 20 *yes/no* questions. A *yes* answer earns the questioner the chance to ask another question; a *no* answer means the next student asks a question. If they haven't guessed it in 20 questions, the student gives them the answer. Each student takes one turn to think of a film or series.

Grammar in context

Ask students to complete the task. Make sure they don't look back at the text on page 115. Refer students to the *Remember* box if they need help.

Then ask students to check their answers by finding the phrases and sentences in the text. Ask them to explain their use.

Remind students that they can find more information in the Grammar reference, Unit 11, page 159.

Answers

1 said (*tell* needs an object)

2 it would continue (when we report a question it is no longer a real question. The word order is like that of a normal statement i.e. subject – verb – object)

Language note

Remind students that the tense of the verbs changes in reported speech, usually going one tense back. The exceptions are when the information is immediately reported (e.g. A: *I'm going to the shops.* B: *What did Peter just say?* C: *He said he's going to the shops.*), for general statements about things which are still true (A: *I always watch* Game of Thrones. B: *He said he always watches* Game of Thrones.) and when the reporting verb is in the present tense (e.g. A: *I love that programme.* B: *He says he loves that programme.*) In these cases, the tense of the verb in the second clause of the statement usually stays the same.

Remind students that the past simple and continuous don't always need to be changed if there is a time context which makes everything clear.

Point out to students that the best way to learn the different grammatical patterns of reporting verbs is to categorise them by pattern.

1 Ask students to complete the exercise. Check answers in open class.

Answers

1 The tour guide said that we **were** the first tourists to visit the forest for many years.

2 The hotel owner told us that the shops were closed **that day** because there was a festival.

3 The captain said that the plane **was** flying at over 800 kilometres per hour.

4 Sally asked the waiter **if the fish was** fresh.

5 The security guard at the airport asked us if we **had packed** our bags ourselves.

6 Mum wanted to know where **we had** been the previous evening.

7 The taxi driver refused **to** take us to our hotel.

8 Marcus denied **to taking** us in the wrong direction.

Extra support

Elicit from students the other time expressions that change apart from *today* → *that day*.

Tell students to check their answers in the Grammar reference.

2 Ask students to complete the exercise. Check answers in open class.

Answers

1 how he was and how his holiday had been.

2 was OK but that he had had a really bad holiday.

3 had had an accident in the mountains and was still in hospital.

4 had happened.

5 had been skiing and someone had crashed into her. She had fallen over and (had) broken her ankle.

6 she was OK.

7 couldn't fly home until the following week, but she'd be OK.

8 to (go to) the cinema on the following Saturday.

9 seeing / that they saw/(should) see the new *Pirates of the Caribbean* film.

10 he had (already) seen it the week before / the previous week.

Extra support

Do the first two questions in open class, eliciting the rules that helped students reach the answer.

THINK | RESEARCH | CULTURE | LEARN | ME

In pairs or small groups, students answer the questions by telling a short story. Elicit some of the stories in open class.

Optional extension

Students write three sentences reporting information from their partner's stories. Elicit the sentences in open class. Ask students to use three different reporting verbs. Ask students to read out some of the most interesting sentences.

Suggested answers

Paul told me that he had twisted his ankle when he was windsurfing.
He explained that his friends had had to carry him to their car.
He said that the doctor had put a bandage on his ankle.

Homework

Assign students Grammar 1 exercises 1, 2 and 3 on page 86 of their Workbook.

OWB

VOCABULARY

Topic vocabulary | Phrasal verbs | Word patterns

→ Student's Book, page 117 SB

Lesson aims

- Understand the correct usage of:
  - words connected with travelling
  - phrasal verbs
  - words + prepositions

Lead-in

Ask each student to write down two interesting questions for another student. Pair the students randomly.

Students ask their partner their questions and note down the exact reply.

Students return to their seats and write down their questions and answers in reported speech, e.g. *I asked David how he was and he said he was fine. I asked him what he had done at the weekend and he told me he had slept a lot.*

Elicit reported questions and answers from students around the class.

Students decide which was the most interesting question.

Words connected with *travelling*

1 3.07 Ask students to complete the exercise. Play the audio for students to listen and check their answers.

Answers/Audioscript

1 Do you know what time we'll *get* to New York?
2 I'll call you when we *arrive* at the port.
3 My dad's going on a business *trip* to China next week.
4 A GPS, or satnav, is handy for working out the best *route* to take.
5 All the *travel* arrangements have been made, so I've just got to pack now and I'll be ready to go!
6 How much is the entry *fee* into the music festival?
7 How much will the taxi *fare* to the airport be, do you think?
8 Make sure you're at the departure *gate* at least 30 minutes before your flight.
9 The train won't be here for another 20 minutes – do you want to stand on the *platform* or wait in the waiting room?
10 Remember to ask if the room has Wi-Fi when you check in at the hotel *reception*.
11 Everyone has to wear a seatbelt, even *passengers* in the back of the car.
12 Roadworks in both directions are making life a misery for *commuters*.

Refer students to the Vocabulary reference, page 167, for more information on topic vocabulary.

Extra support

Check the pronunciation of the following words: *excursion* /ɪk'skɜː(r)ʃ(ə)n/, *route* /ruːt/ (UK), /rut/, /raʊt/ (US), *voyage* /'vɔɪɪdʒ/ and *commuters* /kə'mjuːtə(r)z/

2 Ask students to complete the exercise. Ask them to compare their sentences in pairs before you elicit some examples in open class.

Suggested answers

I usually reach school at 8:55 am.
When we're on holiday, we're going on an excursion to see where they filmed *Avatar*.
The flight to the UK takes about three hours from Madrid.
My journey to school takes about 30 minutes by bus.
The highlight of my holiday was a ride in a balloon.
The voyage from Europe to Australia by sea takes up to 40 days.
I'm going to buy my concert ticket online because it'll be quicker.
I'll meet you at the entrance to the cinema at 8 pm.

Phrasal verbs

3 3.08 Ask students to complete the exercise. Play the audio for students to listen and check their answers.

Answers/Audioscript

1 We've definitely gone the wrong way. Do you think we should *turn round*?
2 Thanks for the lift. If you could just *drop* me *off* by the library, that'd be great.
3 There's a café at the other end of the beach. Let's *head for* that, shall we?
4 The taxi is going to *pick* us *up* at 7 o'clock in the morning.
5 We all went to the station to *see* Ed *off*. It was really exciting!
6 We're hoping to *get away* for a couple of days next weekend if Angie's free.
7 Please *check out* of the hotel by 11 am on the morning of your departure.
8 To be at the port by nine, we'll have to *set out* from here at half past six.

Refer students to the Vocabulary reference, page 168, for more information on phrasal verbs.

Optional extension

Give each student one of the phrasal verbs and ask them to write a question using it, e.g. *Have you ever had to **turn round** because you were going the wrong way?*

Go round the class checking the questions are correct. Then tell the students to mingle and ask five different students their question. Students return to their seats and report the most interesting replies to their partner using reported speech, e.g. *Amy told me that she had had to turn round once because she had forgotten her lunch!*

Words + prepositions

4 3.09 Ask students to complete the exercise. Play the audio for students to listen and check their answers.

Answers/Audioscript

1 I'm *looking forward to* going on the adventure holiday because I'm really *keen on* experiencing new things.

2 This travel visa's *valid for* the next three months.

3 The beach was so *crowded with* sunbathers that we decided to leave.

4 On holiday, it's important that nobody has the chance to *interfere with* your luggage.

5 If we get *separated from* each other, let's meet back at the hotel in an hour.

6 There was a sign in the bathroom *warning* us *against* drinking the tap water.

7 This app is *useful for* translating different words and phrases into the local language.

8 There's *no point in* getting *upset over* the delay – there's nothing we can *do about* it.

Mixed ability

Supply less confident students with a list of possible answers from which to select: *against, for, from, in, over, to, with*. Students who finish early can think of who the speaker might be in sentences 1–8 and what the context might be.

Suggested answers

1 A traveller before they travel.

2 A person who issues travel visas talking to a traveller.

3 A tourist on holiday.

4 A parent talking to their children before they travel.

5 Two travellers exploring a new city.

6 A traveller talking to a friend about their hotel or a restaurant.

7 A traveller explaining a new translation app.

8 Two travellers at an airport. Their plane is delayed.

Refer students to the Vocabulary reference, page 168, for more information on word patterns.

SAY IT RIGHT

Stress in phrasal verbs (4) TRC

For the *Say it right* pronunciation activity and instructions, go to the Teacher's Resource Centre.

THINK | RESEARCH | CULTURE | LEARN | **ME**

In pairs or small groups, students discuss their answers to the questions. Elicit examples in open class.

Homework

OWB

Assign students Vocabulary exercises 1, 2 and 3 on pages 86–87 of their Workbook.

LISTENING
Sentence completion

→ Student's Book, page 118 SB

Lesson aims

- Focus on sentence completion
- Practise a sentence-completion exam task

Lead-in

Play a game to recycle the phrasal verbs from the previous lesson (*drop off, get away, head for, pick up, see off, turn round*).

Divide the class into two teams. Write a phrasal verb on the board and ask teams to think of a grammatically correct sentence using it.

The first team to write a sentence and hold it up gets a point.

After you have used all the phrasal verbs, the team with the most points is the winner.

1 In pairs or as a group, students ask and answer the questions. Elicit ideas from different students around the class.

Suggested answers

1 The man is cycling. It looks like he is travelling a long way. Students' own answers.

2 Students' own answers

2 Ask students to complete the exercise. Ask them to compare their answers in pairs before you check them in open class.

Answers

1 problems **2** occurrence **3** broke down **4** chased **5** impressed **6** pay (more) attention to **7** expressed (himself) **8** become disorientated **9** deal with **10** trip

Extra support

If dictionaries or internet access are available, let students research any vocabulary they don't understand.

3 Ask students to complete the task. Elicit ideas in open class.

Suggested answers

1 difficulties, challenges, obstacles
2 episode, happening
3 stopped working
4 followed, tracked
5 motivated, inspired
6 be conscious of, observe
7 spoke, wrote, kept in touch, transmitted (information)
8 lose one's way, stray (off course), go adrift, become confused
9 contend with, face (up to), confront
10 voyage, adventure, expedition

OPTIMISE YOUR EXAM

Sentence completion

Ask students to read the tips.

- Encourage students to use any time they have before the audio starts to select the options which are grammatically possible and are logical. For example, in the exam task in Exercise 4, only C and H fit both grammatically and logically with question 1.
- Students should listen carefully to when the parts relating to sentence beginnings 1–8 appear. It is likely they will be worded differently to what is written, although the basic meaning will be conveyed. This is why students should be anticipating synonyms, as they practised in exercises 2 and 3.
- Point out that paraphrases of the sentence endings that are not used will probably appear in the audio but will not follow on correctly from any of the sentence beginnings.
- Remind students to use the second listening to check their answers.

Exam task

4 3.10 Play the track for students to listen and complete the exercise. Don't check answers at this stage, as students will listen again to check in Exercise 5.

5 3.10 Play the track again for students to listen and check their answers to Exercise 4. In open class, check the answers and discuss the specific clues that helped them choose them.

Answers

1 C (*Tom Davies, … who spent 174 days cycling around the world*)
2 H (*… avoiding various countries and trouble spots on the way*)
3 A (*… positive memories were of the people he met … the hospitality, warmth and help he received from strangers when he broke down*)
4 F (*… in the Australian Nullarbor desert, it was the strong winds that slowed him down.*)
5 J (*When you're cycling up to six or seven hours a day it's obviously really important to eat big meals …*)
6 B (*… you could sense exactly how he was feeling and how much energy he had from the way he wrote.*)
7 D (*In India, he didn't feel that drivers cared much about cyclists like him.*)
8 G (*It seems he was chased by dogs in almost every country he visited …*)

Extra support

Allow students extra time before they listen to discuss which of the options A–J are possible with the sentence beginnings 1–8.

Cultural note

Tell students that they can learn more about **Tom Davies** at tomdaviesrtw.com.

Myanmar (officially the Republic of the Union of Myanmar and formerly known as Burma) is a sovereign state in South East Asia bordered by Bangladesh, India, China, Laos and Thailand.

THINK | **RESEARCH** | CULTURE | LEARN | ME

If you have access to the internet, students can research information in class. Alternatively, they could prepare this for homework and present their information at the start of the next lesson.

Homework

Assign students Listening exercises 1 and 2 on page 88 of their Workbook. OWB

GRAMMAR 2
Indirect questions

→ Student's Book, page 119 SB

Lesson aims

- Understand the correct usage of indirect questions
- Practise using indirect questions

Lead-in

Play ***Noughts and crosses***. Draw a large 3 by 3 grid on the board. Number the boxes 1 to 9 and write the following words in the boxes: *trip, travel, journey, excursion, flight, arrive, commuters, fee, voyage*.

Divide the class into two teams, X and O. Flip a coin to see which team goes first.

In order for the team to receive the X or the O for the box they have chosen, they must make a sentence using the word correctly.

Alternate between the teams until one team has a line of three Xs or Os, or it is a draw.

Grammar in context

Ask students to complete the task. Check answers in open class. Ask students to read more about indirect questions in the *Remember* box.

Remind students that they can find more information in the Grammar reference, Unit 11, page 160.

Answers

1 No (It looks like the language of speculation and expressing uncertainty, but here it is used to make a polite request – a request for information)

2 No The first one doesn't (because it doesn't start like a question), but the second one does (because it does start like a question)

3 No

Language note

Indirect questions

Point out that we use indirect questions to make direct questions sound more polite. You could demonstrate this by asking one student: *What's your favourite sport? When's your birthday?* Ask another student: *Could you tell me what your favourite sport is? I'd like to know when your birthday is.* Ask students: *Which sounded more polite? Which type would you hear in a job interview?* (the second).

Elicit a list of introductory phrases that are used to create indirect questions and write them on the board. Add any that students miss. With each phrase, ask students if it should have a question mark or not.

Encourage the students to copy the following list in their notebooks.

With a question mark: *Do you know …? Can/Could you tell me …?*

Without a question mark: *I'd be grateful if …, I wonder …, I was wondering …, I'd be interested to know …*

1 Ask students to complete the exercise. Check answers in open class.

Answers

1 can/could **2** wonder / was wondering / 'd be grateful
3 can/could **4** if/whether **5** grateful **6** if/whether

2 Ask students to complete the exercise. Students compare their answers in pairs before checking in open class.

Answers

1 I'd be grateful if you could tell me whether there are any places left on the studio tour.

2 I wonder if you know why the trip was cancelled.

3 Could you tell me what time we land in Moscow?

4 Do you know if/whether I can change my hotel reservation?

3 Ask students to complete the exercise. Ask them to compare their answers in pairs before you check them in open class. Note that there are quite a lot of different ways of rewriting the questions.

Suggested answers

1 **Could** you tell me where they filmed the new *Star Wars* film?

2 Can/Could you let us/me **know** whether/if we're going to arrive on time? / We/I'd like to **know** if/whether we are going to arrive on time. / I wonder if / Do you **know** whether we are going to arrive on time?

3 **Can** you tell me / let me know why you decided to travel around the world by bike?

4 Could you **tell** me how I get to the station? / I wonder if you could **tell** me how I get to the station.

Optional extension

Ask each student to write three direct questions they might ask if they were buying a plane ticket.

Students exchange their questions with another student. Both students rewrite their partner's questions as indirect questions and then ask their questions.

For example:
Could I buy a ticket to France here, please?
Which airport does the plane arrive at?
How much does it cost?

Students exchange their questions with another student. Both students rewrite their partner's questions as indirect questions then ask their questions. For example:
I'd like to know if I could buy a ticket to France here, please.
Do you know which airport the plane arrives at?
Could you tell me how much it costs?

THINK | RESEARCH | **CULTURE** | LEARN | ME

In pairs or small groups, students discuss the question. Elicit ideas in open class.

Homework

OWB

Assign students Grammar 2 exercises 1 and 2 on page 87 of their Workbook.

SPEAKING
Interview

→ Student's Book, page 120 SB

Lesson aims

- Focus on answering questions promptly
- Answer personal questions

The *Talk2Me* video in this unit focuses on holidays. People talk about which types of holidays they prefer and why. Students make notes as they watch the video and then listen out for phrases the speakers use to give themselves time to think. The video can be used in one of two ways:

Flipped classroom

Flipped classroom option

Using this approach, students watch the video and complete the exercises for homework. This prepares students for the speaking lesson by introducing them to the topic and the key phrases to use in the exam task. Teachers who use this method will find they have more class time to spend on activating the target language and developing fluency for the final task.

Talk2Me worksheet

Ask students to also complete the *Talk2Me* worksheet on the Resource Centre for more detailed comprehension exercises and more practice of the key phrases.

Classroom option

1 Ask students to spend a minute or two reading the instructions. Play the *Talk2Me* video for students to complete the exercise. Play the video again, if necessary, before checking their answers.

Language note

Tell students that it is natural to hesitate and use the expressions in the *Phrase expert* box, but they should only be used when the students need time to think. They shouldn't be used robotically after every question!

2 Play the *Talk2Me* video again, so students write the name of the person who says the phrases in the *Phrase expert* box. Pause the video from time to time if necessary. Check answers in open class.

Talk2Me worksheet

Ask students to also complete the *Talk2Me* worksheet on the Resource Centre for more detailed comprehension exercises and more practice of the key phrases.

Answers

The transcript and answer key for the *Talk2Me* video exercises and Worksheet can be found on the Teacher's Resource Centre.

Lead-in

In pairs, students play ***Just a minute***. They speak for 60 seconds, trying not to hesitate, repeat any content words or deviate from the subject. Their partner times them. Students then swap roles. Possible topics: *My best holiday. My worst holiday. What I did last summer. My favourite city.*

3 Ask students to complete the exercise. Elicit answers from different students around the class.

Possible answers

Sightseeing holiday: Advantages: You can take great photos, seeing the unique sights of a city is interesting. Disadvantages: It can be expensive if you pay for a tour guide or a sightseeing bus; if you walk it can be tiring.

Beach holiday: Advantages: It's free to go to the beach. You can get a suntan. It's relaxing. You can swim and play games on the beach. Disadvantages: You need good weather. Beach holiday destinations are very popular – you might have to share the beach with lots of people!

Optional extension

In pairs, or small groups, students think of other types of holiday and the advantages and disadvantages of going on them.

4 Ask students to complete the exercise. Elicit answers from different students around the class.

Extra support

Do the first example in open class and write the students' ideas on the board. This will help students with the phrasing of the remaining answers.

Answers

1 difficult question **2** see **3** thought about **4** kind of person **5** tempted **6** honest

Optional extension

In pairs, students role play the conversation twice, taking turns to be A and B.

OPTIMISE YOUR EXAM

Interview

Ask students to read the tips.

- Point out that, in many official oral exams, candidates may be asked questions that they haven't prepared for. They will need to respond promptly as marks will be lost for hesitating excessively.
- Explain that it is better to use a phrase such as those in the *Phrase expert* box to give themselves some time to think, than either saying nothing or just going 'er'.
- Explain to students that it will take time for these phrases to become natural and that some are more appropriate than others for certain questions. For example:
  A: *Where are you from?*
  B: *That's an interesting question!* ✗
  A: *If you could live abroad, where would you choose to live?*
  B: *That's an difficult question!* ✓
- Explain that students will be given credit for extending their sentences rather than giving short answers. An effective way to do this is by adding reasons, details or context to an answer. For example, to the question *What do you like to do in your free time?* a good answer would be:
  That's easy. I love blogging. I have been blogging since I was ten (CONTEXT). I love it because I can express my feelings and it's great when people respond to my posts (REASONS). My blog is called 'More than a student' (DETAILS).

Exam task

5 In pairs, ask students to do the task. Walk round and monitor students, noting down appropriate and inappropriate use of the phrases to go over in a feedback session at the end of the activity. Go through any errors you noted down on the board with students, eliciting corrections from them where possible.

Extra support

Before students attempt the task, give them some time to read through the questions and decide which phrases from the *Phrase expert* box they could use.

Optional extension

Students write their own interesting, difficult or unusual questions to ask. Then the students mingle or work in small groups asking and answering their questions. At the end of the activity students could vote on the most interesting, difficult or unusual question.

Homework

OWB

Assign students Speaking exercises 1, 2 and 3 on pages 88–89 of their Workbook.

USE OF ENGLISH

Word formation | Sentence transformation

→ Student's Book, page 121 SB

Lesson aims

- Focus on word formation and practise a word-formation exam task
- Focus on sentence transformation and practise a sentence-transformation exam task

Lead-in

Give each student a piece of paper and ask them to write an interesting direct question on the topic of holidays.

Collect the pieces of paper and give one to each student.

Each student rewrites the question as an indirect question.

Tell students to stand up and ask their question to three other students.

1 Ask students to complete the exercise. Elicit answers from different students around the class.

Answers

1 1, 5 **2** 3, 4, 6, 7 **3** All of them

Cultural note

Service Civil International (SCI) is an international non-governmental voluntary service organisation. It has 45 branches and a number of partner organisations worldwide. In Great Britain it is known as International Voluntary Service. The organisation was founded in 1920 by a Swiss engineer called Pierre Cérésole. It is based on the idea that people should work together to help others and live peacefully.

OPTIMISE YOUR EXAM

Word formation

Ask students to read the tips.

- Remind students to read the whole text first. Sometimes students will be able to guess the word simply from the context given.
- Remind students that to discover the form of the word, they must look carefully at the words before and after the gap. Do they need a noun, a verb, an adjective or an adverb?
- Point out to students that they do not lose marks for an incorrect answer, so they should always guess. If they know it is a noun, they could experiment with suffixes of other nouns that they know, e.g. *-tion*, *-al*, *-ness*, *-ity*, *-ment*, *-ant*.
- Reading the text with the words in place will reveal answers which don't sound right.
- Encourage students to read as much as possible. The more reading they do, the more word forms they will become familiar with.

Refer students to the Vocabulary reference, page 168, for more information on word formation.

▼ Exam task

2 Ask students to complete the exercise. Ask them to compare their answers in pairs before you check them in open class.

Answers

1 meaningful **2** helping **3** activities **4** Participants **5** valuable **6** Applications **7** arrangements **8** hugely

3 Ask students to complete the exercise. Elicit answers from different students around the class.

Answers

1 1 **2** 4, 5, 6 **3** 2, 3, 5 **4** 4

OPTIMISE YOUR EXAM

Sentence transformation

Ask students to read the tip.

- Point out that when doing a sentence transformation, students should always try to think what is being tested, as practised in Exercise 3. They should look carefully at the position of the information in both sentences and notice any slight change in wording.
- Passives, reported speech and comparative structures are often tested in sentence transformation as well as phrasal verbs. Students often have to change the form of a word in the given sentence, e.g. from verb or adjective to noun or to an *-ing* form after a preposition.
- Remind students to count the number of words they have written and check carefully that their answer includes all the information in the first sentence.

▼ Exam task

4 Ask students to complete the exercise. Ask them to compare their answers in pairs before you check them in open class.

Answers

1 picked Will up at/from / picked up Will at/from
2 was told not to
3 asked Dionne if/whether she was
4 warned you against/about losing your
5 apologised for not meeting Greg
6 is no point (in) getting

Homework

Assign students Use of English exercises 1, 2 and 3 on page 89 of their Workbook. OWB

WRITING
A letter / An email

→ Student's Book, pages 122–123 SB

Lesson aims

- Focus on language in a letter or an email
- Plan and write an informal email

Lead-in

Write these words in large letters spread out on the board: *A ZOO, AN ART GALLERY, A SCIENCE MUSEUM, A NATURE WALK IN THE COUNTRYSIDE, A HISTORIC HOUSE.*

Ask student to discuss in pairs what they would like or dislike about going on a school trip to these places.

Allow three to four minutes for students to discuss the questions before eliciting ideas in open class.

1 In pairs or as a group, students answer the questions. Elicit answers in open class.

Answers

Students' own answers

2 Ask students to complete the exercise. Ask them to compare their answers in pairs before you check them in open class.

Suggested answers

1 *Hey, It was great to, thanks, got to, Well, great, got back, tons of homework, I can't wait!, Bye for now!*

2 Grammar: Contractions (*I can't believe …, I don't like …, I'd better go …, I've got …, I'm going …, I can't wait!, I'll write*)

Punctuation: Exclamation marks (*Hey Carrie!, … scary!, I can't wait! Bye for now!*); Dashes (*paragraphs 1 and 2*)

3 Ask students to complete the exercise. Check answers in open class.

Suggested answers

1 was **2** bought (accept 'received' if they can explain the situation) **3** was given, received **4** became/were **5** caught **6** persuaded/forced **7** obtain/purchase **8** arrive at / reach **9** find **10** entered/boarded

OPTIMISE YOUR EXAM

A letter / An email

Ask students to read the tips.

- Tell students that when they read the task they should notice who they are writing to and what type of text it is (this will determine the layout of the text, its style, language and the level of formality needed). They should also underline all the information that they have to include (content) and how they should communicate it (e.g. explain, tell, compare, etc.).
- Remind students that in an informal letter/email they should not include formal vocabulary, expressions or linking words, but they should still use a variety of different words and phrases.

For more information on writing informal letters/emails, refer students to the Writing reference, page 171.

Exam task

4 Ask students to complete the exercise individually. Then ask them to discuss their ideas in pairs. Walk round, helping students and monitoring for accuracy.

5 Plan Ask students to complete the paragraph plan. You may want to look at students' plans, if this is possible, to check them and give advice and suggestions for improvement before students take the next step.

Extra support

Students look at each other's plans and exchange ideas and suggestions.

6 Write Ask students to write their email in an appropriate style in 140–190 words. Depending on time, it may be a good idea to set this and the subsequent checklist exercise for homework.

7 Check Ask students to complete the checklist before they hand in their email.

Homework OWB

Assign students Writing exercises 1, 2, 3 and 4 on page 90 of their Workbook and Progress check 11 on page 91.

12 Achieve the impossible

UNIT AIMS

Exam preparation in Unit 12:

- identify synonyms
- identify speakers' attitudes in short extracts
- check understanding and interrupt in a discussion
- understand different parts of speech and use them correctly in a word-formation exercise
- read for gist in a multiple-choice cloze exercise
- make a recommendation in a review

TEACHER'S PRESENTATION KIT

- *Talk2Me* videos
- Speaking test videos
- Class and Workbook audio
- Workbook pages and answer key

UNIT OVERVIEW

Student's Book / Digital Student's Book SB		Workbook / Online Workbook OWB
LESSON / EXAM TASK	**EXAM SKILLS / LANGUAGE FOCUS**	**CONSOLIDATION**
Reading **Multiple matching**	Identifying synonyms (3) A magazine article	Workbook, pp 92–93, Exercises 1, 2, 3, 4 Unit 12, Reading, Exercises 1, 2, 3, 4
Grammar 1	Inversions	Workbook, p 94, Exercises 1, 2, 3 Unit 12, Grammar 1, Exercises 1, 2, 3
Vocabulary	Easily-confused words Phrasal verbs Idioms with *keep* and *lose*	Workbook, pp 94–95, Exercises 1, 2, 3, 4 Unit 12, Vocabulary, Exercises 1, 2, 3, 4
Listening **Multiple choice (extracts)**	Listening for opinion and attitude (2)	Workbook, p 96, Exercises 1, 2, 3 Unit 12, Listening, Exercises 1, 2, 3
Grammar 2	Cleft sentences	Workbook, p 95, Exercises 1, 2, 3 Unit 12, Grammar 2, Exercises 1, 2, 3
Speaking **Discussion**	Managing a discussion	Workbook, pp 96–97, Exercises 1, 2 Unit 12, Speaking, Exercises 1, 2
Use of English **Word formation** **Multiple-choice cloze**	Parts of speech Reading for gist	Workbook, p 97, Exercises 1, 2 Unit 12, Use of English, Exercises 1, 2
Writing **A review**	Using your imagination	Workbook, p 98, Exercises 1, 2, 3 Unit 12, Writing, Exercises 1, 2, 3
Progress check	Check language progress for Units 11 and 12	Workbook, p 99, Progress check and Cumulative progress Progress check and Cumulative progress

Additional material

PRESENTATION KIT	TEACHER'S / STUDENT'S RESOURCE CENTRE RC	TEST GENERATOR
Talk2Me video *Sorry, do you mean …?*	**Unit 12 worksheets:** *Optimise your grammar* (Standard and Higher), *Optimise your vocabulary* (Standard and Higher), *Talk2Me* video, *Say it right* **Units 11–12 worksheets:** CLIL, Culture, Everyday English (TRC only), Grammar communication (TRC only)	Unit Test 12 (Standard and Higher) End-of-year Test (Standard and Higher)

READING

Multiple matching | A magazine extract

→ Student's Book, pages 124–125 SB

Lesson aims

- Focus on multiple matching
- Practise a multiple-matching exam task

Lead-in

Ask the students to look at the unit title ***Achieve the impossible***, and ask them what they think it means (*manage to do something that nobody thought would actually be possible; to succeed in accomplishing an amazing achievement*). Ask students what they think the lesson is going to be about (*feats and achievements*). Explain that a *feat* is an achievement that is difficult or impressive, so to *achieve the impossible* is quite a feat.

Draw students' attention to the photo and ask if anyone knows what the man is doing. (He is walking a high wire or tightrope.) Ask, *What are the odds that he will fall?* (make sure students understand that *odds* means *chances, probability or likelihood*.)

1 In pairs or as a group, students answer the questions. Elicit answers in open class and try to develop a class discussion on the topic.

Answers

Students' own answers

2 Ask students to complete the exercise. Ask them to compare their answers in pairs before you check them in open class.

Answers

1 c **2** e **3** d **4** a

3 Ask students to complete the exercise. Ask them to compare their answers in pairs before you check them in open class.

Answers

1 c **2** f **3** a **4** e

b and d are not needed

OPTIMISE YOUR EXAM

Multiple matching

Ask students to read the tips.

- When students read the text for the first time they will notice the general differences between the texts. They do not need to understand every word.
- Remind students that underlining the key words in each question will help them identify synonyms in the text, as they practised in Exercise 3. This will, in turn, help them decide on their answer.
- Point out that all the information contained in the question, and not just one part, must appear in the text.
- Remind students that they can complete the answers in a multiple-matching task in any order.

Fast finishers

Ask fast finishers to identify the specific words or phrases which have a similar meaning and write them in their notebooks.

Suggested answers

didn't receive = missed out on
official schooling = formal education
was educated = was brought up
appreciate the natural world = respect the land
keep on = continue
research = investigating
was taught = learnt
deal with everyday situations = valuable life skills

▼ Exam task

4 3.11 **Note: The reading text is also available on the audio CD. You may want to have students listen and read the text before doing the exam task.**

Ask students to complete the exercise. Ask them to compare their answers in pairs before you check them in open class. Ask students to explain their evidence.

Answers

1 B (*… she is now teaching other young people about one of these skills: leadership … Mursal's message in her classes is particularly aimed at young women and their empowerment in the local and global community. Rarely do a few skateboards lead to such an inspirational outcome!*)
2 A (*Although he missed out on any formal education for several years, he finally returned to school …*)
3 C (*Not only will the prize money allow her to continue her research …*)
4 B (*As a result, she has learnt valuable life skills …*)
5 D (*Despite his fame, Xiuhtezcatl likes to do the same things that most young people do …*)
6 A (*His education was eventually fully funded by the local government.*)
7 D (*… he was brought up to respect the land …*)
8 B (*… represented Afghanistan's non-profit organisation Skateistan at a global conference in Doha, Qatar.*)
9 C (*Olivia designed an economical test which not only offered results in 30 minutes but also used a card which can store antibodies for up to a week without refrigeration … a considerable improvement on current tests …*)
10 A (*He started observing cars in his local town and by using his natural mechanical skills he worked out how to motorise his toys.*)

5 Ask students to complete the exercise. Check answers in open class.

Answers

at the forefront (adj phr): in a leading or important position
came up with (phr v): to think of something such as an idea or a plan
composure (n): the feeling of being calm, confident, and relaxed
empower (v): give someone more control over their life or more power to do something
encouraged by (v + prep): given confidence or hope by something or someone
orphaned (adj): having no parents because they are dead
outcome (n): the final result of a process, meeting, activity, etc.
spread awareness (v phr): distribute knowledge or understanding of a subject, issue or situation over a large area

Optional extension

Ask students which of the four young people they thought was the most inspiring.

Ask students if they can think of any other examples of inspiring young people.

Homework

OWB

Assign students Reading exercises 1, 2, 3 and 4 on page 92 of their Workbook.

GRAMMAR 1
Inversions

→ Student's Book, page 126 SB

Lesson aims

- Understand the correct usage of inversions
- Practise using inversions

Lead-in

Play ***Twenty questions***. In groups of three or four, one student thinks of a film, book, TV series, etc. that is about an amazing achievement or someone succeeding against all the odds. The other students take turns trying to guess it by asking up to 20 *yes/no* questions. A *yes* answer earns the questioner the chance to ask another question; a *no* answer means the next student asks a question. If they haven't guessed it after 20 questions, the student gives them the answer.

Each student takes one turn to think of a film, book or TV series.

Grammar in context

Ask students to complete the task. Refer them to the *Remember* box if they need help.

Then ask students to check their answers by finding the sentences in the extract on page 125.

Remind students that they can find more information in the Grammar reference, Unit 12, page 160.

Answers

1 b **2** a

Language note

Explain that inversion is used in formal texts or speech when we want to emphasise the adverbial. It is also used in writing to make what we write more interesting or dramatic.

Highlight that *hardly* is followed by *when*, while *no sooner* is followed by *than* (*sooner* is the comparative form of *soon*). Other adverbials that use *when* are *barely* and *scarcely*.

Point out that *hardly*, *no sooner*, etc. are followed by the past perfect to emphasise that one event quickly followed another.

1 Ask students to complete the exercise. Check answers in open class.

Answers

1 Hardly had I reached (*I had hardly reached* is also possible)
2 No sooner had we taken
3 Little did we realise
4 Only when we found
5 Not only did we lose
6 Seldom do

Mixed ability

Check the answers to Exercise 1. Divide the class into A and B pairs, mixing up higher and lower level students. Tell Student A to read out the first sentences in 1–6 and the sentence prompt. Student B tries to formulate the second sentence without looking at their notes. If the answer is correct, Student B continues. If they make a mistake, Student A has a turn, starting again from sentence 1. The aim of the game is for both students to go through all the sentence transformations in one go without making any mistakes.

2 Ask students to complete the exercise. Ask them to compare their answers in pairs before you check them in open class.

Answers

1 *Sixteen-year-olds rarely sail around the world*
Rarely do sixteen-year-olds sail around the world

2 *... but she didn't know how it would end up.*
Little did she know how it would end up.

3 *She had never had to face such difficult conditions so far from land.*
Never had she had to face such difficult conditions so far from land.

4 *Immediately after she had done this, the winds became stronger again and caused more damage.*
No sooner had she done this than the winds became stronger again and caused more damage.

5 *When her satellite phone failed, and her sail broke and ended up in the sea, Abby knew that she would have to set off her emergency satellite beacons.*
Only when her satellite phone failed, and her sail broke and ended up in the sea, did Abby know that she would have to set off her emergency satellite beacons.

6 *A 16-year-old has seldom had such a brave story to tell.*
Seldom has a 16-year-old had such a brave story to tell.

Mixed ability

If less confident students haven't located the six sentences in the text after a few minutes, or are finding it difficult, elicit the six sentences from the whole class so the students can dedicate more time to practising using inversion. Ask more confident students who finish early to select three new items of vocabulary, look them up in their dictionaries and write them up on the board, with definitions.

Optional extension

Students write three personalised sentences using inversion. Elicit the sentences in open class.

Homework

OWB

Assign students Grammar 1 exercises 1, 2 and 3 on page 94 of their Workbook.

VOCABULARY
Topic vocabulary | Phrasal verbs | Idioms

→ Student's Book, page 127 SB

Lesson aims

- Understand the correct usage of:
  - easily-confused words
  - phrasal verbs
  - idioms with *keep* and *lose*

Lead-in

Write these three sentences on the board.

1 ______ had I got home when my mum asked me if I had done my homework.

2 ______ have I taught such a wonderful class.

3 ______ did I know that the man I saw outside was a famous actor.

Ask students to work in pairs and think of all the possible words or phrases that could fill the gaps.

Answers
1 Hardly, Barely, Scarcely **2** Never, Rarely, Seldom **3** Little

Optional extension

Students write their own inverted sentences with gaps for another student to complete.

Easily-confused words

1 3.12 Ask students to complete the exercise. Play the audio for students to listen and check their answers.

Answers/Audioscript

1 Despite his talent, Van Gogh was relatively *unknown* during his lifetime.
2 Jesse James was an *infamous* outlaw in the Wild West.
3 It took a huge *effort* to get to the top of the mountain.
4 You'll be rewarded for all the hard *work* you've put in this term.
5 Don't give up. I'm sure you'll *achieve* your goal one day.
6 To *succeed* in passing the exam, you need to focus on what's important.
7 If you *fail* the exam, don't let it stop you from following your dreams.
8 Some people become more determined when they *lose* a contest.

Refer students to the Vocabulary reference, page 168, for more information on topic vocabulary.

Extra support

Check the pronunciation of the following words: *infamous* /'ɪnfəməs/, *earn* /ɜː(r)n/ and *succeed* /sək'siːd/.

2 Ask students to complete the exercise. Ask them to compare their sentences in pairs before you elicit some examples in open class.

Suggested answers

The restaurant by our house is **famed** for its seafood.
My brother is unemployed and looking for a **job**.
My dad **earns** quite a lot of money in his job.
Yesterday I **missed** the bus and was late for school.

3 Ask students to complete the exercise. Ask them to compare their answers in pairs before you check them in open class.

Answers
1 effort **2** has achieved **3** unknown **4** fail **5** succeed **6** missed **7** job **8** lost

Fast finishers

Ask fast finishers to write two more sentences with a gap which must be filled by a vocabulary item from Exercise 1. Students read their sentences aloud making a 'beep' sound when they reach the gap. The other students have to say what the missing word is.

Phrasal verbs

4 3.13 Ask students to complete the exercise. Play the audio for students to listen and check their answers.

Answers/Audioscript

start or make something start: spark off, set off
prevent, keep away: cut off, rope off
finish, complete: finish off, log off
remove: shave off, wipe off

Extra support

Put the following words on the board: *spark*, *beard*, *rope* and *wipe*. Elicit the meaning from the class, giving your own definitions and examples to clarify meaning if necessary.

Refer students to the Vocabulary reference, page 168, for more information on phrasal verbs.

Optional extension

Ask students to put the phrasal verbs from Exercise 4 into personalised sentences.

Ask students to share their sentences in open class.

Idioms with *keep* and *lose*

5 3.14 Ask students to complete the exercise. Play the audio for students to listen and check their answers.

Answers/Audioscript

1 If you don't *lose your nerve*, you'll reach your goal!

2 Try to *keep sight of* what you want to achieve at all times.

3 Make sure you *keep your head* during all the excitement and you'll have a good chance of winning.

4 Try to focus your energy and not *lose your temper* during the game.

5 I was determined to *keep my word* and do what I had promised to do.

6 When you really concentrate on a task, it's easy to *lose track of* time.

Refer students to the Vocabulary reference, page 168, for more information on idioms.

Optional extension

Tell students to ask each other questions using the idioms. Put the following prompts on the board for support:

When was the last time …

Do you usually …

Have you ever …

Do you know someone who …

Homework

Assign students Vocabulary exercises 1, 2, 3 and 4 on pages 94–95 of their Workbook.

OWB

LISTENING

Multiple choice (extracts)

→ Student's Book, page 128 SB

Lesson aims

- Focus on multiple choice (extracts)
- Practise a multiple-choice (extracts) exam task

Lead-in

Play ***Back to the board***. Divide the class into two teams. Ask a volunteer from team A to sit with his/her back to the board, facing their team. Choose words, phrasal verbs or idioms from the previous lesson and write the words on the board one by one. Team A defines the word for the volunteer student to guess in one minute. After one minute, it is the other team's turn to define a word, and so on. The team that describes the most words in one minute wins the round.

1 In pairs or as a group, students ask and answer the questions. Elicit ideas from different students around the class.

Answers

Students' own answers

2 Ask students to complete the exercise. Ask them to compare their answers in pairs before you check them in open class.

Answers

never (2B), totally (2C), most (question 3), mainly (question 5), particularly (question 6), most (question 7)

3 Ask students to complete the exercise. Check answers in open class.

Answers

1 most **2** totally/mainly **3** particularly **4** never/mainly **5** mainly

OPTIMISE YOUR EXAM

Multiple choice (extracts)

Ask students to read the tips.

- Encourage students to use any time they have before the audio starts to underline key words in the questions, especially the adverbs, which they looked at in Exercise 2.
- Remind students that when the question mentions the feelings of the speaker, as in question 1 in Exercise 4, they should listen carefully to the tone, pitch, volume and speed of the delivery, as well as the words. How a speaker says something can tell them a lot about the speaker's attitude.
- Point out that in many exam tasks like this one, students hear each section twice before they go on to hear the next one. Remind students to use the second listening to check their answers as well as to double check that the answers they have eliminated are definitely incorrect options.

Exam task

4 3.15 Play the track for students to listen and complete the exercise. Don't check answers at this stage, as students will listen again to check in Exercise 5.

Extra support

Before you play the track again, ask students to discuss in pairs the possible answers and try to exclude one of the options in each situation, saying why they have eliminated it. Don't give away the answers at this point. When you check the answers in Exercise 5, ask students to say which option they excluded on the first listening and if they were right.

5 3.15 Play the track again for students to listen and check their answers to Exercise 4. In open class, check the answers and discuss the specific clues that helped them choose them.

Answers

1 B (*I was really pleased that my mum came … she's terrified of getting on a plane, isn't she? … I know. It was the first time she had flown anywhere for over 30 years. I know how difficult it was for her but she was amazing. She didn't complain once.*)

2 B (*… the first blind athlete to qualify for the regular Olympics.*)

3 A (*It was the way everyone else reacted that felt really good. That made it feel like I'd done something special … Just being treated like a hero for a day was enough of a reward!*)

4 A (*I was sorry when I had to put the book down, though.*)

5 C (*But the first thing you notice when you come here is the main road that runs just a few metres away from the site. It's just unbelievable. This should be a quiet place to enjoy the stones, but instead it's really noisy.*)

6 B (*It's that refusal to consider failure that makes him a great hero.*)

7 C (*What I did, a 24-hour trek, was really hard. But when you're doing it for charity, you have to carry on, no matter what. That thought keeps you going, in spite of difficulties.*)

8 C (*… what is really remarkable is the fact that he was deaf when he wrote it.*)

Mixed ability

Give students a copy of the audioscript.

Ask less confident students to underline the distractors in the listening to help them understand more about the kind of traps examiners set.

Ask higher-level students to select three new words or phrases, look them up in their dictionaries and write them up on the board, with definitions.

THINK | RESEARCH | CULTURE | **LEARN** | ME

In pairs, students discuss the questions. Elicit answers in open class and offer any advice that the students have not considered.

Homework

OWB

Assign students Listening exercises 1, 2 and 3 on page 96 of their Workbook.

GRAMMAR 2
Cleft sentences

→ Student's Book, page 129 SB

Lesson aims

- Understand the correct usage of cleft sentences
- Practise using cleft sentences

Lead-in

Write this sentence stem on the board and ask students to work in pairs to think of ways to complete the sentence: *What I like about English is …*

Elicit suggested sentences from the students and accept all reasonable suggestions. Only correct the sentences when the grammar is incorrect.

Tell students that the sentences they have formed are all cleft sentences, and that they are going to look at these in more detail in the lesson.

Grammar in context

Ask students to complete the task. Refer them to the *Remember* box if they need help. Check answers in open class.

Remind students that they can find more information in the Grammar reference, Unit 12, page 160.

Answers

1 b **2** a

Language note

Cleft sentences

Explain to students that cleft sentences, like inversion, are a way of adding emphasis.

They emphasise what we want to say by focusing on a particular part of the sentence.

Cleft sentences that begin with *It* focus directly on what we want to emphasise. *It's John I like (not Adam).*

Cleft sentences that use *what* (or other question words) delay the important information until the end of the sentence which keeps the reader/listener's attention. *What I really like about John is his sense of humour.*

Cleft sentences are often found in writing where we cannot use intonation for emphasis, but they are also often used in speech.

1 Ask students to complete the exercise. Ask them to compare their answers in pairs before you check them in open class.

Answers

1 is that **2** It **3** is that **4** that **5** is that **6** only

2 Ask students to complete the exercise. Check answers in open class.

Answers

1 That, What **2 what**, that **3 which**, why **4 It**, What **5 when**, until **6 do I love**, I love

3 Ask students to complete the exercise. Do the first one together as an example if you think your students need this. Ask students to compare their answers in pairs before you check them in open class.

Answers

1 What impresses you when you see the Burj Khalifa is that it is so tall. / What you are impressed by when you see the Burj Khalifa is that it is so tall.

2 It is the engineering process involved that is really incredible.

3 It is not until you visit the observation deck on the 124th floor that you realise what a feat it is.

4 What is incredible is that the spire was built inside the tower and then lifted into position.

5 What most people don't know is that it is based on the shape of a flower.

6 It was not until the building was finished that it was named Burj Khalifa.

Optional extension

Students think of a building they think is impressive and write three cleft sentences about it.

Suggested answers

What I love about Big Ben is the sound of the clock.

The reason why I like the Sagrada Familia is that it has many different styles.

What I like about the Eiffel Tower is the simple design.

SAY IT RIGHT

Intonation in cleft sentences

TRC

For the *Say it right* pronunciation activity and instructions, go to the Teacher's Resource Centre.

THINK | RESEARCH | **CULTURE** | LEARN | ME

In pairs or small groups, students discuss the questions. Elicit ideas in open class.

Homework

OWB

Assign students Grammar 2 exercises 1, 2 and 3 on page 95 of their Workbook.

SPEAKING

Discussion

→ Student's Book, page 130 SB

Lesson aims

- Focus on checking understanding and interrupting
- Practise having a discussion

The *Talk2Me* video in this unit focuses on being famous. People talk about the advantages and disadvantages of being famous. Students make notes as they watch the video and then listen out for phrases for interrupting or for checking understanding. The video can be used in one of two ways:

Flipped classroom

Flipped classroom option

Using this approach, students watch the video and complete the exercises for homework. This prepares students for the speaking lesson by introducing them to the topic and the key phrases to use in the exam task. Teachers who use this method will find they have more class time to spend on activating the target language and developing fluency for the final task.

***Talk2Me* worksheet**

Ask students to also complete the *Talk2Me* worksheet on the Resource Centre for more detailed comprehension exercises and more practice of the key phrases.

Classroom option

1 Ask students to spend a minute or two reading the questions. Play the *Talk2Me* video for students to complete the exercise. Play the video again, if necessary, before checking their answers.

2 Play the *Talk2Me* video again, so students rewrite the sentences with the correct words. Pause the video from time to time if necessary. Check answers in open class.

***Talk2Me* worksheet**

Ask students to also complete the *Talk2Me* worksheet on the Resource Centre for more detailed comprehension exercises and more practice of the key phrases.

Answers

The transcript and answer key for the *Talk2Me* video exercises and Worksheet can be found on the Teacher's Resource Centre.

Cultural note

Tell students that in some countries it is considered rude to interrupt when someone is speaking. However, when it is necessary, it is important to be polite. Raising the hand slightly and saying one of the phrases in the *Phrase expert* box firmly and confidently will be enough to stop the other speaker enough to get your point into the conversation. Other phrases like *Excuse me*; *One moment*; *Wait* and *Hang on* can also be used to get the speakers attention.

Lead-in

Play ***Twenty questions***. In groups of three or four, one student thinks of a famous person and the other students take turns trying to guess it by asking up to 20 *yes/no* questions. A *yes* answer earns the questioner the chance to ask another question; a *no* answer means the next student asks a question. If they haven't guessed it in 20 questions the student gives them the answer. Each student takes one turn to think of a famous person.

3 Ask students to discuss the statements. Set a time limit of two minutes before eliciting answers from different students around the class.

Answers

Students' own answers

4 Ask students to make notes and compare in pairs. Elicit answers from different students around the class.

OPTIMISE YOUR EXAM

Discussion

Ask students to read the tips.

- Remind students that in many official oral exams examiners give candidates marks for interactive communication. Often candidates have to interact with a partner in a discussion-type activity in which they may need to interrupt their partner to clarify meaning or to contribute to the discussion.
- Explain that it is better to use a phrase to interrupt politely, such as those in the *Phrase expert* box, than simply talking over their partner. If candidates interrupt impolitely they may lose marks for insensitive turn-taking.
- In the same way, it is important that candidates do not dominate the discussion by speaking all the time. They should involve their partner by asking them questions such as, *What do you think?* or *Do you feel the same?*.
- Remind students that if they don't understand their partner's idea, they should ask for clarification using the phrases in the *Phrase expert* box. Having clarified the meaning, students should respond to their partner's idea before giving their own.

▼ Exam task

5 In groups of three, ask students to do the task. Walk round and monitor them, praising them when they interrupt politely. Take notes to go over in a feedback session at the end of the activity. Go through any errors you noted down on the board with students, eliciting corrections from them where possible.

Extra support

Before students attempt the task, give them some time to review the *Phrase expert* box to remind themselves of the phrases for interruption and clarification.

Optional extension

Repeat the activity twice with a different student taking the role of the examiner. To also give more realistic exam practice, you could do the exam task under real exam conditions allowing four minutes for students to complete the task.

Homework

OWB

Assign students Speaking exercises 1 and 2 on pages 96–97 of their Workbook.

USE OF ENGLISH

Word formation | Multiple-choice cloze

→ Student's Book, page 131 SB

Lesson aims

- Focus on word formation and practise a word-formation exam task
- Focus on multiple-choice cloze and practise a multiple-choice cloze exam task

Lead-in

Write ten words on the board and ask students to write as many derivatives from each of the words as possible. Set a time limit of two minutes. You could set this up as a competitive activity and have students work in small groups. The group with the most correct words is the winner.

Suggested words: *allow, belief, educate, friend, know, nation, nature, power, success, use.*

1 Ask students to complete the exercise. Elicit answers from different students around the class.

Answers

1 wide: width(s); able: ability(-ies), inability(-ies), disability(-ies); capable: capability(-ies), incapability(-ies), capacity(-ies), incapacity(-ies)

2 celebrate: celebration(s), celebrity(-ies); accomplish: accomplishment(s)

3 program: programmed, programming; child: childish, childlike, childless; mathematics: mathematical

OPTIMISE YOUR EXAM

Word formation

Ask students to read the tip.

- Spend some time reviewing which parts of speech are to be likely to be tested in word-formation tasks (*nouns, adjectives, verbs, adverbs*).
- Noun forms that might be tested are: singular (e.g. *person*), plural (e.g. *people*), uncountable (e.g. *advice*), nouns for people (e.g. *advisors*), gerunds as nouns (e.g. *advising*).
- Adjective forms that might be tested are: positive (e.g. *happy*), negative (e.g. *unhappy*), comparative (e.g. *happier*), superlative (e.g. *happiest*).
- Explain that adverbs are usually formed by adding *-ly* to the adjective, except for irregular adverbs (e.g. *good – well, fast – fast, hard – hard*, etc.).
- Verb forms that might be tested are: the infinitive (e.g. *eat*), the gerund (e.g. *eating*), the third person singular (e.g. *eats*), the present participle (e.g. *eating*), the past simple (e.g. *ate*), the past participle (e.g. *eaten*).
- Encourage students to categorise vocabulary in their notebooks according to which prefix or suffix the word can take, to help them become familiar with these word forms.

Refer students to the Vocabulary reference, page 168, for more information on word formation.

Exam task

2 Ask students to complete the exercise. Ask them to compare their answers in pairs before you check them in open class.

Answers

1 celebrations **2** widely **3** programmer **4** childhood **5** disability **6** mathematician **7** accomplishment **8** capabilities

3 Ask students to complete the exercise. Elicit answers from different students around the class.

Answers

1 Gaps 1, 3, 6, 7 and 8 test vocabulary from the unit. Gaps 2, 4 and 5 test grammar from the unit.

2 a phrasal verb

3 *keep sight of, keep your head, keep your word*

Optional extension

Ask students: *What are the opposites of the three expressions with keep?*

Answers

lose sight of, lose your head, not keep your word

OPTIMISE YOUR EXAM

Multiple-choice cloze

Ask students to read the tips.

- In an exam, students should always read the text for general understanding first. Remind them that when they have finished the task, they should read the text again and make sure it makes sense with all the answers in place.
- If students don't know the answer, they should first eliminate the wrong answers and then use their intuition by saying the options, and if one 'sounds right', they should go for that one.
- Remind students that the more they read in English, the easier this type of exam task will become because they will become more familiar with common collocations, vocabulary and structures.

Exam task

4 Ask students to complete the exercise. Ask them to compare their answers in pairs before you check them in open class.

Answers

1 D **2** A **3** B **4** C **5** C **6** B/C **7** A **8** C

Fast finishers

Write these definitions on the board and ask students to find the words or phrases in the text in Exercise 4 that match them.

1 *being lighter than air, and moving slowly through it*

2 *flights into space*

3 *a situation in which people, teams, businesses, etc. compete with one another*

Answers

1 floating **2** missions **3** rivalry

Homework

OWB

Assign students Use of English exercises 1 and 2 on page 97 of their Workbook.

WRITING
A review

→ Student's Book, pages 132–133 SB

Lesson aims

- Focus on language in a review
- Plan and write a review of a place

Lead-in

Explain to students that in this lesson they will be looking at a review. Ask students to work in pairs and write down as many things that a review could be about as they can think of in 90 seconds. Elicit different answers in open class. Ask which type of reviews students read most often.

Suggested answers

A book, a film, a TV series, a restaurant, a hotel, a museum, an art gallery, a tourist destination, a computer game, an attraction, a play, a show, a concert, a song, an album, an electronic device, a service.

1 In pairs or as a group, students answer the questions. Elicit answers in open class.

Answers

Students' own answers

2 Ask students to complete the exercise. Ask them to compare their answer in pairs before you check it in open class.

Answer

The writer has used structure b.

3 Ask students to complete the exercise. Check the answer in open class.

Answer

Structure c could also be used.

4 Ask students to complete the exercise. Check answers in open class.

Suggested answers

The skywalk is a kind of bridge made out of steel and glass and it sticks out over the Grand Canyon in the USA.

... a drop of 1,200 metres!

... not only does the ticket include transport and a meal, but you also get a certificate to show you visited.

... you are not allowed to take your own camera onto the skywalk.

OPTIMISE YOUR EXAM

A review

Ask students to read the tips.

- Point out to students that they can make their review more interesting to the reader by using a range of adjectives. Highlight examples in the text (*amazing, impressive, incredible, expensive, reasonable, fantastic*).
- Tell students not to worry whether any facts they include in their review are accurate or not as this would make no difference to their mark in an exam. An English exam is a test of English, not of general knowledge.
- Explain that offering a balance of positive and negative points makes a review more believable to the reader.
- Remind students that clearly stating their opinion and recommendation in the final paragraph is vital because, in real life, readers often look at the last paragraph of a review first to see what the general opinion is.

For more information on writing reviews, refer students to the Writing reference, page 170.

Exam task

5 Ask students to complete the exercise individually. Then ask them to discuss their ideas in pairs. Walk round, helping students and monitoring for accuracy.

6 **Plan** Ask students to complete the paragraph plan using their notes from Exercise 5. You may want to look at students' plans, if possible, to check them and give advice and suggestions for improvement before students take the next step.

Extra support

Students look at each other's plans and exchange ideas and suggestions.

7 **Write** Ask students to write their review in an appropriate style in 140–190 words. Depending on time, it may be a good idea to set this and the subsequent checklist exercise for homework.

8 **Check** Ask students to complete the checklist before they hand in their review.

Homework

OWB

Assign students Writing exercises 1, 2 and 3 on page 98 of their Workbook and Progress check 12 on page 99.

Answers PROGRESS CHECK Units 11–12

Exercise 1
1 flights **2** helpful **3** celebrations **4** arrangements **5** ability **6** valuable **7** meaningfully **8** accomplishment

Exercise 2
1 do I like – I like
2 is the entrance to the Underground – the entrance to the Underground is
3 ✓
4 what – that
5 ago – before
6 I knew – did I know
7 to tell – telling
8 was until – was not / wasn't until
9 when – than
10 only was – was only

Exercise 3
1 trip **2** effort **3** fee **4** route **5** reach **6** fail **7** point **8** word **9** unknown **10** track

Exercise 4
1 logged off **2** cut off **3** turn around **4** made for **5** check out **6** roped off **7** set off **8** get away **9** drop off **10** pick (us) up

Exercise 5
1 had the phone begun
2 finishing off / you finish off your homework
3 was not / wasn't until she left
4 only was I exhausted but
5 not to lose your temper
6 did people see what

OPTIMISE YOUR EXAMS

The *Optimise your exams* pages are designed to give your students extra training in exam tasks. Each task includes OPTIMISE boxes, which contain tips for students. Remind students to read these boxes before they start each of the exam tasks.

Students can work on the tasks in class or for homework, and the tasks can be done at whatever stage you feel is most appropriate for your class.

Your students should complete these pages before they move on to the Practice test in the Workbook.

READING SB pages 136–137

1

Suggested answers:

stories/fiction, advertisements, letters, reviews, messages, informational material, brochures, guides, manuals

2

1 Multiple-choice questions:
1 C **2** E **3** D **4** A **5** B

2 Gapped text:
1 D **2** A **3** E **4** B **5** C

3 Multiple matching:
1 C **2** A **3** E **4** B **5** D

3

Students read the instructions and the text for a maximum of two minutes.

4

Students' own answers

5

1 Wordspotting: student has jumped to a conclusion quickly because of similar words in the text

2 Student has missed the word *main* in the root question which is the key word, and the line: *The big pull for the new audience …* in the text

3 Student has focused on specific phrases but has missed the whole sense of the message, as Ryan uses linking word of contrast *but* and then adds reason at the end. Students need to read the whole section and not just get bogged down in phrases with similar meaning

6

4 C **5** D **6** D

LISTENING SB pages 138–139

1

1 two friends, a film and the actors' performances

2 a teacher, a class presentation

3 a teenager, a difficult situation in the mountains

2

Suggested answers:

1 What do the <u>two friends agree</u> about? The actors could have put more emotion into their acting.

2 <u>Why</u> is the <u>teacher talking</u> to the <u>class</u>? To give students advice on how to plan a presentation.

3 <u>How</u> does the <u>teenager feel</u> about the <u>experience</u>? Scared at first, but then felt it was worth it at the end.

3

Students' own answers

4

1 B **2** C **3** C

5

You'll hear a <u>student</u> called Suzanne Wilson talking about a <u>volunteer project</u> in the <u>Canary Islands</u> in <u>Spain</u>. For questions 1–10 <u>complete the sentences</u> with a <u>word or short phrase</u>.

6

Students' own answers

7

1 conservationist – conservation / marine conservation

2 strong relationships with species – strong relationships

3 camaflage – camouflage

4 19 days – 90 days

5 hard shell – correct answer

6 nesting sights – nesting sites

8

1 student didn't fill in the exact words they heard

2 student didn't read what came before and after the gap to decide how many words were needed

3 student didn't check spelling

4 student didn't fill in the exact words they heard

5 correct answer

6 student didn't check spelling

9

7 daily running **8** insight **9** kayaking, horse-riding **10** take initiative in teams

SPEAKING SB pages 140–143

1

A 3, 7 **B** 2, 6 **C** 1, 4, 5

2–4

The transcript and answer key for the Speaking test video can be found on the Teacher's Resource Centre.

5

Suggested answers:

1 Well, in the first photo you are learning alone because the students are listening individually to the teacher, so you have to concentrate more, but the good point about the second photo is that you learn from others, I mean, you have to cooperate and listen too.

2 Regarding the question, I think the people in the first photo might be feeling really stressed because it's a very crowded station and they can't move very easily, whereas in the second one she seems to be relaxed, happy, she's smiling. She is waiting to travel but she seems calm.

6

Students' own answers

7

Suggested answers:

1 I'd prefer to be in the second situation because it's a more relaxed way to study, for example, with your friends, and you're also out in the fresh air in a nice environment. The more formal situation in class is best when you have to study for exams and it's a good idea to have the teacher there to help you revise, but studying for, say, project work is definitely better in the second photo. So, yes, that's where I'd prefer to be.

2 Where I live the public transport is quite good because it's cheap and it's also pretty efficient. I'd say there is a good underground and bus service which is used by a lot of people. This is why more people use it than taking their car and that's important because it helps stop traffic pollution. But I also think cycling would be a good way to travel around, although we need more cycle lanes in the area.

8

Students' own answers

9–11

The transcript and answer key for the Speaking test video can be found on the Teacher's Resource Centre.

12

Students should tick: 2, 3, 5, 6

13–14

The transcript and answer key for the Speaking test video can be found on the Teacher's Resource Centre.

USE OF ENGLISH SB pages 144–145

1

A 4 **B** 3 **C** 1 **D** 2

2

1 B, C, D **2** B, C, D **3** B, C, D **4** A, B, D **5** A **6** A **7** C **8** A, B, C, D

3

1 noun: 1, 8

2 adjective: 2, 4, 6, 7

3 adverb: 3

4 verb: 5

4

1 incorrect – determination. The answer should be a noun, not an adjective. **2** correct **3** incorrect – extremely. Spelling **4** incorrect – undeniable. The answer should be a negative adjective.

5

5 starring **6** advisable **7** surprising **8** creativity

6

1 Student error: too many words, Correct answer: suggested (that) we buy/bought / suggested buying

2 Student error: verb in wrong form, Correct answer: looking forward to taking

3 Student error: incorrect phrasal verb wording and incorrect grammar, Correct answer: can't figure out

7

4 wouldn't have gone

5 wish I'd studied / wish I had studied

6 is thought to be

WRITING SB pages 146–147

1

1 T **2** F: the first part is compulsory and it is an essay **3** T **4** F: it's a good idea to spend a short time, 5–10 minutes, working on a plan for each piece of writing as this will help organise and structure ideas/paragraphs, etc. **5** T **6** F: if candidates write too much they could lose marks for including information that isn't needed. If they write too little, but still include all the relevant information, they won't lose marks. **7** T

2

Students' own answers

3

Suggested answers:

1 The style and level of language accuracy is excellent for a formal letter but the task is an email to a friend and should be less formal, use contractions and more idiomatic expressions where possible.

If you want my advice, I wouldn't sign up for something which might stress you more. I also wouldn't worry too much about how your decision could affect the others. People are often sympathetic in the end.

2 There are errors with narrative tenses and adjectives, and adverbs could be included to make the descriptions more varied.

Claire couldn't believe that the room had been chosen for a special party. It was really horrible – tiny, quite cold and with hardly any light. What was she going to do? She had truly wanted the event to be so special and had already invited over fifty people but there wasn't room to fit everyone. It was such a cramped space!

3 There are some language errors and the ideas can be linked together better with a wider use of vocabulary. There needs to be a recommendation at the end.

In spite of all the difficulties, the main actor manages to overcome all obstacles by the end of the film, mainly because she is such a strong personality. She is also extremely honest, which is why the other characters forgive her. The film is a must-see; I highly recommend it.

4

In your English class you have been talking about <u>**young**</u> <u>people</u> and <u>health</u>. Now your English teacher has asked you to <u>write an essay</u> for homework.

Write the essay <u>**using all the notes**</u> and giving <u>reasons</u> from <u>**your point of view**</u>.

Some <u>people think</u> that <u>**nowadays**</u> <u>young people</u> are not as <u>fit and healthy</u> as they were <u>**in the past**</u>. What's <u>**your opinion**</u>?

Notes

Write about: **1** <u>exercise and diet</u>

2 <u>medicine and illness</u>

3 .... (<u>**your own ideas**</u>)

5

Introduction: use of technology and social media

Young people in the past: better diet, less fast food, more time in natural environment, more time walking and less time in cars and public transport

Young people today: technology and social media, fast food

6

1 C **2** A **3** D **4** B

7

Students should tick: A, C, D

8

healthy, can frequently, illness, to, In the past, themselves, fast food, physical, In spite of the fact that, balanced, sedentary, prefer to stay, of

New paragraphs: Today, young people…, In past time…, Despite…, To sum up

Workbook Answer Key

UNIT 1

Pages 4–5 **Reading**

Exercise 1
1 F **2** B **3** D **4** G **5** C **6** A **7** E

Exercise 2
A Not only that, but it's great for reducing stress, keeping the brain active and improving your strength and flexibility.
B It's a valuable skill too, and one which could lead to a great career or allow you to earn some money.
C It's basically treasure hunting in places of interest or natural beauty.
D The idea of this is to for you all to try ones you don't have or haven't used for ages.
E They are a fantastic opportunity to get experience of taking part in live shows.
F This involves learning a skill that everyone will find useful.
G They often have the best information about free and cheap events in your area.

Exercise 3
1 D **2** G **3** C **4** A **5** E **6** B

Exercise 4
1 accessible **2** the earth **3** competitive **4** a must **5** swap **6** outlet **7** venues **8** enhancing

Page 6 **Grammar 1**

Exercise 1
Singular countable nouns: friend, idea, internet, theatre
Plural countable nouns: actors, courses, film-makers, films
Uncountable nouns: accommodation, advice, fear, jeans, leisure, shopping
Nouns that can be countable and uncountable: exercise, experience, glasses, gym, paper, tea, wood

Exercise 2
1 a **2** – **3** – **4** – **5** the **6** a **7** a **8** the **9** an **10** – **11** the **12** an

Page 6 **Vocabulary**

Exercise 1
1 screenplay **2** broadcast **3** cast **4** audience **5** satellite **6** producer **7** programme **8** sitcom **9** series **10** channel **11** flop **12** demand

Exercise 2
1 a **2** c **3** b **4** b **5** c **6** a **7** b

Exercise 3
1 do **2** have **3** make **4** take **5** making **6** take **7** do **8** have (also possible 'take') **9** take (also possible 'have') **10** do **11** take (also possible 'have') **12** have

Page 7 **Grammar 2**

Exercise 1
1 a **2** b **3** b **4** c **5** a **6** b **7** a **8** c

Exercise 2
1 a little **2** Both / Both of **3** a few **4** neither of **5** every

Exercise 3
1 wasn't / was not much information **2** either of us **3** only a few minutes **4** a few of the actors

Page 8 **Listening**

Exercise 1
a) possible – you need a noun here that collocates with 'go on'
b) not possible – the gap needs to contain a type of material
c) possible – you need an adjective here
d) possible – you need a noun that can go with 'depend on'
e) not possible – the gap should contain a comparative form

Exercise 2
Students' own answers

Exercise 3
1 camping holiday **2** supportive **3** days **4** plastic **5** annoying **6** safe **7** next summer **8** decide **9** motivation **10** less important

Page 8 **Speaking**

Exercise 1
1 three **2** average **3** often **4** general **5** least **6** routine **7** ever **8** involve **9** twice **10** normal **11** On **12** quite

Exercise 2
1 a **2** b **3** a **4** a **5** b **6** a

Exercise 3
Students' own answers

Page 9 **Use of English**

Exercise 1
satisfy, satisfaction, satisfying, satisfactory
educate, education, educational, educated
impress, impression, impressive
create, creation, creativity, creative
depend, dependence, dependent
act, activity, action, active
-, ability, **able**
-, **health**, healthy
1 unsatisfying, unsatisfactory, uneducational, uneducated, unimpressive, uncreative, independent, inactive, unable, unhealthy
2 Yes. Nouns with *-ion* (satisfaction, education, impression, creation, action) and *-ity* (activity, ability). Adjectives with *-ive* (impressive, creative, active).

Exercise 2
1 activity **2** ability **3** independence **4** impressive **5** satisfaction **6** creativity **7** healthier **8** education

Page 10 **Writing**

Exercise 1
1 fairly informal **2** should **3** an opinion

Exercise 2
1 Have you ever wanted a hobby you could take with you anywhere? Why are podcasts so great? So, why not give it a go?
2 It's great fun when you get into it! It's as easy as that! ... you won't regret it! You'd be amazed at what you can find! ... you won't want to stop!
3 download one of the many free apps, Take (my advice), Check out (the most popular podcasts online)
4 first of all, secondly, finally

Exercise 3
1 get into **2** dip into **3** check out **4** get going

Exercise 4
Students' own answers

Page 11 **Progress check**

Exercise 1
1 overcame **2** sitcoms **3** act out **4** trailer **5** flop **6** chill out **7** comes out / is coming out **8** cast

Exercise 2
1 some **2** the **3** None **4** a bit of **5** All of **6** – **7** Every **8** a little

Cumulative progress

Exercise 3
1 a **2** c **3** c **4** d **5** a **6** a **7** b **8** c

UNIT 2

Pages 12–13 **Reading**

Exercise 1
1 E **2** C **3** F **4** B **5** G **6** D

Exercise 2
1 a **2** a **3** b **4** b **5** a **6** b

Exercise 3
1 C **2** D **3** A **4** A **5** B **6** A

Page 14 **Grammar 1**

Exercise 1
1 knew **2** want **3** didn't / did not / couldn't / could not complete **4** doesn't / does not care **5** aim **6** freeze **7** left **8** Did you forget **9** don't / do not see **10** looks / is/'s looking **11** Do you recognise **12** see

Exercise 2
1 used to think **2** would do **3** is not / isn't used to teaching **4** got used to wearing **5** did not / didn't use to teach **6** he is / he's getting used to **7** Did you use to be **8** are used to working

Page 14 **Vocabulary**

Exercise 1
1 licence **2** qualifications **3** revise **4** ✓ **5** lecturer **6** coach **7** undergraduate **8** ✓

Exercise 2
1 came up with, look up **2** speak up, ended up **3** dig up, used up **4** creep up behind, hurry up **5** caught up with, set up

Exercise 3
1 g **2** d **3** j **4** b **5** h **6** c **7** a **8** e **9** i **10** f

Page 15 **Grammar 2**

Exercise 1
1 had had **2** haven't met **3** had already left **4** hadn't brought **5** Have they begun **6** have spoken **7** had drawn **8** have studied **9** Had they prepared

Exercise 2
1 just **2** for **3** By the time **4** already **5** ever **6** since **7** yet **8** Once **9** been **10** Up to that point

Page 16 **Listening**

Exercise 1
Agreement: I can't see why not. I know! Me neither! Mine too. No doubt about that. Oh yes, totally! Sounds good to me.
Disagreement: I can't see why not. Oh, I wouldn't say that.
Partial agreement: I wouldn't go that far. Yes, to some extent, I suppose.

Exercise 3
1 Me neither **2** Not at all **3** You can't be serious **4** Mine too

Exercise 4
1 C **2** A **3** A **4** B **5** C **6** B **7** A **8** B

Page 17 **Speaking**

Exercise 1
1 absolutely **2** Neither **3** a point **4** too

Exercise 2
1 disagree **2** right **3** don't **4** suppose

Page 17 **Use of English**

Exercise 1
1 got used to **2** didn't use to **3** enjoy **4** being **5** weren't used to **6** working

Exercise 2
1a) 's / is nothing wrong with **1b)** need to concentrate on finding
2a) is experienced in teaching **2b)** succeeded in passing
3a) was criticised for not encouraging **3b)** are interested in learning

Exercise 3
1 had read the book before **2** has decided against going **3** isn't / is not used to teaching **4** paying attention to **5** used to be

Page 18 **Writing**

Exercise 1
1 In my opinion, In my view, It seems to me, I would argue that
2 as, because, for example, that is, this is why, since, such as

Exercise 2
He disagrees.

Exercise 3
1 Apprenticeships are a good thing for young people because they can learn practical skills.
2 They can be more independent since they also earn money. / Since they also earn money, they can be more independent.
3 Not all young people want to go to university, some want to start working or learn in a different way. This is why apprenticeships are a great solution.
4 I would argue that doing an apprenticeship is a good idea as you get the qualifications you know employers want.
5 You get into employment quicker if you do an apprenticeship. In my opinion, this means that there is more opportunity to progress in your career.

Exercise 4
Students' own answers

Page 19 **Progress check**

Exercise 1
1 had never seen **2** used to **3** hasn't driven **4** Have you bought **5** use to take **6** hated **7** has been **8** get used to **9** had spoken **10** left

Exercise 2
1 licence, passed, ended up **2** interested in, degree, lecturers, undergraduates **3** certificate, dig it up, succeeded in **4** wrong with, graduates

Cumulative progress

Exercise 3
1 mathematical **2** logically **3** unable **4** inability **5** difficulty **6** Creative **7** impressive **8** existence

UNIT 3

Pages 20–21 **Reading**

Exercise 1
1 the percentage of the world's population without access to safe drinking water
2 the age Elif was when she succeeded in making a bioplastic
3 the percentage of carbon emissions caused by deforestation
4 the percentage of families in developing countries with no access to electricity
5 the (least) number of hours the battery lasts
6 the number of tons of banana peel thrown away every day in Thailand
7 the size in km^2 of the Tembé territory
8 the amount of dollars raised by Topher White's crowdfunding

Exercise 2
1 D **2** C **3** A **4** C **5** B **6** B **7** A **8** D **9** B **10** C

Exercise 3
1 intrigued **2** experimentation **3** moulded **4** loggers **5** alert **6** sustainable **7** prompted **8** access **9** running costs

Page 22 **Grammar 1**

Exercise 1
1 hadn't been working **2** was working **3** has it been doing **4** You're always looking **5** has been charging **6** had been wondering **7** weren't using **8** isn't working

Exercise 2
1 's/has been making **2** 'm/am working **3** were doing **4** Have you been waiting **5** are/'re flying **6** had/'d been studying

Exercise 3
1 had/'d been surfing **2** has/'s been developing **3** Were they delivering **4** am/'m not using **5** have not / haven't been getting **6** was following **7** are not / aren't serving **8** had you been writing

Page 22 **Vocabulary**

Exercise 1
1 develop, create **2** discover, invent **3** manufacture, produce **4** appliances, machine **5** engines, motors **6** remote control, tools

Exercise 2
1 c **2** f **3** a **4** b **5** e **6** d

Exercise 3
1 speed **2** performance **3** priority **4** definition **5** award **6** time **7** secret **8** speed **9** tech **10** powered

Page 23 **Grammar 2**

Exercise 1
1 much **2** widest **3** the nicest **4** less expensive

Exercise 2
1 more **2** least **3** than **4** as **5** much

Exercise 3
1 better **2** long as **3** harder **4** the most advanced **5** higher than **6** (much) more common **7** the most serious **8** the best

Page 24 **Listening**

Exercise 1
1 wonder **2** sure **3** keen **4** appeal **5** surprised **6** tend
1 d **2** f **3** a **4** c **5** b **6** e

Exercise 2
1 D **2** G **3** B **4** H **5** E **6** A **7** C **8** F

Exercise 3
1 D **2** G **3** B **4** E **5** A

Page 24 **Speaking**

Exercise 1
1 D **2** C **3** C **4** C

Exercise 2
1 far **2** whereas **3** as **4** stressed **5** easier **6** less

Page 25 **Use of English**

Exercise 1
1 drum **2** push/carry **3** carrying **4** switch **5** brought **6** think

Exercise 2
1 in **2** on **3** out **4** into **5** out **6** up

Exercise 3
1 C **2** A **3** B **4** C **5** D **6** A **7** D **8** B

Page 26 **Writing**

Exercise 1
1 positive **2** weight **3** recommendation

Exercise 2
1 B **2** D **3** A **4** C

Exercise 3
Students' own answers

Page 27 **Progress check**

Exercise 1
1 high, engines, top **2** came up with, remote control **3** coming on, develop, manufacture **4** figure out, tools **5** machine, carrying out **6** appliance, plugged in

Exercise 2
1 have/'ve been learning **2** Were you watching **3** had/'d been driving **4** isn't / is not studying **5** The most expensive **6** more reliable than **7** aren't / are not as good **8** the worst

Cumulative progress

Exercise 3
1 as **2** take **3** interested **4** carry **5** would **6** many **7** both **8** as

UNIT 4

Pages 28–29 **Reading**

Exercise 1
1 C **2** E **3** A **4** F **5** D **6** B

Exercise 2
1 b, c **2** a, b **3** a, b **4** b, c **5** a, b **6** a, c **7** a, b **8** b, c

Exercise 3
1 He helped the poor. **2** It was very daring. **3** A film. **4** Their popularity. **5** Their motivation.

Page 30 **Grammar 1**

Exercise 1
1 won't **2** finishes **3** has tested **4** Is he going to **5** have gone **6** Shall **7** are making **8** arrive

Exercise 2
1 going, will **2** does, Shall **3** has, soon **4** is, have **5** are, until

Exercise 3
1 correct **2** correct **3** will have been working **4** will be examining **5** correct **6** will have released

Page 30 **Vocabulary**

Exercise 1
1 trial **2** accused **3** innocent **4** jury **5** evidence **6** guilty **7** judge **8** fine **9** imprisonment **10** victim **11** verdict **12** justice

Exercise 2
1 b **2** e **3** h **4** c **5** f **6** d **7** a **8** g

Exercise 3
1 rate **2** youth **3** correct **4** correct **5** hate **6** correct **7** correct **8** scene **9** petty

Page 31 **Grammar 2**

Exercise 1
1 cut **2** don't / do not go **3** works **4** use **5** don't / do not start **6** 'll/will arrest **7** 'll/will feel **8** won't / will not charge **9** finding **10** scream

Exercise 2
1 a **2** b **3** a **4** b **5** a

Page 32 **Listening**

Exercise 1
1 c **2** f **3** a **4** e **5** d **6** b

Exercise 2
1 fans **2** realistic **3** end **4** approach **5** solve **6** frightening **7** unhappiness **8** mysterious

Exercise 3
1 F **2** T **3** T **4** T **5** F **6** F **7** T **8** F

Page 32 **Speaking**

Exercise 1
1 a **2** c **3** b **4** a **5** b **6** c

Exercise 2
1 A **2** B **3** B **4** A **5** B **6** A

Exercise 3
Asking for agreement or an opinion: Don't you agree? what's your opinion? What do you think?
Introducing your view: As I see it, It's hard to say, but …, Personally, In my opinion, I'd say that, To my mind, I don't think it matters if

Page 33 **Use of English**

Exercise 1
1 a **2** c **3** b **4** c **5** a **6** b

Exercise 2
1 as long as **2** will/'ll have been investigating **3** in case you need **4** unless you want to go **5** provided that you are

Page 34 **Writing**

Exercise 1
1 formal **2** opinion, examples **3** finish, first

Exercise 2
1 F **2** T **3** F

Exercise 3
1 To my mind, It seems to me that … As far as I'm concerned, in my view **2** such as, for example **3** In conclusion **4** Dear Editor, Yours truly,

Exercise 4
Students' own answers

Page 35 **Progress check**

Exercise 1
1 evidence guilty victim judge **2** rate, Youth, wave, petty **3** held up, made for, got away with, let her off

Exercise 2
1 will not **2** going to find out **3** leave **4** will have been writing **5** will be watching **6** unless **7** don't find **8** put **9** Provided **10** if

Cumulative progress

Exercise 3
1 A **2** C **3** D **4** B **5** D **6** B **7** C **8** A

UNIT 5

Pages 36–37 **Reading**

Exercise 1
1 T **2** F **3** F **4** T

Exercise 2
1 D **2** F **3** A **4** E **5** G **6** B **7** C

Exercise 3
1 D **2** F **3** C **4** A **5** G **6** B

Exercise 4
1 treating **2** integral **3** incidents **4** desirable **5** gracious **6** asset **7** envious **8** opponents

Page 38 **Grammar 1**

Exercise 1
1 shouldn't **2** shouldn't have been **3** you're not allowed **4** must **5** don't have to watch **6** could

Exercise 2
1 could (also possible 'can') **2** couldn't **3** should have **4** will be able **5** allowed **6** may (also possible 'can') **7** need **8** isn't allowed **9** to **10** can **11** is allowed to (also possible 'can') **12** mustn't (also possible 'can't') **13** can't (also possible 'couldn't') **14** don't have to

Exercise 3
1 able **2** could **3** have **4** should

Page 38 **Vocabulary**

Exercise 1
1 course **2** beat **3** track **4** pitch **5** draw **6** court **7** win **8** rink

Exercise 2
1 racket **2** competitors **3** rod **4** viewers **5** cue **6** stick **7** referee **8** spectators

Exercise 3
1c **2**f **3**j **4**d **5**h **6**a **7**e **8**g **9**b **10**i

Page 39 **Grammar 2**

Exercise 1
1 b **2** a **3** c **4** b **5** c **6** a

Exercise 2
1 must be **2** might not have known **3** should have been leading **4** must have been **5** ought to be

***Page 40* Listening**

Exercise 1
1 sports **2** Best Teen Blog **3** subscribers **4** show **5** soap opera, singing contest **6** presenters

Exercise 2
1 C **2** B **3** A **4** B **5** C **6** A **7** C

***Page 40* Speaking**

Exercise 1
1 e **2** g **3** f **4** b **5** d **6** a **7** c

Exercise 2
1 must **2** could **3** can't **4** have been **5** be **6** Maybe

Exercise 3
1 must be watching **2** seem to be enjoying **3** may have been riding **4** could have lost **5** might have been competing **6** must be

***Page 41* Use of English**

Exercise 1
succeed, success, successful
benefit, benefit, beneficial
protect, protection, protective, protected
value, value, valuable
challenge, challenge, challenging
1 protect **2** benefit, value, challenge **3** successfully, beneficially, protectively, valuably, challengingly **4** successfully, beneficially

Exercise 2
1 confidence **2** achievement **3** winner **4** unexpected **5** unfortunate **6** challenging **7** successfully **8** valuable

***Page 42* Writing**

Exercise 1
1 formal, exclamation marks **2** complete **3** set phrases **4** paragraph

Exercise 2
1 request for **2** consider **3** would argue **4** In fact **5** propose **6** Because of **7** look forward to

Exercise 3
1 … do not want/wish … For this reason, … **2** I am writing in response to … **3** I would like to put forward a few … **4** Please let me know … regarding … **5** Yours sincerely, **6** My final suggestion is to propose …

Exercise 4
1 b **2** c **3** a
Students' own answers

***Page 43* Progress check**

Exercise 1
1 c **2** b **3** c **4** d **5** b **6** a **7** d **8** a

Exercise 2
1 shouldn't **2** can't **3** may **4** don't have to **5** needn't **6** allowed to **7** ought to **8** will be able to

Cumulative progress

Exercise 3
1 with/of **2** score **3** differences **4** of **5** allowed **6** to **7** used **8** take

UNIT 6

***Pages 44-45* Reading**

Exercise 1
1 Josie **2** Simon **3** Robbie **4** Grace

Exercise 2
1 b **2** a **3** c **4** b **5** a **6** c

Exercise 3
1 T – Increasingly, though, people prefer … **2** F – Probably the hardest thing … **3** F – The training is quite … **4** T – I love music, and … **5** F – I work freelance and … **6** T – It cost £875 but … **7** F – It's a brilliant way … **8** F – I've got my first …

Exercise 4
1 ratings **2** promoting **3** job satisfaction **4** relate (well) to **5** deadlines **6** initiative **7** get (my) big break **8** focusing on

***Page 46* Grammar 1**

Exercise 1
1 b **2** b **3** c **4** b **5** c **6** a **7** c **8** b

Exercise 2
1 helping, to help, help **2** find, finding, to find **3** sending, to send, send **4** to look, looking, look **5** go, going, to go

***Page 46* Vocabulary**

Exercise 1
1 resigned, bonus **2** on strike, wages **3** retired, salary **4** off sick, tips **5** unemployed, on maternity leave

Exercise 2
1 b **2** d **3** a **4** e **5** c **6** h **7** g **8** f

Exercise 3
1 went abroad, got a placement **2** getting ready, went bankrupt **3** got fired / got the sack, went quiet **4** went missing, got upset / went crazy **5** got lost, got the impression

***Page 47* Grammar 2**

Exercise 1
1 c **2** a **3** c **4** b **5** a **6** b

Exercise 2
1 i **2** c **3** f **4** b **5** g **6** e **7** h **8** a **9** j **10** d

***Page 48* Listening**

Exercise 1
1 programme **2** increase **3** difficult **4** train **5** win **6** foreign **7** shop **8** give a job to

Exercise 2
1 ~~youth~~ employment **2** than ~~over~~ **3** qualification > qualification<u>s</u> **4** to give ~~to~~ **5** work > job **6** rather > prefer

Exercise 3
1 university **2** fifty/50 **3** qualification **4** well **5** earn money **6** employer **7** unemployment **8** holidays **9** manager **10** benefits from

***Page 48* Speaking**

Exercise 1
1 Let's **2** working **3** suggest **4** move **5** why

Exercise 2
1 working in a shop **2** tutoring **3** dog walking **4** working as a waiter **5** babysitting

Exercise 3
1 5 (babysitting) **2** 1 (working in a shop), 2 (tutoring) **3** 3 (dog walking), 4 (working as a waiter)

***Page 49* Use of English**

Exercise 1
1 intend **2** get **3** suited **4** focus **5** drop **6** lead **7** imagine **8** adjust

Exercise 2
1 with **2** at **3** on **4** to **5** of **6** in **7** off **8** or

Exercise 3
1 D **2** A **3** C **4** A **5** B **6** C **7** D **8** A

***Page 50* Writing**

Exercise 1
1 Hope that helps!, You don't need any special training! **2** Cheers, Dan, Dear Maria **3** I was glad to hear that …, Thanks for your letter.

Exercise 2
1 F **2** T **3** F **4** T

Exercise 3
Students' own answers

Exercise 4
Students' own answers

***Page 51* Progress check**

Exercise 1
1 copy in, get, upset **2** resign, get, salary **3** lay off, go, on strike **4** get ahead, burn out, getting **5** bonus, went, sack

Exercise 2
1 fancy **2** getting **3** worked **4** in order **5** prefer **6** giving **7** show **8** attending **9** to work **10** be

Cumulative progress

Exercise 3
1 protection **2** employment **3** apprenticeship **4** unfairly **5** complaint **6** relationships **7** guilty **8** imprisonment

UNIT 7

Pages 52–53 Reading

Exercise 1
Students should tick: 1,4, 6

Exercise 2
1 C **2** G **3** E **4** A **5** F **6** D

Exercise 3
1 g **2** d **3** a **4** e **5** h **6** c **7** b **8** f

Page 54 Grammar 1

Exercise 1
1 myself **2** ourselves **3** itself **4** herself **5** themselves **6** yourself **7** himself **8** yourselves

Exercise 2
1 There's **2** It **3** it **4** there **5** it **6** one **7** it **8** one **9** anyone **10** something **11** anywhere **12** Somebody

Page 54 Vocabulary

Exercise 1
1 illustration **2** conductor **3** exhibition **4** set **5** choreographer **6** abstract **7** auction **8** stage

Exercise 2
1 d **2** a **3** f **4** b **5** e **6** c

Exercise 3
1 act **2** part **3** scenes **4** act **5** stage **6** canvas

Page 55 Grammar 2

Exercise 1
1 However **2** many **3** such **4** spite **5** too **6** Although (also possible 'though') **7** even **8** so **9** much/far **10** despite **11** though **12** much/far **13** enough

Exercise 2
1 it was such an awesome **2** in spite of the fact **3** far too big to fit **4** even though he did not / didn't **5** is talented enough to become

Page 56 Listening

Exercise 1
1 c **2** e **3** a **4** f **5** b **6** d

Exercise 2
1 Why don't we **2** How on earth **3** I can't get **4** I wish they wouldn't **5** You should try **6** Could you do

Exercise 3
1 B **2** A **3** C **4** B **5** C **6** A **7** C **8** B

Page 56 Speaking

Exercise 1
1 T **2** C **3** T **4** T **5** C **6** C **7** T **8** C

Exercise 2
1 as, I wouldn't mind **2** If I had to choose, go or, reason why, interested in **3** Although, I'd rather, I'd prefer

Exercise 3
Students should tick both statements

Page 57 Use of English

Exercise 1
1 b **2** b **3** a **4** a **5** b

Exercise 2
1 grown on me **2** in spite of **3** made the costumes herself **4** was such a boring **5** has been found

Exercise 3
1 far too expensive **2** draw up **3** such a small/low number of **4** despite the fact that

Page 58 Writing

Exercise 1
1 one or two **2** attention **3** short **4** feel **5** title **6** vary **7** plot

Exercise 2
1 Focus is on one character (Gina). She is made believable by involving us in her dreams.
2 Drama added by the second sentence (Was this really where her life would change forever?) – it's possible her life will change, but we don't know why or how.
3 Could it be real? It would be worth a fortune!
4 Gina is 'devastated', the market is in an area of town that is 'run-down' and 'unfamiliar'.
5 The title suggests the story could either turn out well or not.
6 Direct speech ('It's yours for just £15'); different tenses ('would change' 'was hoping' 'she'd dreamt' 'strode'); exclamation mark ('It would be worth a fortune!')
7 Plot – contrast between the bad news at the bank, and the possible 'treasure';
Ending – we still don't know if it is going to be a real Alexander Calder necklace.

Exercise 3
Students' own answers

Exercise 4
Students' own answers

Page 59 Progress check

Exercise 1
1 stage **2** hard act to follow **3** turned out **4** grew on **5** played a part **6** choreographer
2 7 exhibitions **8** masterpieces **9** illustrations **10** abstract **11** installations **12** behind the scenes

Exercise 2
1 There **2** yourself **3** anywhere **4** one **5** something **6** far too **7** Despite **8** However **9** such a **10** too many **11** old enough **12** so

Cumulative progress

Exercise 3
1 B **2** C **3** A **4** D **5** C **6** D **7** A **8** C

UNIT 8

Pages 60–61 Reading

Exercise 1
1 D **2** A **3** C **4** B

Exercise 2
1 B **2** D **3** A **4** B **5** C **6** C **7** A **8** D **9** B **10** D

Exercise 3
1 edible **2** impact **3** stage **4** promotes **5** benefit from **6** refuge **7** stimulating **8** released

Page 62 Grammar 1

Exercise 1
1 would happen **2** hadn't been **3** went **4** Had **5** had locked **6** didn't burn **7** have been **8** have filmed

Exercise 2
1 we protected, wouldn't / would not have died out **2** you were, would/'d know what was **3** hadn't / had not destroyed, would have **4** had/'d realised, would have got **5** not gone (also possible 'been'), wouldn't / would not have seen **6** would/'d be, had told

Exercise 3
1 If the ship hadn't / had not hit a reef, it wouldn't / would not have torn a hole in it.
2 Had the crew not been tired, the accident wouldn't / would not have happened.
3 If a storm hadn't / had not hit the area, the oil wouldn't / would not have spread widely.
4 Had the oil not covered the coastline, thousands of animals wouldn't / would not have died.
5 If all of the oil had gone, many Alaskan beaches wouldn't / would not still be polluted.
6 If we could remove it, the beaches would be clean again.

Page 63 Vocabulary

Exercise 1
1 warming **2** effect **3** energy **4** waste **5** footprint **6** change **7** layer **8** development

Exercise 2
1 h **2** a **3** c **4** e **5** d **6** f **7** g **8** b

Exercise 3
1 of **2** by **3** to **4** by **5** from **6** to

Page 63 Grammar 2

Exercise 1
1 invested **2** do **3** bought **4** shared **5** leave **6** could

Exercise 2
1 wouldn't / would not waste **2** hadn't / had not struck **3** didn't / did not leave **4** took **5** had/'d started **6** could go

Page 64 Listening

Exercise 1
1 c **2** e **3** a **4** b **5** d

Exercise 2
1 D **2** G **3** A **4** H **5** F **6** B **7** E **8** C

Exercise 3
1 G **2** D **3** F **4** A **5** B

Page 64 **Speaking**

Exercise 1
1 f **2** c **3** h **4** a **5** d **6** g **7** b **8** e

Exercise 2
1 more importantly **2** And there's another thing **3** The good thing about **4** Having said that **5** as well as **6** This is why **7** In addition **8** Apart from that

Page 65 **Use of English**

Exercise 1
1 ADJ **2** ADV **3** ADJ **4** ADJ **5** N **6** V **7** N **8** N

Exercise 2
1 unrecognisable **2** industrially **3** observant **4** futuristic **5** conservation **6** tightened **7** coverage **8** affordability

Exercise 3
1 genetic **2** biologically **3** threaten **4** sustainability **5** unpredictable **6** storage **7** dominant **8** preservation

Page 66 **Writing**

Exercise 1
1 should **2** specific **3** is

Exercise 2
1 F (The writer uses phrases to directly address the reader and connect with them, e.g. If you're anything like me … Perhaps you also …. In my experience …).
2 T (The writer says that a school garden 'supports the development of life skills').
3 F (The second main point is that school gardens 'help students learn about the world they live in' and make them aware of 'the importance of food choices, personal health and well-being').

Exercise 3
1 Many students don't get enough exercise so driving to school is not a good idea.
2 Students could use other forms of transport such as cycling, walking or using a scooter to get exercise.
3 Car shares are a good idea due to the fact that they reduce the number of cars on the road.
4 Car shares are good for the environment because they also reduce pollution.

Exercise 4
Students' own answers

Page 67 **Progress check**

Exercise 1
1 ozone layer **2** protected from **3** exposed to **4** do away with global warming **6** Climate change **7** die out **8** carbon footprint **9** renewable energy **10** harmful to **11** run out **12** waste of **13** throw away **14** chopped down

Exercise 2
1 hadn't / had not thrown away **2** wouldn't / would not take / hadn't / had not taken **3** started **4** would happen **5** had/'d thought **6** planted **7** watched **8** were **9** could swim **10** had/'d developed

Cumulative progress

Exercise 3
1 there **2** out **3** run **4** working **5** worse **6** toxic **7** so **8** existed

UNIT 9

Pages 68–69 **Reading**

Exercise 1
a 4 **b** 2 **c** 6 **d** 5 **e** 1 **f** 3

Exercise 2
1 D **2** D **3** B **4** A **5** A **6** B

Exercise 3
1 sparked **2** illusion **3** restricted **4** justified **5** identify with **6** comforting **7** realities **8** eager

Page 70 **Grammar 1**

Exercise 1
1 a **2** b **3** b **4** c **5** a **6** a **7** b **8** c

Exercise 2
1 Have (you) been bitten **2** to be developed **3** can be taught **4** was started **5** is held **6** are given / will be given **7** will be instructed **8** have been published **9** are encouraged / will be encouraged **10** is judged / will be judged **11** are presented / will be presented **12** are being accepted

Page 70 **Vocabulary**

Exercise 1
1 science **2** tragedy **3** graphic **4** critic **5** novelist **6** editor **7** crime **8** legend

Exercise 2
1 c **2** f **3** a **4** d **5** g **6** b **7** e **8** h

Exercise 3
1 tell **2** ✓ **3** ✓ **4** tell **5** speaks **6** telling **7** say **8** ✓ **9** ✓ **10** Speak **11** told **12** ✓ **13** tells

Page 71 **Grammar 2**

Exercise 1
1 got **2** deleted **3** delivered **4** cleaned **5** signed **6** will have **7** published **8** had

Exercise 2
1 We have had the books delivered to our home. **2** They are having/getting the catalogues printed today. **3** He had his subscription to the magazine cancelled. **4** I am going to have/get my article published in a newspaper. **5** The journalist had her laptop stolen. **6** I will get/have my autobiography written by a ghostwriter.

Page 72 **Listening**

Exercise 1
1 NS **2** NS **3** F **4** NS **5** F **6** F

Exercise 2
1 F **2** T **3** NS **4** T **5** NS **6** T **7** NS **8** F

Page 72 **Speaking**

Exercise 1
1 Not yet, but I'd like to go one day. **2** Unfortunately, the story was very confusing. **3** I'd say crime fiction is my favourite. **4** I've got a few actually. **5** I think I was disappointed more than anything else. **6** Looking back now, I would say yes.

Exercise 2
1 Have you ever met a famous person? **2** Could you tell me what happened? **3** I couldn't believe **4** How did you feel? **5** I felt excited. **6** What did you do? **7** Unfortunately **8** I felt nervous **9** Looking back now **10** What can you tell me about him? **11** I was really surprised

Page 73 **Use of English**

Exercise 1
1 c **2** b **3** c **4** a **5** b **6** a **7** c **8** b

Exercise 2
1 B **2** D **3** C **4** A **5** D **6** B **7** C **8** A

Page 74 **Writing**

Exercise 1
1 picture **2** feels, adverbs **3** direct speech **4** dramatic

Exercise 2
Students should underline:
1 showed, hadn't expected, was taking, 've broken
2 expert, chilly, glorious, scared, tricky …
3 smoothly, really, crossly, hard, wildly, hardly, shakily
4 'Stop there!' *'You can do this!'*
5 … but then disaster struck. Would I make it to the top?

Exercise 3
Students' own answers

Page 75 **Progress check**

Exercise 1
1 playwrights **2** legends **3** tragedies **4** fantasy **5** novelist **6** graphic **7** read **8** put **9** get **10** tell **11** brings **12** say

Exercise 2
1 hasn't been **2** has had **3** get it **4** can only be **5** is believed **6** had **7** as **8** being sold

Cumulative progress

Exercise 3
1 variety **2** global **3** unknown **4** apparent **5** professional **6** lonely/alone **7** poorly **8** warnings

UNIT 10

Pages 76–77 Reading

Exercise 1
1 F **2** T **3** F **4** F

Exercise 2
1 B **2** C **3** D **4** B **5** A **6** A

Exercise 3
1 funding **2** donate **3** shortage **4** affect **5** leading **6** breakthrough **7** tackle **8** impact

Page 78 Grammar 1

Exercise 1
1 where **2** ✓ **3** why **4** which/that **5** whose **6** ✓ **7** which **8** ✓

Exercise 2
1 which/that **2** why **3** where **4** which/that **5** when **6** who/that **7** whose

Exercise 3
1 which **2** which/that **3** – **4** where **5** who/that **6** whose **7** –

Page 78 Vocabulary

Exercise 1
1 cashpoint **2** PIN **3** discount **4** credit cards **5** cash **6** till **7** change **8** receipt **9** refund **10** bill

Exercise 2
1 switch **2** slept **3** put **4** press **5** carrying **6** started/picked **7** pick **8** decide

Exercise 3
1 make **2** getting **3** made **4** make **5** went **6** making **7** does **8** make

Page 79 Grammar 2

Exercise 1
1 sold **2** lost **3** Wanted **4** spoken **5** Looking **6** Installed **7** Bought **8** Having

Exercise 2
1 Bought online, the watch was a cheap copy. **2** Reduced in the sales, the T-shirts quickly sold out. **3** The person serving us didn't know how to use the till. **4** The police spoke to the people selling at the market about theft. **5** Unable to find the receipt, Jane couldn't get a refund. **6** Having tried on the boots / the boots on, he bought them.

Page 80 Listening

Exercise 1
1a **2**b **3**b **4**b **5**a **6**b **7**b **8**a

Exercise 2
1C **2**A **3**A **4**B **5**C **6**C **7**B

Page 80 Speaking

Exercise 1
1 g, j **2** e, a **3** d, i **4** c, b **5** h, f

Exercise 2
1 I think we should **2** which **3** for **4** make **5** choose **6** To

Page 81 Use of English

Exercise 1
1P **2**V **3**RP **4**N **5**P **6**RP **7**N **8**V

Exercise 2
1 on **2** doing **3** when **4** card **5** on **6** whose **7** loss **8** got

Exercise 3
1 which/that **2** on **3** where **4** why **5** makes **6** get **7** make **8** go

Page 82 Writing

Exercise 1
1 structure **2** first, both sides **3** final, different

Exercise 2
1 question **2** difficult **3** believe **4** such **5** instance **6** conclude **7** emphasise

Exercise 3
1 sides **2** that/how **3** sum **4** argue **5** said **6** For

Exercise 4
introduce a point: There are two sides to this question, and … However, I don't see that … This is a difficult question, and I would argue that … Having said that …
give an example: For example, …
conclude the essay: To sum up, I believe that …

Exercise 5
Students' own answers

Page 83 Progress check

Exercise 1
1 a **2** b **3** c **4** b **5** a **6** c **7** b **8** a

Exercise 2
1 having tried **2** which **3** Driven **4** – **5** Made **6** where **7** worn **8** shown

Cumulative progress

Exercise 3
1 C **2** A **3** D **4** B **5** D **6** A **7** C **8** B

UNIT 11

Pages 84–85 Reading

Exercise 1
1 C **2** E **3** A **4** F **5** B **6** D

Exercise 2
1 too **2** Instead **3** For a start **4** As a result, Consequently

Exercise 3
1 F **2** C **3** G **4** B **5** A **6** D

Exercise 4
1 b **2** f **3** h **4** c **5** a **6** e **7** g **8** d

Page 86 Grammar 1

Exercise 1
1 told to me > told me **2** do I like > if/whether I liked **3** the week previous > the week before / the previous week **4** were they > they were **5** has > had **6** would the festival > the festival would **7** would it > it would **8** must > had to

Exercise 2
1 not to go **2** to help **3** stealing / having stolen **4** to explore **5** to give **6** on driving **7** to apply

Exercise 3
1 informed me (that) Kim was, at that moment **2** promised to send, the next/following day **3** congratulated me on winning their **4** ordered the boys to get off the/that bus then / at that time **5** advised him to buy, his trip **6** denied leaving her litter, the previous day / the day before **7** announced (that) he was going, that morning **8** agreed to sell us their

Page 86 Vocabulary

Exercise 1
1 got, reception, trips **2** passengers, gate, flight **3** route, commuters, arrived **4** reached, journey/ride, platform **5** entrance, fare, ride/journey **6** travel, fees, tickets **7** voyage, excursions

Exercise 2
1 g **2** d **3** f **4** c **5** a **6** h **7** b **8** e

Exercise 3
1 in, for **2** about, with, from **3** about, to **4** with, about **5** on, for

Page 87 Grammar 2

Exercise 1
1 opens **2** whether the flight is delayed **3** I'd be **4** the bank is closed **5** the music festival starts **6** if I can **7** my room will **8** Would **9** was **10** whether the tour has

Exercise 2
1 c **2** a **3** e **4** h **5** f **6** g **7** d **8** b

Page 88 Listening

Exercise 1
1 basics **2** make an effort **3** disagreements **4** visual image **5** keep a record **6** navigate **7** device **8** prevent **9** works **10** online **11** communicate **12** following

Exercise 2
1 D **2** H **3** F **4** A **5** J **6** B **7** E **8** G

Page 88 Speaking

Exercise 1
A see **B** thought about **C** a difficult **D** the kind of person **E** sure about **F** tempted **G** hard **H** honest

Exercise 2
1 G **2** E **3** A **4** C **5** H **6** B **7** F **8** D

Exercise 3
1 good and bad points about travelling by boat **2** Yes **3** Let's see **4** Yes; seeing dolphins while travelling by boat **5** On the other hand

Page 89 Use of English

Exercise 1
1 RS **2** WP **3** DS **4** PV

Exercise 2
1 if she had read that **2** was crowded with **3** have been waiting here **4** set out

Exercise 3
1 am/'m looking forward to sailing **2** advised me to go to **3** had checked out **4** ordered us not to leave **5** was no point in using **6** didn't / did not see Tom yesterday

Page 90 **Writing**

Exercise 1
1 task, organise **2** answer, relevant

Exercise 2
Students should underline three of the following:
1 I bet / really cool / loads / gulp! **2** lucky you! / So, … / Well, … / Can't wait! / Tell you / promise!

Exercise 3
1 You should check out the museum.
2 There's loads to see in the city. / There are loads of things to see in the city.
3 I've got to get to the café in half an hour.
4 I'm going to the coast next weekend – I can't wait!
5 I can't believe you saw a tarantula!
6 It's a cool place to chill out.

Exercise 4
Students' own answers

Page 91 **Progress check**

Exercise 1
1 arrive, get **2** trips, flights **3** travel, journeys **4** fare, ticket **5** entrance, gate **6** platform, commuters

Exercise 2
1 b **2** c **3** a **4** b **5** a **6** c **7** c **8** b

Cumulative progress

Exercise 3
1 whose **2** off **3** behind **4** have **5** top/main **6** about **7** get **8** act

UNIT 12

Pages 92–93 **Reading**

Exercise 1
1 The age Dipa was when she qualified for the Olympics.
2 The year Dipa won a bronze medal at the Commonwealth Games.
3 The age Abraham was when he joined the Children's Parliament.
4 The year the Children's Law was passed in Liberia.
5 The age Francesco was when he had his accident.
6 The amount of money raised by children in America who had heard about Kendall.
7 The number of bikes provided by Kendall's charity.

Exercise 2
1 c **2** f **3** d **4** e **5** a **6** b

Exercise 3
1 B **2** D **3** B **4** A **5** C **6** C **7** D **8** A **9** B **10** D

Exercise 4
1 determined **2** inspire **3** campaigned **4** implemented **5** ambassador **6** spinal cord injuries **7** orphans **8** transplant surgery

Page 94 **Grammar 1**

Exercise 1
1 c **2** a **3** b **4** c **5** a **6** b **7** c **8** b

Exercise 2
1 d **2** f **3** b **4** g **5** a **6** c **7** e

Exercise 3
1 ~~does all the temperature~~ does the temperature fall **2** ~~the winners get~~ do the winners get **3** ~~the app had been~~ had the app been **4** ~~they didn't realise~~ did they realise **5** ~~Not only~~ Rarely/Seldom/Never **6** ~~these species will~~ will these species **7** ~~and~~ than **8** ~~we learnt~~ did we learn

Page 94 **Vocabulary**

Exercise 1
1 achieve **2** job **3** earned **4** miss **5** work **6** effort **7** succeed **8** famed **9** failed **10** unknown

Exercise 2
1 set **2** cut **3** logged **4** wiped

Exercise 3
1 finished **2** roped **3** shave **4** sparked

Exercise 4
1 word **2** temper **3** sight **4** track **5** nerve **6** head

Page 95 **Grammar 2**

Exercise 1
1 What **2** was only **3** is **4** what **5** why **6** I admire

Exercise 2
Students should put a cross after sentences: b, d, f

Exercise 3
1 It was in June when/that **2** The reason (why) they came was **3** What we need are **4** What the volunteers did was (to) **5** It was only when **6** What you notice about it is that **7** What I enjoyed most (of all) was **8** It wasn't until I got there that

Page 96 **Listening**

Exercise 1
1 most **2** completely **3** greatly **4** quite **5** particularly **6** mainly

Exercise 2
1 quite **2** particularly **3** completely **4** most **5** mainly **6** greatly

Exercise 3
1 A **2** B **3** C **4** B **5** C **6** C **7** B **8** A

Page 96 **Speaking**

Exercise 1
1 Sorry to interrupt, but **2** So, what you're saying is **3** Sorry, do you mean **4** Can I just say **5** I think you mean **6** Sorry, but I don't get your point.

Exercise 2
1 D **2** C **3** F **4** A **5** E **6** B

Page 97 **Use of English**

Exercise 1
1 temper **2** word **3** cut **4** sooner **5** only **6** that **7** lose **8** kept

Exercise 2
1 B **2** D **3** C **4** A **5** B **6** C **7** D **8** A

Page 98 **Writing**

Exercise 1
1 features **2** reaction **3** facts **4** recommendation, final

Exercise 2
Students' own answers

Exercise 3
Students' own answers

Page 99 **Progress check**

Exercise 1
1 famed **2** effort **3** earn **4** failed **5** logged **6** wiped **7** cut **8** sight **9** nerve

Exercise 2
1 had he attempted **2** wasn't until / was only when **3** only can he draw, but **4** reason (why) they sailed the world was **5** do you find **6** I noticed was that **7** sooner had she written her novel than **8** was only when I saw his collection that

Cumulative progress

Exercise 3
1 achievement **2** unknown **3** inventor **4** primarily **5** communication(s) **6** wireless **7** impressive **8** satisfaction

Audioscripts

UNIT 1 | STUDENT 'S BOOK

1.01 | Reading, page 5, Exercise 4

1 F One piece of advice he offers to young people wanting to get into film-making is to just go for it.

2 D There's no point taking Hollywood on at its own game.

3 A They'll teach you how to plan, shoot and edit your film to get the best results.

4 G You'll get nowhere if you wait until you find the perfect place to shoot or get perfect weather.

5 B This involves showing it to a small audience to see how they react.

6 E They are often free to enter and many of them focus on movies made by teenage film-makers.

1.05 | Listening, page 8, Exercises 4 and 5

I have quite an unusual free-time activity, I suppose, but it's a lot of fun. I love the circus and my activity is learning circus skills. It includes things like acrobatics and tightrope walking. My favourite activity though, is riding a unicycle, that's a bicycle with one wheel. I belong to a local circus club with other young people.

I didn't really know what modern circuses were like until I went to see one with one of my relatives when I was 11. I was expecting a traditional circus, with elephants and lions, but the modern circus is very different. There aren't any animals and people perform amazing tricks and artistic routines. It's much more exciting.

None of my family knew anything about the circus, so they were a bit curious when I started asking if I could join a circus club. I promised it wouldn't affect my schoolwork, and they could see how passionate I was about it. In the end, both my parents agreed to let me join and I started to learn some simple skills.

At first, it can be quite hard, and a lot of people give up in the early stages. You need physical strength for some of the skills, and I didn't have much at the beginning! Without that, you get very tired very quickly, especially with certain skills like riding a unicycle. I found that running helped. It was something that my circus skills teacher advised me to take up. I try to go out and do a couple of miles every few days. Once you get into the habit, it's not so bad, although it can be hard work on cold winter mornings!

Once you have the basic skill, like walking along a tightrope, then you need to learn a routine. This is a whole performance, involving a number of different tricks. When you're learning a new routine, I find it helps to do it slowly at first. That way, you can remember how each trick leads into another. Then you can do it faster once you're confident that you know what you're doing.

After a few weeks of practice, I like to try a new routine out on people, maybe with a short performance in the streets. People like to see someone doing a few tricks while they're out shopping. And it doesn't matter if you make a mistake because new people are always passing! I was really nervous for my first ever performance and I'm sure lots of things went wrong. But people were really encouraging, and it made me determined to learn how to perform better.

At the moment, I'm getting ready to learn a new skill, which I want to add to my shows. If I can juggle, then I think that'll make my tricks and performances even more impressive. Riding a unicycle is great, but doing it while you do something else is even more entertaining. And you have to remember that circus skills are all about entertainment. To entertain people, you don't just need the right circus skills. People have to find you interesting as well. That's one of the hardest parts for a lot of performers.

Once I've mastered a few skills, I'd love to get some experience as a clown. That would let me use everything I know. And there's no feeling like making people laugh. I would recommend it as an activity for everyone who enjoys performing.

UNIT 2 | STUDENT 'S BOOK

1.11 | Listening, page 18, Exercises 4 and 5

1 You hear two friends talking about doing an online course.

Boy: So, that's it. The last lesson over. Shame – I'm going to miss it. I really learnt a lot, didn't you?

Girl: Well, I wouldn't say that, to be honest, but it did help clear up a few things I wasn't sure about.

Boy: Well you've always been much better at computer programming than me anyway. I think I've really improved. You can't fault the instructor though.

Girl: No, not at all. She was great. Really kind, helpful and knowledgeable.

Boy: And doing it online was much easier than I'd thought it would be. I'd definitely recommend online learning.

Girl: Oh yeah, totally. It's a great way to improve your skills.

2 You overhear a girl talking on the phone about a new arts and sports centre.

No, it's in Waverly Street. Next to the supermarket – yeah, that's right. Anyway, I popped in on my way to the cinema the other night and it's lovely – they've done it really well. I picked up some leaflets, which I'll show you. They have tons of things. I've already signed up for their Monday-night dance class for teenagers – looks really good – but of course you have violin lessons on Mondays, don't you? I reckon you'll like their winter weekend drama course – it's just your thing. I think they even put on a show at the end. They also do things like aerobics and step, which you might be interested in, but we can think about those when we look at the leaflets together. I'll bring them round later.

3 You hear two teachers talking about an exam.

Teacher 1: Well, that was a bit tough, wasn't it? I'm not sure I'd like to have taken that when I was 14.

Teacher 2: Me neither! Most of them looked terrified, the poor things. Though Debbie and Alex didn't seem too bothered by it.

Teacher 1: I know! Debbie even finished early. Though she did say afterwards that she thought a few of the questions were unfair. I wouldn't go that far, but …

Teacher 2: Well, she might be right. I'll sit down this evening and go through it in more detail. One thing's for sure – it's always been a lot easier in the past.

Teacher 1: Oh, no doubt about that. This time last year they all came out with big smiles on their faces. Do you remember?

4 You hear part of an interview with a professional magician.

Interviewer: And we're very glad to have with us in the studio Sue Clarkson, also known as Mrs Magic, who's a professional magician. Sue, thanks for coming in.

Sue: Thank you for having me. You know, it's lovely to be here again because I was in this very studio ten years ago today, and you asked me then if I thought I could make a career out of magic – and here I am today!

Interviewer: I remember it well. Has your typical working day changed since those days?

Sue: Well, to some extent, I suppose, but not too much. I still do a lot of children's parties – but I also do corporate events too these days. You know, for companies and businesses. They love it. But I'm taking a break from all of that for a few weeks to offer some free magic lessons to disabled children. And of course every good magician needs an audience, so the children will be performing for free every Sunday evening for the next month in the town hall. It would be great if some of your listeners could come along and support.

Interviewer: I'm sure they will!

5 You hear a boy talking about learning to ride a bike.

Well, it must have been about ten years ago. Yeah, I guess I was about five. My sister used to ride round and round the garden really fast, and I was so jealous! I was so excited when my mum and dad gave me my own bike for my birthday. I wouldn't exactly say dad taught me, but he really did encourage me to try to work it out for myself, and I'll never forget that. I got there eventually. I was so proud of myself – I couldn't wait to show my mum I'd learnt how to do it. She was really pleased for me.

6 You hear two friends talking about revising for an exam.

Boy: So, we've got two more evenings before the chemistry exam. Shall we revise at my place tonight and your place tomorrow?

Girl: I can't see why not. Sounds good to me. I'm really not convinced we'll get it all done in two evenings though. It's the whole year's notes. It's pages and pages!

Boy: No need to worry. I've got a plan. We'll need a couple more people though. Any objections if I invite Al and Claire to study with us?

Girl: Not at all! I want to know more about your plan, though!

Boy: Sure!

7 You hear a teacher talking about a charity event.

Everyone, can I have your attention for a minute? Thanks. So, as you all know, we had the fantastic sponsored walk yesterday to raise money for a number of local charities, and I hope you all enjoyed it as much as I did – I'm sure you did! Well, we've now counted all the money we brought in, and you should all be very proud of yourselves as it's a fantastic £3,000 – far more than last year. So very, very well done everyone. Now I know a few of you still have to actually collect the cash from people who've sponsored you, so if you could bring that in to school by the end of the week, that would be perfect. Thanks again.

8 You hear two friends talking about an adventure weekend.

Boy: It looks brilliant, doesn't it? It's got rock-climbing, abseiling, bridge-building. Just my kind of thing.

Girl: Mine too! I'm sure my parents will be keen for me to go. What about yours?

Boy: Oh yes, they won't mind. As long as it's not too expensive. I guess we need to have the exact costs before we ask them.

Girl: Yeah – let's get that tomorrow. I can call them. Then we'll go from there.

Boy: And when it's all sorted, we can let Susie and Jess and the others know and they can come too, if they like.

Girl: Great idea! I can't wait!

UNIT 3 | STUDENT'S BOOK

1.17 | Listening, page 30, Exercises 2 and 3

Speaker 1

Invest In Me! is a great programme to watch, but I'm not sure that it's the best way of finding businesses to invest in.

Speaker 2

That's not very useful. I'd be surprised if they want to invest in that.

Speaker 3

Well, I'm not particularly keen on business, so it doesn't really appeal to me.

Speaker 4

I tend to think that they usually only invest in products and businesses that are already successful.

Speaker 5

I wonder if your product would be better if it was more portable.

Speaker 6

I can't imagine why anyone would invest in this product.

1.18 | Listening, page 30, Exercises 5 and 6

Speaker 1

Darren, hi. I'm Laura. So – well done! Impressive. It ticks all the boxes in terms of its look and feel, and it clearly fills a need. I don't think there's anything like it on the market, at the moment. But what really swings it for me is how you can take this idea and widen its appeal for people on holiday, different industries, even kids at school. They'd each need something slightly different, but it wouldn't be difficult to adapt. So, I think the potential is huge, and I'm going to make you an offer.

Speaker 2

Right. Interesting. I actually can't imagine that enough people are going to be willing to pay for this, Darren. You're asking a lot of money for something that's quite simple. And it's easy to copy as well. You're going to have a lot of competition soon, too. And I don't think you're going to be able to compete with the big players, who'll do it cheaper. So, I'm impressed with you, and how you've only used the very best plastic and metal putting this device together, but I'm afraid I won't be investing, so I'm out.

Speaker 3

I'm not particularly keen on how this looks, to be honest, Darren. I think its styling is a little old-fashioned, I'd say. It certainly doesn't really appeal to me, and I don't think it would appeal to my kids either really. But that we can fix. Also, I wonder if you should make it slightly smaller. It's not the easiest thing to carry around with you, is it? What I would say though is that operating it really is very simple indeed. And that I think gives you an edge. So, it needs work in terms of its design, but I'm a designer – that's what I do – and I'd like to work with you. So I'm going to make you an offer too.

Speaker 4

Hi Darren. My name's Phil. Darren, some of the people who come in here over-engineer their inventions. Do you know what I mean? They make them more complex and complicated than they need to be, sometimes adding features that aren't really necessary at all. I'm not sure if you're a genius or just lucky, but every single feature you've included does the job that it's supposed to do – and they're all important jobs at that. Personally, now I've seen this, I don't know how I've managed to live without one for so long. I want one. I think all my friends will want one. And for that reason, Darren, I want to make you an offer.

Speaker 5

Darren, it's obviously clever, and you've put a lot of thought into it, but I think you should have considered the business side of things a bit more carefully. I'd be surprised if you sell a thousand units this year – and I don't just mean in this country. All round the world. And you need to be selling a lot more than that for me to get a return on my investment. And I don't mean it's too expensive. I don't think it is. Quite the opposite, in fact. I'd say your pricing's spot on. Very reasonable. But you haven't worked out how to increase your production, and you haven't figured out your sales model. I just don't think you're ready for this investment yet. So, good luck, but I'm not going to invest. I'm out.

UNIT 4 | STUDENT'S BOOK

1.23 | Listening, page 40, Exercises 4 and 5

Interviewer: Hello, and welcome to *Stories of the Week*. My guest today is Serena Jackson, who organises mystery weekends. She's going to tell us what they are and why they've become so popular. Serena, welcome.

Serena: Thank you. It's good to be here.

Interviewer: Now, let's start by explaining what a mystery weekend actually is.

Serena: Yes, well, the idea has its origins in the classic detective fiction of the 1920s and 30s. During that period, which some have called the Golden Age of detective fiction, writers such as Agatha Christie, wrote novels about crimes that took place in large country houses. The guests who are staying at the country house are all suspects in the crime, and there's always a detective who finally solves the mystery. The stories were sometimes called 'whodunnits', because the reader tries to work out who has done the crime.

Interviewer: So, what happens on your mystery weekends?

Serena: Well, our mysetery weekends take place at a large hotel in the country. The guests arrive, and are shown to their rooms. There, they find instructions and costumes. Each of them plays a different character. When they come down to dinner, they learn that there has been a crime and no-one is allowed to leave the hotel. Actors play the main characters and the guests have to collect evidence by watching the actors, listening to their conversations, and by exploring the hotel. Finally, they are asked who they think is guilty of the crime, and the mystery is solved. It's usually a lot of fun.

Interviewer: It definitely sounds like a lot of fun! These mystery weekends are aimed at an older audience. What about events for teenagers?

Serena: Often, whole families come along, enjoy working together and get involved in the mystery weekends, but for those teenagers who fancy having a go at being an amateur detective, there's so much on offer. Some companies organise themed birthday parties where party-goers play the characters, in costume of course, and a detective host turns up to direct the entertainment. An easier option is to do it yourself and play a mystery board game with your friends. In contrast to the mystery weekends, it's the guests who are the main characters and one of you will be the criminal!

Interviewer: Sounds exciting! Why do you think this kind of event is popular?

Serena: For the same reasons that all crime stories are popular. First of all, there's the pleasure of playing the detective. We love to look for clues, test out our own theories and try to be cleverer than the criminal. If you work out the solution, you get a lot of satisfaction from it. Apart from that, we have a very deep desire to see justice done. When someone is the victim of a crime, it goes against the rules that society lives by. We want to see the offender caught and punished. We all hate to see someone get away with an offence.

Interviewer: I see! So, tell us Serena, what skills do you need to be successful at these events?

Serena: Ah, that's a very good question. One essential characteristic is the ability to think outside the box. By that I mean that you shouldn't just accept the obvious solution to a problem. You'll be given all kinds of false clues and you need to be able to see what is relevant and what's irrelevant. Often, it's the crazy ideas that help you find the solution!

Interviewer: That's great advice. Do you think events and games like these will always be popular?

Serena: Oh, yes. In our everyday lives, we face so many complicated problems. We turn on the TV news or read a newspaper and it can seem as if the world is full of crime and other negative issues. In a way, events such as these give you the chance to get away to a time and place that seems simpler than today, when the only thing you had to worry about was one simple crime and who had done it!

UNIT 5 | STUDENT'S BOOK

1.24 | Reading, page 49, Exercise 5

1 D Surprisingly, video games can often help us to master these.

2 G They constantly place obstacles in your path until you reach the solution.

3 A This may help you to make more informed choices in the real world.

4 E You need to decide what to build, how to use resources effectively and which strategies work.

5 C You shouldn't give out personal information about yourself to someone you don't know.

6 F As well as developing life skills, having excellent computer skills could also help you with a future career.

1.30 | Listening, page 52, Exercise 2

Interviewer: I'm joined now in the studio by 15-year-old Adam Carter, who's the captain of the Eastbrook under-16s football team. Adam, thanks for coming in.

Adam: It's nice to be here!

Interviewer: Now, Adam, I could have invited you in because your team's doing rather well this season, or perhaps because as captain you're a very good role model for other teenagers, but in fact the main reason we asked you here today is to talk about some of the exciting changes that have happened to your team in the last couple of years. It must have been an interesting time.

Adam: It certainly has been!

Interviewer: Take us back to how it all began.

Adam: Well, two years ago, I was in the Eastbrook under-16s boys' team, and my sister Rachel was in the girls' team. We'd often kick a ball around together in the garden, so we just wondered one day – why don't our teams ever play each other? You know, my team only played other boys' teams, and Rachel's team only played other girls' teams. We just thought it was a bit strange. You know, we do PE together at school, so why not football too? So – we talked to all our team members, and agreed to try an experiment.

1.31 | Listening, page 52, Exercises 4 and 5

Interviewer: I'm joined now in the studio by 15-year-old Adam Carter, who's the captain of the Eastbrook under-16s football team. Adam, thanks for coming in.

Adam: It's nice to be here!

Interviewer: Now, Adam, I could have invited you in because your team's doing rather well this season, or perhaps because as captain you're a very good role model for other teenagers, but in fact the main reason we asked you here today is to talk about some of the exciting changes that have happened to your team in the last couple of years. It must have been an interesting time.

Adam: It certainly has been!

Interviewer: Take us back to how it all began.

Adam: Well, two years ago, I was in the Eastbrook under-16s boys' team, and my sister Rachel was in the girls' team. We'd often kick a ball around together in the garden, so we just wondered one day – why don't our teams ever play each other? You know, my team only played other boys' teams, and Rachel's team only played other girls' teams. We just thought it was a bit strange. You know, we do PE together at school, so why not football too? So – we talked to all our team members, and agreed to try an experiment.

Interviewer: Girls and boys playing together?

Adam: Yes. Well, we decided to do it in two stages, which is exactly what happened. For a year – last year – we kept the teams separate in that there was still an all-girls team and an all-boys team, but we'd play against each other once or twice a week.

Interviewer: OK. And how did that go?

Adam: It was a great success. I'd been a bit worried that the boys would beat the girls every match but fortunately they were far too good for that. Interestingly, it was pretty evenly split – they're clearly not a pushover.

Interviewer: And this year?

Adam: This year we've gone to stage two, where we've completely merged the two teams, so we've got boys and girls playing alongside each other. Because of the numbers, we've got an A team and a B team, and they're fairly evenly split in terms of the number of boys and girls in each one.

Interviewer: Now, that's a huge change in a short period of time. Some people must have been worried it wouldn't work out.

Adam: Yes – well, actually, I don't think any of the actual players – boys or girls – thought it was a bad idea. I can't remember anyone saying we shouldn't try it, but some of our parents tried to talk us out of it. Their basic argument was that boys are stronger than girls so it wouldn't be fair, but as I said, that's proved not to be the case at all.

Interviewer: You must have faced a few practical problems along the way?

Adam: One or two. Quite a few people said to us: you're going to have problems with changing rooms and things like that, but to be honest, where we usually play – Eastbrook football field – there aren't any changing rooms anyway. At the end of a game, you put your tracksuit on, go home and have a shower at home. So actually it hasn't really been a problem at all in that respect.

Interviewer: So, you're now one team – well, two teams, A and B, but you know what I mean. You're one mixed team. My question is – who do you play against? Are there other mixed teams out there? There can't be many.

Adam: Ha! No, not many! But we're encouraging a few teams to give it a try, and I think they're looking at us and seriously considering it now. In terms of who we play, we'll play anyone who wants to play us, so under-16 boys-only teams, under-16 girls-only teams if they want to, under-16 mixed teams if they exist. We don't care – as long as they don't care! We're trying to organise a local tournament though solely for mixed teams. Hopefully, that'll encourage a few more to get started.

Interviewer: Now, you're the captain this year, aren't you? Can you see there being a female captain at some point in the future?

Adam: Absolutely! I really hope there will be. This is my last year in the team of course, as I'll be 16 next year, so they'll be looking for a new captain. I can't see any reason at all why it couldn't be a girl – as long as they're the best person for the job, of course. I think that's really what we've all discovered. It's about doing your best, being the best, not whether you're a boy or a girl.

Interviewer: And on that note, let me thank you for coming in, and wish you and your team all the very best.

Adam: Thanks for inviting me.

UNIT 6 | STUDENT'S BOOK

2.06 | Listening, page 62, Exercises 2 and 5

Hello, everyone. I'm Kerry and I'm a careers adviser. That means that I go into schools and colleges and speak to young people about the choices they face and the career options open to them. I give them information about different occupations in order to help them make better choices.

However, my main starting point is not the occupations but the young people themselves. I believe it's really important to understand yourself before you look for positions in the world of work. Your skills and your personality traits need to match up with the kind of career path you intend to follow. One tool that I use with young people to guide them in this area is a SWOT analysis. That's S-W-O-T. Each letter stands for an important area that you need to think about.

S stands for 'strengths'. Essentially, this refers to things that you are good at. This might be one of your school subjects, such as ability in maths, or it might be a broader skill, such as getting on well with people. I encourage young people to look at all aspects of their lives and to identify as many strengths as they can. Often, people can be surprised by what they discover about themselves once they start to make a list. For example, last week I had a discussion with a teenager who just couldn't think of any strengths. After talking to him for a while, I learnt that he played a lot of video games. Playing these games involved skills such as strategic planning and using maps, and demonstrated some important personality traits, like determination. Eventually, he realised that he did have a number of strengths and we were able to go on from there.

W stands for 'weaknesses'. We all have tasks that we prefer not to do. Personally, I can't stand filling in forms. Sometimes I make myself busy with other work so as not to do it. That's a weakness. You have to be honest with yourself about what you find difficult and what you would rather not do. You might have the idea in your head that you want to be a doctor, but if you are shy and don't like meeting new people, then it might be a disadvantage in that profession. A list of your weaknesses helps to clarify either what occupations you might avoid, or what areas you may need to get better in.

O stands for 'opportunities'. This refers to anything that can help you use your strengths to achieve your goal. For example, if you are good with animals, and a vet has a surgery in your area, then that could be a good opportunity for you to volunteer and get some experience. Or perhaps through your family you know someone who does a job you're interested in. You may have the opportunity to benefit from their experience to find out more about different positions within a certain profession.

T stands for 'threats'. These are obstacles or difficulties that might prevent you from achieving your goal. Threats may involve a lack of resources. For instance, it's very challenging to become a pilot if you can't afford the training. And if your chosen profession involves going to university, that may be very difficult if there are a limited number of university places in your region or in your country.

After doing a SWOT analysis and making lists of key points under each heading, the young people I work with have a much clearer idea of what they need to do to get where they want to be. Now let's look at a couple of examples in more detail.

UNIT 7 | STUDENT'S BOOK

2.07 | Reading, page 71, Exercise 5

1 F by fishing nets that the artist saw when travelling

2 G they are moving the light and patterns around on the sculpture itself

3 A we've discovered that it is full of light this week

4 E to bring art to all kinds of people and age groups

5 B of the litter dumped in our seas and take more care of our environment

6 D all this is free and you make friends in the crowd

2.11 | Listening, page 74, Exercise 2

Extract 1

I'm not quite sure what to do, Joel, to tell you the truth. Can I ask your opinion?

Extract 2

Well, it's difficult. I've got this bit over here which is supposed to be a dark corner, so I've been colouring it with this pencil but it's got so dark that it's practically black. I'm not sure what I can do about it now.

Extract 3

I'd get a rubber and rub – very gently though – over the dark area. I think that might make it lighter. It's worth a try, I'd say.

Extract 4

We'd only gone in because we were passing and Matt saw the sign outside and thought it sounded interesting – neither of us had ever been to one before, you see – and there were all these people, and so many things on display. I couldn't believe it.

Extract 5

I would be looking forward to it, except the person sitting two rows in front of me has got such a big hat on I can't see anything at all! It's really annoying.

Extract 6

So, shall we do it on cave paintings, then? There's loads of stuff online about them, and they're really interesting.

2.12 | Listening, page 74, Exercises 4 and 5

1 You hear two people talking in an art class.

Joel: Are you all right, Chloe? You look confused.

Chloe: I'm not quite sure what to do, Joel, to tell you the truth. Can I ask your opinion?

Joel: Sure. What's the problem?

Chloe: Well, it's difficult. I've got this bit over here which is supposed to be a dark corner, so I've been colouring it with this pencil but it's got so dark that it's practically black. I'm not sure what I can do about it now. What do you think? Do you think I should start again?

Joel: That seems a bit extreme. You don't really have time, anyway. Ummm … you said it's pencil. I'd get a rubber and rub – very gently though – over the dark area. I think that might make it lighter. It's worth a try, I'd say.

Chloe: I'm really not sure that's going to work. I think it'll just make it worse, won't it?

Joel: Well, to be honest, I'm not sure you've got any other options. Give it a go and see what happens.

2 You hear a woman talking about an auction she went to.

Well, it was wonderful, to be honest. We'd only gone in because we were passing and Matt saw the sign outside and thought it sounded interesting – neither of us had ever been to one before, you see – and there were all these people, and so many things on display. I couldn't believe it. They also had a catalogue with all the pieces in. I looked through it, but Matt didn't want to, really. It started at half past two and although there were so many people there, not that many people actually bid for things. I didn't have enough money on me to bid for much but there was one thing, a beautiful silver ring. I couldn't resist it. I got it for £20 – I was so pleased. I'll show it to you.

3 You hear two people talking about a work of art.

Jez: This is why you brought me here, is it?

Megan: Yes! This is Sea and Land, by Martin Davis. It's even better than I expected.

Jez: Well, I don't know enough about modern art and installations to comment, really, but I'm not sure I can see what all the fuss is about. It's just a video screen and some flashing lights, isn't it?

Megan: You're too old-fashioned to understand modern art – that's your problem! I'm not even going to try and bother to change your mind, but at least let me enjoy it for a moment.

Jez: Absolutely! Just tell me what you're enjoying about it …

Megan: Well, look. It's about the relationship between the sea and the land – things from the sea washing up on the shore, things from the land polluting the waters. You can see that through the images coming up on the screen. And the lights create an atmosphere of pain and suffering, and yet beauty at the same time. It's very powerful.

Jez: Right.

4 You hear a conversation in a shop.

Shop assistant: Hi there. Can I help you with anything?

Customer: Yes, actually. I'm looking for a present for my niece – she's 13 and she's really into arts and crafts.

Shop assistant: OK – so she likes making things. It's quite a broad area. Do you know if she has any specific interests – painting, photography, origami, those kind of things?

Customer: Origami – that's paper folding, isn't it? I think she likes that, yes.

Shop assistant: Well, we've got some lovely packs here. This one's for quite young children, but this one here's for teenagers. It's got hundreds of different things you can make – animal figures, buildings, loads of different things.

Customer: That sounds great. How much is it?

Shop assistant: 14.99.

Customer: That's great. I'll take it. Thanks.

6 You hear part of a documentary on TV about a famous painting.

Today, of course, it's recognised as a masterpiece but, back then, 400 years ago, it caused a scandal when people first heard about it. Some people called for it to be burnt or destroyed, others for the artist, Drogin, to be imprisoned. Despite these difficulties, Drogin exhibited the painting in Paris, and it was there that critics began to recognise its greatness. Within a few years, it was rightly considered one of the greatest paintings of the century. Interestingly, it was considered to be such an important piece that for 30 years, no member of the public was allowed to view it. And that was nothing to do with the original scandal at all.

6 You hear a conversation at a concert.

Charlotte: I'm looking forward to this. It should be starting soon.

Greg: I would be looking forward to it, except the person sitting two rows in front of me has got such a big hat on I can't see anything at all! It's really annoying.

Charlotte: Oh yes. Do you want to swap places?

Greg: That won't help, will it? Then you won't be able to see.

Charlotte: Maybe we can move. There are some empty seats over there.

Greg: No, the tickets have got seat numbers on. Not everyone's come in yet. It could be that those tickets have been sold. I'll be all right.

Charlotte: Look, why don't you ask her to take it off. I'm sure she won't mind.

Greg: No, I don't want to cause any trouble. I'll see how it goes.

Charlotte: Well, I'm happy to ask her, even if you aren't.

Greg: Well, if you really don't mind …

7 You hear part of an interview with a teenage artist.

Interviewer: Monica, what got you into sculpture in the first place?

Monica: My dad had a book of pictures of sculptures by Henry Moore, the famous sculptor, and I spent hours looking at them. I loved – still love – the incredible rounded shapes he makes. Whether it's human figures or animals or abstract shapes, there's something fascinating about his work. I've always been attracted to it, and as soon as I got the chance I started learning the techniques behind sculpture.

Interviewer: And how did you get the chance?

Monica: I moved to a school which specialises in art and design, and luckily they offer sculpture as part of the curriculum. For me, it was wonderful.

8 You hear two friends talking about a project for school.

Boy: So, shall we do it on cave paintings, then? There's loads of stuff online about them, and they're really interesting. And they've been in the news recently because of that new cave they've found with pictures of animals – those paintings are really, really old. I think it's a good choice.

Girl: I agree. I'm not sure it'll be easy, however. Mr Radley wants us mainly to write text, not paste in pictures. It's quite difficult to write about cave paintings without including pictures of them, isn't it? That's my only concern, really.

Boy: Yeah, that's true. And we do have to write 500 words. Maybe there's something better we can focus on.

UNIT 8 | STUDENT'S BOOK

2.17 | Listening, page 84, Exercises 4 and 5

Speaker 1

I got involved in a really interesting project which I saw online. They were looking for people who wanted to travel to Nepal, stay with a local family and learn about their water needs. That's something I've always been very passionate about and I wish I had got involved sooner. Too many people around the world don't have enough clean water and it's time we did something about it. The idea of the project was to help with planning small hydropower stations, which would meet the energy needs of local people. The family I stayed with, who lived in a remote area, really looked after me well and I was so grateful because sometimes I really felt a long way from home.

Speaker 2

Our headteacher decided it was time for the school to go green and asked for volunteers who were interested in helping. I put myself forward and so did my friend Ellie. The head reassured us that we didn't need to be experts, which was a relief. She asked us to come up with suggestions that the school governors could consider. Ellie and I realised that the school has a lot of roof space, so we thought solar panels might work and help to reduce the amount of fossil fuels we use. It was really satisfying when the school governors agreed and the project went ahead. Now all the heating and hot water in the school is provided by renewable energy, which makes me feel proud to have been involved.

Speaker 3

The project I was involved in was organised by a group called WindAid. They build wind turbines around the world to provide clean energy to communities who have never had electricity. Imagine how thrilled I was to go to a tiny village in the mountains of Peru and start work on putting a turbine up. Once the turbines are up and running, the villagers have light and can even start using computers to help them in their businesses. Of course, there are technical experts who lead the projects, but there's plenty for everyone else to do, from digging holes to entertaining the local children! I learnt a lot about myself and what I'm capable of, which is one of the reasons I recommend it to other people.

Speaker 4

When I heard that they were planning to build a wave energy farm off the coast where I live, I knew there would be some local opposition. People who live in the area were concerned that it might spoil the view, but I felt it was the right thing to do. The local council held a public meeting about it, and I got involved in the campaign to explain the positives to people.

I'm really not the most confident speaker in the world, but I pushed myself and was really glad that I met the challenge. In the end, I got up in front of 200 people and explained why I thought it would bring benefits to the area. It seemed to go well, so fingers crossed!

Speaker 5

Geothermal energy comes from the heat deep under the surface of the Earth. You have to drill down a couple of miles to reach the hot rock, and you send down water that comes back very hot. In the long term, I'm sure it's going to form part of our renewable energy strategy. The project I was involved in was in the north of England, where they're just beginning to explore the idea. My job was to interview local people and find out about their attitudes towards geothermal energy. I wish more people knew about geothermal energy. If they were better informed, perhaps more research would be done into it. I found, though, that local people were largely ignorant of how much of a difference it would make if we really used it properly.

UNIT 9 | STUDENT'S BOOK

2.18 | Reading, page 92, Exercise 2

Vanity Fair is set in the early 1800s and it's a classic novel of romance and adventure. The main characters are Amelia Sedley, a warm-hearted but innocent person and Becky Sharpe, the selfish protagonist. Amelia is from a rich family but Becky is poor. Before being sent to teach and look after Sir Pitt Crawley's daughters, Becky stays with the Sedley family where she meets Jos, Amelia's brother, who falls in love with her and George Osborne, a family friend who is interested in Amelia. While she is with the Sedleys, Becky secretly marries Sir Pitt's son, Captain Rawdon Crawley. Meanwhile, the Sedleys have lost their money and George's rich father forbids him to marry Amelia. Dobbin, George's best friend who admires Amelia, persuades George to marry her and consequently, George's father refuses to leave him any money when he dies.

2.23 | Listening, page 96, Exercises 4 and 5

Interviewer: Today, I'm joined in the studio by three students, Marcia, Laura and Ashraf. Hello and welcome.

Students: Hi.

Interviewer: Now, you've just completed what sounds like a fascinating school project about invented languages in books and films. Marcia, if I can start with you. Can you explain why authors invent languages?

Marcia: Yes, sure. Well, there are lots of examples in books and films where an author or scriptwriter wants to create a new world or a new country with its own geography, culture and history. And sometimes, in order to make it seem as believable as possible for the audience, authors go one step further, and create a whole new language for the characters from that place to use.

Interviewer: I suppose it makes a change from everyone speaking English all the time.

Marcia: Exactly. In science-fiction and fantasy genres, it can help the reader or viewer to inhabit the world and really believe in it, which is crucial in these types of books and films.

Interviewer: So, can you give us some examples from these genres?

Marcia: Yes, well, I guess at the moment, Dothraki, from TV's *Game of Thrones* is the most famous example. It's already got 4,000 words and its own language-learning app!

Interviewer: Ha! That's really impressive! So, is this the first time people have tried to learn an invented language?

Marcia: Oh no. Dothraki has got a long way to go to catch up with Klingon, which is probably the most famous invented language in science fiction.

Interviewer: Klingon? What on earth is that?

Marcia: Well, it was created for the Star Trek films in the 1980s. The Klingons were a race of aliens, but when they started 'speaking' in the first Star Trek film in 1979, the actors playing them just made a few random noises that didn't make any sense.

Interviewer: So, hardly a fully developed language then?

Marcia: No, but what's really interesting is that a few years later when they made another film, the producers and director were so serious about creating a realistic language that they had a language created for the film by Mark Okrand, a linguistic expert. The result was a language that initially had around 1,500 words, and its own strict grammar and pronunciation rules. And since its initial invention, the Klingon vocabulary has doubled to about 3,000 words. There is even a Klingon translation of Shakespeare's *Hamlet*!

Interviewer: That's remarkable. Do you know how many people can actually speak Klingon?

Marcia: It's hard to say, but there is a fascinating story about a man in the USA who tried to raise his son to be bilingual in English and Klingon.

Interviewer: Oh dear, poor lad … Anyway, thanks Marcia. So, Ashraf, is it just science-fiction and fantasy writers that like to invent languages?

Ashraf: Well, no it isn't. Some writers use invented languages not so much to create a new world but more to make a point about the state of the world they are writing about.

Interviewer: What do you mean?

Ashraf: Well, George Orwell's *1984* is a good example of this. It was written in the 1940s about an all-powerful state which wants to control every aspect of a person's life, including how they speak and therefore think. The state introduces Newspeak, which isn't really a new language like Klingon or Dothraki, but is a simplified version of English with all the feeling, beauty and passion removed, as well as many of the negative words. Over time, more and more words are removed from the dictionary, which gets smaller with each new edition. So eventually, people no longer have the vocabulary to think complex thoughts or imagine new ideas.

Interviewer: Thanks Ashraf. Finally, Laura, what invented languages did you look at?

Laura: Well, actually, I decided not to look at invented languages as such, but instead at how certain writers invented words that have become part of our language.

Interviewer: OK, that's quite different. So, which writers did you look at and what words have they given us?

Laura: Well, unsurprisingly, William Shakespeare is the writer who has given most words to the English language. He was the first person to use certain nouns as verbs, such as 'bet', he turned verbs into adjectives, for example 'accused', he added suffixes and prefixes to make words like 'fashionable' or 'worthless', or just invented new ones like 'gossip'. In fact, he invented over 1,700 words that are still in use today.

Interviewer: Well, thanks to all of you for joining me today. It's been fascinating, and I've certainly learnt a lot.

Students: Thanks.

UNIT 10 | STUDENT'S BOOK

3.05 | Listening, page 106, Exercises 4 and 5

Jenny: On today's *Blog Watch*, I'm joined by Simon Pollard, a keen blogger who's recently posted a great piece about some very lucky people. Isn't that right, Simon?

Simon: Hi Jenny. Well, some of them were very lucky, yes, others less so.

Jenny: So, tell us about the blog post. Who are these people and what luck did they have?

Simon: The post, 'Lucky Finds', is really about the stories of people whose lives change very suddenly after finding something that turns out to be extremely valuable, or not. It isn't really a post about making a fortune, but more about how people react to this amazing luck and how obsessed they become.

Jenny: Can you tell us about some of these stories then?

Simon: Well, one of my favourite ones happened in a field in the Suffolk countryside in the UK. And it all started when a farmer called Peter Whatling lost a hammer.

Jenny: OK …

Simon: Well, it must have been quite an important hammer, because he called his friend, Eric, and asked him to help look for it.

Jenny: Right. And did they find the farmer's precious hammer?

Simon: Ha, ha. Not to begin with. But they did find some very old silver spoons, gold jewellery, and ancient coins.

Jenny: Wow, and what did the farmer do?

Simon: Not being the owner of the land, the farmer thought it was right to tell the landowners, the local council. They immediately sent a team of archeologists to the field and the next day they dug up a huge amount of Roman treasure, including over 500 gold coins and 14,000 silver coins.

Jenny: Wow! So, who owned the treasure?

Simon: Well, under British law, buried treasure becomes the property of the state.

Jenny: So, Eric and the farmer didn't receive anything for finding it?

Simon: Far from it. The treasure went to the British Museum but Eric was paid £1.75 million for discovering it.

Jenny: Ah and what about the farmer?

Simon: Being a good friend of the farmer, he agreed to give him half of the money.

Jenny: What a wonderful story that is.

Simon: Yes, unfortunately, not all the stories have happy endings. In the same year that Eric struck lucky in a farmer's field, over in the USA, Teri Horton went into a local second-hand shop to buy a friend of hers a gift. In there she found a very large and strange painting. Thinking it was funny, she decided to buy it there and then for $5.

Jenny: Don't tell me it was some lost masterpiece.

Simon: Well, having bought it and taken it home, her friend wasn't keen on it so Teri kept it for herself before eventually deciding to try and sell it. But after having seen it, a local art teacher thought it could be by the famous American modern artist Jackson Pollock.

Jenny: I don't think I've heard of him.

Simon: No, neither had Teri. But she soon had. A painting by Jackson Pollock can sell for over $100 million, provided that you can convince someone that it is an original. And this can be extremely difficult. Some art experts came to look at the painting, but none of them was sure about it being genuine. Eventually, she asked an expert at studying crime scenes to have a look at it and he was convinced that he had found one of the artist's fingerprints on it.

Jenny: Oh wow! So Teri's painting was an original?

Simon: If only it were that easy. The art world still isn't sure about Teri's painting, which remains locked up in a warehouse as she carries on trying to convince them of its value.

Jenny: OK, let's have one more story.

Simon: OK, one of the luckiest people I came across was a man in the USA who made a living buying and selling metal. At a sale he spotted a large golden egg with a beautifully made clock inside it. At over $13,000 it was a very expensive item, but being sure he could make some money from it, he bought it.

Jenny: That's a big risk.

Simon: You would think so. But the egg was made of gold, and the man guessed that even if it wasn't worth much more, he could still make a profit selling all the gold.

Jenny: So, what happened?

Simon: Well, before selling it, the man decided to do some research. It turned out that the golden egg was actually made by the famous jeweller Fabergé for the Russian royal family in the 19th century.

Jenny: And this time everyone was sure it was real?

Simon: Without a doubt. In fact, he soon sold it to a collector for $33 million.

Jenny: Well, thanks for joining us today.

UNIT 11 | STUDENT'S BOOK

3.06 | Reading, page 115, Exercise 4

1 E All of these places were used for sets in *Game of Thrones*.

2 B Initially, he'd been disappointed as the producers didn't take him on for a part.

3 G Northern Ireland has also benefited from the same series and with an increase in tourism, the economy is sure to start growing.

4 A Brendan had been unemployed for more than three years.

5 D Finally, the cost of filming here compared to the United States is lower.

6 C In 2015, the UK alone was making as much as £140 million from screen tourism, according to film consultancy services.

3.10 | Listening, page 118, Exercises 4 and 5

Holly: It's now time for our weekly roundup of the best travel blogs. I'm joined today by the young travel blogger of the year, Justin Caxton. Hi Justin. Good to have you back on the show.

Justin: Thanks, Holly. It's nice to be back.

Holly: So, I guess you must have read hundreds of travel blogs. I wonder if you could tell us what you look for in a blog?

Justin: Well, yes, I have. They range from tourists who just want to tell their friends and family about their holiday or adventure, to explorers writing about journeys through some of the world's most remote and dangerous places. But personally, I'm really interested in stories from ordinary people who have been on extraordinary adventures or done amazing challenges.

Holly: So, what have you got for us this week then?

Justin: Well, there was one blog that I couldn't stop reading. It's the amazing story of Tom Davies, a 19-year-old from London who in 2015 spent 174 days cycling around the world.

Holly: 174 days? Incredible! And do you know how far he cycled?

Justin: About 29,000 kilometres. It really was a phenomenal journey, most of which Tom did on his own.

Holly: So, where did his adventure take him?

Justin: Well, because of political problems, visa problems and general concerns for his safety, Tom did the journey in a number of stages, avoiding various countries and trouble spots on the way. He set off from London, and then followed a route across France and Italy and down through the Balkans until he eventually arrived in Istanbul. He then picked up the journey again in Mumbai, India, and cycled all the way to Kolkata. After that he did a couple of stages across South East Asia, setting out from Myanmar and making for Singapore, then it was on to Australia, New Zealand, and the USA before finishing off back in Europe, through Portugal and Spain.

Holly: Well, I'm exhausted just hearing about it.

Justin: Ha, ha. On the blog he writes about the details of the trip, including what the weather was like, the food he ate, the places he visited and the things that happened. It's a great read, and really inspiring.

Holly: I can imagine! So, can you tell us about some of the highs and lows of his adventure?

Justin: Well, reading the blog you get the feeling that his most positive memories were of the people he met. He often talks of the hospitality, warmth and help he received from strangers when he broke down, especially in places like India. And obviously, you can't go on such a journey without being impressed by the natural beauty of the world and Tom was no exception, clearly enjoying the views in places such as New Zealand and the USA.

Holly: And what about some of the difficulties that he faced?

Justin: Well, he often writes about the extreme weather that he faced. He began his journey in Europe in the middle of winter and had to endure a lot of rain, wind and snow on his journey across the continent, which clearly had a really negative effect on his spirits. In India it was the heat that affected him most, and in the Australian Nullarbor desert, it was the strong winds that slowed him down. Food also features often in his blog posts. When you're cycling up to six or seven hours a day it's obviously really important to eat big meals, which in some countries was a little harder than others.

Holly: Do you know if he got sick at all?

Justin: Yes, he did. This was mainly due to the food he ate. He became very ill in Italy, and then again in India. But what was interesting was that you could sense exactly how he was feeling and how much energy he had from the way he wrote. As you read through his blog, you experience the highs and lows with him.

Holly: And what other dangers did he face?

Justin: Well, it seems that the biggest dangers he faced were from the other road users. In India, he didn't feel that drivers cared much about cyclists like him. In one angry post about how bad the experience was, he invited anyone who disagreed with him to spend a few weeks cycling across India. It's a good point, which is hard to argue against.

Holly: Yes, I'm sure.

Justin: He also had some scary and not so scary encounters with animals. It seems he was chased by dogs in almost every country he visited – which must have been frightening – he encountered monkeys in Asia, and found himself racing an emu in the Australian outback.

Holly: Woah, no way! And are there any photos on the blog?

Justin: Yes, there are plenty. Although Tom admits that his photos may not be the best quality, they do provide a really interesting insight to his journey, the places he visited and the people he met.

Holly: So, how does he finish?

Justin: The last day, day 174, he cycled from Winchester in the south of England back home to London, finishing the ride on the street where he lives. Over a hundred of his family and close friends were there to welcome him home, which must have been really incredible. As Tom got off his bike he described it as 'the best feeling in the world'.

Holly: How wonderful!

Justin: Definitely! But best of all, not only was he the youngest person to cycle around the world, during his trip he also raised over £50,000 for charity.

Holly: What an amazing achievement, and an extraordinary young man.

UNIT 12 | STUDENT'S BOOK

3.15 | Listening, page 128, Exercises 4 and 5

1 You hear two friends talking about an important day.

Woman: I was really pleased that my mum came. It was such a long way but I would have been really disappointed if she hadn't come to our family reunion.

Man: How did she get there?

Woman: Well, it was too far to drive, so she came by plane.

Man: Really? But she's terrified of getting on a plane, isn't she?

Woman: I know. It was the first time she had flown anywhere for over 30 years. I know how difficult it was for her but she was amazing. She didn't complain once.

Man: How did she manage to do it?

Woman: Well, she went on a course earlier this year to help get over her fear. It really helped her to relax and understand how safe it is.

Man: That's great. I'm so happy for you.

Woman: Yes, it was really special. And now she wants to travel the world.

2 You hear a news report about a woman.

Sport now, and as expected the disabled athlete, Monica Holmes, has qualified for the Olympic team. Monica needed a time well under her personal best to meet the qualification standard, and she managed it with ease. It'll come as a birthday present to herself on the day she turns twenty-five to be the first blind athlete to qualify for the regular Olympics. Her coach suggests that she's in with a real chance of getting to the final, and Monica will now join the rest of the Olympic athletics squad for training.

3 You hear a boy telling a friend about rescuing someone.

Boy: It was awesome, but really scary as well. You never think you're going to be in that situation and you never know how you're going to react.

Girl: It's a good job you reacted like you did. You must be really proud of yourself for diving in without worrying about your own safety like that.

Boy: Well, you know, I didn't feel like a hero or anything, although I guess I had a sense of achievement. It was the way everyone else reacted that felt really good. That made it feel like I'd done something special.

Girl: What about the woman?

Boy: Oh, she wanted to give me something, but I turned it down. Just being treated like a hero for a day was enough of a reward!

4 You overhear a girl talking about a book she has read.

So, I finished that book, you know about the moon landings and what an amazing achievement they were. It was hard going in places, just because it got quite technical. I was sorry when I had to put the book down, though. The writer really carries you along with the story of the race between the Americans and the Russians. It was such a dangerous journey, and it's a relief when everyone finally gets back to Earth in one piece. I'll lend it to you when I see you.

5 You hear part of a programme on an extraordinary place.

It's an amazing construction and the most important archeological site in the country. And there is still a great deal of mystery about how and why it was built, something which may never be fully explained. But the first thing you notice when you come here is the main road that runs just a few metres away from the site. It's just unbelievable. This should be a quiet place to enjoy the stones, but instead it's really noisy. I'd really like to recommend this but to be honest, there are lots of other much nicer ancient sites to visit.

6 You hear a teacher talking about someone he admires.

In the history of Antarctic exploration, one of the figures who stands out is Ernest Shackleton. I've always found his story fascinating. He wasn't a great scientist or a great navigator, but he had a talent for getting the best from his men. They didn't always think he was the easiest or the kindest leader, but when the expedition went wrong, he was the perfect person to be in charge. When their ship, the *Endurance*, got stuck in the ice and sank, Shackleton and five others sailed a lifeboat 800 miles to get help for the rest of his men. It's that refusal to consider failure that makes him a great hero.

7 You hear a girl talking about something she did for charity.

My main hope is that I've inspired other people to do something worthwhile. What I did, a 24-hour trek, was really hard. But when you're doing it for charity, you have to carry on, no matter what. That thought keeps you going, in spite of difficulties. There was a big group of us doing it, and everyone encouraged and supported each other along the way. There was a huge sense of achievement at the finish, knowing that we've made a difference to some people's lives. But you don't have to do what I did, there are lots of things you can do to make a difference.

8 You hear part of an interview with a musician.

Interviewer: You've just recorded a new version of Beethoven's ninth symphony. Can you tell us why you chose this work?

Musician: Well, it's so beautiful, so powerful and emotional. I've been fascinated by it for many years. And as both a singer and a musician, I was attracted to how he introduces singing into the final part. In fact, it was quite a surprise when I found out that this was the first major symphony that used voices.

Interviewer: That's not the only thing that is unusual about the work, is it?

Musician: No, what is really remarkable is the fact that he was deaf when he wrote it. When you think about that, it's a huge achievement.

Interviewer: Definitely. And what did people think about it when they first heard it?

Musician: A lot of people thought it was his greatest work of all, although at the time some critics didn't like the singing, which isn't much of a surprise.

OPTIMISE YOUR EXAMS STUDENT'S BOOK

3.16 | Listening, page 138, Exercise 1

1

Boy: I think it really reflected exactly what they had to go through and how tough the whole experience was. It was shot brilliantly.

Girl: Hmmm, maybe up to a point. The actors had obviously been well trained for all the action but a lot of elements were missing, like transmitting each person's feelings and what they were thinking individually …

2

Teacher: So, I'd say just pick a topic that you feel comfortable talking about in front of the class. This means you won't need to spend hours doing research or any specialised reading.

3

Boy: On the last trip we did I remember we went hiking through this really steep, rocky gorge. I was pretty scared but my oldest cousin kept me going, telling me about how when we got through the most dangerous bit of the climb we'd have this amazing view of a huge lake right across the valley.

3.17 | Listening, page 138, Exercises 2 and 4

Extract 1

You will hear two friends talking about a recent trip to the cinema.

Boy: Did you go and see that film about those people who survived in the desert for 10 days? I thought the story was amazing.

Girl: Yeah, I read about it online and it sounded really inspirational, but the film was a bit disappointing. I felt let down.

Boy: Really? I think it really reflected exactly what they had to go through and how tough the whole experience was. It was shot brilliantly.

Girl: Hmmm, maybe up to a point. The actors had obviously been well trained for all the action but a lot of elements were missing, like transmitting each person's feelings and what they were thinking individually …

Boy: Well, I'm sure that's even difficult for an actor if you haven't lived through an experience like that, but yes, perhaps they could have put a bit more emotion into it.

Girl: Exactly, less focus on the survival techniques and more on people's reactions.

Extract 2

You'll hear a teacher talking to their class.

When you're planning this project you'll need to think about including something from your own personal experience, something anecdotal. So, imagine you have to tell your audience about it in your own words and try to make it surprising and get some humour into your presentation too. You really mustn't just research any topic of interest online and copy ideas from websites. So, I'd say just pick a topic that you feel comfortable talking about in front of the class. This means you won't need to spend hours doing research or any specialised reading. My advice is to spend time working out a good plan and then practise what you're going to say with someone else who can listen to you and give you feedback before you do it in class.

Extract 3

You'll hear a teenager talking about an outdoor activity.

My cousins and I go off to the mountains together every summer holiday, which is cool as we always have fun together. On the last trip we did, I remember we went hiking through this really steep, rocky gorge. I was pretty scared but my oldest cousin kept me going, telling me about how when we got through the most dangerous bit of the climb, we'd have this amazing view of a huge lake right across the valley. I was worried I wasn't as fit as he was and I secretly wanted to give up but in the end, I did it. I couldn't believe it! It really was worth it … just for the amazing scenery we finally saw.

3.18 | Listening, page 139, Exercise 7

Part 1

If you're interested in sea life and marine biology, like me, then I recommend going on a volunteer trip to Tenerife in the Canary Islands. Last summer was my final year before starting university and my school organised for some of us to go and work with a marine conservation organisation. And, guess what? We really did get to see some amazing marine life, including bottlenose dolphins, pilot whales, turtles and a lot of different species of birds. Interestingly, there are as many as 24 species that migrate through the waters of the Canary Islands at different points in the year, so you're pretty much guaranteed to see something from one of the organisation's marine life watching boats.

Before I tell you a bit more about volunteering, here are a few facts that I learnt about some of the marine life while I was there. Bottlenose dolphins, which we saw regularly, are commonly found world-wide and often form strong relationships with other species and even with humans. Children usually love them as they seem to have a sort of smiley, happy expression underneath their long forehead. They have dark grey skin on top but are lighter grey underneath which helps them to camouflage themselves.

When you see them in the water, it's an impressive sight and they can go as fast as 30 kilometres an hour. I was so excited that I actually got to see real dolphins in the wild! They eat about 15 kilograms of food a day and their diet is made up of different kinds of fish, as well as squid and octopus. It's vital that we protect them because research shows that over 50% of captured dolphins will die after around 90 days in captivity. This is mainly because their skin is sensitive, so if they get cut or bruised, an infection can break out almost immediately. And if they are caught and then transported somewhere, the shock can be psychologically and physically devastating for them. So, I don't need to remind you of how important it is keep this species in its natural habitat.

Apart from the dolphins, we were also able to see turtles on some of the diving sessions we did. There are quite a lot of different varieties that pass through the Canaries, but I was struck by how beautiful the Atlantic green turtle was. They are the biggest sea turtles with a hard shell and can grow to approximately 100 centimetres in length. They can be seen in tropical and sub-tropical waters all over the world and they live off sea-grass and algae. But this turtle is also under threat and is becoming an endangered species, generally because they are losing their nesting sites and natural environment as a result of illegal poaching, dynamite fishing and other types of human interference. I have to say that going on this study-volunteer programme really did make me more aware of how vulnerable our natural world can be.

3.19 | Listening, page 139, Exercise 9

Part 1

Now I'll tell you something about the volunteer programme and how it works. The conservation organisation has a farmhouse where the volunteers stay. Our group was there for ten days and they provide you with accommodation and food. It's good fun and you have to get involved with the daily running of the place, cooking in small groups and of course there is a rota for cleaning up too. Young people come from all over the world so you get to meet and make new friends.

There are three main volunteering areas, which include going out on the dolphin and whale watching boats, where you get involved with collecting data about marine life. Then there is a research centre where all the data is processed and analysed. This was especially interesting for me as you get hands-on experience with expert teams who give you an insight into how to manage a research project.

Then there's an Information Centre which has an area for volunteers. This is where you have contact with the public and find out more about the marine life watching community, and environmental campaigns. It has fantastic multi-media resources … some of the photos and videos that tourists donate to the organisation are really useful for research purposes. Apart from the volunteering work, you also have the opportunity to enjoy other activities such as diving, canyoning, kayaking or horse-riding.

Finally, it's worth thinking about what it takes to volunteer on a programme like this. You need to be committed to conservation but really any person who has a positive attitude and is willing to work hard, collaborate and take the initiative in teams can make the most of an experience like this.

Now, does anyone have any questions?

UNIT 1 | WORKBOOK

01 | Listening, page 8, Exercise 3

People are always surprised when I tell them about my hobby … well, it's my passion really. I've not only learnt some useful skills through doing it, but it's also made me much more self-confident.

I never really thought I'd enjoy a water sport because I don't like swimming or sailing, but last year I went camping with my family and we stayed near a lake. I tried kayaking with my cousin and we both loved it. For me that was that – from then on I was hooked.

When we came home, my parents allowed me to join a local club. Since then, they've been really supportive. I was worried they might try to persuade me to stop kayaking, but they're delighted I've found something I love doing. The club is on a lake and I go kayaking most days – in all seasons! Some people only go in spring and summer, but I've found that if I dress warmly enough, I can kayak in all weathers, even on freezing winter days.

Nowadays, kayaks are made of wood, plastic or fibreglass, although the earliest ones, built by the Inuits in North America, were made of animal skins over a whalebone frame. I've got my own kayak now – it's a one-person kayak, although you can get ones for two or three people. Mine is made of plastic so it's light and strong.

Not long after I started, I tried kayaking in a two-person kayak, but I didn't enjoy it as much. If you don't paddle together at the same time, the kayak can become quite unstable. It's tricky to get in rhythm with someone else. It used to drive me mad, it was really annoying! I was much happier kayaking by myself.

When you watch it, kayaking can seem deceptively easy. You get in the kayak and paddle off … right? Wrong! It's harder than it seems because the most essential thing to learn is water safety. You have to learn to rescue yourself and others. When you start lessons, it's quite hair-raising because they involve capsizing the canoe, so you go *upside down* in the water, and then turning it over again, so you come *out* of the water. Unless you master that, you're not allowed out. Luckily, my instructor was great, so we learnt the basic safety techniques pretty quickly. Then we moved on to paddling skills – that's how you move in different directions.

Now that I'm proficient, I've been looking into doing some white-water kayaking next summer. It's basically kayaking down rapids on a river, but while I feel really confident kayaking on lakes and even in the sea, I'm not convinced that I'd enjoy going down rapids. You have to make split-second decisions and I'd be nervous about making a serious mistake. I think you have to be pretty cool-headed and love excitement to do it.

I take part in competitions now. At the moment I'm getting ready for one – that means a lot of hard training, in and out of the water. I go to a gym twice a week to do exercises to improve the muscles in my back, legs and arms. If you want to get better, you need to really build up your upper-body strength as well as your general fitness level. I get up at 5 am every day to fit in all the training, and sometimes it's hard to stay motivated, but my instructor is really encouraging.

If I won any of the races in the competition, I'd be delighted, but that's not why I do it. When I'm out on the water alone and when I get into the flow of the movement, that's much more important to me than winning a competition … it feels simply amazing.

UNIT 2 | WORKBOOK

02 | Listening, page 16, Exercise 3

A: That Zumba class was a killer! I'm not as fit as I used to be, that's for sure.

B: Me neither! I haven't got the energy to go swimming now. Would you mind if we just went straight home?

A: Not at all. I'll just call my brother and he can pick us up outside the gym. Unless you'd prefer to walk …

B: You can't be serious! I can't even stand up!

A: No, I was only joking. Of course we're not going to walk. My feet are killing me!

B: Mine too!

03 | Listening, page 16, Exercise 4

1 You hear two friends talking after a Zumba class.

Woman 1: That Zumba class was a killer! I'm not as fit as I used to be, that's for sure.

Woman 2: Me neither! I haven't got the energy to go swimming now. Would you mind if we just went straight home?

Woman 1: Not at all. I'll just call my brother and he can pick us up outside the gym. Unless you'd prefer to walk …

Woman 2: You can't be serious! I can't even stand up!

Woman 1: No, I was only joking. Of course we're not going to walk. My feet are killing me!

Woman 2: Mine too!

2 You overhear a boy talking on the phone about a judo club.

You know I've always wanted to take up judo – yes, that's right, judo – not karate, no. Anyway, now that the football season is over, I think it's a good time to start. And I thought you might be interested too. I've got the leaflet here – hang on a second – yeah, listen to this: 'Afternoon classes Monday to Friday. Weekends nine to five.' See? We can go to the club during the week and again on Saturday and Sunday. You just need a suit and a belt. … What? No, a white belt, of course, we're just beginners! Black is for the experts. … Oh, you want to earn a black belt? [*laughs*] Why not?

3 You hear two girls talking about a driving lesson.

Girl 1: Did you make any mistakes? Were you nervous? You didn't hit anything, did you?

Girl 2: Hit? Of course, not! It wasn't as bad as you think. For a start I didn't drive on public roads. It was just a track for learners.

Girl 1: Oh, that doesn't sound very exciting.

Girl 2: Actually, it was, because I hadn't driven before. The instructor explained that I should stay off the roads until I get some experience and confidence.

Girl 1: Well, OK … I see her point.

Girl 2: Yes, it makes sense. Anyway, I got to drive and turn, and reverse. Next week … parking!

4 You hear part of an interview with a life coach.

Interviewer: Thanks for joining us, Damien.

Man: It's my pleasure. I'm a big fan of the show, so I'm really delighted to be here.

Interviewer: You're a life coach. Interesting! How exactly do you coach lives?

Man: Well, I help people to achieve their goals. Just like a trainer helps an athlete, a life coach works to improve people's lives or careers.

Interviewer: And you've made a film about it? Is that right?

Man: Ah, not quite. There's this Hollywood director. He's making a comedy about a loser and a life coach and he asked for my help.

All I did was read the script and make some suggestions.

Interviewer: Well, I can't wait to see it!

5 You hear a girl talking about a pet.

I mean, I was just walking back from the shops and he started following me. Kind of shyly at first, with his head hung low, and then he became a bit bolder, even barking at some other scary-looking strays. We named him Grandpa because he was old, and we tried to teach him some manners, like waiting patiently for his food without begging. But he couldn't change that habit – not that it mattered, we loved him anyway. What he did learn to do though, and quite well, was bring in the post and other stuff. Our postman can take credit for that, but I don't know how he got him to do it!

6 You hear two friends talking about a job.

Boy 1: You'll never believe it! I was just named employee of the month at work!

Boy 2: Great! Keep that up and you could become the boss in no time.

Boy 1: I wouldn't go that far! I'm just the guy who cooks the chips.

Boy 2: Everyone's got to start somewhere, Liam. Today French fries, tomorrow your own restaurant.

Boy 1: That's true enough, but I don't see my future in burgers and fries. The police force – now that's where I want to be. Solving crimes and protecting people.

Boy 2: That's funny. I can't imagine you as a police officer.

7 You hear a teacher talking about graffiti.

Teacher: Listen up, please. This is a reminder about the graffiti removal. As no-one has come forward about the damage – yes, damage, it certainly isn't art – you will all be responsible for the clean-up. Now, I know you'd rather stay at home to watch videos or update your Facebook, or whatever it is you do when you're not here … but I expect to see you bright and early on Saturday morning. Don't forget a sturdy pair of gloves and a wire brush. And I don't want to hear any whining – the graffiti didn't spray itself on the walls; some of you know who was responsible but have chosen to keep quiet. You only have yourselves to blame. Have I made myself clear?

Students: Yes, sir.

8 You hear two boys talking about a survival weekend.

Boy 1: I can't wait. It's going to be great. Living in the wild, building our own shelters, catching fish, cooking over a campfire. We'll be like Bear Grylls on TV!

Boy 2: Look, it all sounds great – and I'd love to go – but have you seen the weather forecast? They're predicting storms this weekend.

Boy 1: Again? It seems like every weekend is ruined by rain.

Boy 2: I know. There's almost no point in planning anything. Maybe we should cancel.

Boy 1: Let's wait till Friday before we do that; you never know … the weather might improve.

Boy 2: OK, fair enough.

UNIT 3 | WORKBOOK

04 | Listening, page 24, Exercise 3

Speaker 1

I'd been waiting for this one, yeah, and saving up my money! Its biggest appeal is the design, for sure. I mean, just look at it … beautiful metal casing, sleek and modern. Nothing like the cheap one I was using before. All in all, I'm really pleased with it. There's just one thing that's not 100 per cent. When I listen to music, there's a bit of static noise from time to time. I wonder if it's something that could be improved. I know some people have had issues with the camera, but that hasn't been my experience. I give it a nine and a half out of ten.

Speaker 2

I don't actually own one, but I've checked it out at the shops. I have to say, the specs are pretty good, at least on paper – it's supposed to have good battery life between charges, which is what you want if you're out and about all day, and the design is great. However, it's awkward to hold and doesn't slip into the pocket of your jeans easily. I tend to think that the smaller ones are better for that reason. So that alone was enough to put me off buying it. I reckon it's a seven out of ten.

Speaker 3

My job keeps me on the go all day. I have to visit clients, make loads of calls and send emails. I demand a lot from my phone, so one that can't keep up doesn't appeal to me. Now, the manufacturer says that the battery should last twelve full hours with normal usage, but I'm not entirely sure I agree with that claim. I've been getting around eight hours before it starts to fade, which is pretty disappointing. I'm not happy that I've had to buy a portable charger for emergencies. For me, it's a six out of ten.

Speaker 4

My eyesight isn't what it used to be, but the nice big screen means I don't have to squint all the time just to compose or read a text. It's really quite a plus for me. Now the bad news: it's not as affordable as other models, but if you keep it for more than a few years, that's not an issue. No, the thing that I'm really not keen on is the settings. It's not easy to use by any means. Honestly, you need a degree in engineering to figure it out! So maybe a five out of ten.

Speaker 5

Frustrated doesn't begin to describe how I feel. I'd gone on holiday and taken loads of photos, as you do. I was impressed with the sharpness of the images, no complaints there, but the video was pretty poor. So when I returned, I contacted the manufacturer about a refund or a replacement. Well, would you believe it, they just weren't prepared to listen. They said it wasn't their problem and to go back to the shop I'd bought it from. If that's how they treat their customers, I'd certainly be surprised if they remained in business. Ten for the phone, zero for the maker!

UNIT 4 | WORKBOOK

05 | Listening, page 32, Exercise 3

Interviewer: Hello listeners and welcome to *Crime Time*. Today our studio guest is crime novel writer George Bailey, who's just released his latest book, *When Will It End?* Welcome to the show, George.

George: Thanks for having me.

Interviewer: Those of us who are admirers of your books know that you spent almost 20 years in the police force. The obvious question is, how much has that influenced your writing?

George: Hugely! And not only as a writer, but as a person too. It's probably made me a good amateur psychologist because I understand people, sometimes better than they understand themselves. As for my writing, I think being a chief investigator was the ideal preparation for crime writing. I was at crime scenes, I searched high and low for clues, I know about forensic science. I interviewed people who had committed crimes and their victims. And I think that experience of witnessing people's anger, fear and regret has contributed greatly to the authentic tone in my books.

Interviewer: How do you write them? Do you make a plan in advance or do you just start writing and see what happens?

George: Some authors like the challenge of writing freely and almost letting the story develop by itself. Me? I'm the opposite. I always have the story with its conclusion in my head before I begin. When I actually put pen to paper, I produce a summary first. Chapter by chapter, it covers what's going to happen all the way to the end where all is revealed. The notes I make are quite detailed and they help to keep the story on track. Otherwise, it's very easy to lose control of it.

Interviewer: Would you say that comes from your work in the police force?

George: Oh, yes, without a doubt, the analytical method is something I learnt as an investigator because in that job, a lot depends on being logical and focused. The plan I use is very helpful when all the little bits and pieces in a crime novel need to fit together. I mean, for example, you need to make sure there's enough evidence in the story to point to a few suspects, without making it too obvious who the killer is. Readers enjoy being kept in suspense until the end about the killer's identity. It seems to ruin their enjoyment if they can easily work it out themselves.

Interviewer: Your stories take place in the quiet English countryside. Why did you choose it as the setting for your crime novels?

George: It doesn't seem the obvious place for criminal activity, does it? The farms and fields, the charming little villages and towns. But it's the contrast between these peaceful small town communities and the violence that takes place there which makes the story more terrifying. As a former police officer I have seen and experienced these contrasts and I assure you that violent crime can happen anywhere.

Interviewer: Do you think that's why crime fiction is so popular? That it reminds us nothing is perfect or as it seems?

George: Yes, I do, because it's about the things happening around us – the injustice and the misery. I hope my books are more than just exciting stories to read during a flight or lying on the beach. I like the idea that a reader might be left thinking about the conditions that exist in the world we live in.

Interviewer: Can you tell us a little about *When Will It End?* which is the fifth book in your series featuring Detective Inspector Giggs?

George: Well, the story begins in an empty old house in the village of Morsley. The elderly man who lived there has recently died. There is a locked, windowless room and no key, which is very puzzling. But when it is finally opened, the actual mystery at the heart of the story also opens. Detective Inspector Giggs has to use all his experience and knowledge to solve a crime that was committed over 20 years before.

Interviewer: It sounds fascinating and I can't wait to read it!

UNIT 5 | WORKBOOK

06 | Listening, page 40, Exercise 1

Interviewer: I'd like you all to welcome 16-year-old Heather Russell to the show today. You might know her from her popular sports blog *Half Time Break*. Heather, thanks for joining us.

Heather: It's great to be here.

Interviewer: First of all, I have to congratulate you on the success of your blog. Not only was it awarded Best Teen Blog, but you've got a record number of subscribers. Well done, that's a great achievement, but there's more, isn't there? You're here today because you've got some very exciting news to share with our listeners.

Heather: I certainly have, and I can hardly believe it myself. I've got my own TV show!

Interviewer: Fantastic! Fill us in on how that came about.

Heather: Well, there's this guy who reads my blog, Tim, and his dad happens to be a producer at Channel 7. He usually does quiz shows and game shows, but the channel wanted to reach a younger audience. So they asked him to come up with a good idea for a show. Not a soap opera or a singing contest. People are sick of those! He figured Tim, being a teenager himself, would be able to help him out. And Tim had a brainwave – a sports show, not with well-known presenters, but with young people, which is a brilliant idea because there isn't anything like that on telly.

07 | Listening, page 40, Exercise 2

Interviewer: I'd like you all to welcome 16-year-old Heather Russell to the show today. You might know her from her popular sports blog *Half Time Break*. Heather, thanks for joining us.

Heather: It's great to be here.

Interviewer: First of all, I have to congratulate you on the success of your blog. Not only was it awarded Best Teen Blog, but you've got a record number of subscribers. Well done, that's a great achievement, but there's more, isn't there? You're here today because you've got some very exciting news to share with our listeners.

Heather: I certainly have, and I can hardly believe it myself. I've got my own TV show!

Interviewer: Fantastic! Fill us in on how that came about.

Heather: Well, there's this guy who reads my blog, Tim, and his dad happens to be a producer at Channel 7. He usually does quiz shows and game shows, but the channel wanted to reach a younger audience. So they asked him to come up with a good idea for a show. Not a soap opera or a singing contest, people are sick of those! He figured Tim, being a teenager himself, would be able to help him out. And Tim had a brainwave – a sports show, not with well-known presenters, but with young people, which is a brilliant idea because there isn't anything like that on telly.

Interviewer: And I suppose he thought of you as he subscribes to your blog. Is that right?

Heather: Exactly. Then Tim's dad arranged a meeting at the TV station. To be honest, I wasn't really sure what they had in mind for the show, but I went along with some ideas of my own. And they loved them!

Interviewer: Can you tell us what they are and what the show will be like? The format isn't a secret, is it?

Heather: Hah, no! Of course I can discuss it. I'll be presenting live from events and talking to players and athletes. We're not focusing on one sport like other shows do. We've got tennis, football, basketball, netball, cycling, swimming … well, pretty much anything that happens in the city! And back at the studio there'll be two other presenters to comment on the action and the results. They're my age too.

Interviewer: That must be so exciting for you, and it sounds like a great show. Have you had any experience interviewing?

Heather: I was the editor of my school newspaper last year, so I got the opportunity to do that, yes. But I'm sure there's a huge difference between interviewing someone for an article and doing it live on air. That'll be a first for me.

Interviewer: I've read your blog, Heather. You're obviously a sports fanatic, but you've got a great sense of humour too. Some of the posts and memes on your site are just hilarious. Is that another reason why Channel 7 wanted you on the show?

Heather: Oh, absolutely! It's going to be very light-hearted with fun videos, you know – the epic fails. Everyone loves those, except the people that are in them! Um, there'll be a live audience and prizes. Oh, and there's no script – none of the presenters will be reading lines. It's just going to be us saying what we think at the time. That can create very funny situations. Or disasters! But I've got my fingers crossed that it all goes smoothly.

Interviewer: Can we talk a little bit about your blog now? Will you give it up when the show starts?

Heather: I've thought about that. Um, yeah, it's going to be hard to juggle school, the show and the blog, but I'll stick with it. I love it and the readers enjoy it too. A lot of work has gone into it too – I mean, you wouldn't believe how many statistics and records I've got on it, from all the major events like the Olympics, the football World Cup … even golf … which no teenager has followed … ever! But it's there just in case someone's interested.

Interviewer: All that knowledge will come in very handy when you're on TV. I think viewers really appreciate it when the sports reporters know what they're talking about. Do you play a sport yourself?

Heather: I used to play more when I was younger – basketball and tennis mainly, but I gave them up when I started cricket. I'm in a girls' team and I'm really enjoying it. If anyone's interested, we're always looking for new players. Just Google Carlton girls' cricket team and you'll find the information.

Interviewer: Is it your favourite sport then?

Heather: To play, yes, but football is my great love. I'm hopeless at it though, but I'm a great spectator!

Interviewer: Well, Heather, it's been great talking to you, and I wish you the best of luck with the show. And to our listeners, *Half Time Break* – the show – starts next month on Channel 7. Be watching!

Heather: Thanks so much.

UNIT 6 | WORKBOOK

08 | Listening, page 48, Exercises 1 and 3

Hi, everyone. My name's Justin and I'm here today to talk to you about Head Start – a government initiative to help young people. You may have heard of it. It's aimed at boosting youth employment. Now, some of you here may have decided against further education at university, so this talk will be of immediate interest to you, I'm sure. And for those of you considering a degree course, though unemployment may not be an issue for you right now, it could become one after you graduate.

So, let me start with some statistics: In the past 12 months, the unemployment rate among 18- to 24-year-olds in this country has risen to an average of 13%. That is unacceptable, and that's why the government set up Head Start three months ago. More than 50 Head Start offices, with over 500 staff, have opened since then and more are planned. Right here in Braxton, we'll be cutting the ribbon next week. You are all welcome to attend and there'll be a handout with details at the end of the talk.

Now, let me explain what Head Start actually does, with some examples. Let's say you're a recent school-leaver, aged 18. You've decided to give university a miss, and are looking for a job. It's tough out there without a qualification or work experience, so at Head Start we make sure you get them. After you register, we interview you to find out what your strengths and interests are. Maybe you're happy to do an apprenticeship or a part-time training course. If that's the case, we connect you with the right people. Or maybe you want to go straight into a job that doesn't require you to have a certificate. There are unskilled jobs out there for you, but I would suggest you think twice about them. Such jobs don't pay well and are often not very satisfying.

Now, with the above example, you're probably thinking, 'Yes, I know that already. What else can you tell me?' Well, here it is: through Head Start, the government will pay you if you undertake an apprenticeship or training course. That's right. You will be able to earn money and develop skills at the same time. It won't be a full-time salary of course, but enough to cover daily expenses such as transport and food. As for unskilled jobs like working in a supermarket or a fast-food restaurant, we pay the employer some money to take you on, and you earn the basic adult wage. It's a win-win situation.

So how does this reduce youth unemployment? Well, young people who know they can earn some money while training are more likely to choose this rather than the other option – the dole. The dole – or, to call it by its proper name, unemployment benefit – is the government payment you receive while you are unemployed. It is supposed to help you out while you're looking for a job. Theoretically, you could stay on the dole forever, but you'll only have enough money for the basics – there'll be no holidays abroad, a nice car or your own home. Those things only come with a good salary. So it's vital to get into the workforce. Once you gain experience, you can start to make a career which, hopefully, will keep you working for many years to come. And even an unskilled worker can work their way up and perhaps become a retail manager.

In the case of unskilled work, employers are happy to take on young people if they cost less to employ. We've received great feedback because everyone benefits from it.

Head Start is investing in youth, and if you'd like more information about the full range of services …

UNIT 7 | WORKBOOK

09 | Listening, page 56, Exercise 2

Extract 1

Why don't we contact the council when we get back to the office?

Extract 2

How on earth was it stolen in broad daylight under the tightest museum security?

Extract 3

I can't get the trees to look natural. I mean, look at them.

Extract 4

I wish they wouldn't do it here. Why in a park of all places?

Extract 5

You should try blending them into this painting.

Extract 6

Could you do me a favour?

10 | Listening, page 56, Exercise 3

1 You hear two friends talking about a play.

Alice: How are the dress rehearsals coming along, Gemma? You must be pretty excited about your first play.

Gemma: I would be if I weren't so anxious, Alice! There's still loads to do – the lights, the costumes, the programmes … and opening night is only two weeks away.

Alice: Is there anything I can do? I don't know much about theatre productions, but I could help with some sewing.

Gemma: Would you really? Well, we are having issues with the fittings. You see, we're using some old costumes – to save a bit of money – but they need alterations. Some are too long and need shortening, and others are too tight. It might be a lot of work. Are you absolutely sure?

Alice: Of course! Bring them over to my place at seven tonight.

Gemma: You're a life saver!

2 You hear part of an interview with a teenage novelist.

Interviewer: Aiden, what would you say to any budding writers out there?

Aiden: Oh, where do I begin? Well, I think you have to keep going and never consider giving up. There'll be times when you're looking at a blank screen, fingers poised over the keyboard, but you have no ideas. Absolutely nothing! You'd be surprised how often that happens to even the most famous authors. It's called writer's block and it can last for months!

Interviewer: And how do you break through that block?

Aiden: A long walk, a night out, binge-watching a great TV series … honestly, just any distraction to take your mind off the problem. It'll clear your head and you can get back to writing.

3 You hear two people talking in a park.

Woman: I can't believe it! Was that there yesterday?

Man: What do you mean?

Woman: Look over there, on that wall near the fountain. I'm sure it wasn't there yesterday when we were having our lunch break.

Man: No, it wasn't. That's new graffiti. We would've noticed something so big.

Woman: And ugly! The council only cleaned that wall a few weeks ago and here it is tagged again. I wish they wouldn't do it here. Why in a park of all places? People come here to relax and, well, to get away from things like graffiti.

Man: Yes, I'm sick of it. It's all over town. Why don't we contact the council when we get back to the office? The sooner it's removed, the better.

4 You hear part of a documentary about a stolen painting.

How on earth was it stolen in broad daylight under the tightest museum security? It had all the makings of a Hollywood film. And the press couldn't get enough of it. There were so many theories. One newspaper even suggested the painting was taken on the orders of a foreign leader. Imagine the stunned reaction when it was discovered, some 10 years later, in a wooden box in the basement. But stranger things were yet to happen. It turns out the thief had abandoned it there – possibly hoping to return at a later, safer time to retrieve it – but for some unknown reason, never did.

5 You hear a conversation on a film set.

Director: Ryan, this is the most important scene in the film. It's when your character discovers the skeleton. How do you think you should play it?

Ryan: Well, I could stand here with a shocked look on my face, eyes open wide, mouth open, like this …

Director: Hmmm, that's kind of predictable. Let's try something else. Why don't you drop the book you're holding and sort of walk backwards a bit? You know, in fear. You're scared of what you've discovered. Terrified!

Ryan: Should I fall backwards too? Would that make it more realistic?

Director: That might work. Give it a go and we'll see. Lights! Camera! Action!

6 You hear two people talking about a statue.

Man: So, we'll put the largest statue directly opposite the windows, right? Loads of people walk past the gallery every day and they'll definitely see it. Once they come inside, they'll wander around and take a look at all the other pieces. And hopefully buy something!

Woman: I agree it'll get people in. But now I'm not so sure it's the best strategy. The thing is, that statue is the most impressive item we have. Nothing else really compares to it. People might be disappointed with the rest of the collection. They shouldn't be, but what if they are?

Man: I see what you mean. Selling all of the pieces is a priority. Let's rethink this.

7 You hear a man talking about a screenwriting workshop he went to.

In the end, I'm really glad I went. My friend Emma, who's studying film directing, had heard about it and thought I'd be interested – she knew I was writing my first screenplay, you see. And we've always joked that I'll write the greatest script ever and she'll direct the film. So there I was at the workshop and a sweet little old lady sat down next to me. I thought she must be lost, so I said, 'Can I help you? Which room are you looking for? This is a screenwriting seminar.' Well, I can't tell you how embarrassed I was. She was actually an Academy Award-winning screenwriter, whose son was giving the seminar. She'd come along to hear him.

8 You hear a conversation in an art class.

Teacher: How are you doing here, Dylan?

Dylan: Not very well actually. Could you do me a favour? Please tell me what you think.

Teacher: What in particular are you having trouble with?

Dylan: I can't get the trees to look natural. I mean, look at them. They're just big green balls on brown sticks. There's no movement, no wind in the leaves, nothing. I can't undo it. I should probably throw it out, but I haven't got another canvas.

Teacher: Not so fast. The problem here is that you've only used one shade of green. You need three or four different greens to create depth and movement. You should try blending them into this painting.

Dylan: Well, OK, if you think it'll work.

UNIT 8 | WORKBOOK

11 | Listening, page 64, Exercise 3

Speaker 1

I didn't know much about habitat loss until I watched a documentary at school as part of our environmental science course. Did you know that it's the biggest threat to biological diversity? Worldwide, forests, plains, rivers, lakes and other places where so many different species live, are disappearing. And it's our fault. By 'our', I mean all humans. We're clearing land to make way for farms, houses and roads. Companies drill for oil and gas under the sea, and there've been catastrophic oil spills with countless animals dying. Is industrial development really more important than living creatures? Shouldn't areas rich with land and marine species be protected by law? It's an important issue because each species, no matter how small, has an important role to play in the ecosystem.

Speaker 2

I've realised the world is connected in more ways than just the internet. A while ago, I was at the beach, walking my dog. It was a bit chilly and there was no-one else around. Well, you wouldn't believe what was on the shore. I mean, normally in winter, it's just seaweed and the odd dead fish. But that day there were empty crisp packets, soft drink bottles, plastic shopping bags – loads of those – even hair combs and shoes! I took a look at the product information and it was in three or four foreign languages that I didn't recognise at all, which really shocked me. It just goes to show how bad the problem is when waste from one country can end up in another.

Speaker 3

We moan a lot about the weather here, don't we? It's too wet and never warm enough. Well, I'm beginning to change my mind about that! I was in Australia last year and I can tell you, extreme heat is much worse than grey skies. Would you believe that for 10 consecutive days the temperature was over 42 degrees? Can you imagine what that's like? It saps you of your energy, not to mention the sunburn you can get. It was a freak heatwave that even the locals weren't used to. What's really worrying is it's becoming more common. Some people have got their heads in the sand if they think climate change isn't happening. It is, and unless it's tackled, it can only get much worse.

Speaker 4

You can sit at home and watch documentaries about the environment. You can even sign online petitions to stop this or support that. Which is all very worthy, I'm sure. But unless you've seen a catastrophe with your own eyes, you'll never be able to understand its impact. Backpacking through Asia a few years ago, I came across a village along the banks of a river. There wasn't a soul around. I found out that a factory upstream had dumped toxic waste into the water. The villagers literally woke up one morning to find they had no clean water, a river full of dead fish and no way to make a living. They were forced to abandon their homes. Imagine being faced with that. What would you do? It really made me think.

Speaker 5

I try to be environmentally aware, but it isn't always easy. Recycling's not a problem. We've got separate bins at home for different kinds of waste. And I'm careful not to let the tap run while I'm brushing my teeth or doing the dishes. But we do fly to nice places for our summer holiday, and that's a massive carbon footprint right there. So every little bit we do seems to be cancelled out by that. Maybe we just don't care enough to change our habits. That's probably true of most people … and it really worries me. Making changes shouldn't be seen as a pain in the neck. Unless we're all fully committed to change, there's not much hope for us, is there?

UNIT 9 | WORKBOOK

12 | Listening, page 72, Exercise 2

Interviewer: Today on *Literary Hour*, I'm joined in the studio by students Peter and Olivia, who recently attended the Teen Writer Boot Camp. Hello and welcome guys.

Peter and Olivia: Hi.

Interviewer: So you two attended a weekend seminar on writing. Peter, let me start with you. What were your reasons for attending the boot camp?

Peter: It sounded like fun and it was! I'm not an aspiring novelist, I'll leave that to Olivia. No, journalism's my thing and the boot camp was ideal. One of the sessions I attended was about writing pieces like long articles and short stories.

Interviewer: Are they different to writing a novel?

Peter: Sort of, yes, but we learnt that the basics are the same. A short story can be very short or a third the length of a novel. You still need to develop characters and a plot with a beginning, middle and end. And you need to give your characters a 'voice'. That means they need to come across as individuals with their own way of communicating and reacting. All of that is on a bigger scale when you're writing a novel. I think the most important difference is in the planning of a novel.

Interviewer: I take it that means being well-organised, does it?

Peter: Exactly. I wouldn't be surprised to learn that some famous authors have huge maps on their wall with the names of characters and places from their book, and arrows showing relationships and that sort of thing. That's probably an extreme example, but you get the idea … some plots are SO complicated!

Interviewer: Yes, indeed. Just think about all the genealogies and places in something like the *Lord of the Rings* trilogy. I'm so impressed that Tolkien managed to keep track of it all. It must have been really difficult – Olivia, would you agree?

Olivia: Absolutely. And unless you've got a really good editor, it would be easy for careless mistakes to slip in. But I like the challenge of novel writing.

Interviewer: Have you written a novel then?

Olivia: It's not finished, but yes, I'm trying to write my first.

Interviewer: That's great! And how has the boot camp helped you?

Olivia: In lots of ways. One really important piece of advice I got was that you have to be prepared to let go. For instance, you may have written a section that you really like because it's funny or you just like the way it sounds. But if it doesn't add to the story, if it doesn't advance the plot, you have to get rid of it. I'm actually rewriting mine now and I think it's much better.

Interviewer: What about short story writing? Peter, can you tell us what you learnt at the boot camp?

Peter: Sure! First of all, we were given the opening of a short story to read, *Metamorphosis* by a Czech writer called Franz Kafka.

Interviewer: Kafka?! That's pretty advanced reading for teenagers!

Peter: Is it? I don't know, we only read the first line, but they say *Metamorphosis* is the greatest short story ever written. So if you're going to learn something, who better to learn it from than the best?

Interviewer: I've read it and the beginning is just astounding. It grabs you and pulls you in. Do you remember it for our listeners?

Peter: [*laughs*] It's kind of hard to forget. OK, so the English translation goes something like this [*clears throat*] *One morning, when Gregor Samsa woke from troubled dreams, he found himself transformed in his bed into a gigantic insect.* Basically, this guy wakes up and discovers he's a man-sized cockroach.

Interviewer: What did you think when you read that?

Peter: I laughed, and then I thought, 'How do you live as a human in an insect body? How do people react to you? Could you ever leave your home? How do you become human again?' And that was the purpose of the exercise. To get us thinking. We were told to consider the implications for this person. Then we wrote our own continuation of the story.

Interviewer: That's a very interesting way to develop the craft. So everyone's imagination was firing. Let me ask you, Olivia, about imagination. How important is it?

Olivia: It's everything. And that was really drilled into us on the course. We also looked at some of the works of Roald Dahl, another very imaginative writer. Did you know that at the start of his career, his style was realistic? Then he developed a much more imaginative style, and children's fiction was the perfect fit for him.

Interviewer: No, I didn't know that. How interesting! And tell me, do you think imagination and I suppose creativity, too, are easy to develop?

Olivia: Anyone can think in an imaginative way, it's just that a lot of people don't, probably because they don't need to. But when you write, it's what makes a story richer. When we were on the course, we did this fun exercise. The instructor put three random items on a table – a balloon, an empty coffee cup and a bike wheel.

Interviewer: Ah, let me guess … you had to work all of them into a story?

Olivia: That's right. And everyone came up with totally different stories from those same three elements. It shows that you can take anything and fit a story around it. It gave me the confidence to look at my own work in a totally new way.

Interviewer: It sounds like it was a very productive weekend! Would you recommend it to any budding writers out there?

Peter: Definitely!

Olivia: Of course!

Interviewer: Thank you so much for being on the show today, guys.

UNIT 10 | WORKBOOK

13 | Listening, page 80, Exercise 2

Alec: Today on *I Blog*, I'm joined by Jade Owens, who recently posted an informative piece about bad luck. Well, that's a creepy topic, Jade!

Jade: Hi, Alec. It certainly is, but fascinating too.

Alec: So tell us about the blog entry. What kind of bad luck are we talking about here?

Jade: The post is called 'Unlucky Finds' and it's about strange curses that are associated with famous treasures and jewels. There are lots of examples of people discovering incredible things, but not being able to enjoy them, for obvious reasons.

Alec: Do you mean like the so-called 'Curse of the Pharaohs' where it's claimed that anyone who disturbs one of the ancient Kings of Egypt will die a horrible death?

Jade: Not necessarily, though that's the worst that can happen. But illness or just bad luck in general too. And actually, it's considered bad luck to disturb any mummy, not just that of a pharaoh. But because the rulers of Egypt were buried surrounded by golden statues, gold furniture, jewellery and precious stones, their tombs were the ones that attracted thieves hoping to strike it lucky. And they definitely did, because we haven't found many that are intact.

Alec: And the most famous example of such a tomb is that of King Tutankhamun.

Jade: Without a doubt. Everyone's heard of it. In the case of Tutankhamun, whose tomb was discovered by archaeologist Howard Carter, it was Carter's financial backer who died. His name was Lord Carnarvon, and he provided the money Carter needed to fund his dig in the Valley of the Kings, in Egypt.

Alec: Lord Carnarvon wasn't the only person associated with the discovery to die, was he? I mean, it wouldn't be creepy otherwise.

Jade: No, it wouldn't. A radiologist who supposedly X-rayed the mummy died of a mysterious illness, a rich American died after visiting the tomb, and one of the workers involved in the dig was said to have died of poisoning. Carnarvon died a year after the discovery, and they say that at the exact moment of his death, all the lights in Cairo mysteriously went out.

Alec: So did all that prove it was real?

Jade: Hardly! Too much exposure to X-rays can be deadly. The American died of pneumonia. The worker could have come into contact with poison regardless of the dig. Carnarvon was bitten on the cheek by a mosquito, and while he was shaving, he made it worse. The bite became infected and he died. None of those deaths were unnatural. As for the lights, it's apparently true, and would be impressive but for the fact that blackouts were very common in Cairo at that time.

Alec: It was just a coincidence then?

Jade: I'd say so. But the interesting thing is, people wanted to believe in it. In fact, Sir Arthur Conan Doyle, the creator of Sherlock Holmes, announced he was convinced Carnarvon had been killed by the Pharaoh's Curse, and the press began to publish wild stories as fact.

Alec: Arthur Conan Doyle? Really? Now, what about Howard Carter, who discovered the tomb? Did anything nasty happen to him?

Jade: You would think so, wouldn't you? I mean, he not only discovered the tomb and physically opened it, but he also removed the mummy of Tutankhamun from the sarcophagus. Yet, he lived until 1939, sixteen years after the discovery.

Alec: Can I ask what drew you to the topic? Was it the mystery surrounding these tales of bad luck?

Jade: To begin with it was. Well, they're fascinating, aren't they? I never believed they were true, though. But I started to wonder why others were so willing to accept them as fact. Even someone like Arthur Conan Doyle!

Alec: Yes, I was quite astounded by that.

Jade: Same here. Because his character Sherlock Holmes is so logical, we just assume that he would be too. Who knows? Maybe he just enjoyed a good mystery as much as the next person. Maybe the story appealed to his imaginative side. Still, it's a huge leap from enjoying a mystery to believing in strange forces.

Alec: I'll say! What other strange tales can you tell us about?

Jade: Well, there's the Koh-i-Noor diamond, which at one time was the largest in the world. The name means 'Mountain of Light' in Persian. According to the curse, whoever owns it will rule the world, but will also have great misfortune. Only a woman can wear it without terrible consequences.

Alec: So no man can own it. What happened to those who didn't heed the warning?

Jade: The son of an emperor was exiled from his kingdom; Shah Jahan, who built the famous Taj Mahal in India, was imprisoned by his son; and a Shah of Persia was murdered.

Alec: Can you tell our listeners what happened to it?

Jade: It belonged to various Indian and Persian rulers, but as you probably know, it ended up here in the UK when India became a British colony in the 1840s. It's in the Tower of London now, part of the Crown Jewels that belong to the British Royal Family. It's in a crown full of diamonds that is displayed there. Ever since the Royal Family have owned it, it has only been worn by the wife of the king, or a ruling queen.

Alec: And no male members of the British Royal Family have ever worn it?

Jade: No, they haven't. Perhaps they're worried about the curse!

Alec: How extraordinary! Well, thanks for joining us today. It's been very informative. Jade's post 'Unlucky Finds' is on her blog at www. …

UNIT 11 | WORKBOOK

14 | Listening, page 88, Exercise 2

Blake: Today on *Tour Guide*, we've got some great information for travellers. Carly Simms, our tech whiz, is here to bring us up-to-date with the best travel apps. It's nice to have you on the show, Carly.

Carly: Thanks, Blake. Hi, everyone.

Blake: I'm really looking forward to this because I'm going to Berlin on holiday next week, and I'm sure your information will come in handy. So what have you got for us?

Carly: Well, as you know, I've been researching travel apps. We've all got internet-enabled phones and gadgets and these apps will make your life on the road a whole lot easier. These six apps will ensure you never get lost, misunderstand anyone, or make costly mistakes with your currency.

Blake: And I've made every one of those mistakes! So what are we starting with?

Carly: The first app is called Citymapper, and as the name suggests, it's got maps.

Blake: I've got Google maps on my phone – I suppose everyone has. Is Citymapper better then?

Carly: Better, no. Different, yes. Google's great and it covers the world, but Citymapper provides information that you might find more important when you're trying to navigate the public transport network, as you will in Berlin. It's easy to use, which is a big plus because you don't want to be fussing with it as the bus you want drives past! There's information about departures in real-time and there are updates about any transport disruptions, such as road works. And it gives you the total price of the journey. At the moment, it's available in around 30 major cities worldwide, including Berlin.

Blake: Perfect! I'll be sure to download it.

Carly: It gets even better, Blake.

Blake: How's that?

Carly: It's absolutely free!

Blake: Fantastic! So take note, listeners, that's Citymapper. What's next, Carly?

Carly: Languages! If you've ever been to a country where English isn't spoken, you'll know what it's like to feel frustrated because you can't communicate. Well, Duolingo is here to help. You can learn the basics before you leave, or you can use it to freshen up your grammar and vocabulary.

Blake: My German is non-existent, so I'd better get to grips with some basics!

Carly: Well, it's always polite to attempt to speak the language wherever you are. Lots of Germans speak English, I'm sure, especially in the big cities like Berlin and Munich, but it's nice to make the effort and at least be able to say *Hello, Goodbye, How much is that?* and *Can I have a pretzel, please?*

Blake: I agree. So how exactly does Duolingo work?

Carly: It's actually very entertaining. It's kind of like a game in that you work your way up through the levels and get points as you advance. There are no teachers involved, it's all self-study, so you won't learn to speak exactly like a native, but as I said, you'll get the basics. It's also free!

Blake: OK, so that covers basic communication with other people, but what about reading?

Carly: Well, Google translate is ideal. If you haven't used it before while travelling, you'll be wondering why you hadn't after I explain what it does. Most people use it to quickly translate texts on their computer, so for example, if I want to read a French article, I can put it through Google and it'll give me a rough English translation. But it's essential for travellers like you, Blake, because it can translate the day-to-day words you come across and all you have to do is hold your camera up to the text, like a sign or a menu, and Google will translate it for you instantly. That's another free one.

Blake: I love it! What's next, Carly? You mentioned something about foreign currency earlier. Lots of people aren't good at maths, and I'm one of them. For some reason, I just can't do the conversions in my head.

Carly: Thank goodness you don't need to. XE currency will take the headache out of foreign exchange. There's a lot of business-related stuff on the site, like the price of gold, but for travellers it can convert every world currency. So no matter where you are, you can see what the local currency is against the British pound. Another great feature is that it works offline by saving the last updated exchange rates. That's really useful if you're in a place with no Wi-Fi or you're low on data.

Blake: I'm definitely going to download that one.

Carly: There's another good one for money, more precisely, for bills. Let's say you're out in a foreign city with friends and you get the bill for your meal. How do you split it? Especially if you're mathematically challenged, like you, Blake! Well, there's Splittr which works out how to share costs between friends. The best thing about it is, no arguments!

Blake: Great! Is that app free too?

Carly: No, but it's not expensive. It's less than £2, I think.

Blake: Carly, this is really great information. Thank you so much!

Carly: Oh, but there's one more app! And it's the perfect way to end your trip. It's called LiveTrekker and it creates a digital journal of your travels.

Blake: How do you mean? Like photos on Instagram?

Carly: No, this is like an interactive map. It tracks your journey with a red line on a map that follows the exact route you take. But that's not all. It can also record your speed and altitude, so adventure travellers will love it. The app supports photos, videos, audio and text that you can add along the way. I suppose it's like a multimedia travel diary. It's free and I can't wait to use it!

Blake: Me too! Wow, what great tips, Carly. I'm sure our listeners are rushing to download …

UNIT 12 | WORKBOOK

15 | Listening, page 96, Exercise 3

1 You hear a news report about an animal.

A heartwarming story now about Ginger the cat and her five kittens. The garage they were living in caught fire and when the fire brigade arrived to put it out, they found Ginger severely burnt, pulling her kittens out of the fire one by one. What's even more remarkable about Ginger's heroic rescue effort is that she had been temporarily blinded by the fire. Incredibly, she touched each of her kittens with her nose to make sure they were all there and alive. Ginger is now being treated by a vet and is expected to make a full recovery, as are her kittens.

2 You hear two friends talking about a presentation.

Girl: Thanks for coming tonight, Josh. I really appreciate it. I hadn't realised what it would be like to give a presentation to a room full of strangers!

Boy: Honestly, you looked really confident up there, like you'd done it a hundred times before.

Girl: I was shaking like a leaf on the inside when I was waiting for my turn to speak. It's strange though how quickly I was able to focus once I was up there. Even those questions from the audience at the end – some were really tough but I answered them well, I think. I have to say though I'm relieved it's over!

3 You overhear a girl talking on the phone about a documentary.

So this guy did an experiment and he was the subject. He ate nothing but fast food three times a day for 30 days. Isn't that crazy! He wanted to examine the effects of eating it. Well, naturally, he gained a lot of weight and developed all sorts of other problems like high cholesterol and blood pressure, but it's what happened to his mind that's even scarier. Towards the end of the experiment, he was unrecognisable. He went from being cheery and positive to tired and moody. It really shows how damaging too much fast food is and it has completely changed the way I think about eating it.

4 You hear part of a programme about famous women.

And now we look at two very different women. Cleopatra, the last queen of Egypt, ruled an empire whereas Marie Curie was a leader in the field of science. Curie left behind an extraordinary legacy that is with us today. She discovered two chemical elements, polonium and radium. Not only that, but she was the first person ever to win two Nobel Prizes. Cleopatra's monuments and palaces have fallen to ruins. Her colourful history and dramatic death by snake bite are all that remain in our memory. Although both were strong female figures in a male-dominated world, more than anything it is Curie's role as an innovator that distinguishes her.

5 You hear a boy telling a friend about a project he worked on.

Boy: When we got to the village, I couldn't believe how warm and welcoming the people were. Then they showed us where they collected their fresh water from. It was a kilometre away!

Girl: How on earth did they manage?

Boy: They carried it, of course, in buckets on their shoulders! Even the children. We tried it ourselves – the full buckets were really heavy.

Girl: But then you built the well in the village.

Boy: Yes! They said we were heroes and I was so proud. It took a week of hard work, but the looks of joy on the children's faces when they realised they wouldn't have to carry the water from the river … well, nothing can compare to that.

6 You hear part of an interview with an art historian.

Interviewer: Can you tell us something about Picasso the person rather than the artist?

Art historian: It's hard to separate the two when talking about artists, particularly an artist as influential as Picasso. Even as a child he was a free spirit who hated being told what to do by authority figures. As you can imagine, this caused some problems at school. For being a disobedient student, he was often sent to a bare room with white walls and a bench to sit on. Any other student would have hated it. What's fascinating is that he welcomed the punishment. He loved it there, because he took a sketch pad with him and drew. He said he could have stayed there forever, drawing without stopping.

7 You hear two friends talking about sports.

Girl: I can't wait for the Olympic Games to start, especially the table tennis.

Boy: Table tennis? I can't say it does anything for me.

Girl: Why not? Table tennis is really exciting! It involves skill and speed!

Boy: I know what you mean, but I think racing is more exciting. When two athletes are competing in a race to see who is the fastest, it draws you in from start to finish. You can't sit down! That's why I prefer track to field events like the long jump. Swimming is the same. I mean, you think someone is going to win and then they're overtaken by someone else who touches first and maybe even breaks a record.

8 You hear a tour guide talking.

I hope you all remembered to wear sturdy shoes because we'll be walking on some very uneven terrain as we approach the site. If not, please be extra careful. Also, please make sure you stick with the group because the site is huge and we don't want to lose anyone. It happened to some teenagers last year and by the time we found them, the museum had closed, and they missed out on seeing one of the most magnificent statues in all antiquity. A real must-see item that I highly recommend …

The *Optimise Practice test* audioscript can be found on the Teacher's Resource Centre.

Macmillan Education
4 Crinan Street
London N1 9XW
A division of Macmillan Publishers Limited

Companies and representatives throughout the world

ISBN 978-0-230-48881-6

Written by Anna Cole and Peter Smith

First published 2017

Text designed by Designers Collective
Typeset by J & D Glover Ltd
Cover design by Designers Collective

The publishers would like to thank the course consultant Karen Ludlow.

The authors and publishers would like to thank the following for permission to reproduce their photographs:
Alamy Stock Photo/Hero Images Inc. p27; **Getty Images**/Daniel Grill p26, Getty Images/iStockphoto/Thinkstock Images/Ridofranz p24

Commissioned photographs by **Creative Listening** p16(tr); **MTJ Media** pp8(tl, tr), 16(l, bl).

Full acknowledgements for photographs in the facsimile pages can be found in the Student's Book and the Workbook.

Printed and bound in Uruguay

2023
26